19-1-0

Aligning Human Resources
and Business Strategy

Aligning Human Resources and Business Strategy

Linda Holbeche

ELSEVIER
BUTTERWORTH
HEINEMANN

AMSTERDAM BOSTON HEIDELBERG LONDON NEW YORK OXFORD
PARIS SAN DIEGO SAN FRANCISCO SINGAPORE SYDNEY TOKYO

*To my loving husband Barney, my parents Elsie and Bill and to
the memory of my parents-in-law, Philippa and Brian*

Elsevier Butterworth-Heinemann
Linacre House, Jordan Hill, Oxford OX2 8DP
30 Corporate Drive, Burlington, MA 01803

First published 1999
Paperback edition 2001
Reprinted 2002 (twice), 2003, 2004 (twice)

Permissions may be sought directly from Elsevier's Science and
Technology Department in Oxford, UK: phone: (+44) (0) 1865 843830;
fax: (+44) (0) 1865 853333; email: permissions@elsevier.co.uk.
You may also complete your request on-line via the Elsevier homepage
(http://www.elsevier.com), by selecting 'Customer Support' and then
'Obtaining Permissions'.

British Library Cataloguing in Publication Data
Holbeche, Linda
   Aligning HR and business strategy
   1. Personnel management   2. Strategic planning
   I. Title
   658.3

ISBN 0 7506 5362 0

For more information on all Butterworth-Heinemann
publications visit our website at www.bh.com

Printed and bound in Great Britain by Biddles Ltd, King's Lynn, Norfolk
Composition by Scribe Design, Gillingham, Kent

Contents

Figures

Foreword by David Hussey

When the term Human Resource Management began to be used, it was intended to be more than a more fashionable job title. The intention was that HRM should take a more strategic role than personnel management. Unfortunately, just as many people in sales became marketing managers overnight and corporate planning departments swapped their titles for strategic management, so many personnel departments took the new name of HRM: in too few cases was the change in name matched by an increase in strategic behaviour. True, more top HRM people are now on the boards of their organizations, but there is more to strategic HRM than this.

The need for strategic HRM has never been greater. Many strategic blunders could have been avoided had competent HRM professionals played a part in the strategy formulation and decision process. But the need for a proactive role goes deeper than this. There is a direct link between employee motivation and behaviour, the creation of value for customers, and increasing shareholder value. There is a clear strategic need which should be led by HRM. Once strategies have been determined, there is another role that only HRM can fulfil, which is to create HR strategies, policies and procedures which work towards the implementation of the corporate strategies and fulfilment of the corporate vision.

Strategic HRM is a hot issue, which has generated some wisdom, much agreement on the need, and a great deal of waffle and hot air. Many of the books on strategic HRM, and there have not been all that many, have argued convincingly about the *why*, but floundered badly over the *how*.

There are eight myths which hamper progress to effective strategic HRM:

Myth 1: If the top HR manager is on the board this is enough to ensure that HRM is strategic.

Myth 2: If HRM is allowed to be proactive when new corporate strategies are considered, this automatically means that all HRM activities will become strategic.

Myth 3: Doing things right automatically means that we are doing the right things: therefore it is enough to apply good professional practice.

Myth 4: Because new HR policies and procedures take a lot of time and effort to implement, they will have a long shelf life.

Myth 5: Evaluation and performance measures are too difficult and expensive for HR activities, and HRM does not need to be subject to such disciplines.

Myth 6: In any case it is not possible to evaluate the results of many HRM actions which should be treated as acts of faith.

Myth 7: Every action we take in HRM is with a concern for the interests of the organization, which means we are strategic.

Myth 8: Line management know that HRM is a valuable value-adding strategic partner which plays an irreplaceable role in the management of the organization.

(from Hussey, D. E. (1996). *Business Driven Human Resource Management*. Wiley, Chichester)

This is why Linda Holbeche's book is important. It explores both the why and the how of strategic HRM. She demonstrates that rhetoric is not enough, by providing clear guidance, and practical solutions to many of the opportunity areas for strategic HRM. The book benefits from the research she has been involved in over the past few years, adding understanding of the issues and solutions that real organizations are facing. Case examples expand the points the book makes.

This is a book which all managers in any area of management, as well as those in HRM, will find very useful as they strive to make HRM a more significant contributor to the strategic success of their organizations.

David Hussey
Visiting Professor in Strategic Management, Nottingham Business
School, Nottingham Trent University
Chief Editor, Croner's Journal of Professional HRM

Foreword by Clive Morton

I applaud Linda's thorough work in putting this comprehensive study together. It is well researched, covering the wide field of literature on the subject and very well supported by case studies, research and the solid experience of the HR professionals in both public and private sectors.

The wide spectrum of HR interfaces covered highlights again and again the clear value added contribution of HR to both the success of today's business and the prospect of business development through HR strategy. At each stage the tension between running the business today and building for tomorrow is highlighted.

Some would say the term 'HR Strategy' is a misnomer, something of no substance. Linda helpfully starts with clear definitions of what it means in both theory and practice, challenging HR to address such questions as:

- What will the competitive marketplace for the company's products, services and labour look like over the next five to ten years?
- What is the company's core competence, especially over the next three to five years?
- What kind of human resources will the organization need in order to compete successfully, or to continue to develop and provide high-quality services?
- What types of HR practices are relevant to building the organization needed for the future?

This challenge to HR to understand the business strategy world is complemented by differing scenarios of potential growth with the *implication* on HR's capacity and challenge:

1 Firms may grow within existing markets: *implication* – HR's capacity to create business cultures through which revenue-enhancing strategies are implemented can be a major source of competitive advantage.
2 If a firm purchases a competitor: *implication* – HR's challenge is to identify the culture which is required for both companies.
3 Firms may grow through existing products in new markets e.g. global: *implication* – HR's role is to facilitate growth, selecting the right local leadership and balancing local and corporate demands.
4 Firms may grow through new products within existing markets: *implication* – HR needs to create a business culture which emphasizes radical innovation and continuous improvement.
5 Firms may grow through new products and new markets: *implication* – HR's role combines the approaches in points 3 and 4 above.

Having dealt with the core issue of the alignment between HR strategy and business strategy Linda develops the theme into the key areas of delivery in a wide-ranging fashion. Each will have appeal to differing audiences; however, my selection of the pinch points that count are first HR's role in encouraging cross boundary working and innovation – Linda pinpoints the issues with a quotation from Jean Lammimann and Michel Syrett.

> Right brain thinking, which exists on a metaphorical and spatial plane, is the stuff of which new ideas are made. It sits uneasily in the context of a management culture founded on a rational process of thought that is presumed to result in informed and effective business decisions.
>
> The foundations on which traditional management is based–rational judgement and decision-making based on sharply expressed definitive ideas – can be counter-intuitive and may shut down all but a fraction of the organisation's creative capability.

Second the limits on HR's ability to influence and align strategy are seen in two crucial areas: communication with line management – where line managers' preoccupations are likely to be short term productivity focused whereas HR may be rather more concerned about longer term or cross-organizational issues. The parallel is made to the Churchillian statement about the British and Americans being 'two nations divided by a common language'.

The other major limitation is over the perception about the value of HR. As Linda says, 'A vicious circle seems to be at work: human resources specialists often seem to be passive and lack confidence, perhaps because they have not been perceived as adding value in the past. Ironically, this might have been because they were too closely associated with employees, rather than with the business decision makers. At a time when employees have been seen as dispensable, the image of HR may also have suffered. Then, perhaps due to a lack of confidence, HR professionals are often accused of being too hesitant, checking for consensus at a time when this is difficult to achieve. When 'checking' behaviour leads to decision-making paralysis, the impression of poor value-added is compounded.'

Breaking out of this cycle in a cash strapped environment can seem impossible and there is a tendency to fall into the 'cobbler's child' syndrome – of not spending time and money on the HR development.

Lastly, the pinch point of M & A activity is dealt with in some depth in terms of key roles, areas of due diligence and the key role of culture. For success in M & A three abilities must be grown:

- The ability to talk with one another.
- The ability to work with one another.
- The ability to learn from one another.

So simple, yet so rarely achieved. It reminds one of the attitude of the Japanese at Komatsu towards suppliers and precisely what HR needs to do with its partners to align people strategy with business strategy.

Dr Clive Morton, OBE
Associate Professor of HRM and Business Strategy, Middlesex University
Chairman, Centre for Tomorrow's Company Research Board
Chairman, AMED – the network of management developers

Preface

So much has been written about the changing role of HR that the reader might wonder why I have sought to add to the debate. It seems that being an HR professional is a tough proposition these days and that there are endless requirements to prove that value is being added by HR interventions. The pressures on the function are enormous and in many cases, resources are thinly stretched. The HR function is frequently accused of being reactive. Yet I believe that the situation need not be so bleak and that HR has potentially the most significant contribution to make of all the functions, if it manages to combine operational excellence with a really strategic approach.

My motivation in researching and writing this book is to find out how excellent professionals are delivering value. That is not to say that I believe that the practitioners featured in this book have a blueprint for success but some of the approaches described here are likely to provide food for thought for other organizations. Similarly, I am not attempting here to address all aspects of a strategic and operational HR agenda. I have focused on some of the performance and developmental issues which I consider key if business and HR strategies are to be aligned. This is not therefore a technical book, but one which highlights what practitioners are doing with respect to strategic recruitment, organizational development, management and international leadership development and change management. I have tried to illustrate the theory with 'live' cases where time permitted, and have included checklists which I hope will be useful to HR teams and line managers in assessing their needs and service provision.

I hope that the ways in which the HR strategists featured in this book are approaching the challenges of aligning business and

HR strategies in their organizations will provide evidence that outstanding value can be added by HR and offer encouragement to practitioners who are finding the quest to add value hard going.

Acknowledgements

I am extremely grateful to all the people, too numerous to mention, who have contributed to this book. These include participants in the various research programmes, and those who have kindly helped us to develop organizational case studies. In particular I would like to thank Dr Candy Albertsson of BP Amoco, Geoff Rogers of Standard Chartered Bank, Anthony J. Booth, CBE, of Ericsson, John Bailey of KPMG, Roger Leek of BNFL, Brian Wisdom and Alison Ainsworth of First Quench, David Waters of Whitbread PLC, Stephen McCafferty of Standard Life, Gary Storer of the NatWest Group, and Professors David Hussey and Clive Morton for their forewords. I am also indebted to Jane Yarnell of the National Air Traffic Services and Leslie Patterson of Dow Corning for their case studies.

I would to thank my colleague Christina Evans for her case study and other fellow Roffey Park researchers including Caroline Glynn, Dr Wendy Hirsh, Marion Devine, Professor Peter Smith, Michel Syrett, Jean Lammiman and John Whatmore whose research is referred to in this book. A **list of the surveys** published by Roffey Park, with details on how to obtain them, appears after the index. I am grateful to other members of the Roffey Park team who have helped in the process of preparing the book for publication, including Pauline Hinds and Krystina Fijalka. Clive Ruffle and the Learning Resource Team at Roffey Park have been very helpful. Thanks are also due to Valerie Hammond, Chief Executive of Roffey Park for her support for this project.

I would like to acknowledge the help of everyone at *Personnel Today*, for their role in the Roffey Park *Personnel Today* (1999) survey, particularly the features editor, Scott Beagrie. *Personnel*

Today is part of an HR Portfolio which includes *Training, Employers' Law and Occupational Health* magazine. It reaches 40,000 senior HR and training managers across the UK's public and private sectors. Extracts from the survey and from the fortnightly award-winning news magazine appear by kind permission.

I should also like to thank Grace Evans and Ailsa Marks of Butterworth-Heinemann for their stimulating encouragement. Finally I should like to thank my family and, in particular, my husband, for their ongoing support and understanding.

I hope that the ways in which the HR strategists featured in this book arc approaching the challenges of aligning business and HR strategies in their organizations will provide evidence that outstanding value can be added by HR and offer encouragement to practitioners who are finding the quest to add value hard going.

Part 1 The need for strategic HRM

1 *Beyond internal consultancy – the need for strategic Human Resources*

> The successful organizations will be those that are able to quickly turn strategy into action: to manage processes intelligently and efficiently: to maximize employee contribution and commitment; and to create the conditions for seamless change (Ulrich, 1998).

As everyone involved in the profession is aware, the role of HR is changing and the value delivered by HR services is being questioned. In some cases, organizations are finding other ways of providing the service which used to be HR's own. BP and BAE Systems are in the vanguard of the 'total' outsourcing of HR administration. US-based IT networking company Cisco Systems has developed a sophisticated intranet system for its own staff which has saved about £1.75 million in 'headcount avoidance', or about 30 HR jobs. According to the solutions architect for Cisco Systems, 'the concept of self-service frees up HR to concentrate on the value-added aspects of the business – analysis, leadership development and so on' (*Personnel Today*, 29 April 1999).

It sometimes seems that working in Human Resources is a no-win situation. We are all familiar with organizational values statements such as 'our people are our greatest asset', yet the reality on the ground is often different. Even in this age of information, when the value of intellectual capital should be becoming more apparent, business priorities, shareholder returns and bottom-line considerations take precedence over employee concerns.

So how is the Personnel function supposed to change this state of affairs? For years, Personnel has struggled to reinvent itself, get close to the customer and add value to the business. We are now supposed to be in the era of HR as a strategic business partner. The trouble is, the expectations of internal customers and of personnel specialists themselves about what HR can and should contribute may not have kept pace with the rhetoric. In many cases, HR professionals are still perceived to be primarily concerned with 'tea and sympathy' issues, or expected to be 'fixers' of line management problems.

The priority given to people issues is usually reflected in the status of personnel or HR professionals. The terms used to describe the function – 'back office', 'support', 'cost centre', even 'internal consultants' – imply something that is non-essential to the organization's business and therefore of lesser value. There are few main boards with a director solely responsible for human resources. Even where this is the case, the actual influence of the HR director can be limited. More often than not, HR is perceived to be a 'junior' member of the board, expected to implement the board's decisions rather than help shape them. Lip service is paid to the importance of aligning personnel and business strategies.

The lack of importance attached to addressing employee needs is most apparent in times of major crisis or opportunity for the business, such as a merger. The Roffey Park mergers research suggests that HR is often only peripherally involved in the due diligence process, let alone shaping the emerging integrated culture of the new organization. Whether this is because senior management does not understand HR's potential contribution, or because of a perceived lack of credibility of the HR team, or a combination of both, is hard to say.

Proving 'added value' in such circumstances is difficult. Indeed, Roffey Park research carried out in 200 organizations over a two-year period in the mid-1990s found that the most endangered occupational group appeared to be junior HR professionals, many of whose jobs disappeared at that time. The most common criticisms were that HR was too reactive, produced piecemeal initiatives and was constantly behind when dealing with key issues. Since that time, many of those HR teams have reshaped their delivery, devolved responsibility for operational personnel issues to line management and set themselves up as internal consultants. The aim was to ensure that the business would benefit from focused solutions, delivered in a timely and effective way.

Yet our latest research continues to suggest that, despite the shift to internal consultancy, HR is still perceived to be reactive, producing too many initiatives which go nowhere or solutions which do not match the need. Some HR professionals are reluctant to devolve responsibilities to the line since this can seem like a loss of professionalism. Furthermore, there can be reluctance among line managers to take on the HR responsibilities devolved to them as part of the shift to an HR consultancy service. This is partly due to the pressures line managers are already under, and making time for additional responsibilities can seem irksome. Some managers feel that they lack the skills required and prefer the idea that there is a function they can turn to, or blame, if problems occur.

Of course, effective consultancy is a highly skilled process and consultancy skills are a vital part of an HR professional's toolkit. In some ways working as an internal consultant can be harder than working as an external consultant since you have a longer-term set of relationships to maintain and perhaps a set of expectations about your function which can help or hinder what you can achieve. Success as an internal consultant is not easy. Yet I am arguing that internal consultancy is not enough in itself to enable HR professionals to really add value.

The changing role of Personnel

Given the growing emphasis on 'people' issues in many organizations, there seems to be a key role for Human Resource professionals in building the organization's capability to cope with ongoing change. Yet in many cases, professionals are not seizing the opportunities, feeling themselves beset by constant budget cuts and a lack of focus on people. What Human Resource professionals are able to deliver seems very dependent on the way their role is perceived within their organization. Typically, in the past, Personnel has been seen as a service deliverer, a management tool and hardly strategic.

In essence, there appears to be a transition in expectations of the HR role. According to research carried out in the mid-1990s, HR practitioners and line managers perceive the need to move on from 'traditional' roles, but the emerging roles are still being developed. The distinctions appear to be broadly as follows:

Traditional	*Emerging*
Reactive	Proactive
Employee advocate	Business partner
Task focus	Task and enablement focus

Operational issues	Strategic issues
Qualitative measures	Quantitative measures
Stability	Constant change
How? (tactical)	Why? (strategic)
Functional integrity	Multi-functional
People as expenses	People as assets

The welfare model (after Tyson and Fell, 1986)

To some extent this can be understood in terms of the evolution of the Personnel function throughout the twentieth century. In the early days of large organizations and organized labour, the function of pay clerk was often carried out by the same person who meted out 'tea and sympathy' as the notion of employee welfare caught on. Usually held by a woman, such posts were regarded as useful tools of management but postholders were not expected to contribute to the development of strategy.

Clerk of works

As the Personnel role evolved it gradually became a more active tool of management. Managing people was certainly 'line' management's responsibility, but 'staff' roles such as Personnel could provide useful specialist support on a range of issues such as pay and conditions, employee welfare, recruitment and selection, etc. To a large extent, these were largely 'maintenance'roles through which the status quo was enshrined in personnel policies and procedures. The role of Personnel was often thought of as the company 'policeman' or clerk of works.

The industrial relations expert

By the mid-1970s and the period of industrial unrest in the UK, the function of personnel was beginning to attract specialists in employee relations, many of them men, who took on the responsibility for leading negotiations with unions and (often militant) staff groups. The tough stances often adopted in these negotiations were reflected elsewhere as organizations were reshaped to meet the needs of the changing workplace. As 'fixers' of company problems such as dealing with major restructurings, redundancy programmes and other 'difficult' tasks, personnel professionals earned the right to be taken seriously as members of management.

At about the same time, the function as a whole began to professionalize its approaches. Spurred on to some extent by the lead set by the then Institute of Personnel Management and counterpart international bodies, specialists in Personnel started to describe themselves as professionals. Membership of the professional body gradually came to be by qualification rather than experience alone.

Personnel as a profession

To some extent, the power of the role grew beyond the original confines of the job. The more Personnel became the specialist repository of information about employees, including senior management, the more it needed to be consulted about any and every issue related to employees. Over time, in some cases, responsibility for managing people appeared to slip away from line managers who would refer to Personnel for everything from a minor disciplinary offence to recruitment. Personnel began to be seen as a power in the land, even if, in most cases, the Personnel director was not a member of the board. The primary function of Personnel was seen to be service delivery and the numbers employed within the function grew accordingly.

In more recent times, the growing demand from various governments for increased accountability, on the one hand, and for better people management, on the other, has to some extent strengthened the hand of those advocating effective training and development. Initiatives such as Investors in People and measurement frameworks such as ISO and the European Foundation for Quality Management (British Excellence Model), have linked 'hard' business results with 'soft' inputs such as leadership. The Institute of Personnel and Development has achieved chartered status. At least at face value, the importance of effective people strategies has been recognized and line managers have been expected to become leaders. External influences such as the Working Time Directive and Fairness at Work initiatives are placing pressure on organizations to address employee needs appropriately. The need for a strategic response to human resource issues will no longer simply be left to the good intentions of managers who feel well disposed to take people issues seriously.

Leveraging human resources has been widely accepted as the key to competitive advantage. However, how much this recognition has been translated into practice and resulted in genuinely changed priorities is debatable. This may perhaps be explained by the general tendency of executives to pay attention first and foremost to the bottom line. Given their responsibilities, this is understandable, as long as their attention does not stop there. In many organizations 'people issues' are way down the agenda, and where they do appear they are often short-term operational problems rather than key areas of attention. Other factors which may explain why people issues are not taken very seriously include expectations of the role of Personnel, the political context within which Personnel specialists are operating and the skills and effectiveness of the specialists themselves.

In recent years, numbers of Personnel specialists have been slashed, often because the function was not perceived to add value. In Roffey Park research carried out in 200 organizations between 1994 and 1996, the numbers of 'junior' personnel professionals fell by 35 per cent. Comments from the sample population suggested that HR professionals perceived the function to be under threat. Typically, the lack of value added was noticeable in the implementation of change, with HR forced into a reactive, 'picking up the pieces' role. Initiative overload, with poor follow-through of key initiatives, were other symptoms of the function's difficulties in many organizations. Personnel professionals grappled with the difficulties of balancing pragmatic solutions with professionalism.

Conversely, of the fifth of our sample population who had been promoted during that time, many were 'senior' Personnel professionals, some of whom were invited to join the board. The idea is that value is better added through targeting specialist support on key internal clients and by devolving other personnel responsibilities to the line, where arguably they belong.

Interestingly, the recent Roffey Park/*Personnel Today* survey (1999) of nearly 200 HR practitioners, found that the picture of HR is perhaps not so bleak after all. If anything, these practitioners appear to see the influence of HR as strong and the function to be growing in size. Roffey Park's Management Agenda Surveys 2000–2001 confirm this trend. Even so, the function does not appear to be focused on strategic matters.

The internal consultant

The evolution of Personnel has continued, with specialists being encouraged to take on the role of consultant to line management and cut down the element of operational service delivery.

- *Is HR in your organization decentralized?*
  Yes/partly   22 per cent
- *Is HR in your organization centralized?*
  Yes/partly   42 per cent
- *Has your HR team grown in size?*
  Yes   57 per cent
- *Has your HR team reduced in size?*
  Yes   34 per cent
- *Is HR spread too thinly?*
  Agree slightly/strongly   63 per cent
- *Has HR been outsourced?*
  Yes/partly   16 per cent
- *Is HR directly represented on the board?*
  Yes   50 per cent
- *Is it true that HR has no influence at board level?*
  Agree slightly/strongly   36 per cent
- *Has responsibility for personnel been devolved to the line?*
  Yes/partly   71 per cent
- *To what extent is there no consistency because
  responsibilities are devolved?*
  To some extent/to a great extent   30 per cent
- *Do HR professionals lack credibility in your organization?*
  Agree slightly/strongly   33 per cent
- *To what extent is HR too reactive?*
  To some extent/to a great extent   61 per cent
- *To what extent does HR spend too much time on trivial matters?*
  To some extent/to a great extent   60 per cent

Roffey Park/Personnel Today Survey, 1999.

Typically, devolution of HR activities to the line is unpopular with line managers who tend to reject the notion of internal consultancy unless they are also continuing to receive service delivery support. Line expectations about what Personnel is meant to deliver may well be rooted in the 'tea and sympathy' or the service delivery phase of evolution. As one line manager in a pharmaceutical company announced to his personnel colleague when she came to tell him about her change of role; 'Don't tell me you're an internal consultant and here to solve my problems. Since you're leaving me to do my own recruitment, **you** are my problem'. Yet in many organizations, responsibility for many aspects of people management has largely passed back to the line. In others, a 'rump' of the core personnel function attempts to provide service delivery while other team members provide internal consultancy.

The danger of working to predominantly short-term management agendas is that the real value which can be added through Personnel, namely the development of effective manpower and succession strategies, skills development and strategic recruitment, gets dissipated at business group level. One Roffey Park research report (November 1998) makes depressing reading on this front. The role of Human Resource professionals in developing processes in some 350 UK organizations still seems anything but strategic. Forty-four per cent of respondents described their HR approaches as piecemeal and another 29 per cent as reactive. Only 18 per cent were seen as helpful.

The drive towards customers and effectiveness sounds laudable, but knee-jerk responses to these demands may mean that ironically the function deprives itself of the means to deliver what is required. In parts of the UK public sector, for instance, the demand for cost savings and efficiency has led to a typical 'client'/'consultant' split within the personnel and training functions. Under Compulsory Competitive Tendering and now Best Value initiatives, parts of the personnel service are often outsourced, preventing real teamworking across the function.

People as assets

These shifts in the shape of the personnel service have coincided with a general rebadging of personnel functions as 'Human Resources', Strategic HRM or Business Partners. The notion that a resource as fragile yet valuable as human beings can be regarded as a 'resource' or fixed asset is curious, to say the least. The use of the term 'resource' stems from attempts by managers and academics to understand the basis of competitive advantage in organizations. Under a resource perspective, three basic types of resource can provide competitive advantage:

*   Physical capital resources which include, for example, the company's finances, equipment, plant, etc.
*   Organizational capital resources which include the firm's structure and systems for controlling
*   Human capital resources which include the skills, competencies, experience and intelligence of employees

Ways of establishing the link between the company's human resources and competitive advantage are explored in Chapter 2.

Yet for all the limitations of the term, it does suggest that people as assets, whether capital or revenue assets, need to be regarded as an investment. In this sense, getting the best out of 'resourceful humans' is perhaps a more appropriate way of thinking about effective people management strategies. People are a potentially more fragile resource, yet one which has greater potential value than other forms of asset. This, despite the well-known Dilbert cartoon which shows the boss recognizing that 'people are no longer our greatest asset – they are now ninth'. The eighth most important was carbon paper! Strategies for adding to the value of the human asset and for effective divestment of that asset, if need be, require a more proactive approach than simply developing and policing policies and procedures.

Raising the game

The challenge for HR practitioners is to focus HR activities on developing aspects of the organization's human resources which can be turned into sustainable competitive advantage. In many organizations, personnel specialists have managed to raise their game. Increasingly, professionals are acting as change agents and are targeting specific aspects of organizational culture which need to change in order to equip their authority for the challenges ahead. In other cases, HR professionals are clearly seen to be operating as business partners with senior management, providing the link between business and organizational strategies, support and challenge to the senior team and developing credible initiatives in a setting of ongoing cost reduction.

Some HR practitioners have reached the national stage. Among the most influential figures in the HR field as chosen by *Personnel Today* are:

* Anne Minto, who as HR director of **Smiths Industries** has a wide network of contacts, knowledge and influence. She has a varied career history including having been deputy director general of the Engineering Employers' Federation.
* Anne Watts, Equal Opportunities Director of **Midland Bank**, is known for her tireless campaigning for equal opportunities and for innovative work/life balance initiatives.

- Clive Morton, previously Director of Learning and Human Resources at **Anglian Water** and now an independent consultant, began his career as a civil engineer and is widely respected for his theories on learning, partnership and communication.
- Bob Mason, HR Director of **British Telecom UK**, has helped turn BT into one of the most progressive employers in terms of its HR policies.
- Stephanie Monk, HR Director at **Granada Group**, sat on the Low Pay Commission and was key in formulating the policy to introduce the minimum wage.

The transition to a more strategic role can be difficult, but it is certainly not impossible. Several of the case studies in this book, featuring the activities of HR practitioners who are making a strategic contribution to their organizations, should offer hope and practical insights into how others have made the transition.

What makes strategic HRM 'more strategic' than HRM?

Strategic HRM has become topical in recent years but definitions as to what is meant by the term vary widely. Shaun Tyson (1995) defines HR strategy as 'the intentions of the corporation, both explicit and covert, toward the management of its employees, expressed through philosophies, policies and practices'. Typically, strategic HRM bridges business strategy and HRM and focuses on the integration of HR with the business and its environment.

Some researchers distinguish between 'hard', traditional HRM and 'soft'. 'Hard' HRM reflects a contingency approach based on the assessment of the best way to manage people in order to achieve business goals in the light of contextual factors. 'Soft' HRM focuses on a high-commitment–high-performance approach to the management of people. One of the key elements of 'soft' HRM is the internal integration of HR policy goals with each other. In the UK, David Guest (1989) incorporated the HR policy goals of strategic integration, commitment, quality and flexibility into a model. He suggests that these HRM policy goals are a package which Purcell (1996) considers to have six common elements:

- Careful recruitment and selection
- Extensive use of systems of communication
- Teamworking with flexible job design
- Emphasis on training and learning
- Involvement in decision making
- Performance appraisal with tight links to contingent pay.

The main rationale for strategic HRM thinking is that by integrating HRM with the business strategy, rather than HR strategies being a separate set of priorities, employees will be managed more effectively, organizational performance will improve and therefore business success will follow. This in itself may not be enough. Tony Grundy (1998) suggests:

> Human Resources Strategy in itself may not be effective. Integrating Corporate Strategy and HR matters into an 'Organization and People Strategy' may prove more successful.

Some researchers (Huselid, Jackson and Schuler, 1997) have argued that technical HRM focuses on building a company's performance, while strategic HRM creates competitive advantage by building HR systems which cannot be imitated. Strategic HRM therefore has a clear focus on implementing strategic change and growing the skill base of the organization to ensure that the organization can compete effectively in the future. Indeed, Stroh and Caligiuri (1998) suggest that strategic HR departments are future-oriented and operate in a manner consistent with the overall business plan in their organizations. Such departments assess the knowledge, skills and abilities needed for the future and institute staffing, appraisal and evaluation, incentives and compensation, training and development to meet those needs.

This also suggests that facilitating organizational learning, both for implementing change and in helping to develop strategy, is a key element of strategic HR. According to this approach, people are a key resource and a critical element in a firm's performance since they build organizational effectiveness. Tony Grundy defines organizational effectiveness as: 'The capacity of the organization to adapt rapidly to its external environment and to meet market and other external demands and with good resulting business performance.'

What remains unclear is how organizations can achieve consistently superior performance via HR strategy. This has led to a focus on measuring the effects of HR activity on business performance, though the range of measures used in different organizations tends to be inconsistent.

'Fit' with business strategy

In the 1980s various thinkers such as Fombrun, Tichy and Devanna (1984) argued that what was important was a tight external fit between the external business strategy and HRM. This contingency approach suggests that for any particular organizational strategy, there will be a matching HR strategy (Figure 1.1).

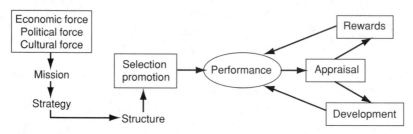

Figure 1.1   *The human resource cycle and 'fit' with business strategy. Based on Devanna et al., 1984*

The belief that the closer the 'fit' between business strategy and organizational functions will result in organizational effectiveness has been challenged in recent times. The challenges relate to the lack of empirical evidence that this close strategic fit will automatically lead to improved effectiveness, and that such approaches do not take into account measures of organizational effectiveness. There are also criticisms that such approaches can be too simplistic in their assumption that the creation of HR strategy inevitably follows the business strategy.

Recent studies (for example, Delaney and Huselid, 1996) claim to have found a statistically significant link between 'bundles' of HR policies and business performance. These bundles of HR practices need to be internally consistent and depend on the organizational logic in that context. A key finding appears to be that in order to obtain best effect, an integrated set of complementary HR practices needs to be implemented. Thus, while individual aspects of 'best practice' are useful for benchmarking purposes, the approaches used must be congruent with the organization's state of development if the real benefit is to be felt. Various studies, including Brewster, Hegewisch and Lockhart (1991) have suggested measures for assessing the strategic importance of HRM, such as whether there is an HR specialist in the top management team, the role of the line in HR responsibilities and the contribution of HR to the development of business strategy.

Operating as a business partner – what do CEOs need from HR?

Defining what being a business partner means in practice involves looking at what the 'partner' requires from the relationship. Assuming that the business partner is line management, looking at what chief executives do not want from HR is as informative as finding out what they require. A small-scale research project in which chief executives talked about what they needed from the function suggests that CEOs do not value an emphasis on professional skills alone. HR professionals need to understand the business and its challenges, as well as be able to translate business strategies into their human resource implications. They need to be able to communicate with executives in ways which demonstrate this understanding.

Similarly, the study suggests that CEOs do not appreciate too great a concern with rules and procedures which results in inappropriate policing and blocking action. The quest for the 'perfect' solution or 'best practice' system is not appreciated either, if such initiatives are not owned by management or do not fit the organization. This means that HR professionals must involve line managers in the development of initiatives which make a difference to how people are managed, developed and rewarded. The well-intentioned new appraisal scheme or competency framework, if developed by HR alone, may be perceived as over-engineered or inappropriate.

One CEO's agenda is illustrated by this brief extract from an interview with the head of a government-supported organization providing a public service in the field of the arts. While not necessarily typical, the following extract perhaps indicates key areas in which HR professionals can provide a partnership approach to addressing key organizational issues.

Q   *What are the issues you have to deal with?*
A

- Board and committee – issues relating to the political profile of the organization, including relationships with ... (external bodies, including funding bodies).
- Internal policy matters – issues relating to the organization culture and the management of change.
- The management of people – including relationships with three different unions
  Management of trading areas within an overall charitable institution.

Q   *Which are the critical ones for your organization?*
A

- The effective recruitment, management and development of people, since the organization depends on the skills and excellence of its staff in all areas.
- Ensuring that the (organization) stays at the cutting edge in all areas. The organization has to perform as market leader and set the highest of standards.

Q   *What are the major challenges for you personally?*
A

- Managing a diverse range of individually talented, but not necessarily like-minded people.
- The management of change which appears to be continuous and ensuring that the very best results are achieved.
- Ensuring a cohesive approach to the introduction of policies across the organization. This is particularly difficult since the organization is made up of several very different cultures. The integration of those cultures and the understanding of those cultures is essential to the organization's success.
- The whole nature of the organization is very short-term. Part of the difficulty I face is marrying the short-term projects that are achieved regularly throughout the year with the more strategic and longer-term policies that need to ensure the overall survival of the organization. I also need to help my managers achieve a better longer-term understanding of where they are going so that they can forward plan more effectively than they do at present.

Q   *What are the constraints of your role?*
A

- Lack of recognition for how important human resources issues are, e.g. the board tends to focus only on financial matters.
- A union that is in the last century. Making change in these areas is very difficult.

- Financial pressures will continue to increase. This will put people/managers under pressure to find alternative/more efficient/different ways of doing things while maintaining the very high standards that the organization operates. There will be a need to ensure the high profile of the operation at every level. This will be essential to persuade our political masters that we are continuing to do an excellent job.
- Time is a major constraint as the organization works at full capacity throughout the year and it often appears one is responding to resolving immediate difficulties rather than carrying out forward planning.

What chief executives appear to require is someone who can translate the organization's needs back into business language and help executives understand what must be done with regard to people if the business strategies are to be achieved. This means that HR professionals need to be able to sense the issues which count, and to have the confidence to relay some potentially tough messages to management about what needs to be done. This is the quality described by Dave Ulrich as 'HR with attitude'. CEOs also need HR to be experts in process skills, able to win commitment and influence within the organization.

This requires an ongoing dialogue with the line business organization and the ability to both plan change and bring others effectively through change. Approaches to achieving this will be examined in Chapter 14. For the HR function, the agenda becomes a simple one – the aim is to be both a contributing member of the management team as well as to create personal and functional capability. Business will then drive the HR agenda rather than HR activity being an end in itself.

Reorienting HR to high added-value contributions

There is an apparent paradox which prevents some HR functions from making strategic contributions. If the basic HR processes such as administrative activities are not in good order, especially on sensitive issues such as executive pay, no strategic contribution is likely to be considered of value until the administrative problem has been fixed. If the problems recur, the credibility of HR teams can be at stake. It is understandable then that many HR teams concentrate on delivering the core processes right without attempting to be proactive with regard to strategy. Perversely, HR teams which concentrate on administration tend to be criticized as being 'reactive' and are regarded as a cost. Processing paperwork, addressing employee concerns and administering personnel policies are time-consuming and energy-hungry. Since a key aim of HR teams must be to improve cost efficiency, business competitiveness and customer service (Ulrich *et al.*, 1995) the paradox must be resolved.

One way of resolving the paradox is by taking good care of routine HR responsibilities through information technology so that HR departments can concentrate on high value-added activities. This means reorienting the HR team to a more strategic approach.

Reengineering HR

A relatively radical approach is to reengineer the HR function. This typically happens when organizations restructure their central functions in order to encourage diversification within the business. Corporate centres are often thought to hold back individual businesses because of their desire for a common culture, or for system compatibility. Corporate centre staff often see their role as managing the concerns of a range of stakeholders including customers, suppliers and employees and community interests. Though these contributions are real they are hard to quantify and the trend to demerge or decentralise functions appears well under way.

Ideally, a more strategic reorientation of HR takes place when the HR team reviews what it would contribute as a function, and how it would structure itself, if HR operated in a 'greenfield site'. Reengineering can target the whole function or just a key HR process. Hammer and Champy (1993) define reengineering as 'utilizing the power of modern information systems to radically redesign processes in order to achieve dramatic improvement in critical performance measures'. Wayne Brockbank of the University of Michigan and Arthur Yeung of San Francisco State University (1998) have identified two main ways of reengineering HR. One is technology driven, where an 'off-the-shelf' system package is used and HR processes redesigned accordingly;

the other is process driven which starts with a process redesign and then has systems custom-built to support the process. Brockbank and Yeung advocate the technology-driven approach because:

- It allows suppliers to provide the technical support available from previous systems
- Since it builds on existing systems, costs should be lower
- Time-consuming technical hitches can be eliminated.

Many Human Resource information systems are built on People Soft and SAP packages.

Cost reduction is a main driver behind HR reengineering efforts. The use of advanced information technology in order to transform the delivery of routine but important administrative activities is leading to greater efficiency and reduced HR-to-employee ratios. This, of course, brings down the cost of service delivery and allows professionals to concentrate on adding value through knowledge-based, problem-solving activities. Companies in the advanced technology sector such as **Apple Computers** and **Hewlett-Packard** have led the field on this form of delivery of operational HR. Another driver is improving the quality and consistency of HR services. In many companies, decentralized decision-making about IT systems has led to a plethora of HR systems being used which do not talk to each other, causing duplication and lost opportunities, especially when carrying out internal talent searches, for example. In situations such as this, IT systems can seem more of a constraint than a help.

One company has completely revamped its separate, people-related systems within a single shared system architecture. People management information has been streamlined, automated and integrated. This means that continuous HR process improvements can be easily incorporated, ensuring that the systems continue to be relevant and supportive to managers. Another company has been able to radically reduce the cycle time in salary planning while increasing accuracy. Other organizations use IT to cope with the process of filling management positions, from forecasting needs to identifying suitable candidates. Increasingly, companies are using telephone and e-mail help desks to answer and process routine enquiries about pay and benefits, medical and retirement plans and other issues where a 'human' response is required.

Reengineering HR processes, and providing user-friendly tools to acquire information on demand, can be helpful to managers who now have devolved responsibility for addressing employee issues directly, without the intervention of HR. Some companies make available on-line self-sufficiency tools such as internal job posting systems, directories of all employees and their locations/contact details, training courses and other important information.

Reengineering can itself be costly, since the hardware, communications infrastructure and applications software need to be appropriate and require a heavy time commitment from staff involved (consultants, HR and IT staff). It is important to pick the right HR process from the outset rather than launch programmes which are too complex or never get completed. Typically, reengineering is triggered by problems with existing systems and the need to address specific goals. Some resistance can be anticipated since reengineering can also present risks to existing systems and threats to jobs. The level of psychological resistance should not be underestimated. When introducing reengineering, therefore, it is important to be clear about why it is needed and how reengineering fits with the overall strategy to achieve business goals.

Transforming HR's role

Winning support for such changes is essential if they are to succeed. Setting clear and realistic goals can help achieve buy-in from top management. Clients need to perceive the benefits to them of supporting the development and implementation of new systems. It is important to develop a centralized system which can flex to local autonomy and the varying needs of the business. Ideally, forming coalitions with internal clients who are champions of change can help create a culture supportive of change within the organization. A steering team, usually consisting of senior HR managers, line and MIS managers, is usually formed at an early stage. This team helps to find out the key concerns of users of the proposed process, works out the problems with the current process, sets new targets for the process and develops an implementation plan.

Implementation teams are formed to provide solutions to each of the proposed processes and action plans and milestones are established. Implementation teams need to be held accountable to clear and measurable targets. Monitoring the processes and communicating results helps maintain support for the change. Once the processes have been reengineered, additional training is generally required to help line managers and HR professionals use the new processes effectively. This can overcome one of the commonest pitfalls which is that users do not understand the new system. Assuming that the new processes are correctly targeted, championed from the top and add value, this allows HR professionals to focus on areas where their contribution can significantly move the organization forward.

What HR can be valued for and should build on

The skills of the HR specialists are key to the effective development and implementation of people strategies. Similarly, HR practitioners can and do adopt a range of roles, variously described as strategist, mentor, talent scout, architect, builder, facilitator, coordinator, champion of change. The art is to have the flexibility and awareness of what is needed in different situations. Many is the HR strategist who takes up a new role in an organization which is apparently ripe for change but has deeply embedded practices which are difficult to shift. The strategist usually experiences great frustration as they see their attempts to bring about change wither away. The pragmatist works within this context to make change happen at the pace which is likely to lead to the embedding of new approaches, rather than seeking to bring about widespread initiatives in order to make their mark.

First and foremost, professionals need to be credible, understanding the business of their organization and able to take appropriate risks. They need to be knowledgeable about HR processes and to monitor and measure effectiveness. More importantly, they need to be able to manage culture, recognizing what needs to be maintained, strengthened or changed, as well as to manage change.

How much HR should be seen to be taking a lead in preparing the organization for change when the way ahead remains uncertain is open to debate. Of course, there are risks in developing an HR strategy in the absence of a business strategy. The usual accusations of being 'out of touch', 'power crazy' or 'ivory tower' are bound to follow. Conversely, waiting for the business strategy to become clear may mean that vital planning time can be lost and HR is once again in catch-up mode.

Part of the problem is that the more highly client focused you are, the more likely it is that you will be delivering solutions which fix that particular client's immediate problem, perhaps at the expense of corporate needs. Typically, internal clients of HR are interested in solving problems which affect them in the short term; they are less interested in what they fear will be the over-engineered corporate solution which is delivered too late to be of real use. There is also the human tendency to reject solutions which are 'not invented here'. Consequently, internal consultants can often find themselves chasing local issues where the business head has seen a 'people problem' and tried to fix it. It can be hard to challenge a powerful player who perceives you to add value only if you do what they say. The focus on short-term issues then sets up the vicious cycle of being unable to produce the bigger wins for the organization in equipping it for its future challenges because you are too busy focusing on, or repairing damage in, the short term.

Yet now more than ever the ability to balance short-term demands with a longer-term perspective is called for. Certain drivers for change are already starting to transform the employment landscape, reversing previous power balances between employers and employees. Globalization is highlighting the need for organizations to manage the development of talent as well as to manage knowledge in complex international networks. Technology and the rapid changes in working practices and skills requirements are enabling employees who are truly employable to command their price and dictate terms to their employers. While line management is responsible for the growth and survival of the business and its employees, HR as a function has potentially a key role to play in partnering the line to prepare their organizations for future challenges. This is where operational effectiveness has to be balanced by a strategic perspective.

This need for balance is demonstrated through one of the major thrusts of strategic thinking in recent years. Hamel and Prahalad's (1994) notion of the core competence of a firm suggests that firms should build their strategies to what they do best. Wayne Brockbank (1997), however, points out that this condemns a firm's strategic thinking to a short-term perspective given that the life span of knowledge is rapidly shrinking.

Brockbank argues that what counts are not the core technical competencies but the core cultural competencies:

> The key core competence, however, is not what a firm does based on what is known, but is, rather, a firm having a culture which encourages flexibility, change, learning, creativity and adaptability to customers.

HR practitioners need to identify the future organization's needs through addressing questions such as:

- What will the competitive marketplace for the company's products, services and labour look like over the next five to ten years?
- What is the company's core competence, especially over the next three to five years?
- What kind of human resources will the organization need in order to compete successfully, or to continue to develop and provide high-quality services?
- What types of HR practices are relevant to building the organization needed for the future?

Towards a strategic HR agenda

A strategic HR agenda is likely to have a number of key goals relating to the attraction, development and retention of talent. This may mean competing for the 'best' employees through developing innovative approaches to careers and rewards. Quality of management is likely to be another key agenda item. This may mean introducing tough and effective assessment and development processes to ensure that the organization has the leadership it needs. The enabling of high performance is likely to be a key target for strategic HRM. This involves understanding how high performance is built and sustained, as well as identifying and eliminating barriers to high performance. This will probably involve addressing those aspects of organizational life which have an adverse effect on people's motivation.

Perhaps the biggest item is also the most diffuse: creating and building organizational climates and cultures which support what the organization wants to do. This may mean bringing about small or substantial changes which can threaten internal clients' comfort zones. Changing cultures will also involve identifying the new aspects of behaviour and practice which will need to be reinforced through reward and recognition.

I am not saying that operational HR is irrelevant but that organizations may increasingly follow the lead set by companies such as **Unisys** and **IBM** who have found innovative solutions to providing an effective administration service to the line while freeing up HR specialists for more strategic work. HR professionals will need to be capable of making the decisions to drive the organization forward. This requires developing a specific skill set as well as the winning the right to contribute strategically because you deliver results. Credibility is often gained or lost on the ability to both shape strategy and implement it. Strategic thinking is clearly essential but the skills of bringing about change extend beyond being able to take a longer-term view. Project management skills and the ability to work successfully in cross-boundary teams can be essential to effective delivery of outcomes.

If HR is to truly become a business partner, specialists need to really understand the business and be able to reflect that understanding in their actions. They do not need to be experts, but they should be able to use creative approaches to designing HR processes which really meet needs. Basic consultancy skills, such as gaining entry and diagnosis, should be part of the professional toolkit. Similarly, part of the art of the HR business partner is knowing when to lead in creating a new people-related process and when to build line ownership by building the corporate from the local. This means that HR has to be on the look-out for useful initiatives which have begun elsewhere in the organization and be able to build greater coherence so as to avoid 'death by a thousand initiatives'.

Bringing about change, above all, requires HR specialists to be able to influence key players and to have the confidence to challenge. This means being politically aware and being prepared to use various forms of power to ensure that strategic people needs are appropriately dealt with. HR has potentially many sources of power, such as the use of information about staff. Being able to use data effectively to make a convincing case is part of the HR toolkit. In **BP Amoco**, Dr Candy Albertsson, for instance, managed to win business support for a new means of assessing high potential by helping executives draw conclusions from competency data gathered from an assessment process (see Chapters 10 and 11). Of course, the most easily available form of power is personal power, which stems largely from an individual's personality. Being respected as a professional, being a team player and being the kind of person who is trusted and to whom people at all levels can turn can be a source of influence and credibility.

Perhaps the core expertise lies in managing ongoing change and working with management to develop a robust and resilient workforce able to thrive on change. HR professionals need to be able to cope well with change and help others to do so. They need to understand their organization's cultures and be able to work out – with others – what needs to be strengthened, because it supports what the organization wants to do and what does need to be changed.

Prioritizing the HR agenda may mean stepping out of the vicious cycle of constant delivery in order to choose the key areas of focus if value is really to be added. Radical choices may or may not be the consequence, but you do not know until you try. According to Keith Walton, a member of **IBM**'s management consulting unit, 'HR is traditionally seen as a cost. If you can separate the operational from the strategic, you can see that the strategic side adds value'.

Checklists on the role of HR

From operational to strategic

Dave Ulrich (1998) defines the domains of strategic HR as follows:

- Employee champion
- Expert in the way work is managed and executed
- Change agent
- Strategic partner
- Administrator

Other work (Radford, 1995) defines the following as key responsibilities of HR:

- Recruitment (including induction) as a strategic activity
- The appraisal process
- Training
- Remuneration
- Management practices and developing new approaches

The following questions are intended to offer the basis for an HR team self-assessment:

Expectations of the role of HR

- What business are we in? What should we be in? Who are our customers?
- How do our customers perceive our services?
- What are managers' and employees' expectations of HR?
- In reengineering processes, what are the implications for roles and responsibilities of HR professionals?
- In what ways can managers and HR specialists work more closely to link strategy and personnel practice?
- If we had fewer services, do we know what trade-offs our customers would be willing to make?

Adding value

- Would you manage HR differently if your personal circumstances were impacted upon directly by bottom-line performance?
- What current organizational or managerial issues, if resolved, could result in substantial business improvement?
- Where do we add value? Proportionately how much time do we spend on value adding activities?
- What is the relationship between cost and value of the work we perform?
- What does our organization need from HR currently – and in the next few years?
- What changes could we make to increase the effectiveness of HR in our organization?
- How will we measure the success of reengineering efforts?
- How will we let people know?
- How should we structure HR to add value?
- What should be the ratio of HR to the line?

Changing the focus of HR

- Where are we now in terms of our HR function?
- How much does IT play a part in our overall HR strategy?
- Who will champion reengineering efforts?
- In what ways will reengineered processes be superior to existing ones?

- In moving from operational to strategic, how should the gap be filled, and by whom?
- If we devolve aspects of HR to the line, how do we maintain consistency?
- How should line managers be prepared for their role?
- What should we offer?
- What new competencies and skills do we need?
- What flexible practices will enable us to shift from operational to strategic?

The influence of HR

- Is HR represented on the management board or involved in actually devising the HR strategy?
- Will the organization give a higher or lower priority to managing people in the next five years?
- If the priority will be lower, what impact will that have on retention of key people?
- If we change what we do, which process would we begin with?
- How will we minimize resistance to change?
- How shall we deal with managers who cannot make the transition?
- Which body makes the strategic decisions in practice?
- How does that body receive information about, and take decisions on, managing people? How is HR involved?

References

Brewster, C., Hegewisch, A. and Lockhart, J. T. (1991). Researching Human Resource Management: methodology of the Price Waterhouse Cranfield Project on European trends. *Personnel Review*, **20**, No.6, 36–40.

Brockbank, W. (1997). HR's future on the way to a presence. *Human Resource Management*, Spring, **36**, No.1, 65–69.

Delaney, J. T. and Huselid, M. A. (1996). The impact of Human Resource Management practices on perceptions of organizational performance. *Academy of Management Journal*, **39**, No.4, 949–969.

Fombrun, C., Tichy, N. M. and Devanna, M. A. (1984). *Framework for HRM. Strategic Human Resource Management*. New York: John Wiley.

Grundy, A. (1998). How are corporate strategy and human resources strategy linked? *Journal of General Management*, **23**, No.3, Spring.

Guest, D. (1989). Personnel and Human Resource Management: Can you tell the difference? *Personnel Management*, January, 48–51.

Hamel, G. and Prahalad, C. K. (1994) *Competing for the Future*. Boston, MA: Harvard Business School Press.

Hammer, M. and Champy, J. (1993). *Reengineering the Corporation*, New York: Harper Business.

Huselid, M. A., Jackson, S. E. and Schuler, R. S. (1997). Technical and strategic Human Resource Management effectiveness as determinants of firm performance. *Academy of Management Journal*, **40**, No.1, 171–188.

Lahteenmaki, S., Storey, J. and Vanhala, S. (1999). HRM and company performance : the use of measurement and the influence of economic cycles. *Human Resource Management Journal*, **8**, No.2.

Purcell, J. (1996). Human resource bundles of best practice: a utopian cul-de-sac? Paper presented at ESRC/BUIRA Seminar Series on Contribution of HR Strategy to Business Performance.

Radford, A. (1995). *Managing People in a Professional Services Firm*. London: IPD.

Storey, J. (1998). Strategic non-HRM – a viable alternative? *Strategic Change*, November.

Stroh, L. and Caligiuri, P. M. (1998). Strategic Human Resources: a new source for competitive advantage in the global arena. *The International Journal of Human Resource Management*, **9**, No.1, February.

Tate, W. (1999). *Demerging Organizations – A guide to best practice*. London: Financial Times Management.

Tyson, S. (1995). *Human Resource Strategy. Towards a General Theory of Human Resource Management*. London: Pitman Publishing.

Tyson, S. and Fell, A. (1986). *Evaluating the Personnel Function*. London: Hutchinson.

Ulrich, D., interviewed by MacLachlan, R. (1998). HR with attitude. *People Management*, 13 August.

Ulrich, D., Brookbank, W., Yeung, A. K. and Lake, D. G. (1995). Human Resource competences: an empirical assessment. *Human Resource management*, Winter.

Yeung, A. K. and Brockbank, W. (1998). Reengineering HR through information technology. *Human Resource Planning*.

The context for strategic Human Resources

A recent report by Washington-based McKinsey Global Institute, reported in *Personnel Today* (1 April 1999) suggests that the UK economy suffers from apparent anomalies in competitiveness. There is still a huge gap in productivity between the UK and other industrial nations. Nevertheless, the long-term prognosis is good. With flexible labour markets and open capital markets, Britain has fewer constraints on growth than many other countries. Lack of awareness of global best practice was one of the issues singled out as contributing to the problem. If Britain manages to remedy the deficiency and close the productivity gap it has a unique opportunity to leap ahead of competing nations in terms of overall growth (Lewis, 1999). This chapter makes use of research findings from two surveys carried out by Roffey Park Management Institute: the *Management Agenda 1998/99*, which is completed by line and HR managers; and a survey of HR managers carried out in 1999 in collaboration with *Personnel Today*.

The changing business environment

No organization is immune from the changing tides of economic, social, political and technological trends. Many of the socio-economic certainties of the twentieth century are crumbling. Marketplaces are becoming ruthlessly competitive as unique technologies, unique physical assets and historic brands are challenged. In the UK, high street giants such as **Sainsbury's** shed jobs during 1999 and Marks & Spencer has been subjected to radical restructuring in 2001 because of falling profits. As the world enters the new millennium, globalization has become a major thrust, when only a decade ago, most UK pundits were predicting only the advent of the 'Euromanager'.

Much manufacturing capability has migrated from the developed world to parts of the developing one. The West is becoming predominantly a service economy, with the UK in particular seeing the development of high technology, financial services and travel and tourism as major growth areas.

Kenichi Ohmae, author of *Triad Power* (1985), suggested that the route to global competitiveness was to establish a presence in each area of the Triad – Japan, the United States and the Pacific, and Europe – and to use each of the three Cs of commitment, creativity and competitiveness. Ohmae points out how globalization will ultimately affect all aspects of a nation's economic life:

> The essence of business strategy is offering better value to customers than the competition in the most cost-effective and sustainable way. But today, thousands of competitors from every corner of the world are able to serve customers well. To develop effective strategy, we as leaders have to understand what's happening in the rest of the world, and reshape our organization to respond accordingly. No leader can hope to guide an enterprise into the future without understanding the commercial, political and social impact of the global economy.

Consumer demands and the need for flexibility

In the UK the 24-hour shopping and service culture is taking root, with changing working patterns an inevitable result. From the customer's point of view, having service available round the clock is the main consideration. For organizations, the need to provide continuous service is leading to experimentation with flexible staffing provision. Some organizations are increasingly using the capability provided by technology to run help desks and other operations on a 'sun-time' basis from different parts of the world. In other cases, organizations are becoming increasingly reliant on different types of flexible worker who can provide the cover required.

The impact of technology

On the technologies front, e-commerce is becoming the 'normal' way to do business. As competition in the service economy becomes more intense – and the financial services industry is a prime example of this – the trend towards market consolidation through acquisitions is often a defensive move to avoid being swallowed up by bigger players. At the same time, major political shifts have opened up vast new markets for capitalist goods and services, such as China, while closing down some 'traditional' ones.

Many pundits argue that we are now in a new industrial era or at least on the verge of the Information Revolution which will take us out of the Machine Age. In the Information Age, the individual is king or queen, with corresponding freedoms of choice. The implications of this are significant:

- Governance of society is mutating
- The very nature of the firm, of the workplace is changing
- Work itself, and the nature of the employment contract, are undergoing major changes.

Governance of society is mutating

In the global electronic economy, investors and fund managers can transfer huge amounts of capital in an instant. This can sometimes lead to the destabilization of a national or regional economy, as happened in East Asia. The global marketplace is indifferent to national borders and many nations have lost much of the sovereignty they once had. According to Professor Anthony Giddens, the 1999 Reith Lecturer, 'globalization is political, technological and cultural, as well as economic'.

'News' can now be relayed around the world instantly, shaping opinions and transforming traditional family and societal values. One impact of globalization appears to be the removal of power and influence from local and national communities into the global arena. Conversely, there appears to be a corresponding push for greater local control of power, for 'subsidiarity' and the right to make decisions at the most local level possible, as witnessed in the UK by the devolution of some political powers to Scotland and Wales. Giddens argues that in a world based upon active communication 'political power based upon authoritarian command can no longer draw upon reserves of traditional deference or respect'. He points out the paradox and political instability inherent in the fact that while many parts of the world are making the transition to democracy, at the same time there is widespread disillusionment with democratic processes.

Opinion polls carried out in various Western countries suggest that people have lost a great deal of trust in their politicians and conventional democratic procedures. Younger people, often described as Generation X, are said to be disaffected and alienated. Giddens suggests that what is needed is a deepening of democracy on a global level. This, he argues, will involve active devolution of power and the use of alternative democratic procedures such as electronic referenda and people's juries. He also suggests a strong democratized civil culture, which markets cannot produce, will be needed. Government, the economy and civil society need to be in balance.

The changing nature of the workplace

These shifts are echoed within organizations. Many organizations are taking issues relating to corruption, inequality and fairness at work very seriously and ethics are now regularly on the HR conference agenda, if not discussed in the boardroom. The debate centres around the relationships between business, society and the public good. Charles Handy (1997) argues that firms must see their roles as contributing to society over the long term, rather than simply increasing shareholder dividends in the short term.

Management teams are being encouraged to take their corporate citizenship roles seriously, and in some cases, executives are rewarded on the basis of how they demonstrate corporate values, including 'corporate citizenship' and 'community involvement'. In some cases, company ombudsmen have been appointed to ensure that fairness is possible for both employers and employees. In other cases, employment legislation requires employers to take their responsibilities to employees seriously. The Working Time Directive and proposed employment law, such as moves to prevent bullying in the workplace, will lead to greater protection for employees against some of the negative effects of modern working conditions.

The need for real leadership

There are other reflections of these environmental trends in an annual survey of issues related to working in organizations, carried out by Roffey Park. The survey, known as the Management Agenda, offers an overview of some of the trends within contemporary organizations, mainly based in the UK. In one example from many in the survey where management appears to be not 'walking the talk', 76 per cent of respondents suggested that management and organizational practices are very much out of sync with espoused values statements. Reward systems were considered particularly contradictory and respondents reported few incentives or sanctions to encourage management to model the values.

Many respondents call for a culture change led by senior management. This appears to be important not only in providing an appropriate climate for high performance but also because of the perceived effect on employee morale of inappropriate leadership behaviours. Several respondents reported that, where senior managers did model organizational values, individual commitment to the organization increased. On the other hand, the disconnection between management rhetoric and practice appears to be a strong reason for people wishing to leave.

Organizational politics

Another key factor of organizational life appears to be the increasingly political environment with which many employees are having to contend. To some extent this can be understood in the context of more fluid organizational structures in which informal political alliances can be a means of getting the job done beyond formal reporting lines. Cross-boundary working also appears to be on the increase. This seems to heighten the possibility of political behaviour since loyalties can be tested when reporting lines become less clear. Many respondents spoke of the importance of developing effective networks not only for getting the job done but also for personal career development purposes. However, the majority of respondents commented on the negative features of working in a political environment, including the adverse effects on job satisfaction.

Mergers and alliances

Ongoing consolidation of the marketplace is particularly noticeable in financial services. In other sectors, strategic alliances seem to be the preferred option with over half the respondents predicting that their organization will develop such an alliance in the near future. 'Virtual' companies are appearing at the centre of loose alliances, linked together with global networks. Transnational organizations appear to be decentralizing and globalizing with the help of technology. Many of the survey respondents are working for organizations which already operate globally and for a third of the sample, globalization appears to be a future trend. However, the comments from some respondents suggest that they may not be as aware of the implications of operating internationally as management writers would recommend.

Changing organizational structures

In the parallel Roffey Park/*Personnel Today* research project looking at Strategic Human Resources, the following results suggest some significant shifts in the way organizations are developing:

- *Is your organization growing in size?*
  To some extent/to a great extent   71 per cent
- *Is your organization involved in strategic alliances?*
  To some extent/to a great extent   78 per cent
- *Is your organization involved in mergers?*
  To some extent/to a great extent   41 per cent
- *To what extent is your organization experiencing change?*
  To some extent/to a great extent   86 per cent
- *To what extent are working practices changing?*
  To some extent/to a great extent   56 per cent
- *To what extent is your organization short-term focused?*
  To some extent/to a great extent   56 per cent

Flatter structures

Many organizations have taken the opportunity to flatten management layers in recent years. Hardly surprisingly, perhaps, there seems to be a slowing down in the number of organizations seeking to delayer but very few respondents see the trend back towards conventional hierarchies getting under way. The emphasis continues to be towards smaller, more flexible units with as few levels of management as possible. Delayering in the 1990s appeared strongly driven by the need for cost savings and the benefits to businesses are being felt in sustained profits. Difficulties arise when the staffing of specific units is too 'lean' to do what is required and when managers fail to provide the required forms of leadership. Equally important, flatter structures appear to highlight some aspects of the changing employment relationship, namely that such structures do not easily lend themselves to conventional promotion opportunities for employees. This can lead to a loss of commitment to the individual organization and a turnover of staff with marketable skills who are still looking for conventional career development opportunities.

Call centres

One of the most significant developments in recent years is the growth of call centres. Employees are usually grouped in large buildings where their performance is carefully monitored. Particularly common in customer service operations, especially in the financial services sector, working in call centres appears to be gaining ground as a form of employment. These have been criticized as being the human equivalent of battery hen conditions, with employees encouraged to conform to rigid standards and conditions, but the trend appears to be that the call centre concept will be extended to service centres.

Internal service centres, offering a wide range of professional expertise, are already used by a number of international organizations to service human resources, finance and other functional needs. Service centres can be based in any geographic location and typically require employees to be multi-lingual, graduates and professionally qualified in their own field. Shared service centres (SSCs) are usually external enterprises set up to manage outsourced non-core business processes. **Kelloggs UK** migrated its European financial processing to a European shared service centre in 1997 and the **BBC** outsourced its financial transaction processing to an SSC in 1998. The SSCs are usually jointly owned by partners and are tied in to ongoing business process reengineering.

The changing nature of work itself

Roffey Park/*Personnel Today* findings:
- *To what extent is job uncertainty ongoing?*
  To some extent/to a great extent   63 per cent
- *To what extent is employee motivation an issue in your organization?*
  To some extent/to a great extent   98 per cent
- *To what extent is retention of key employees an issue for your organization?*
  To some extent/to a great extent   85 per cent
- *How much does your organization need to attract fresh blood?*
  To some extent/to a great extent   77 per cent

According to this survey, some of the biggest issues affecting employees in all sectors are motivation and retention. HR also has the challenge of attracting new talent to the organization.

The notion of a 'nine-to-five' full-time role is rapidly being superseded by different organizational realities. The concept of permanent employment as a 'right' has been replaced by employment being due to having marketable skills. The trend towards 'core' workers who remain in an organization's employ and 'peripheral' workers who are outsourced appears to have taken hold. Routine office and production work can now be exported anywhere around the world or carried out electronically. As organizations continue their quest to cut wages bills and increase quality, low-skilled workers in the West are effectively having to compete for jobs against highly skilled workers based in developing countries whose employment costs are much lower.

Knowledge workers

Ian Angell (1999), Professor of Information Systems at the London School of Economics, suggests that the Information Age will not simply counterbalance the removal of 'old' jobs with the creation of new ones. What will be required in employees is 'intellectual muscle' which will be hard to develop and even more difficult for employers to track down and retain:

> Growth is created from the intellect of knowledge workers, not from the labour of low grade service and production workers. Growth has been decoupled from employment.

He suggests that survival by adding value will be a new form of natural selection.

While there is general acknowledgement of the importance of knowledge workers, the sharing of knowledge around organizations, which is generally considered key to leveraging that knowledge, remains problematic. The restructurings of the 1990s have broken up central teams who typically looked after corporate knowledge. The tendency within business units is for isolationist attitudes to come to the fore which can lead to wasted effort and duplication as well as untapped opportunities. The organizational issues related to the management of knowledge are examined in Chapter 16.

The role of the manager

> * *To what extent does your organization experience inappropriate leadership and management styles?*
>   To some extent/to a great extent   72 per cent
>
> *The Management Agenda*

A few years ago managers seemed an endangered species as they appeared to represent organizational superfluity – in an empowerment context it was argued, were 'checkers checking checkers' necessary? Perhaps the reality is that managers are more needed than ever, but that their role is changing. No longer are they expected to be the 'first among equals' or the technical expert. The current trend in management thinking is to see the manager as a helper rather than a problem-solving hero. In all sectors managers are being encouraged to take on the role of coach, whether or not they have appropriate skills for this. However, the trend is firmly in place with professionals and technical managers increasingly expected to take some responsibility for people management. There is a greater emphasis on teamworking, for instance.

The role of managers is becoming increasingly complex due to the variety of forms of contract to which employees and contractors are working. Managing a departmental team of full-time workers is becoming a thing of the past as managers are increasingly required to act as organizational 'glue' between workers of all kinds. The nature of the individuals being managed is changing too. Highly skilled knowledge workers generally do not take kindly to being managed, and are very critical of management if their needs are not met. Managers then have the tricky task of managing performance, raising standards and gaining commitment from people over whom they may have no direct line reporting control and whose technical skills are likely to be superior to those of the manager.

Teamworking

> * *To what extent is your organization encouraging the development of teamworking?*
>   To some extent/to a great extent   78 per cent
>
> *The Management Agenda*

Team working appears to be extensive with the majority of respondents working in some form of team, typically on a project basis. An increasingly prevalent form of teamworking is cross-functional or cross-boundary with 63 per cent of respondents in the Management Agenda survey working in such teams. Cross-boundary working will be explored in Chapter 6. Working in teams appears to be a major source of satisfaction and skills development for the majority of respondents, though it is recognized by many that multiple skills are required to work effectively in today's teams.

'Virtual' teams appear to be gaining ground. They typically come together around specific business issues or opportunities and tend to be project based. They rely on the convergence of a number of complex technologies and can be based almost anywhere. Virtual enterprises tend to disband when their task is finished, or relocate to areas where there is least regulation or most profit.

Use of technology

In Roffey Park's survey, electronic mail is used by 73 per cent of respondents, even though some of these users did not have direct access to the technology. Typically, people suggested that they now spend considerable periods in front of a screen rather than talking with people, even if they are in the next office. There were numerous comments from people lamenting the advent of electronic means of communication. People suggested that they found face-to-face communication the most effective means of communicating but that voice- and e-mail were now the favoured forms used at work.

E-mail in particular came in for comments which suggest that the benefits of technology can easily be outweighed by their drawbacks if used ineptly. Among the positives, it appears that the more widespread use of technology is beginning to make smarter ways of working possible. Communication too appears to have increased since the advent of electronic mail, in quantity if not quality. On the other hand, numerous comments suggest that much of the information conveyed by electronic mail is irrelevant at best and at worst can add to the work pressures and stress which many people are experiencing. People complained about being deluged with unnecessary data via e-mail and voice-mail. A study in the UK by Gallup (see Buckingham and

Coffman, 1999) suggested that individuals are interrupted every 10 minutes on average by incoming messages to which they are expected to respond. Keeping track of, and making progress towards key targets can be very difficult in such circumstances. Many respondents comment on the negative impact of electronic mail on people's ability to relate to others. The bluntness of some messages causes offence and there is a call from many respondents for a new form of etiquette which takes modern means of communication into account.

Flexible working

Flexibility has become a buzzword in the 1990s referring to both the need for organizations to structure themselves so that they are highly responsive to the changing environment and the effect this has on the nature of employment. Currently around 29 per cent of UK employees work part-time or in some other form of flexible working pattern.

In most of the organizations in the Roffey Park surveys, flexible working accounts for up to 25 per cent of the workforce. Part-time and shift working is, of course, well established in the retail and leisure industries. The number of part-time jobs is increasing faster than full-time ones. By 2006, the number of individuals working part-time is expected to increase to 31 per cent as a result of both organizational and individual needs.

This change in the employment model towards a more flexible one, with an increasing proportion of short-term contracts, is a challenge which HR and line managers are starting to face. However, the management of a flexible workforce will mean more accurate planning and corresponding changes in HR systems and thinking. In the Roffey Park surveys, the most common form of flexible working on offer was part-time work, followed by fixed-term contracts. Job shares are also on the increase, but are still relatively rare in professional roles. Less common are term-time only working, 'key-time' working, voluntary reduced hours, associate schemes, etc.

Certain groups of people in the Roffey Park Agenda survey (often employees of long standing) preferred to work flexibly. These included people returning from long-term sickness, staff who have to travel long distances to get to work, individuals wanting to give more time to interests outside work and single people with a need for more time than money. The majority of people wishing to work flexibly were working mothers or individuals wanting to take time out to study. Working fathers and people with caring responsibilities, especially for elderly relatives, were also keen to work flexibly.

The idea appears to be gaining ground that a much wider range of jobs can be based away from an office environment, thanks to technology. Working from home is increasing in some sectors including IT and employees are generally well equipped with the relevant technology to make teleworking feasible. Companies such as BT, who supply the electronic infrastructure and are introducing other technologies such as Solstra to enable people to work from home, have seen this side of their business grow significantly in recent years.

Telecommuting produces a number of benefits for organizations. It allows office buildings to be disposed of and their capital released. It also means that people are more likely to focus on their job when they are meant to be working since there are fewer 'social' distractions. However, there is some evidence that, despite the benefits to many telecommuting employees, such as being spared the physical commute to the office, some feel a sense of loss of the community aspect of organizations.

Many respondents predict the ongoing outsourcing of non-core activities. For managers, to the challenge of managing a more flexible workforce which includes greater numbers of contractors and temporary staff will be added the need to manage knowledge when staff have no strong loyalty to the organization. This is perhaps an area with which many organizations represented in the Roffey Park sample have yet to cope. Relatively few appear to have strategies for managing intellectual capital or see knowledge management as a priority.

Demands on employees

Career issues

For employees looking to move up the career ladder, flatter structures do not just shift the goalposts – they kick them down. Many staff have found their career has reached a plateau earlier than they expected. Instead of being promoted, they have to accept lateral moves in a culture that regards sideways moves as negative. In a situation where jobs are in short supply, lack of career development opportunities might seem to be a small price to pay for ongoing employment. The problem is that there is increasing evidence of the effect of employee morale on employee performance and organizational viability. Rather than being a 'personnel' issue, the challenges relating to career development are now a business issue. Not least is the significant lessening of employee commitment to the organization, due to a perceived reduction of career opportunities. This is leading to turnover, especially in jobs requiring specialized skills and which can command high market rates. Career issues will be examined in Chapter 9.

Stress

> • *To what extent is work/life balance an issue in your organization?*
>   To some extent/to a great extent   77 per cent

In the Management Agendas 1998–2001 there appeared to be widespread stress among respondents caused by long hours, uncertain employment prospects and unclear expectations. This range of pressure is creating a new 'stress-busting' industry. City workers can now enjoy holistic therapy treatment during lunch periods and some firms are hiring specialists in Indian head massage to provide relief to employees at their desks. Agenda respondents report ongoing heavy demands made on them by employers. There appear to be constantly rising expectations of employees with regard to both the quality and quantity of output, as well as a requirement that employees will learn new skills and do more with less. Long hours are still the norm in respondents' organizations. Despite these demanding conditions, the majority of respondents report themselves as still being relatively loyal to their employers.

Interestingly, although these conditions appear to be general, regardless of sector, the way in which people are responding to them appears to polarize into two broad reactions. On the one hand, in 1998 the majority of people still perceive the additional pressures on them to be stressful. Ninety-one per cent spoke of increased stress affecting relationships. Several groups of comments refer to the way in which unreasonable workloads can result in quality being compromized, as well as wear and tear on the individual. Some people report that their health has suffered as a result of heavy workloads and lack of balance between work and other parts of their lives. This negative situation is compounded when there appears to be a lack of recognition of the problem, and of employees' achievements, by the line manager and the organization.

Yet the survey suggests that 'balance' means different things to different people. Almost a third of respondents felt that the increased demands made on them had a positive aspect since they provided a developmental 'stretch'. Comments in this case suggested that individuals believe that the organization is getting the best out of them and that their own ability has been recognized. There is a sense that for some people, the increase in pressure and responsibilities is enabling them to realize some of their potential. One comment however is typical of many: 'responsibilities are growing faster than rewards'.

Management style and the chance for personal development appear to be two factors which relate closely to whether people perceive the pressures on them to be positive or negative. Years on from the first delayering projects, organizations are beginning to see the effects of new structures on their people. Often introduced in order to achieve greater efficiencies and improved customer service, flatter structures can, in theory at least, lead to improved productivity and enhanced individual and team performance. In practice it would seem that the implementation of flatter structures has lowered employee morale and created large gaps in existing frameworks for rewarding and developing staff in some cases.

The extent to which people feel able to grow and 'empowered' to do their jobs appears to be closely linked to job satisfaction and resilience to extra pressure. Many of the people who considered the added pressure on them to be negative spoke of inappropriate management styles still preventing empowerment from being a reality. Typically, comments suggested that relatively conventional command and control management styles in which managers believe that they have the solution to problems remain the order of the day.

On the other hand, many of those who perceived the pressures to be positive spoke of the stimulus provided by increased challenge, broader roles and the opportunity to develop others. These they found helpful to their personal development. Indeed the vast majority of respondents (95 per cent) considered that they have developed in the last year, largely through informal means as well as training. This may be linked to the fact that 86 per cent of respondents stated that their role has changed in the last two years, bringing greater variety, responsibility and a more strategic focus than before. The changing roles were not necessarily brought about by skilful management interventions or by succession planning but by organizational growth and structure change in many cases.

On the whole the respondents agreed that the extra work pressures called on employees to make sacrifices, particularly with respect to their home life and spending time with their children. A third of respondents suggested that their health had suffered. However, many admitted that their own ambition was a key driver and that they were to some extent prepared to collude with their employers over such conditions in order to make career progress. Arguably, this is an area where responsible employers can provide clear and unequivocal support for better balance, rather than appearing to endorse the principle of work/life balance but do nothing to make reality match the aspiration.

This is where the combination of lack of recognition, increased workloads, poor management and lack of career opportunities have prompted 57 per cent of managers in the Management Agenda survey to contemplate changing their jobs. People are being expected to continuously raise standards and output levels, develop new skills and do more with less. In some cases, managers are voluntarily 'downshifting', i.e. stepping off the career ladder, or in some cases leaving paid employment altogether, in order to 'get a life'. Others are subject to pressures which can undermine their performance. The real impact of such stresses will be felt on business results and many organizations are now beginning to address the question of enabling employees to have balance.

What can HR do about balance?

HR has a significant role to play in ensuring that their organizations are enabling employees to have some form of balance. Developing employee-friendly policies is part of the solution, but such policies need to be owned by employees and senior managers if they are to become a reality. Some of the more interesting practice on this front comes from America. In the USA, stressed-out employees of **Boston City Council** have an automated phone system which screens calls for depression. Callers listen to recorded descriptions of how they feel ranging from 'I get tired for no reason' to 'I feel others would be better off if I were dead'. They punch the appropriate number and hear a recorded diagnosis that urges severe cases to seek counselling (*London Evening Standard*, May 1999).

In the UK, the 1999 Employer of the Year finalists included organizations such as **Watford Borough Council** which has developed clear family-friendly policies that are supportive of flexible working and provide childcare vouchers. **Littlewoods** recognizes that employees have a life (and dependents) outside work. The company policies allow people to change conditions as their circumstances change, for instance with elder care arrangements. Job shares are encouraged and time off for emergencies is considered normal so that people do not have to resort to subterfuge to deal with a family crisis. **Business Express**, which is part of the Littlewoods group, offers employees five days' paid leave for family reasons each year. Fathers have ten days' paternity leave as a right. Having this as a right means that employees are more likely to be open about their needs rather than simply taking 'sick' leave. This means that the organization can plan for the leave and avoid unexpected downtime.

In the USA, casual-lifestyle retailer **Eddie Bauer** uses its work/life programmes to help employees lead more productive and balanced lives. The firm has won many accolades for its approaches to employee support including being named as one of the 'Best Companies to Work For' by *Washington CEO* magazine. In 1993 the HR team wanted to create a flexible work environment plus offer an exceptional benefits package in order to make Eddie Bauer an employer of choice. HR has produced a package of benefits which covers routine and non-routine challenges of work and home. The firm's management believes that the investment more than pays for itself because many of the programmes reduce health-care costs. The Employee Assistance programme offers a Child and Elder Care consulting and referral service, referrals for personal counselling and legal and financial assistance to both employees and their family members. Among other initiatives introduced are:

*   Balance Day, a free day once a year when employees can 'call in well'. This is in addition to normal time off

- As well as the usual array of benefits, extras include a casual dress code and alternative transport options such as preferred parking for carpools
- Its *Customized Work Environment* programme offers options such as job sharing, a compressed workweek and telecommuting
- It offers a plan which allows employees to enjoy group buying power for mortgage loan discounts
- Emergency child care.

Employers with employee-friendly policies argue that these policies are helping the business, as well as employees. In the case of Eddie Bauer, the work/life programmes have led to fewer sick days, less absenteeism and lower healthcare costs. **Lloyds TSB**'s policies are based on the belief that by offering employees peace of mind they are more likely to see greater productivity. By encouraging an overt and planned approach to leave for family issues, the company can also plan and arrange appropriate cover. Retention is also improved since people appreciate working for a supportive employer. Offering people the chance for a balance between work and personal life therefore makes good business sense.

The future

Among the future trends most commonly suggested by Agenda respondents was business growth being achieved through strategic alliances. There was widespread recognition that certain key skills will be required of employees working in such alliances including influencing, political and strategic thinking skills. Managers in particular are considered to have increasingly complex responsibilities as the nature of the workforce changes. Although there has been no apparent tidal wave of flexible working, the trend towards outsourcing, managing contractors, part-time and temporary staff appears to be well established. As this trend continues, organizations may need to consider reviewing how well they currently manage their flexible workforce and identify ways to create mutual commitment and benefits. Christina Evans' (1998) ongoing research into ways in which organizations and employees can get the best out of a flexible workforce offers some pointers as to how they might do this.

Efficiency and higher productivity are not enough to guarantee the competitive advantage of any organization. Those which are likely to be successful will be companies that continuously produce new products and services and where innovation is a 'natural' ingredient of every role. Transformational leadership, as exercized by senior management, will be a key ingredient in enabling organizations to achieve innovative solutions to business problems. Leadership will continue to grow in importance, especially when leaders are able to establish an environment in which innovation can flourish.

Conclusion

What is becoming clear is that organizations will need creativity, innovation and continuous renewal if they are to sustain themselves and their success. They will need to manage rapid and complex change and be able to make both the formal and informal systems work to the benefit of the organization. In this changing context, the strategic HRM contribution is essential. The HR professional should be in touch with the effects of change from the employee angle and can anticipate some of the priorities that will need to be addressed if organizations are to attract and retain a knowledgeable and committed workforce. HR policies and practices which lead to the strategic development of the organization for sustainable success will be invaluable.

The importance of learning for both the organization and the individual is greater than ever. The rise of the knowledge worker places a reliance on the skills of employees to an extent perhaps not seen before. It seems clear that the implications of the management of 'intellectual capital' in the 'post-industrial age' have not yet been fully grasped by some managers. The importance of managers using appropriate management styles to enable effective work practices is underscored by the Agenda survey. The 'turn-off' factor of inappropriate management styles is a primary reason for people wishing to leave their organizations. The challenge for managers is to be able to harness employees' initiative and commitment through appropriate support and direction. They therefore need to act consistently with organizational purpose and value statements – an area where the survey suggests considerable room for improvement.

Similarly, the ongoing demands for quality and productivity have produced unprecedented pressures on many parts of the UK workforce which may be unsustainable. The long hours culture and demanding roles causes many employees to experience a lack of balance with their personal lives, whereas for others this is a price they are prepared to pay for career advancement. Indeed, some people find the more demanding roles have given them a chance for significant personal development which has enhanced their job satisfaction. However, this suggests the need for creative career strategies if these well-rounded individuals are going to be tempted to stay with their organizations in the long term. Retaining key players is likely to be a major challenge in many organizations.

The increased use of technology also has this double-edged quality. On the one hand, technology can result in improved communication and better ways of working. On the other, without a well-thought-out strategy for effective use of electronic communications in particular, the result can be to add to existing pressures on employees. The increasing complexity of work and the real employability of people with the relevant 'knowledge' skills suggests that employees will be unlikely to tolerate working conditions which do not satisfy their needs. Employees are making themselves increasingly employable, with or without the help of their organizations. Their enhanced skills, including strategic thinking, and their recognition of the importance of managing their own career suggest that people recognize that they have a choice. Many of the managers in our survey are actively considering leaving their organizations. Organizations wishing to retain their knowledge workers will need to address the issues of balance, flexibility, learning, careers as well as management development. They will also need to find ways of maximizing the knowledge present in the ever more fluid organization structures and turn that knowledge to competitive advantage. The question of whether and how this can be achieved will be explored in Chapter 16.

Checklists on organizational design

Globalization

Research carried out for the International Personnel Association (1998) suggests that the three critical aspects of people management to the success of multinational companies in the global arena are as follows:

- The adoption of flexible management policies and practices worldwide
- The inclusion of the HR function as a strategic business partner in global business
- The development of global leaders.

An article by Linda Stroh and Paula Caligiuri (1998) suggests that 'successful multi-national corporations recognize the value in having global managers with the expertise to anticipate the organization's markets and to respond proactively. These organizations have learned that leaders who are flexible and open to the demands of the global market have made possible the organization's international business success'.

- How does your organization manage across borders, i.e. is your organization predominantly
  - Domestic
  - Multi-domestic
  - A simple export organization
  - Using local agents
  - International
  - Truly globalized with a complex web of businesses, joint ventures and alliances across most of the world's economies?
- What is the impact of globalization, i.e. should HR be centralized, decentralized or a combination?
- What are the main ways in which international employees are deployed, e.g. on short-term assignments, expatriate postings, etc?.

Dealing with ethical dilemmas

- What ethical dilemmas exist at, and between, the following levels – corporate/organization, business unit, managerial, individual?
- What differences in values exist between those organizational levels?
- What potential conflicts exist between local and corporate cultures?
- How is authority held – formally/institutionally/informally?

- How can differences between local and corporate cultures be worked through?
- What is the role of HR in dealing with ethical dilemmas?

Flexible working

- What types of flexible working will enable the organization to meet its needs? What forms can help employees and can we accommodate these?
- What help will managers need in managing the flexible workforce?
- What form of training is received and how will this be carried out?
- How will communications and HR processes be tailored to ensure that flexible workers feel fully involved and committed to the organization?
- What team building will be required when new forms of team, especially 'virtual' teams, are set up?
- How can we enable employees – full-time or 'flexible' – to manage the new generation of knowledge through learning?

Balance

- How will we find out what 'balance' means to different groups of employees?
- What role will senior managers need to take in changing a 'long hours' culture?
- What innovative approaches can we develop to create an employee-friendly culture?
- What other forms of reinforcement need to be in place within HR systems to ensure that employee-friendly policies are implemented?

References

Angell, I. (1999). Brave new world. *Tempus*, Issue 15.
Buckingham, M. and Coffman, C. (1999). What is a great workplace? A weekly summary of Gallup's discoveries about great managers and great workplaces. *The Gallup Poll – Managing.*
DfEE, *Labour Market Skills and Trends, 1997–8.*

Evans, C. (1996, 1997) *Managing the Flexible Workforce*. Roffey Park Management Institute.

Giddens, A. (1999). The BBC Reith Lectures, 1999, *BBC Radio 4 Home, BBC Homepage*.

Glynn, C. (1998). *Work–Life Balance*. Roffey Park Management Institute.

Glynn, C. and Holbeche, L. (1998, 1999). *The Management Agenda*. Roffey Park Management Institute.

Handy, C. (1997). *The Empty Raincoat*. London: Hutchinson.

Holbeche, L. (1998). *High Flyers and Succession Planning*. Roffey Park Management Institute.

Lewis, J. (1999). Mind the gap. *Personnel Today*, 1 April.

Ohmae, K. (1985). *Triad Power*. New York: Free Press.

Stroh, L. K. and Caligiuri, P. M. (1998). Increasing global competitiveness through effective people management. *Journal of World Business*, **33**, No.1.

3   *Measuring the impact of strategic HRM*

> The only HR actions which have value in any organization are those which contribute to the achievement of its goals (Phelps, 1998).

For many Human Resource practitioners, it's an act of faith that people management is a key factor in determining profitability. Whether that view is shared by management team colleagues is a different matter. The drive to achieve shareholder value or cost-effective public services means that management teams typically focus on widening the gap between revenue and costs, usually by driving down costs in the short term. In recent years this has often entailed restructuring, downsizing, delayering, revising work practices and replacing human skills with technological solutions.

In countless organizations, lip service is paid to the idea that people are the key resource of an organization. This is where decisions which result in treating 'our greatest asset' as disposable chattels lead to justified employee cynicism when the reality of executive priorities hits home. Often in those same organizations, HR practitioners are under pressure to prove that value is being added by HR activities.

Even when well-meaning executives are sincere in their belief that employees count, they are often at a loss as to how to translate this belief into policies and practices which work well, both for the business and for individuals. Implementing effective people management and knowing which approaches are working is difficult enough; assessing how much effective people management impacts on the bottom line is even more difficult.

Part of the problem is that the dominant means of measuring and assessing organizational success are quantitative and financial. After all, what is valued, or seen as critical, tends to be what is measured and reported. So much of what is reported as 'fact', i.e. financial performance data, fails to explain how the figures have been achieved. Since so many people management practices are intangible, and are therefore treated as invisible or 'soft', evidence of the link between these practices and business results often appears indirect and non-explicit. Without 'hard' proof of the link with business results, belief that good people management is critical can remain at the 'hunch' level.

Even though strategists often condemn the narrow focus on financial data as 'driving with the rearview mirror', the general trend among management teams and boards is to set measures which track familiar sorts of data. These may seem to offer fewer risks than those which appear unproven, especially when the only company results which tend to be publicly reported are the short-term bottom line. Of course, setting measures based solely on 'lag', i.e. retrospective performance, is unlikely to lead to business success in changing times. The real challenge is to identify and report on the parameters for future success – the 'lead' measures – as well meeting the needs for control in the here and now.

The business case for addressing employee needs

The growing recognition that financial performance is based on various other forms of performance – almost all of which are carried out by human beings – is evident in the growth of performance-measurement models. Acceptance of the business case for investing in the 'soft' employee issues, such as communications and training, appears to be accelerating. In the UK, the Investors in People movement has long highlighted the importance of employees to economic and social success and the number of organizations seeking to achieve or maintain their IIP status is growing. IIP has become a prestigious accolade and many of the leading organizations in all sectors can now claim to have achieved IIP status. Indeed, the UK Labour Party has achieved IIP accreditation and government departments are being encouraged to gain IIP status. This is to be achieved against a backdrop of ongoing change and the reshaping of public services to achieve greater cohesion, 'customer' focus and efficiency. This suggests a clear recognition that good people management practices will be a key feature in achieving the UK government's objectives.

Arie de Geus, the world-renowned strategic planner, contends that 'economic' companies whose focus is predominantly short term and bottom-line driven are likely to be outpaced by so-called 'living' companies which base their decisions on the company's and employees' potential as a living entity (see Chambers, 1997). He argues that if managers wish to extend a company's life span, they must focus on developing brain-rich companies which can adapt to a changing environment. This involves forming relationships with employees and using conservative financing to govern their growth.

Indeed, Professor Jeffrey Pfeffer (1995) of the Stanford Graduate School of Business argues that the basis for competitive success has changed. In a rapidly changing marketplace, deregulation of industries such as the airlines, telecommunications and the financial services has led to a proliferation of competition from many quarters. Protected markets are disappearing and the technologically driven demand for ever more innovative products makes many products quickly obsolete. Traditional sources of competitive advantage such as investing heavily in capital equipment or aiming for economies of scale have become less important in this era of mass customization. Customers want goods and services which are tailored to their needs but they do not wish to pay premium prices for those goods. For Jeffrey Pfeffer 'what remains as a source of competitive advantage, in part because it is difficult to imitate and in part because other sources of success have been eroded by competition, is organizational culture and capability, embodied in the workforce'.

If Pfeffer's assertion is correct, the importance of strategic Human Resource activity should not be underestimated. In the UK there is also increasing research evidence that there are substantial returns to managing the workforce effectively. The CIPD commissioned research which was carried out by the Institute of Work Psychology at Sheffield University and the Centre for Economic Performance at the London School of Economics. The findings suggest a strong link between good people management practice and business results. The research, carried out in more than 100 medium-sized UK firms, found that people management is not only essential to the success of an organization but also that it outstrips technology, quality and competitive strategy in its impact on the bottom line (see Pfeffer, 1995).

The CIPD findings suggest that good personnel policies and practices can improve productivity and performance by enhancing skills and giving people responsibility for making the best use of their skills. The research confirms strong ties between attitudes and performance and highlights two areas of HR practice which above all relate to improvements in productivity and profitability. These are the acquisition and development of skills (through induction, training, selection and appraisal practices) and job design (as assessed by the degree of teamwork, flexibility, autonomy, responsibility, problem solving and variety). In the firms studied it became evident that enabling employees to use their creativity in practical ways, leading to business innovation and improvements, was a feature of the more successful companies. Ironically, the average cycle time in many organizations is so short that employees' roles are constrained, preventing the realization of some of the capability of employees.

Predictors of business results

Employee satisfaction

The CIPD research also highlighted the predictive nature of employee satisfaction for business results. Satisfaction was based on many aspects of working life, such as recognition for good work, pay and conditions and relationships with supervisors and team members. This indicates that effective people management is about more than traditional HR practices such as training and has to take into account a wide range of aspects of employee satisfaction, including employee needs for growth and development. While the job satisfaction of individuals is typically a poor indicator of performance, the researchers found that it is the overall levels of satisfaction across staff which seem to affect business performance.

The organization as community

Another predictor of business success is how employees see their company as a community, where people feel socially included rather than alienated. In particular, the more successful organizations in the research were ones where there was a positive 'human relations' climate brought about by concern for welfare, the removal of status barriers, good communication, high-quality training and respect for employees. **Kwik-Fit**, for example, enjoys a high reputation within the motor repair industry for honest dealing and excellent customer service. The company's substantial sales and profit growth reflect the customer reaction to Kwik-Fit and its services. Employees are encouraged to delight the customer and have the freedom to respond to immediate customer requirements. Each Kwik-Fit location builds links with the local community and has a high degree of delegation of responsibility so that small groups can make a difference. It remains to be seen whether the 'community' feel of Kwik-Fit's operations can be maintained since its recent acquisition by Ford.

Research by the Gallup Organization about Great Managers and Great Workplaces (Buckingham and Coffman, 1990) also suggests that measures linked with employee satisfaction, such as turnover, are predictive of profitability. Gallup's research had a focus on four outcome variables: employee retention, customer satisfaction, productivity and profitability. Researchers noticed that organizational excellence was based on high-performing workgroups, rather than the organization as a whole. They found that a number of situational factors such as pay, parking, etc. which are often elements of an organizational strategy, do not make a difference to the most productive workgroups in the companies studied. What did matter were a number of factors which are more firmly the responsibility of managers, with HR support.

The right roles and recognition

These factors included employees being clear what is expected of them through the setting of explicit expectations by the manager. However, individuals need to find their own way of achieving these expectations if they are to feel ownership of their job. Managers therefore need to be able to judge how to help each employee take responsibility and be able to get the best out of the different members of their teams. Employees also need to have access to the resources and equipment to do their work effectively. They need to be offered roles which make the best use of their talents and matching the right person to the right job is a challenge for many managers. The support of HR in developing processes to enable managers to make the best use of talent can be vital. This is particularly the case with another key factor – helping people to develop. The researchers also found that praise and recognition are critical: 'the new knowledge-based worker relies and depends upon praise and recognition as the means of defining what is valued by the organization.'

Holistic frameworks – the Business Excellence Model and the Balanced Scorecard

Recognition that effective performance management is key to the achievement of business results has been popularized in two influential models which have been adopted by many organizations to good effect. The Business Excellence model, used by **BNFL** as a guiding template, suggests clear links between business outputs (results) and organizational inputs, such as leadership and effective people management. The model provides a means of measuring and tracking the impact of employee-related initiatives on the bottom line.

BNFL's core business involves nuclear fuel reprocessing. The nuclear industry is consolidating and BNFL's international operations have increased following mergers with Magnox Electric and Westinghouse Electric. BNFL is playing a major role in reshaping the industry and currently has 10 per cent of the world's annual fuel cycle and clean-up market and provides around 8 per cent of the UK's energy needs.

Within BNFL it is recognized that, as a knowledge-based organization, the core competencies such as operating in political and regulated nuclear environments are highly complex and difficult to acquire. The organization has a long-term perspective and relationships with clients last many years. Bringing about change in such a context can be challenging. On the 'outputs' side of the Business Excellence model, the organization's strategic priorities include being world class in safety and plant operation and reducing the cost base by 25 per cent.

To achieve these outputs some changes in working practices and other aspects of the organization's culture will be required. Roger Leek, formerly Head of Human Resources at BNFL, took the lead on the strategic priority to transform performance and behaviour from the rather institutionalized, 'civil service' approach to one which maintains controls but allows individuals to contribute to the full. Measures have been set around both the 'outputs' and the 'enablers' so that progress can be tracked. The Business Excellence model is being used to measure all aspects of a set of integrated HR processes, including training and development. For more details of how the processes work, see Chapter 4. Roger sees this process of culture change taking three to five years and it is already underway in BNFL.

Similarly, the Balanced Scorecard 'translates an organization's mission and strategy into a comprehensive set of performance measures that provides the framework for a strategic measurement and management system' (Kaplan and Norton, 1998). The scorecard typically shows how the financial bottom line of an organization is not obtained as a simple accounting exercise but that performance is needed in each of several perspectives if financial success is to be achieved. First and foremost, all these key areas need to be pulling in the same direction – that of the vision and strategy of the organization. Strategic goals, critical success factors and measures need to be established in all scorecard areas.

The Scorecard perspectives are:

- Customers, and the activities required to ensure that service matches customer needs as well as the vision
- Learning and growth, and the activities required to build sustainable growth
- Internal business processes and the careful prioritization of key business processes at which the organization can excel
- Financial, and the activities required to succeed financially in the eyes of shareholders.

The Scorecard is dynamic and should reflect the specific needs of an organization at a point in time. Indeed, different parts of an organization may have different scorecards depending on their circumstances and priorities. In some organizations, the scorecard notion is used to develop real-time personal scorecards. Some parts of the corporate Scorecard may have greater priority at some times more than at others. Following their merger in 1996, **Royal and SunAlliance** had large amounts of differing IS/IT applications and infrastructure. The challenge was to consolidate these, especially in the context of post-merger retention issues. The UK **Life and Pensions Group** used the Business

Excellence model to set the IT vision and to set up improvement initiatives. They are also establishing and implementing a Balanced Scorecard set of IT measures linked to the Business Excellence model.

The key message behind these models is that financial success does not occur in a vacuum and that all areas of the Scorecard have to be attended to if success is to be maintained. They therefore need to be carefully measured, tracked and potentially require investment. **BP Chemicals** introduced its version of the Balanced Scorecard in 1994 and has successfully cascaded it throughout the organization. The current focus is on creating a learning organization by using networking, IT and knowledge management to share ideas. The main aim of this knowledge strategy is to improve Balanced Scorecard results.

The Executive Scorecard

This scorecard has been devized by **Saratoga Europe**, part of Saratoga Worldwide, to examine the same perspectives as the Balanced Scorecard but viewed from an HR focus. Saratoga has amassed a databank of human resource measures and benchmark data from its client group. The assumption is that 'anything we do with people in any organizational setting ought to have some output and eventual impact upon results'. Data is gathered against some ninety human resource measures to assess impact on:

- Improved production
- Cost reduction
- Quicker cycle times
- Improved quality
- Positive reactions from human beings.

The Saratoga measures, both quantitative and qualitative, are grouped under the following categories of key human resource activities in which there are clear measures of success:

- Organizational effectiveness (revenue, cost, profit and added value per employee)
- Compensation and benefits
- Recruitment
- Absenteeism and turnover

- Training and development
- Occupational health and safety.

The assumption is that if employees are working effectively, they will add value through their positive effect on customers, who will in turn purchase more and produce a positive impact on the bottom line and, where appropriate, improved shareholder value. These can be measured through increased revenue growth, customer retention, etc. Conversely, where employee commitment and competence are low, there is likely to be a negative effect on the bottom line. Indicative measures would include negative customer reaction, absenteeism, turnover, etc. The Saratoga approach is to use researched people criteria incorporating internal performance trends and external benchmarks to develop a strategic improvement cycle. Client organizations can then benchmark themselves against other organizations to assess their relative positions. Typical target positioning includes revenue per employee – top 25 per cent and cost per employee – bottom 25 per cent.

How can HR add value?

The pressure on HR departments to prove that they add value tends to push practitioners into a measurement frenzy. One way to avoid becoming lost in a bureaucratic muddle of measures which are difficult to make sense of is to use a tool such as Activity Based Costing of the HR function. This approach focuses on identifying the key activities to be measured and checking the potential knock-on effects on other aspects of HR provision of measuring only certain activities to avoid 'skewing' the data. In the UK the **East Sussex Police Force** was subject, like all other UK police forces, to government-imposed targets and measures on response times to emergencies. What the East Sussex police noticed was that, in order to comply with response targets, they were having to drive faster than was advisable and the number of accidents involving police vehicles rose. The police took the decision to revise the government targets at local level so that they could achieve an acceptable response time with far fewer accidents.

HR activities regarded as key should be linked with other organizational functions to develop clarity about how HR contributes to performance in other parts of the organization. These measures are then integrated to produce a holistic picture of how HR's contribution is integral to the success of other parts of the business. The emphasis should be on measuring the impact of HR-related policies and actions using business language.

Calculating the return on investment from HR is extremely difficult, even with a superficially straightforward equation such as:

$$\text{ROI} = \frac{\text{Benefit} - \text{Cost}}{\text{Cost} \times 100\%}$$

This kind of equation is usually applied to apparently discrete areas of HR activity such as the evaluation of training. The difficulty with trying to prove the real and longer-term differences which training and other HR activities can make to an organization's effectiveness is that there are so many other variables to take into account. Therefore, making firm claims about the value of an individual activity can seem specious to people who need to be convinced by numbers. That is not to say that measuring activities and trying to assess the effect of HR interventions is a waste of time. However, measurement should ideally be used to help HR select the functions and processes for action which are real priorities for the business and where there is the maximum possibility of creating a direct impact on the bottom line.

Take a notoriously 'loose' concept such as empowerment, for instance. Effective empowerment initiatives are aimed at improving an organization's bottom line by giving employees the freedom to make decisions and by treating employees as partners. Unfortunately many organizations do not achieve this goal because they fail to measure empowerment and link it to their costs and profit. HR has a key role to play in ensuring that management understands what empowerment is really about and that measures are set which are linked to strategic goals and processes as well as to individual accountability. HR also needs to identify and set in place ways of tracking the impact of other elements known to be essential to the success of empowerment programmes such as stable leadership at the top, few redundancies, profit sharing and power-sharing schemes and emphasis on innovation at all levels.

Ideally, all HR activity should be classified according to the level of importance and impact on the organization (Figure 3.1).

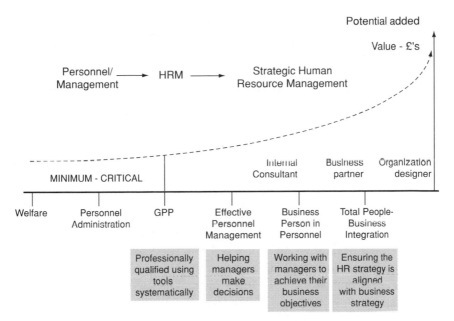

Figure 3.1   *Moving up the HR ROI scale. Source: Paul Kearns,* The Bottom Line HR Function, *Chandos (Oxford), 2001*

This would allow practitioners to determine which are activities are core, which are administrative, which are critical. Taking a hard look at which activities must remain an essential part of the HR portfolio and which might be outsourced is a first step. Working out the relative costs and payback periods for the investment made is a next step. Of course, much strategic HR activity, whether it is change management, succession planning, or training and development, has much longer payback periods than the normal business cycle. Nevertheless, the payback of HR activities should result in significant competitive advantage for the organization. Maurice Phelps (1998) of **Saratoga Europe** suggests that 'payback means measurable improved performance, and for your people that payback can only show through in improved organizational performance'. This means demonstrating an improving performance relationship against others competing in the same markets and servicing the same customers.

This is where HR practitioners who feel obliged to justify their existence need to master the art of collecting and presenting people-related data in a way which makes clear the business benefits of investing in longer-term returns in order to secure the organization's future viability. Employee behaviour needs to be measured in output terms, so that the links with hard business performance can be understood.

Similarly, HR needs to be able to apply risk management techniques to the different aspects of HR strategies. What would happen if recruitment were not carried out strategically, but dealt with in a stop-gap way? What would be the cost of failing to retain groups of key workers during a period of organizational turbulence? What would be the dangers to the organization of not developing individuals with the organizational knowledge as well as the skills to be the future business leaders? A key area of business partnership for HR is to translate employee-related policies into practice in a way which really makes a difference to the business and its employees. These policies need to help establish the link between what the business aims to achieve and the way in which employees are managed and enabled to achieve those aims. The policies should reflect the organization's strategy at the highest level, with detailed HR goals, targets and measures cascading from this.

Benchmarking

Part of the business of data gathering is to know how well your HR provision compares with the 'best' HR practices elsewhere and for this, benchmarking can be a useful tool. Benchmarking gains a bad press when organizations use it for the purposes of copying 'best practice' from one organization and try to apply the ideas wholesale in another. However, benchmarking can be a means of finding out what exactly is meant by 'added value' in different contexts, how this is measured and HR's role in adding that value.

Benchmarking is, in general terms, the comparison of aspects of one organization's business or practices with those of other organizations. It should be an ongoing process of measuring products, services and operating practices against competitors or those considered as market leaders and is a very much linked to a philosophy of continuous improvement. Benchmarking is often specifically aimed at comparing product quality so that improvements to one's own processes can be identified and implemented. In some cases, comparisons are made with firms whose products may not be the same. So a computer firm, for example, might compare its indicators with those of a biscuit manufacturer.

Aspects of the organization's processes are compared to find where other firms gain speed, efficiency, quality or cost savings from their process.

Benchmarking allows organizations to identify where in their own processes there is duplication, waste or superior practices. Typical areas for benchmarking operations include:

- Customer service levels
- Inventory control
- Inventory management
- Quality process
- Purchasing practices etc.

International companies often benchmark on their perceived company image, especially the value of the brand and the place it occupies in the minds of customers. Benchmarking usually focuses on existing products and services, so at best it might be described as helpful in enabling organizations to catch up with good practice.

If HR and line managers are trying to understand how other firms run their operations, a benchmarking audit can provide useful insights into 'good' practice. Typically, such an audit is based on finding out:

- What does the organization do?
- Who are its customers?
- Where is it located – national, regional, international?
- What is its corporate strategy?

Then explore its operations by looking at:

- Supply-chain linkage
- Quality and just-in-time philosophy and policies
- Forecasting procedures
- Inventory management
- Work environment, physical organization and layout
- Technology used
- Financial status
- Customer relations.

However, benchmarking rarely gives insights into planned future developments which might be modifications of what you are being shown. Despite this, information provided by other companies can often seem impressive to busy line managers. Benchmarking HR services allows you to identify how appropriate your HR provision is to the needs of your business relative to other HR providers, and to position your HR service along a sliding scale. This can then steer you towards useful targets for improvement, and/or supply information which can be used to justify what you propose.

With respect to benchmarking the Human Resource function and activities, it is important to identify the key HR drivers and performance indicators so that a meaningful set of measures can be developed. By gathering internal client feedback about existing HR processes, performance and practices, and documenting these, the critical success factors within the HR function can be prioritized and the appropriate focus for benchmarking can be selected.

The area for benchmarking should be chosen with care. Pick a specific aspect of the HR organization or operation which needs improving. This may be internal client relationships and satisfaction levels, delivery time for a service etc. Review your own process to fully understand how the current procedures work and choose another organization which excels at that specific aspect. The people who are going to be involved in implementing improvements should be involved in the benchmarking visits. Visits should be short and reciprocal – you should at least be willing to answer questions which you wish to ask the other company. The data provided through benchmarking should be used for internal purposes only and treated as confidential.

HR benchmarking often focuses on issues such as:

- Ratio of HR to line staff
- Management levels of HR staff
- Involvement in management decision-making and types of decision on which HR contribution is sought
- Relationships with line management
- How HR processes operate
- How HR is structured – centrally, decentralized etc.
- Roles of HR staff, e.g. consultancy, administrative – numbers and skill levels of those in roles
- How HR operates as a team, especially in an international organization
- Accuracy rates for aspects of operational HR, e.g. monthly salary operations

- Retention rates for key worker groups
- Percentage of new recruits who are still with the organization after six months
- Forms of succession planning
- Use of technology by HR
- Training provision – types of training provided, percentage of salary bill spent on training, how training budgets are controlled
- Evaluation practices.

Although generally carried out with external organizations, internal benchmarking can also be helpful in large companies for spreading awareness of how good results can and are being achieved in different parts of the business. This can be very relevant to specific areas of HR interest such as spreading good practice on team communication, for example. The use of such internal benchmarks can be motivating for those identified within the organization as having a 'world-class' approach to some aspect of people management.

The service–profit chain

The link between investment in people, providing technology to support front-line workers, improved training and recruitment practices and profitability is most apparent in service organizations. The 'new economics of service' are perhaps most evident in a number of US companies such as **Taco Bell** and **MCI**, where a radical shift has occurred in the way they manage and measure success. This involves making customers and employees paramount. The techniques used assess the impact of employee satisfaction, loyalty and productivity on the value of products and services delivered. This in turn is calibrated against building customer satisfaction and growth of customer loyalty. It has been estimated, for instance, that the lifetime value to a fast-food retailer of a loyal pizza eater can be $8000. These techniques put a 'hard' financial value on 'soft' measures.

According to a *Harvard Business Review* article by Heskett *et al.* (1994), the service–profit chain clarifies the links between the following:

- Customer loyalty drives profitability and growth
- Customer satisfaction drives customer loyalty

- Value drives customer satisfaction
- Employee productivity drives value
- Employee loyalty drives productivity
- Employee satisfaction drives loyalty
- Internal quality drives employee satisfaction
- Leadership underlies the chain's success. Leaders of successful service companies emphasize by their words and actions the importance of each employee and customer.

In the UK, Julian Richer has turned **Richer Sounds** into the biggest and most profitable hi-fi retailer in the country, with the highest sales per square foot of any retailer in the world. Richer's recipe for Richer Sounds is to recruit the right people, motivate them and provide them with the training they need to provide excellent customer service. He suggests that good management is 'all about achieving the right balance between control and motivation'. In other words, staff are set clear standards and robust procedures. All staff are engaged in continuous improvement through learning. Reward systems are aligned to behaviours which the organization values and wishes to encourage, such as innovation and outstanding customer service. Richer argues that it is possible to achieve a happy balance between strong central control and empowerment – and have both.

So clear is the mandate to staff that customer satisfaction is key to business success that employees are given a degree of freedom in using their initiative to ensure that customers' needs are met. Bureaucracy is kept to an absolute minimum so that speedy action can delight customers. Richer also consults staff widely on business and employee issues. As he tells staff: 'It is your responsibility to tell us what you think. We want to improve the business continually, and we can't do so unless you tell us where we are going wrong.' Employees also have the satisfaction of seeing many of their suggestions implemented.

Performance is measured weekly against a range of criteria including obvious ones such as sales and customer service. Julian Richer and members of his management team personally go though the figures each week with store managers in a third of the shops. Other measures include both positive matters such as whether staff met for suggestion brainstorming sessions, and the number of suggestions from individual employees put through, as well as negative aspects such as absenteeism. Central departments are also measured on their (internal) customer service such as the way they answer the phone. This close attention to measures means that any deviation from desired outcomes can be tackled immediately.

In the USA, companies such as **Xerox** are attempting to quantify customer satisfaction. Xerox has polled 480,000 customers annually regarding product and service satisfaction using a 5-point scale from 5 (high) to 1 (low). They have found that providing excellent service (gaining a 5) was significantly more likely to lead to repeat business than giving good service (scoring a 4). Xerox aims to create 'apostles' who are so delighted with the service they have received that they tell others and convert sceptics. They also want to avoid 'terrorists' or unhappy customers who speak out against a poorly delivered service. Other organizations have also calculated that the real 'cost of quality' is more dramatically linked to the lost opportunities caused by an unhappy customer spreading bad news about the company than to the loss of that customer alone. Xerox recognizes that the key to customer satisfaction involves ensuring employee satisfaction and giving people the behavioural and other tools they need to do their job.

Human Resource processes and activities can and do affect every element of the service-profit chain to profitability. Employee loyalty has a direct cost to businesses when employee turnover is the consequence of a lessening of loyalty. These costs are not only the losses incurred by the cost of recruiting and training replacements but also the loss of productivity and decreased customer satisfaction when valued employees leave. The impact on customer relationships can be huge. Members of the Harvard Business School faculty have put a cumulative loss of at least $2.5 million in commissions on the unscheduled departure of a valued broker from a securities firm.

Many research surveys, including my own, have suggested that dissatisfied employees are more likely to express the intention to leave a company. Conversely, satisfied employees are more likely to stay. At **Sun Microsystems UK** employee turnover in a highly competitive labour market was cut to 4 per cent due to imaginative career and other development opportunities and correspondingly high levels of employee satisfaction. Another key factor which drives employee satisfaction is internal quality which links with employees' perceptions of their ability to meet customer needs. This is where employees have the systems and other resources they need to do their job and where thought is put into identifying how to help employees to provide the most professional service. In some companies dedicated phone lines are used to answer employees' questions, remedy situations and alert senior managers to potential problems to be addressed.

MCI carried out a study of seven telephone customer service centres and found clear relationships between employee satisfaction, customer satisfaction and customer intentions to continue to use MCI services. Factors relating to job satisfaction included:

- The job itself
- Training
- Pay
- Advancement fairness
- Treatment with respect and dignity
- Teamwork
- Company interest in employee well-being.

All these factors are areas for strategic HR intervention and a shared responsibility between HR and the line. Another American Company, **Taco Bell**, a subsidiary of Pepsi-Co, has integrated measurement data about profit by unit, market manager, zone etc. with the results of customer exit interviews. They found that those stores which were the top performers on customer service also outperformed the others on all measures. Consequently, managers' compensation in company-owned stores is now closely linked to both customer satisfaction and profits.

Above all, perhaps the single biggest element underlying the chain's success is leadership commitment to developing a corporate culture which centres around service. Such leaders make their priorities evident in their behaviours, such as spending time listening to customers and employees, and by the attention paid to selecting, tracking and enabling employees to provide excellent service. Corporate value statements about customer service are not enough – senior managers' behaviour and their focus on employees and customers appear to make the difference.

The Sears turnaround

Perhaps one of the most well-known examples of a business turnaround using the employee–customer–profit model is that of the US retailer **Sears Roebuck and Company**, which is documented in a *Harvard Business Review* article by Rucci *et al.* (1998). In 1992, following a period of steady and serious business losses, the new head of the merchandising group, Arthur Martinez, instituted a turnaround plan which benefited from the willing support of employees who were keen to make the business successful and from the residual loyalty of customers to the Sears brand, despite low levels of customer satisfaction. The company's service strategy was revamped, store operations were reengineered and there was a heavy emphasis on training, incentives and the elimination of unnecessary administration for sales staff. A range of other business initiatives, including Sunday deliveries, contributed to the superb results achieved by 1993 (a sales increase of more than 9 per cent in existing stores and market share gains in a number of major goods).

The initial business turnaround was used as the springboard for more fundamental change so as to avoid the dangers of complacency identified as a primary source of failure of so-called 'excellent' companies by Peters and Waterman (1982). While the turnaround strategy had been implemented in a conventional 'top-down' way, Martinez saw the need to engage managers' and employees' hearts and minds in developing the company's future. A strong driving vision to achieve world-class status was established. The team at headquarters in Phoenix created an algorithm *work* × *shop* = *invest*. This emphasized the point that for Sears to succeed financially, the stores had to be a compelling place to work (i.e. that employees would be highly motivated) and to shop (that the best merchandise alone would not ensure the company's success). This became known as the three C's – 'to be a compelling place to work, to shop, to invest'.

Task forces were established to explore issues relating to financial performance, innovation, values, customers and employees. The innovation group did external benchmarking. Employees in the Values group were involved in gathering the views of all 80,000 of their colleagues to identify the six core values which Sears employees felt strongly about. These included honesty, trust and respect for the individual. The customer task force studied customer surveys going back several years and found that, broadly speaking, customers wanted Sears to succeed. The Employee group conducted a survey and found that employees were generally proud to work for Sears.

The data gathered by all the task forces was used to establish goals, including to build customer loyalty and to provide excellent customer service by hiring and holding on to the best employees. Specific objectives were developed to achieve these goals.

Measurement was a key feature in ensuring that the turnaround was not a flash in the pan. The task force data provided preliminary measures within each of the three elements of the vision. So, under *A compelling place to work* were measures relating to personal growth and development, empowered teams etc. Under *A compelling place to shop* were measures relating to customer needs being met and customer satisfaction. Under *A compelling place to invest* were financial measures linked to revenue growth, sales per square foot, inventory turnover etc. The Phoenix team wanted to see if there were any links between the three areas of measurement. During 1995 metrics of every kind were gathered and causal pathway modelling applied to establish cause and effect.

The result of this analysis was that clear links were established between employee attitudes and customer service, employee turnover and the likelihood that employees would recommend Sears to their contacts. A key discovery was the positive impact of an employee's ability to see the connection between his or her own role and the company's strategic objectives. Managers began to see how a change in training or business awareness could have a direct impact on revenues. Another key finding was that attitude towards the job and towards the company had a greater effect on employee loyalty and service to customers than all the other dimensions measured. These became the main focus of subsequent ongoing employee surveys which are based on a revised model of the employee–customer–profit chain. The measurement of Total Performance Indicators or TPI has become embedded in the Sears culture.

Having isolated the 'soft' issues which make a difference to the 'hard' business results, Sears can now see that a 5-point improvement in employee attitudes will drive a 1.3-point improvement in customer satisfaction which in turn will lead to a 0.5 per cent improvement in revenue growth. The TPI model has proved sufficiently accurate for Sears that it can be used for predicting business performance – based on employee attitudes.

Measures alone were not sufficient to achieve maintained high performance. A major training and learning initiative was launched to change the perceptions and attitudes of the workforce, help employees understand how the business worked and to improve their own approach to customer service. 'Learning maps' were used which informed employees of the changing economic and social context of retailing. The goal was economic and business literacy. Town hall meetings built on the learning and converted it into action.

Sears management recognized the importance of leadership to the development and maintenance of a high service culture. A leadership model was developed which incorporated every aspect of the transformation, including operational competence. The fifteen top executives identified the skills and qualities they looked for in appraising their direct reports and from this data, twelve leadership skills were agreed, to be used as the basis for promotion, recruiting and selecting future leaders. The skills are assessed using 360-degree feedback and form the basis of leadership training. All courses at the Sears University are linked to one or more of the twelve leadership skills and more than 40 000 managers have now been trained.

In a further move to align managers' behaviour to the direction of the company, the rewards and compensation of executives have been altered so that long-term incentives are now based on non-financial as well as financial measures. This is based on the reliability of the TPI as a leading indicator of business performance. These combined efforts to create customer satisfaction through improving employee satisfaction are paying off through handsome increases in revenues and vastly increased market capitalization.

Strategic planning in Dow Corning

This case study is prepared by Leslie Patterson, HR Director, **Dow Corning**. Leslie describes how a strategic HR planning framework is used to align business and organizational strategies in Dow Corning.

Dow Corning company profile

Created in 1943 by Corning Glass Works (now Corning, Incoporated) and The Dow Chemical Company, Dow Corning was organized to explore the potential of silicones, materials that combine the temperature and chemical resistance of glass and the versatility of plastics. In little more than a half-century, that exploration has resulted in over 10 000 products and speciality materials used by about 50 000 customers worldwide representing virtually every major industry. Headquarters are in Midland, Michigan, USA, with area headquarters located in Brussels, Belgium, and Tokyo, Japan. Dow Corning has 8300 employees worldwide with 1800 in Europe. 2000 revenues were $2.75 billion with a net income of $104.6 million.

Strategic HR planning process

Description

Strategic HR Planning (SHRP) was developed by Professor Wayne Brockbank of the University of Michigan. It looks at the linkages between business strategy and human resource management and assesses the degree to which these are in alignment. The closer the alignment, the better the organizational responsiveness will be and hence the ability to adapt to customer needs and maintain competitive advantage (see Figure 3.2).

Desired outcomes

- The articulation of the *culture, behaviours* and *competencies* which are necessary to ensure successful execution of business strategy.

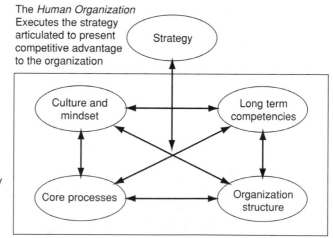

The *Human Organization* Executes the strategy articulated to present competitive advantage to the organization

The SHRP focuses on alignment of HR processes to create the ideal culture and mindset to achieve the business strategy

The performance of a system is not the sum of the performances of its parts taken separately, but the *product of their interactions*

Figure 3.2   *The components of the ideal human organization*

Figure 3.3 *The strategic HR planning process*

- The development of a *plan* of *HR initiatives* to enable the desired culture, behaviours and competencies to become more prevalent in the organization (see Figure 3.3).

Case study

In 1993, Dow Corning restructured into three geographic areas (the Americas, Europe and Asia) and two business groups:

- Core Products Business Group (CPBG) to produce the backbone technology, dimethylsiloxane, and deliver fluids, rubber, sealant and silicone at the lowest possible total cost
- The Advanced Materials Industries Group (AMIG) to grow current sales and profit while focusing on the acceleration of long-term growth of silicon-based materials.

In 1997, the European CPBG general manager approached HR for help with what he believed was a communications problem. He explained that he was concerned about the poor perception of CPBG as compared to AMIG and felt the time had come for the CPBG board to take some action to reverse the situation. Examples of what he wanted to change were:

- The AMIG business had a much more positive culture; they called themselves the 'amigos', turning their AMIG acronym into an appealing name. How could CPBG do the same?
- CPBG was losing good employees to AMIG and it was becoming difficult to attract high potentials to CPBG. How could CPBG reverse this trend?

In checking whether the same phenomena were occurring in the other geographic areas, several differences were noted. In the Americas, for example, there were more employees leaving AMIG and going to CPBG than in the other direction. Further probing uncovered the following:

- Although CPBG was a global term, the scope in Europe and the Americas was different. The Americas CPBG also included the semiconductor business, the highest growth sector at the time.
- CPBG and AMIG had different measures linked to variable compensation plans: AMIG goals were linked to sales of new products and CPBG's to manufacturing site quality goals. Pressure from AMIG to get new products out faster had resulted in some manufacturing problems. CPBG 'blamed' AMIG for under-performance on CPBG targets while AMIG targets were being met.
- AMIG was generally perceived as the 'place to be if you want to get on in Dow Corning'. The perception was that AMIG was outperforming CPBG yet the business results did not reflect this.

The main conclusion from the research was that while communications were going to be part of the solution they were not the real problem. It was agreed that it was time to check that the CPBG culture was aligned to the needs of CPBG's external customers and that the HR processes were providing the appropriate reinforcement and reward. The process used to do this was the HR Strategic Planning Process developed by Professor Wayne Brockbank of the University of Michigan which had already been used with some success with several groups in Dow Corning.

Over the course of several sessions with the CPBG board in 1997–8, the following three organizational characteristics for the CPBG culture and mindset were identified:

- Honest winners
- Confident change agents
- Customer maniacs.

These characteristics were the distillation of many long hours of reflection and discussion. However, not all were unanimously accepted. For instance, the use of 'maniacs' caused much debate. For some, this was too strong a word and had negative overtones. For others, it was good because it sent a strong message and attracted attention.

For each characteristic, we then did a gap analysis (on a scale of 1 to 5) of the extent to which it was aligned with the current culture and the impact (high, medium, low) it would have on the key business strategies if it were fully aligned. Table 3.1 is a summary of this assessment.

The next step was to assess the three characteristics against HR practices using a quality function deployment (QFD) analysis to check:

- The degree of alignment *today* (1 = aligned; 3 = not aligned)
- The potential impact if the HR practice were fully aligned (1 = low; 3 = high).

The results are shown in Table 3.2.

At this point in the CPBG process, Dow Corning announced a new corporate direction: to become a customer-driven company.

Table 3.1 *Integration of organizational characteristics with business strategies*

Business strategies	*Organizational characteristics*		
	Customer maniac	*Honest winner*	*Confident change agent*
Business strategy #1	H	H	M
Business strategy #2	H	H	H
Business strategy #3	H	H	M
Business strategy #4	M	H	H
Business strategy #5	L	H	H
Gap analysis	0 – CPBG-wide	2	1
(1 = low; 5 = high)	3 – some parts		

Table 3.2 *Assessment of organizational characteristics against HR practices*

HR practices	Impact – honest winner	Impact – customer maniacs	Impact – confident change agents
Recruitment	4	4	6
Promotions	6	9	6
Outplacement/redeployment	9	4	9
Appraisal	6	9	6
Rewards and recognition	9	9	9
Training	6	9	2
Developing	6	9	6
Benchmarking	6	6	3
Communications	9	6	6
IT systems design	?	6	3
Organizational structure	4	6	9
Reengineering	6	9	6
Physical setting	2	4	6
Leadership	6	9	6

Notes
- Rewards and recognition were the only HR practice with '9' in all cells
- Outplacement (redeployment) which had a '9' for two characteristics
- Customer maniacs has highest number of 9s (seven versus three for the other two characteristics) which reflects and reinforces the gap analysis where customer maniacs score.

External research showed that key drivers of customer satisfaction were employees who displayed the following behaviours:

Able to build relationships
- Listen, learn and work together with our customers to anticipate their needs

Act with a sense of urgency
- Our customers' priorities are ours: speeding up internal processes is a must

Display a can-do attitude
- Focus the full force of our talents on our customers and 'make things happen'

Act with integrity
- Inspire long-term trust in line with our values.

The closeness of the research findings to the three CPBG characteristics did not go unnoticed by the CPBG board and it gave them added confidence that they were on the right track! Indeed, initial discomfort with the use of 'maniac' turned into positive acceptance. However, before going into detailed action planning, the CPBG board felt it was time to do a reality check and share their thinking with CPBG employees. These sessions provided useful input on the content but, more importantly, they served as an essential step in change management by engaging CPBG employees in the process and by role modelling the leadership's interactive approach to communications. Feedback was very positive and typical comments included: 'These sessions are an indication that the process has started' and 'I feel like we are participating in our customer-driven company program.'

The output of the process was a project charter entitled 'Creating a Customer-Driven Organization in CPBG–Europe' with the purpose of developing a culture of unswerving devotion to customers and their satisfaction. Specific initiatives covered the HR practices of leadership, appraisal, development and reward and recognition. The subsequent restructuring of the corporation in late 1998/early 1999 resulted in the disbandment of the CPBG and AMIG businesses but the pioneering work started by the CPBG board members has continued in the new organization.

Case study summary

The work with CPBG provided many benefits and learning at different levels:

- Professor Brockbank's process provided a structured methodology for making tangible and clear to management the linkages between external customers, business strategies, company culture and HR practices.
- CPBG understood that they were not competing with AMIG for the same resources.
- The CPBG board accepted that creation of the appropriate culture to achieve their business goals was a leadership responsibility.
- Completing the Brockbank process was in itself an excellent teambuilding exercise for the CPBG board and illustrated the key role of sponsorship in change management.

Update

In the two years since this case study was written, the strategic HR planning process has become fully integrated into the annual corporate planning and budgeting process at Dow Corning. All business units complete a critical review of the alignment of business strategy with their human organization and the projects resulting from this SHRP process are prioritized as part of the overall planning process. While the model used today is no longer Brockbank's but Noel Tichy's Ideas–Values–Emotional Energy–Edge model*, the fundamental point remains: a key determinant of balanced growth for any organization is its human resource system. For HR, the challenge is to ensure that the HR processes for staffing, performance management, rewards and development which make up the human resource system are mutually reinforcing and aligned to the business direction.

Material in this case study © Leslie Patterson, Organizational Effectiveness Europe, Dow Corning.

Conclusion

HR is under pressure to demonstrate a payback from HR activities, whether these are team building, innovation or family-friendly initiatives, culture change or total quality management. The extent to which this pressure is felt in any organization is a reflection of the organization's culture. Senior line managers too are under pressure to achieve outstanding performance measured in bottom line terms. The partnership between line and HR needs to result in a workforce with the skills and motivation to help the organization survive and thrive in an increasingly competitive environment.

Senior managers have a vital role in creating an organization which views investment in people management as a source of competitive advantage. In service organizations in particular, managers need to manage their investment in people – both customers and employees – and set both qualitative as well as quantitative measures to assess the impact of that investment.

*For more detailed description of the model, refer to *Leadership Engine – How Winning Companies Build Leaders at Every Level* by Noel Tichy, Harper Collins 1997, and *Every Business is a Growth Business* by Noel Tichy and Ram Charan, Times Books 1998.

Employee commitment and confidence are key determinants of employee behaviour. Research suggests that these can be measurably improved if managers focus on enabling skills development and creating a community in which employees feel able and willing to give of their best.

HR needs to focus their activity on areas which are critical to the business in the short and medium term. Though I shall argue later that many of HR's critical interventions do not lend themselves to easy measurement in the short term, the extent to which unmeasured activities will continue to be seen as justifiable in the long term is questionable. HR practitioners need to prioritize the areas which will make a difference to their organization and identify, measure and track the effect of the initiatives they put in place to address these. Whichever measurement framework or guiding principle is used, HR should be in a position to identify the few things which must be managed in order to produce the biggest benefits. Profitability depends not only on assigning financial value to 'soft' measures but also on linking those different measures into a complete service–profit picture.

Collaboration between HR and other managers is extremely important. A shared vision and an agreed set of bottom line objectives are starting points. A joint belief in the vital nature of people-related activities is imperative to an organization's success. Both parties need to recognize that HR activities are crucial to achieving their mutual objectives and ensure that both are involved in the setting of the strategic business, and therefore HR, agenda at an early enough stage. Perhaps then the value of HR's contribution can speak for itself.

Measurement checklists

Customer value

- How does your organization define loyal customers?
- How do you understand changing customer demands and why customers defect?
- Are customer satisfaction data gathered in an objective, consistent and regular way?
- Where are the listening posts for obtaining customer (and employee) feedback in your organization?

- How is information concerning customer satisfaction used to solve customer problems?
- How is information about customers' perceptions of value shared with those responsible for designing a product or service?
- How will changing customer needs affect the competencies required of employees?
- How do you measure service value?

Employee value

- How do you measure employee productivity?
- How do you create employee loyalty and what is the right level of employee retention?
- Is employee satisfaction measured in ways which can be linked to similar measures of customer satisfaction sufficiently frequently that trends can be established for management use?
- Are employee-selection criteria and methods geared to what customers as well as managers believe to be important?
- Do employees know who their (internal or external) customers are?
- Are employees satisfied with the support (technical and personal) they receive to do their job?
- To what extent are your organization's leaders energetic, participative, good listeners, motivational and able to walk the talk by personally demonstrating the organization's values?
- How much time and effort is put in by senior managers to creating a culture centred around service to customers and fellow employees?

Use of measurement

- In order to survive, what must your organization do over the next three years?
- How clear are the strategic challenges to the HR team, and employees as a whole?
- Do you use measurement to challenge assumptions, check health or to cause compliance?
- Are the measures used 'lag' i.e. based on standard operating data which assumes the status quo, or 'lead' i.e. are you measuring the areas which you believe will make a difference to the organization in the future?

• To what extent are measures of customer satisfaction, customer loyalty and the quality of service output used to recognize and reward employees?

References

Buckingham, M. and Coffman, C. (1999). What is a Great Workplace? A weekly summary of Gallup's discoveries about Great Managers and Great Workplaces. *The Gallup Poll – Managing.*

Chambers, N. (1997). Does the bell toll for your living company? (interview with Arie de Geus), *HR Focus, 74,* No.10, October.

Ettorre, B. (1997). The empowerment gap: hype vs. reality, *HR Focus, 74,* No.7, July.

Heskett, J. L., Jones, T. O., Loveman, G. W., Sasser, W. E. and Schlesinger, L. A. (1994). Putting the service–profit chain to work, *Harvard Business Review*, March–April.

Institute of Personnel and Development (1999). *Training and development in Britain, 1999: The First IPD Annual Report,* April.

Kaplan, R. S. and Norton, D. P. (1998). Using the Balanced Scorecard as a strategic management system', *Harvard Business Review*, January–February.

Kearns, P. (1998). Moving up the HR ROI scale, *Financial Times*.

Kirkpatrick, D. (1996). Revisiting Kirkpatrick's four-level model, *Training and Development*, January.

Patterson, M., West, M., Lawthorn, R. and Nickell, S. (1997). *The Impact of People Management Practices*, London: IPD.

Peters, T. (1992). *Liberation Management.* London: Macmillan.

Peters, T. and Waterman, R. II. (1982). *In Search of Excellence.* New York: Harper Business.

Pfeffer, J. (1995). People, capability and competitive success, *Management Development Review*, 8, No.5, 6–10.

Phelps, M. (1998). The Executive Scorecard: Achieving competitive Advantage through HR benchmarking, *The International Journal of Business Transformation*, 1, No.4, April.

Richer, J. (1995). *The Richer Way,* Emap Business Communications.

Rucci, A. J., Kirn, S. P. and Quinn, R. T. (1998). The employee–customer–profit chain at Sears, *Harvard Business Review*, January–February.

In the 1990s the key is not just having the right strategy, but being able to execute, to implement the strategy – having, in other words, effective operational capabilities (Pfeffer, 1995).

The main focus of this chapter is on exploring what is meant by corporate strategy and the links between that and HR strategy. In the previous two chapters we have looked at what is meant by organizational effectiveness. We will start by considering approaches to strategy and then assess the implications for HR strategies.

Approaches to developing corporate strategy

One of the key challenges for the leaders of any organization is to provide a sense of direction and a focus for the organization's activities. Ideally, strategic direction involves creating a situation in organizations where the present is being driven from the future, rather than simply being seen as an extrapolation from the past. In changing times there is a greater need for clarity of business direction than in more stable times when the status quo provides employees with guidance as to what is expected of them. If employees are to be able to contribute their skills in the most effective way in order to realize business aims, it helps if people know what these aims are. People need to know what they are expected to do and why.

Some organizations make clear their medium-term aspirations through vision and mission statements. In the absence of vision, people often gain their understanding of where the organization is going from statements about its purpose, however ill defined, from statements of business values and other broad ways of indicating what the organization is about and where it is heading. In some organizations, the business direction is made clear in strategic imperatives and the business plan.

Of course, corporate strategies tend not to be made in isolation – they should take into account the changing needs of external stakeholders such as customers, the changing business environment, including markets, and the critical resources needed to carry out the strategic aims. These critical resources include such factors as capital and technology, and increasingly rely on people – their brain power, access to information and ability to learn new approaches.

In conventional corporate planning, management teams often carry out an environmental analysis using a tool such as the PEST model (an analysis of the changing Political, Economic, Sociological and Technological factors currently or potentially affecting their organization and its stakeholders). Typical factors relate to the economy – local, worldwide or specific to particular geographic regions; to the political climate, such as key international events. Other factors might include social and industry trends, changing demographics, emerging technology and shifting competitor behaviour. The potential impact of these changes on existing strategy as well as potential threats and business opportunities can be assessed.

One international construction company, for instance, had a small sub-business involving the reclamation of poisoned land by removing the spoilt earth to landfill sites. The company recognized that the Green movement was becoming highly influential in Europe in the early 1990s. They were able to see opportunities for a more environmentally friendly operation using bioremediation. This has become a useful and profitable part of the company's portfolio.

An environmental analysis is often followed by a look at the strengths and weaknesses of the organization in relation to these threats and opportunities (a SWOT analysis) so that the potential impact on the organization of possible changes in strategy can be gauged. Such an analysis should take into account the impact of changes on customers, shareholders, management, employees, suppliers, unions and the financial community. Ways of minimizing risk are identified.

This assumes a three-pronged approach to strategy – that having carried out an analysis, strategic choices are made which are then implemented. Models of strategic processes are often linear, sequential and apparently rational. Managers undertaking corporate planning are encouraged to answer broad questions:

- Where are we now?
- Where do we want to get to? What is our future vision?
- How shall we get there?

Thompson and Strickland (1998) suggest a set of five phases as follows:

1 Defining the business and establishing a strategic mission
2 Setting strategic objectives and performance targets
3 Formulating a strategy to achieve the target objectives and performance
4 Implementing and executing the strategic plan
5 Evaluating performance and reformulating the strategic plan and/or its implementation.

Planned versus emergent

These classical planned approaches to devising and implementing strategy are based on fairly mechanistic models of organization and assume that the future can be known, predicted and to some extent controlled by managers. The emphasis is on intention, or strategic intent, stability and return to equilibrium. Success is thought to depend on extensive planning and design, often using external consultants, accurate anticipation of resistance to change and skill at overcoming this resistance.

Several conditions need to be in place for a planned approach to strategy to be realized. There needs to be a relatively predictable or stable environment where economic conditions, competitors or government actions are unlikely to significantly affect the organization's ability to achieve its plan. There also needs to be a consistent adherence to the vision or plan within the organization over a long time. This implies that the critical mass of the organization is aligned and working to achieve the same future state. This is often where planned approaches break down due to a combination of internal rivalries between business units, different time spans among 'support' functions such as Personnel and IT and lack of integration of objectives across business units. The organization needs to have sufficient resources (e.g. money, skill, time, technology) and leadership to deploy these resources effectively in order to achieve the plan. Communication and control methods need to be sufficiently robust to prevent re-interpretation of the planned future state within the organization.

The benefits of such approaches are apparent clarity and the ability to monitor progress. The downsides are that the plan can become paramount, even when circumstances change and the strategy should change. Similarly, the relatively top-down approach generally used with such approaches often leaves those who are left to implement the plan feeling that they have had no say in creating it. The cost is a potential loss of employee ideas and commitment to the plan.

In many organizations, the day-to-day reality of the strategic process is somewhat different. When everything is in flux, having a clear direction can be difficult. Change, rather than being seen as linear, can appear cyclical, especially to employees who have worked with the organization for any length of time and may have 'seen it all before'. Often, in the absence of strong central direction, small project groups or business teams start to introduce new practices and initiatives, many of which relate to the customer. There is often real enthusiasm and commitment to what they are doing among members of project teams but the downside can be that such activities are not coordinated and can lead to duplication or political clamp-downs.

Such emergent approaches arise from the irrational side of organizations, such as political processes and other elements of the informal system. New order typically emerges rather than being designed or externally driven or hierarchically controlled. When smoking was generally banned in public places and places of work it might have been assumed that smoking would die out. Instead, some of the most firmly established and collaborative networks (which include people at all levels in an organization) are now to be found among smokers who have found themselves relegated to taking their smoking breaks at the doorstep.

The assumptions behind emergent approaches to strategy and change is that the future is inherently unknowable and that key organizational results often occur through the enhancement of random or unexpected events. Based on ideas from complexity and chaos theories, emergence involves seeing organizations as networks of multiple feedback loops which are so complex that no individual or small group is likely to see the 'whole picture'. The benefits of such approaches are that, if tapped for the benefit of the organization, the ideas of small groups and individuals can contribute vastly to keeping corporate strategy in touch with the needs of customers and the changing marketplace. Of course, because these seemingly *ad hoc* activities are driven by people who have a sense of ownership of their ideas, levels of motivation in such groups are usually high. Front-line staff in particular usually have a range of insights into changing customer needs and the subtle shifts in the market but their ideas and input may not be sought by management.

A classic example of a strategy which emerged as the result of learning by listening to the customer, paying attention to the reasons for success and failure, reinforcing success and thinking creatively about different distribution channels is the **Honda Motorcycles'** entry into the US market (the Honda case study is described in Pascale, 1995). The strategy which emerged of selling their small motorcycles through general stores was very far from Honda's original intention of selling large motorcycles through established dealers.

However, emergence is not at the polar opposite of planned change, i.e. random action, but rather reconciles the two. Organizations need both planned approaches which are sufficiently flexible and adaptable that they can cope with changing circumstances and the seemingly haphazard proliferation of activities in which employees are developing new ideas. The challenge is to get the best of both approaches, perhaps by coordinating apparently disparate initiatives and helping people to see where linkages may occur. Where there is no clear organization vision, a sense of direction can emerge from creating coherence among different initiatives by increasing the flow of information between project groups. This coherence can provide a guiding framework for further activities. Where there is a clear business direction, helping task groups to see how they are contributing to the whole can create a sense of momentum, purpose and involvement.

Creating the conditions in which change can occur

The role of the manager then is to create conditions in which change can occur. Managers need to pay attention to their environments and the threats and opportunities they contain, as much as to their own plans. They need to raise their awareness of how they interpret events – particularly the assumptions which they use – as a key feature of their own and organizational learning. Managers can encourage the creation of fluid, adaptive organizations through increasing information flows, improving processes, changing structures and enabling people to develop the skills required to work in them. In the same way, managers should be sensitive to the people processes they use such as the extent to which they involve people in decision making, delegate work etc. Managers should communicate their long-term intentions in terms of broad purpose and principle, rather than detailed plans, as only broad principles will stimulate the creativity, learning and adaptability of those in closest contact with the environment.

Whichever approach is used to provide clarity about the future direction, the real challenge is trying to ensure that every aspect of the organization, especially employees, are working in the same direction. Alignment involves knowing what the organization's purpose is and then ensuring that performance is built into it. In other words, every employee's performance should contribute to the achievement of the strategy.

Aligning the organization to the business direction

The principle of alignment is that every aspect of an organization's activities should be integrated and pull in the same direction – to the achievement of corporate goals. In an ideal world, the organization's mission and goals should be translated into its business and strategic plan. These need to reflect the organization's values to prevent employees from being pulled in different directions. Systems and structures which are created need to reflect the values at a very detailed level. Achieving the strategy or vision relies on the performance of people within the organization which in turn calls for high levels of motivation and commitment among employees. Employee performance needs to reflect the mission, goals and values and, if excellent performance is required, there must be opportunities for employees to gain ownership and satisfaction from what they do. Alignment needs to happen at an organizational, team and individual level.

All too often, however, visions and other direction-setting messages are obscure and what people really get their steer from is the behaviour of people around them, especially that of senior managers. People infer what is expected of them from the organization's culture, by the way people are treated and by what management appears to value and reward. Where there is a mismatch between what is espoused, such as teamwork, and what is practised, people will believe what they see. Similarly, if the only way an organization rewards is by promoting a privileged few, people who are not promoted are unlikely to believe feedback that they are doing a good job. Management practices which are at odds with espoused values cause employee cynicism and eat away at motivation. At every level, gaps between organizational rhetoric and reality need to be identified and addressed.

Alignment frameworks

There are many conceptual models which suggest how different aspects of an organization interlink with others. One of the best known is the McKinsey framework, also known as the 'Seven S' model. This and other frameworks allow a gap analysis to be made at any point in time to ascertain whether all aspects of the organization are pulling in the same direction.

An interesting distinction is drawn between the so-called 'hard triangle' of strategy, systems and structure and the 'soft square' of staff, style, skills and shared values. Typically, it is the hard triangle which excites executives and around which most money is spent on consultants. Redesigning the organization's structures is not enough if change is to be really embedded. All the seven Ss need attention. People need to be helped to develop the skills and the motivation to work in new structures and with changed working practices. They need to understand why they are being asked to do these things, which is where change without a clear rationale can be so demotivating for employees.

Management and employee styles of operating may need to be adjusted. Organizations which are introducing process working or a greater customer focus may need to help staff to develop appropriate behaviours. Command and control styles of management may seem out of place if the business strategy and a lean structure call for empowered employees. In an ideal workplace, the structure should affect organizational performance to the extent that skilled and motivated employees are directly involved in determining what work is performed and how it will be carried out. However, more commonly, internal contradictions between elements of an organization lead to poor performance. Information systems and reward systems may undercut one another if people are paid only for what they know. There is therefore little incentive to share information with others.

Alignment frameworks are particularly useful when change is being implemented in one aspect of the organization. Inevitably there will be knock-on effects on other parts of the system and, if these can be anticipated and dealt with proactively, difficulties can be lessened. Importantly, when an organization's mission or strategies appear to change course, this can cause conflict with previously shared values. The Roffey Park research into careers (Holbeche, 1995) highlighted how bitterly some employees resented the apparent shifts in the culture of the UK National Health Service over the last decade. Rather than adjust to a greater managerial culture, many employees left and joined the private sector where there were fewer mixed messages about the organization's mission as well as better pay.

Within the overall business strategy there may be some broad cultural thrusts, such as teamworking which affect most employees in some way. People management systems need to be revised to reflect teamworking if this how the organization is intending to achieve its business goals. This means managing the performance of teams in the organization and clarifying what they are collectively expected to achieve. Team performance guides need to be developed and complemented by team development plans. Similarly, team rewards and performance measures need to reinforce messages about the importance of teamworking. The argument goes that if you don't measure desired performance such as teamworking, it won't happen.

Alignment also has to take into account the specific stage that the organization has reached. Is this a mature company with a few 'cash cow' services in great need of innovation and overhaul? Is this an organization which is in a start-up phase and where recruitment, setting up systems and processes are likely to be priorities? Similarly, is the organization's market share shrinking, or going into a growth phase? Several general avenues of growth have been identified by Gertz and Baptista (1995) as follows:

1   Firms may grow within existing markets: *implication* – HR's capacity to create business cultures through which revenue-enhancing strategies are implemented can be a major source of competitive advantage
2   If a firm purchases a competitor: *implication* – HR's challenge is to identify the culture which is required for both companies
3   Firms may grow through existing products in new markets e.g. global: *implication* – HR's role is to facilitate growth, selecting the right local leadership and balancing local and corporate demands
4   Firms may grow through new products within existing markets: *implication* – HR needs to create a business culture which emphasizes radical innovation and continuous improvement
5   Firms may grow through new products and new markets: *implication* – HR's role combines the approaches in (3) and (4).

Building competitive advantage

A major worldwide survey conducted under the auspices of IBM and Towers Perrin entitled *Priorities for Gaining Competitive Advantage* has identified several key groupings of HRM policies and practices which have been linked to competitive advantage:

*   *Culture*
    Promoting an empowerment culture
    Promoting diversity and an equality culture
*   *Organizational structure and control*
    Emphasis on flexible organizations/work practices
    Emphasis on utilizing IT to structure the organization
    Emphasis on horizontal management
    Emphasis on increasing and promoting customer service
    Emphasis on rewarding innovation/creativity
    Link between pay and individual performance
    Shared benefits, risks and pay for team performance
*   *Resourcing*
    Emphasis on external resourcing
    Emphasis on internal resourcing – training and careers
    Emphasis on internal resourcing – managing outflows

- *Communication/corporate responsibility*
  Emphasis on communication
  Emphasis on corporate responsibility.

Each of these elements is interrelated to the others. If one element is at odds with the others, no matter how clear the strategy, mixed messages will get in the way of implementation. HR planning can ensure that the key elements are integrated into a focused plan for building competitive advantage through people.

How can HR strategies be fully aligned?

Of course, in setting business strategies, line managers need to be fully in tune with what their customers say they want from the organization. The same is true of HR strategies, except that such strategies may have to be attuned to the needs of each organizational unit. HR and line managers need to think through the kind of culture needed in each unit if the people in that unit are to be able to deliver the business strategy.

What makes a difference to the delivery of business strategy is people's behaviours. So, for instance, all the 'customer focus' in the world is no use if clients perceive that the company's representative is rude to them over the phone. HR needs to think through the behavioural character desired of employees. This includes both behaviours which the company wants to encourage and dysfunctional behaviours which the company wishes to stop. HR also needs to think through the HR processes which are aligned to that behaviour. This will include issues such as recruitment, training, resources, location, working environment etc. Working through these issues with line managers in a systematic way helps line managers to see the link between managing the cultural aspects of the organization and achieving business goals.

Major action plans can establish what the HR team needs to do next to make the change happen. These plans need to be developed with the management team and can be both short and long term. Changing the structure, for instance, can be a short-term measure while changing the culture can take several years and may need to be phased.

Aligning HR and business strategies through HR planning

Strategic planning is a key tool for HR. One definition is implied in the much quoted conversation between Alice and the Cheshire Cat in Lewis Carroll's *Alice in Wonderland*:

> 'Would you tell me please, which way I should go from here?'
> 'That depends a good deal on where you want to get to,' said the cat.
> 'I don't much care where,' said Alice.
> 'Then it doesn't matter which way you go', said the cat.

Tony Grundy (1998) defines HR strategy as 'the plans, programmes and intentions to develop the human capability of an organization to meet the future needs of its external and internal environment'. HR strategy may be planned, emergent or some combination of these. Research by Tyson and Witcher (1994) as well as Grundy suggests that emergent HR strategy may be damaging to organizational effectiveness. Other research projects also suggest that the more planned and timely the implementation of HR strategies, the more value is perceived to be added to the business.

There are many reasons why many HR teams do not take a planned approach. Some HR teams may prefer working in an emergent way and would rather wait until there is a clear business strategy on which to model the HR strategy. This may be a long wait and opportunities for adding value may be missed. Some teams fear criticism of being seen to create their own policy in the absence of business strategy, on the one hand, or being seen to drive business strategy, on the other. The sheer complexity of the links which need to be managed between HR strategy and organizational effectiveness may mean that the overall focus of the delivery is diffuse and therefore not appreciated. Similarly, periods of ongoing change and active organizational politics can cause the links to be undermined. This may be a question of ownership of the HR strategy and where it sits in the organizational structure.

However, Lam and Schaubroeck's (1998) research suggests that leaders in firms with relatively highly formalized HR planning are more likely to perceive its usefulness compared with those firms where the HR strategic objectives are less clear. In strategic HRM, planning needs to go beyond being focused on operations and control. Whether a formal or informal approach is used, the important thing is to keep the plan simple. As HR teams move towards a strategic HRM approach, the need for integration among the different HR practices increases. These clear objectives are then likely to be useful in strategic planning activities, helping the organization to enhance organizational performance, rather than simply being a means of making the case for more resources.

HR planning is critical to the effective development of strategy since it should identify gaps and surpluses in capabilities as well as issues of utilization of talent. Indeed so central is this identification of organizational capability considered by some researchers that they argue for an enhanced role for HR planning in overall strategic planning. Various researchers have suggested that the most effective links are made when HR strategy as such disappears and is more fully integrated into other resource strategies supporting the operational management process.

This would mean that the role of HR would be to facilitate the development of an organizational strategy which is owned and developed by line managers. This would probably be issue based and directly linked to the business strategy. Indeed, Tony Grundy argues that the key role of a strategic HRM function is to facilitate Organization and People strategy, together with joint coordination with line management of strategic programmes such as management development and succession planning.

The effectiveness of HR planning very much depends on the organizational context. HR planning objectives are likely to be contingent upon different competitive strategies and different organizations will therefore be unlikely to use identical approaches to similar issues. However, unless the objectives are clear, building commitment to the strategy among line managers and employees is difficult. Lam and Schaubroek (1998) suggest three different kinds of HR objectives:

- *Operational* – which seek to identify current capabilities and trends with short-term requirements in mind
- *Traditional* – which attempt to incorporate forecasts about the numbers of employees and their skill types to meet longer-term demands. This type of planning needs to take account of career development, succession planning, exter-

nal recruitment and appraisal data. It can establish whether
it is possible for the organization to achieve its strategic
objectives

- *Strategic* – which is where HR planning provides valuable
  data and is carried out as an integral part of the overall strategic planning process. This involves line managers in developing and evaluating HR practices since this approach
  recognizes that those who are most knowledgeable about the
  workforce should be involved in building commitment to the
  strategy across the organization. Often the main thrust of
  strategic HR planning is finding ways to establish and maintain core competencies.

Typical objectives associated with different areas of HR
responsibility (after Lam and Schaubroek) include:

- *Maximum strategic impact*
  Align HR practices with business objectives
  Conduct development programmes to support strategic
  changes
  Carry out job analyses for long-term objectives
  Improve HR adaptability on changing environment
  Enhance workforce capability and motivation
- *Coordinate*
  Improve coordination between various HR functions
  Improve team effectiveness
  Improve HR project management
  Develop compensation and benefit programmes
  Coordinate any potential HR problems
  Integrate diverse HR functions and operations
- *Communicate*
  Communicate HR policies inside the organization
  Improve management acceptance of current HR policies
  Improve employee involvement and understanding of HR
  Conduct job analyses for long-term objectives
  Communicate HR policies outside the company
- *Control*
  Clarify budget and resources availability
  Manage personnel-related costs
  Improve HR budget control
  Improve HR resource procedures and control
  Review HR operations procedures

Alignment through organization development

Corporate strategy usually involves reviewing the business the organization is in, or wants to be in and its relative competitive positioning in the marketplace. This allows a strategic intent to be developed. A review is then carried out of the human capabilities through which competitive advantage can be achieved, enabling the organization to compete in a distinctive and sustainable way.

In the financial services sector in the UK, increased competition has led to pressure for greater efficiency in operations and more responsiveness to customer needs. At **NatWest Group**, a major revision of the brand has taken place and managers have recognized that employees not only represent the brand, but that their behaviours and approaches need to be aligned to the brand image. There is therefore a strategic thrust to enhance the brand and ensure that customers perceive no gap between the marketing image and the service they receive. The company is in a state of rapid transformation as it seeks to develop new products and services and gain internal efficiencies.

The decentralized structure has led to a wide range of management practices in different business units and little sharing of good practice across the organization. An organization development team at the centre of the organization has the challenge of helping to bring about change, as well as creating greater coherence across the organization while not diminishing the autonomy of the business units. This delicate balancing act is achieved by ensuring that the heads of the different business units are fully involved in developing the OD strategy and can perceive the potential value added by the unit to their own operations.

The OD team, led by Gary Storer, is aiming to focus its delivery on a few key areas. These include strategy and planning, organization and management, culture and values, people and performance. Learning and change will be at the heart of all OD activities and provide inner coherence to the OD strategy. The team consists of experienced OD practitioners who have both internal consultancy and business experience. The OD strategy is as follows:

Our focus is on:
• Change in organizations and culture
• Organizations and team effectiveness
• Leadership and management processes

- Organizational learning and corporate knowledge

Our Outputs will be:
- Involvement in major change initiatives
- Supporting business management and major functions
- Developing change skills in the company
- Evaluating organization effectiveness

Our methods include:
- Consultancy and facilitation
- Project management
- Education and training

backed up with:
- New management tools and processes
- Diagnostic audits and surveys
- Seminars, case studies and information networks
- Best practice action research.

Clear lines of communication exist between the OD team and those responsible for providing training, management and leadership development and succession planning. While at any point in time, the specific focus of the team's activity within this general remit will be tailored to the needs of a particular business unit, the core thrusts remain the same and have a corporate perspective. The team can then pursue major corporate projects while working within different business units to help them achieve their local OD objectives, such as managing a specific change process.

The clarity of outputs means that the team will be able to measure their achievements and gain client feedback which can feed further into the ongoing development of strategy. It could be argued that a coordinated organizational strategy such as this could be the joint starting point for developing corporate strategy.

Aligning the structure of HR with the organizational strategy

In recent years, many central HR teams in large organizations have decreased in size. There has been a noticeable shift to consultancy-type roles with many HR responsibilities devolved to the line. Operational HR roles have been the most endangered, with parts of the operation, such as pay and even recruitment, outsourced. Many organizations have experienced problems with quality and the current trend appears to be to take back into the centre the areas of operations which leave HR most exposed if they go wrong. This includes areas such as executive compensation and bonus arrangements. To some extent, these consultancy-type relationships have left HR with less direct power, but where the influence of HR is strong, the function is seen as central. The converse is also true.

The most common HR structures appear to concentrate the strategic roles in the corporate centre, leaving operational support to the line being provided through divisional support units. Where such devolved support units exist, they sometimes report back to the head of HR, and are therefore clearly maintaining a strong professional link, while other units report to the divisional director, maintaining only a dotted-line relationship with the head of HR. In some cases, call centres and help desks have been established to ensure that operational HR support of some kind is available to line managers who may not have a regular HR contact. **Unisys** has established an international on-line service centre which provides solutions to HR issues in a way which meets 'local' as well as corporate requirements.

As units devolve there can be tensions which the function attempts to resolve in different ways. The centre can come to be seen as increasingly peripheral as most strategic decision making takes place in the business units. This can be particularly challenging when HR attempts to take a corporate perspective on the development of high potential talent, for instance, since business heads can be reluctant to share information with the centre which might cause them to lose a 'star' employee to another region. One organization's approach to resolving such tensions is described in the case study about Dr Candy Albertsson of **BP Amoco** in Chapter 11. Similarly, the market nature of relationships within which some HR teams operate can prove a barrier to a meaningful relationship with line managers. Some organizations are overcoming this difficulty by avoiding internal charging systems.

Empowerment

Empowerment has become a cliché and a discredited one at that in some quarters. The main reason according to Barbara Ettore

(1997) is the myths surrounding it. If empowerment is supposed to be defined as an employee's ability to solve problems, make decisions and take actions based on those decisions, management has encouraged the first two but has failed to allow the third. Often the real dilemma for executives is whether to trust employees. The management assumption is that workers cannot fully understand the impact of their actions on the organization's bottom line. This assumption is based on the relative lack of information received by workers which would give them a clear insight into how their actions affect the whole operation, stretching from the business strategy and work processes to customers, shareholders, suppliers etc.

This is where empowerment without alignment with strategy and information is likely to backfire. Yet the benefits of empowerment can outweigh the risks. Empowered organizations are more likely than others to respond quickly to ideas and suggestions, enable managers to make their own decisions without having to rely on headquarters and put customers' needs first. Empowerment needs to be aligned to the strategic aims of the organization so that employees can direct their solutions to real business issues. Typically, employees need to be clear about what the customer wants, the part their own role plays and what shareholders are looking for. Characteristically, in empowered organizations, good ideas are rewarded effectively and authority is appropriately delegated as far down the organization as possible. Systems are a supportive framework rather than a set of constraints and employees work to broad principles rather than rules. Companies like **Levi-Strauss**, **Hewlett-Packard** and **Nordstrom** are among high-performing organizations which practise aligned and informed empowerment. But, as Ettore points out, 'as with all initiatives, if management is not committed and if HR is not a strategic function, it will fail'.

Aligning training and development to business strategy

Benchmarking is often used to identify organizations considered to be 'best in class' on particular aspects of their strategy or implementation. Training and development benchmarks often focus on the amount of money invested in T&D activity. These figures vary widely among employers but US surveys during the last decade suggest that a disproportionate expenditure, i.e. those who spend more than 1.5 per cent of their payroll on T&D, is made by just 0.5 per cent of all US employers. These few organizations recognize that having a workforce with high skill levels is a primary source of competitive advantage. In these exemplary organizations, T&D is strongly aligned to the strategic leadership and planning processes of the business. The primary focus of such training is on creating readiness and flexibility through training supervisors, managers and executives since it is these individuals who set the tone for the rest of the organization.

Typical of the 'best practice' benchmark organizations is that they:

- Create a systematic link between business strategy and the T&D system. T&D targets are reviewed at least annually to ensure that they are still on track with changing business requirements
- T&D executives take a full part in the strategic planning process, ensuring that strategic goals take into account the availability of the talent needed to carry out the goals
- Information support systems are also integrated into the strategic planning process

Links between training and development activity and the business strategy depend very much on whether training is an integral part of the HR strategy and whether this is itself fully aligned to business needs. Depending on the type of competitive strategy in use, different analytical links can exist. Strategies geared to the life cycle of the organization need employees and especially management styles to be adapted to changing conditions. Those which focus on competitive positioning through differentiation are likely to place a greater emphasis on process innovation and specialization of distinctive skills. Similarly, strategies focused on realizing strategic intent are likely to lead to competency definitions which help the organization to compete effectively.

Research carried out in the UK (Poole and Jenkins, 1996) suggests that core elements in the development of competitive advantage in respondents' organizations were:

- Management development
- Career development

- The development of high-potential employees
- Support for continuous training and retraining.

Clearly, human resource development as well as management is an essential part for building sustainable competitive advantage. Training can help in the creation of a more productive, skilled and adaptable workforce.

Strategic alignment through competencies

Ensuring alignment relies on excellent performance management so that people are clear what their roles are, what is expected of them and how that might change. A competency framework is a useful way of aligning HR processes to the business strategy. In this section we look at some processes for defining and using competencies. Practical examples follow later in this chapter, and also in Chapter 8, where the focus is on developing talent within an organization.

Competencies are often defined as 'a particular attribute that people have that collectively helps to develop the capability of the individual and the organization'. If you adjust competencies so that they are continually aligned to the business strategy, the likelihood of people's behaviour being in line with what the business needs at any point in time is high. If these are reflected in the performance standards the organization is seeking to achieve, the link between skilled behaviour and outputs is evident.

They are a means of describing the kinds of behaviours and approaches which should enable the organization to achieve its business objectives and should draw employees' attention to things which need to be commonly applied. So, for instance, as organizations require people to work across boundaries, there is a need for clarity on what effective cross-boundary team working looks like. Defining the competency can help those involved become more aware of the implications for the way they work. By definition, competencies are temporary and need a review process built in to check that they are still linked with current business strategies. General competencies are a means of ensuring consistency across the organization through the creation of a common language to describe performance. In addition, professional and functionally specific technical competencies make up the typical competence framework.

Performance management of the 1990s has mainly focused on activity management. Competencies should be a means of defining where the 20 per cent of effort needs to be put in order to achieve an 80 per cent return. However, if competencies are used mechanistically, or are not 'owned' by the people for whom they have been defined, it is unlikely that they will produce the benefits of clarity since they will not be used. There is an increasing awareness that people's needs must be taken into account if they are to be motivated to carry out activities to a high standard. A competence framework needs to be a means of addressing both organizational requirements for performance and individual needs for development, achievement and recognition.

Defining competencies

Ideally, a competence framework should enable employees to understand what the organization as a whole, what teams and individuals need to be good at to achieve the organization's objectives. Defining competencies can be a developmental process for those involved. For instance, in most organizations managers are required to manage change, even though they may not relish change much themselves. Involving managers in defining or reviewing competencies can be a useful way of acclimatizing them to change and help them to recognize the ways in which they can enable others to succeed by the 'new rules'.

Competencies can be identified in a number of ways and to a number of levels. Typical techniques used include repertory grid and critical incident interviews. In defining competencies it is important to start with what customers expect, create plans to give the customers what they expect, define which activities are required to achieve those plans, and then identify the skills, knowledge and behaviour needed to carry out these activities. Standards and measures can then be applied so that performance can be more closely managed.

Competencies usually relate to a mix of strategic foci, the things the organization is trying to do or must protect, and those things which are critical to moving the organization's culture in the desired direction. Typically, the first level is to interpret the organization's purpose or values into competency statements. Another level is where the focus is on a few key or core competencies which are essential if the organization's business strategy is to be realized. A third level, identified by Prahalad and Hamel

(1995), is the way in which the organization's core competence differentiates it from competitors.

Competencies should ideally be defined in terms of knowledge, skills and experience. What really matters is how people use their ability in the workplace – it is their actual behaviour which counts. The behaviours should be defined so that people are aware of what really effective behaviour looks like. Typically, competencies include some descriptor statements or 'anchor points' so that the graduation of skilled behaviour is obvious. Another common element in many competency schemes has been the emphasis on standards. In the UK in particular this approach has been evident in the range of government-backed initiatives in competency-based schemes such as NVQs and the MCI competencies themselves. To some extent this approach has become rather discredited since the attempt to measure competence standards can appear a bureaucratic process.

Using competencies

Defining competencies is not enough, however. People often need help in becoming effective at them. Ideally, the competency framework should enable development plans to be created for all three levels: organizational, team and individual. At an organizational level, competencies can be a means of ensuring that the values are really lived if they are integrated into other HR processes. The trend towards competency-based pay systems is not yet well established in the UK but various organizations such as the former **Glaxo-Wellcome** have experimented with them in recent years. At an individual level, having the clarity afforded by the competencies should in theory allow people to be clear about how they can add value through their role.

For managers, performance management should also be easier, as should targeted recruitment against competency-based role descriptions. Role profiles can be developed at an individual and a team level. These can then provide a focus for development, performance management and recognition. Self-assessment and feedback processes such as 360 degrees can be developed around the competency-based profiles. These are increasingly used for appraisal and development purposes such as personal and team development. Typically, they are used in leadership training and subsets such as training managers to be coaches. Development can then be focused on things which matter.

Competencies can therefore help achieve alignment between the organization's strategy and teams and individuals. Competence frameworks should ideally be tailored to the organization, using simple and relevant language. As many people as possible who will be implementing competencies should be involved in their design. Good targeting of the key activities can ensure that people are focused on the important things and rewarded for them. The Balanced Scorecard can be a helpful means of identifying appropriate measures from the point of view of various stakeholders. Good management information is important, as is continuous improvement and a learning culture.

Integrating HR processes at BNFL

Since this book was first published, BNFL has experienced varying business fortunes. However, BNFL is taking a systematic approach to changing the organization's culture from a public sector mentality to one which combines international commercial acumen with the highest safety standards. BNFL are using competencies as the heart of an integrated set of HR processes (see Figure 4.1) to help

Figure 4.1   *The competency framework for BNFL*

bring about this culture change over the next three to five years (see Chapter 2). To facilitate new working practices, the organization has been delayered from ten hierarchical levels, with their grades and titles, to five.

Each of the levels in the structure – executives, business leaders, managers and professionals, team leaders and team members – has had competencies identified which are unique to them but there are, of course, interconnecting strands. Technical competencies complement the behavioural competencies and are based on differentiators of outstanding performance. The competencies identified for each group were benchmarked against other international organizations and 'stretched' to make them more competitive.

Integrating competencies into other HR processes

BNFL is investing heavily in training and development as a key means of raising awareness and changing attitudes. Specific programmes have been devised for each level. It is recognized that effective leadership is key to the culture change and executives and business leaders have the chance to take part in international management development at IMD in Lausanne. The IMD programme is designed around the senior manager behavioural competencies such as 'creating future success', 'driving and improving business' and 'sustaining success'.

Training and development is only part of the picture, however. It is recognized that if change is to be sustained, the competency framework should genuinely help people do their jobs in a way which meets the strategic priorities. The competencies have therefore been used to overhaul the performance management process and methods of working. Another important tool introduced in 1998 to help bring about culture change is 360-degree feedback. This initiative represents a massive commitment and is resource hungry but is considered a vital part of creating awareness of the need for change and practical insights into what and how to change. The questionnaires focus on behavioural competencies with the emphasis for senior managers on leadership. The executive group piloted this and all the other HR processes.

The 360-degree activity will be compulsory and annual for executives, business leaders and participants on development programmes or workshops and will be offered every two years to other groups. So far, 300 people have gone through the process, receiving feedback from an unlimited number of direct reports and peers as well as their boss. Feedback is presented in a formal portfolio with an overall summary by competency cluster, detailed feedback against each competency and verbatim written comments which tend to be the most direct. Feedback is facilitated by HR or a line manager who has received in-depth training for this role. The feedback is used purely for developmental purposes and the individual owns the feedback. However, individuals are encouraged to share the feedback at least with their line manager so that development needs can be agreed. Coaching, as a competency for all line managers, has become a key requirement of the role.

The process of sharing the feedback, especially with peers and direct reports, leads to sustained changes in behaviour. The next steps will be to review and update the competencies every two years and establish norm data for benchmarking purposes and to validate development programmes. The 360-degree process will be automated, which should reduce costs and enable the instrument to be 'kept fresh' as business needs change.

The 'Beyond 2000' HR strategy will see the integration of reward and benefits which will complement and reinforce the move to the new culture. This will take time and work is currently under way to codify the new behaviours into revised terms and conditions. Other planned areas of integration will be career and succession planning, with future leaders recruited and developed in line with the organization's vision and the related behavioural competencies.

Aligning HR strategies in UK local government

No-one who works in the sector needs to be reminded that local government, along with the rest of the UK public sector, has been subject to unprecedented change in recent years. In common with organizations of all sectors, local government has had to respond to the increase in competition, the requirement for greater customer focus, the advent of new technology and demands for more cost-effective services. In addition, various governments have exerted pressure on local government to deliver the central government agenda in the context of local democracy, leading to an ongoing squeeze on funding.

Local government has responded to these demands in a number of ways. During the 1990s, compulsory competitive tendering, though now somewhat discredited, reflected the belief that injecting an element of competition into service provision would be beneficial to the (council) taxpayer. Councils have slimmed down, outsourced non-core activities and focused on improving quality. New, flatter organizational structures, working practices such as teamworking and the end to the 'job for life' are typical organizational responses. Employees are familiar now with the concept that job security is not to be relied on and that career management is their responsibility.

Local government is subject, however, to a greater shift than simply the demand for greater cost-effectiveness. The wider political landscape of the UK constitution is changing rapidly. The recent reforms of local government, including the revising of the central/local government relationship and moves towards greater local democracy such as the new London Mayor role, the creation of the Scottish Parliament and the Welsh Assembly raise questions about the future role of local government. The ongoing pressure for reform is evident in the Best Value initiative which aims to ensure that the taxpayer receives cost-effective and efficient local services, delivered by the most appropriate provider. For local government, this will mean re-examining how services are delivered, evaluating provision, creating partnerships with other providers and making tough decisions about what remains the responsibility of officials to deliver.

The implications of Best Value

Of course, working out the real implications of Best Value for any one council is fraught with difficulty. In these 'lean organization' days, few authorities have the resources to plough through the sheer volume of paperwork being generated by the Best Value industry and many officials and elected members seem to be still working out the implications for their council. This may be because the very nature of a new initiative is full of ambiguity. However, another factor may be the initiative-weariness of many officials who tend to regard Best Value as just another buzz phrase which will be flavour of the year before being quietly dropped. Getting to grips with the potential implications and opportunities may therefore not seem worth the effort.

Working with management teams from different sectors I am struck by the regularity with which senior local government officials will say that they have no time for strategic thinking and that strategy is not the role of officials anyway. They may be right, but as managers of still relatively large groups of employees, management teams have a responsibility to both manage change and provide stability where they can. Staff who have heard the term 'Best Value' are frequently jumping to the conclusion, in the absence of alternative clear messages, that job cuts are an inevitable consequence of the initiative.

And who can blame them for a pessimistic interpretation? While other public sector providers appear to be responding positively to the opportunities inherent in Best Value (one housing association, for instance, has recently redefined its role as moving from being rent collectors to being social enablers), many local government staff appear to be suffering the after-effects of one change too many. Stress, overwork, uncertainty and lack of promotion prospects are reducing employee commitment at a time when there is increasing recognition that the skills and ideas of the workforce are the real competitive asset of an organization.

While it may be difficult for management teams to exercise real leadership in the political context of local government, many pundits agree that employees need a clear sense of where the organization is going, and what their role is within the changing context. According to Lorraine Trainer, head of Human Resources at **Coutts Group**,

> When managers are not told where the organization is headed, they cannot lead others towards it. We must ensure the organization has a clear vision of the future and what we want to develop people for; otherwise, the appraisal is like looking into the rear-view mirror of a car. In the past, it was to fit people for hierarchical jobs. Now people have to keep adding skills so that they are flexible and can move with the times.

While many local authorities are unlikely to see a voluntary outflow of large numbers of staff, the bigger threat implicit in a lack of commitment is the strong link between uncertainty and lack of creativity. In the Roffey Park research on the human aspects of mergers (Devine, Hirsh and Holbeche, 1998) there were several instances where employees in the acquired companies, who were unsure of their future and the new way of doing things, effectively closed down their creative ideas and projects. This phenomenon became known as 'burying the babies' – at least until the future looked more secure.

Yet the future need not look so bleak. Even gurus of downsizing such as Stephen Roach have recognized that ongoing staff cuts not only damage morale but weaken the organization's capability to deliver its services. Roach is quoted as saying

> If you compete by building, you have a future. If you compete by cutting, you don't. In the end there is only one way out: upgrading the quality of the workforce'.

Indeed, the **Local Government Association's** response to the Best Value consultation process suggests that employees will be the key to best value.

> The government recognizes that if services are to be responsive to the needs of their customers, then those who deliver them have a key role to play: a well trained and motivated workforce will underpin efficient and effective local services.

The LGA's recommendations include approaching Best Value with extensive staff involvement and consultation. Job security and secure pension rights should be key features of quality employment which in turn leads to quality service provision.

Implementing Best Value – the Human Resource contribution

So if the key to successful implementation of Best Value is a well-motivated, trained and skilled staff, how is this to be achieved and what is the role of Personnel in ensuring that the organization has the staff it needs in order to achieve its aims? Let's start by looking at staff motivation. Research carried out in all sectors by Roffey Park (Holbeche, 1997) and elsewhere in recent years suggests that when certain factors are present, change is more likely to be viewed negatively by employees. These include:

- Where there is an external requirement for change
- Where there is a constrained, unsupportive environment
- When change is extensive and apparently never-ending

- When change appears not to have the wholehearted backing of the CEO
- Where there is a radical shift in the organization's mission
- When change appears to be introduced mainly to reduce headcount.

Perhaps inevitably, some of these factors may be present when introducing Best Value. In such circumstances, employee motivation is likely to be dented. Of course, employee motivation is not the sole responsibility of Human Resource professionals. Yet, at the very least, HR needs to be aware of the implicit paradoxes common to many change programmes which can severely affect the motivation levels of their internal clients. The more the emphasis appears to be exclusively on the external client, the less staff will perceive that they are in receipt of Best Value themselves. How can staff interests and customer interests be better linked? How can a culture of positive change be created in which people positively welcome change and introduce improvements based on their understanding of the problems?

The more change is the order of the day, the less value and honour is granted to a previous *modus operandi*. This can lead people to feel that their work to date is not valued. How much change is actually needed and what can be stabilized which is highly effective? How much can success be celebrated and previous practices publicly ended and mourned/celebrated? Employees in local government often appear to have a strong 'vocational' calling – they appear to care about providing good service. Yet countless government messages imply that employees need carrot or stick approaches to encourage them to reach higher levels of performance. How much can change initiatives be managed in a way which harnesses employees' latent creativity and goodwill and takes a less dismissive view of peoples' motivation? Similarly, many change programmes are essentially short term in focus and can effectively skew the organization's longer-term capability for which Human Resource professionals are responsible, at least in part. How can both short- and long-term organizational needs be addressed under Best Value?

Best Value – addressing employee needs

So if people genuinely are the key to successful implementation of Best Value, perhaps focusing on one broad topic will help to illustrate how short- and long-term needs can be reconciled. Some of the biggest issues affecting staff motivation are about careers. Much has been written about the changing psychological contract. There appears to be widespread recognition of the idea that the notion of a job for life and promotion prospects has been replaced by that of employability. Staff are expected to be flexible, develop broader skill sets, take responsibility for managing their own careers and be prepared to be dispensable if their skills are no longer needed!

Avoiding mixed messages

To some extent, our research suggests that some people are adjusting to these ideas and are finding increased satisfaction in new roles with greater responsibility and chance for development. These are the very attitudes which will be valuable under Best Value, where employees who find new ways of using skills and expertise will be key to the organization's success. However, our research also suggests that moves towards empowerment can be seriously undermined by mixed organizational messages which feed employee cynicism. If employees find that their employer makes it impossible for them to develop new skills or to manage their own career even at the same level, they may find the notion of employability somewhat hollow, especially if promotion continues to exist for the chosen few.

Similarly, if people are to be encouraged and enabled to learn new skills, it follows that a management style which is supportive of empowerment and judicious risk-taking will be called for. Typically, a major source of employee cynicism is where the behaviour of managers is out of kilter with what the organization is trying to achieve – where the 'walk' does not match the 'talk'. Command-and-control styles of management and blame cultures may be somewhat at odds with Best Value approaches. A key focus for Personnel may therefore need to be senior management training, including the development of a wide range of management styles.

Systems will also have to be brought in line with Best Value and integrated with the organization's strategies. Performance-related pay, when targeted on areas which are not central to Best Value, can undermine outputs. Reward systems will need to reflect the collaborative outcomes required within Best Value. Lack of communication or overload of data can disable organizational efforts to lead staff in a new direction. Council members and officials will need to take stock of how their authority will respond, clarify how this differs from current ways of doing things and provide constant reinforcement of the direction, together with news of the progress being made towards key targets.

Staff will need support as they develop the required skills and approaches. People need to know what is the reason for the change, what the implications of Best Value are for them and what is required for future 'success'. Our research suggests that employees may well be motivated to learn new things since the most common motivating factors for employees in all sectors appear to be challenge, having the chance to achieve, gaining breadth, depth or both, and recognition for their performance and development.

Clearly it would be unrealistic to assume that Human Resource professionals should find themselves responsible for providing all aspects of staff development and recognition – especially since many 'corporate' recognition schemes appear not to be very motivating. Line managers also have a vital role to play here. Setting stretching targets for staff members, providing coaching and recognition when the individual delivers the desired outcomes should all be parts of the line managers' toolkit. Yet so often these basic aspects of people management are missing. Human Resource professionals have a responsibility for providing the training and tools to line managers to enable them to manage people effectively.

The skills for future success

Dave Ulrich (1998) suggests that organizational success will spring from capabilities such as speed, responsiveness, agility, learning capacity and employee competence. As the **Local Government Association's** statement of objectives on Best Value notes, unlocking the knowledge and creativity of staff is the key to innovation and continuous improvement.

The kinds of skills which individuals are likely to find useful in changing times seem fairly common to organizations of all sectors. Roffey Park research has found a remarkable similarity among respondents in recent surveys who recognize the need to develop high-level political influencing skills. This is the ability to make things happen by understanding the informal system, and bringing about change without formal authority. Strategic thinking is needed at all levels, so that people can understand the implications of change and work in partnership with the organization to deliver strategic solutions. IT skills, financial and broader business awareness should enable staff to understand the mechanics of what the organization needs to do as well as take shrewd risks based on informed judgement. Leadership and change management should be core skills for any manager, especially those in senior positions. Entrepreneurial skills and creative thinking should enable people to find innovative solutions and make things happen.

Training may be part of the answer, but in many cases these skills need to be developed on the job through effective use of mentors, peer coaching, challenging assignments and learning review processes. Competency-based approaches to development may make it possible for people to have learning opportunities in different parts of the organization from areas to which they had access in the past. Helping people to develop their skills and employability calls for a strategic approach, with a longer-term perspective but firmly rooted in the here and now. Trials of different approaches, well evaluated to assess what works, can deliver results in the short term and avoid the danger of paralysis while officials wait for the way ahead to become clear.

Delivering Best Value to and through employees

So if change under Best Value is to be managed skilfully, a partnership approach between management and HR is called for. The business strategy for delivering Best Value needs to be clear and the HR strategies which support this must be directly linked to the business intention. Key targets for strategic activity with regard to employees include:

- Improve communications
- Clarify career tracks
- Develop people
- Provide feedback and recognition
- Ensure balance
- Involve people.

Most importantly, developing an open, problem-solving climate can not only equip people for learning what is appropriate in the short term but can also provide the basis for ongoing change in the longer term. This involves understanding your current culture, breaking established patterns which are counterproductive, setting new standards and giving people the chance to exercise new skills. In addition, some sacred cows may need to be challenged. New ways of working which are positive and moving in the 'right' direction should be stabilized and achievements celebrated. People's roles should be linked to the business imperative so that everyone knows where they fit in, and what role they have to play in ensuring successful service delivery which really represents best value. As Dave Ulrich says:

> The successful organizations will be those that are able to quickly turn strategy into action: to manage processes intelligently and efficiently: to maximize employee contribution and commitment; and to create the conditions for seamless change.

Alignment Checklists

Managing the business environment

In what way does the way we interact with the external environment add value to the management of our workforce?

- How aware are we of the business environment in which we are operating? What are the economic/political, social, demographic, technological, competitor and consumer trends?
- What is the potential strength of the impact of these trends on our organization?
- What influence do we exercise in the local business environment through lobbying and communicating in the local language?

Defining and analysing the organization

Does the organization enable us to build a sustainable competitive advantage?

- Is the organization's purpose linked to the structure and the work to be done and is the purpose evident in all aspects of goals, plans, measures?

- Is there a clear 'arrival point' when we can declare a 'victory'?
- To what extent do corporate values drive behaviours and guide decisions?
- Does the shape of the organization – its size, the numbers employed, the numbers at each level or grade, the types of hierarchy and spans of control – support what the organization wants to achieve?
- Flexibility – how do our structure and contractual arrangements enable us to respond to change and integrate with the marketplace?
- Retaining talent – does job design offer employees scope for development? How do we measure motivation and morale? How do we interpret turnover and absence indicators?
- How well integrated are leadership, values and behaviours? HR practices and policies?
- How well have staffing practices, training and development as well as performance management been aligned to culture and strategy?
- How well aligned are communications to culture?
- How well aligned is the organization design to what we are trying to achieve?

Productivity and labour costs

How are we ensuring the highest possible rate of return on our investment in people for profitability?

- Workforce investment – what are the options, costs and short-term/long-term payback we can expect?
- Are the costs of running the organization – the HR and distribution, and productivity measures – clear and controlled?
- Productivity measures – what are the ratios, measurement and controls we can use?
- Budgeting and control – what workforce planning and budgeting methods, headcount control and other key indicators can we use?
- Incentive scheme development – what should we take into account in designing these schemes? What measures of effectiveness are appropriate and how will we calculate the cost versus the benefit to the business?

Workforce planning

Do we have the workforce to implement the business plan?

- Workforce planning – how do we evaluate existing human resources against future requirements (numbers, abilities, skills, experience)? How do we identify gaps and surpluses? What retention indicators can we use?
- Resourcing – how will we ensure that our strategy addresses the needs of the external environment, internal talent and retention policies?
- How will we make up gaps in the workforce – through (re)training, recruitment, development or a combination? What are the key short- and medium-term gaps we will need to fill?
- How will we deal with surpluses of employees – through retraining, relocation, redundancy?
- Career planning – how will we provide assessment (of abilities, skills, competencies), counselling and development?
- Succession planning – what forms will we use? Focused on a minority or building up a cadre? What processes will support these plans?

References

Appleyard, B. (1999). No time like the present, *Sunday Times*, 28 February.

Devine, M , Hirsh, W. and Holbeche, L. (1998). *Mergers and Acquisitions: Getting the People Bit Right*. Roffey Park Management Institute.

Ettorre, B. (1997). The empowerment gap : hype vs. reality, *HR Focus*, 74, No.7 July.

Gertz, D. L. and Baptista, J. (1995). *Grow to be Great, Breaking the Downsizing Cycle*. New York: Free Press.

Grundy, A. (1998). How are corporate strategy and Human Resources strategy linked? *Journal of General Management*, 23, No.3, Spring.

Holbeche, L. (1995). *Career Development in Flatter Structures – Organizational Practices*. Roffey Park Management Institute.

Holbeche, L. (1997). *Career Development: managing the impact of flatter structures on careers*, Oxford: Butterworth-Heinemann.

IBM Corporation and Towers Perrin (1994). *Priorities for Gaining*

Competitive Advantage, quoted in Poole, M. and Jenkins, G. (1996). Competitiveness and human resource policies, *Journal of General Management*, **22**, No.2, Winter.

Lam, S. S. K. and Schaubroeck, J. (1998). Integrating HR planning and organizational strategy, *Human Resource Journal*, **8**, No.3, 5–19.

Pascale, R. T. (1995). The Honda Effect. In Mintzberg, H., Quinn, J. B., and Ghoshal, S. (eds): *The Strategy Process*, Englewood Cliffs, NJ: Prentice Hall.

Prahalad, C. K. and Hamel, G. (1995). The core competence of the corporation. In Mintzberg, H., Quinn, J. B. and Ghoshal, S. (eds), *The Strategy Process*. Englewood Cliffs, NJ: Prentice Hall.

Pfeffer, J. (1995). People, capability and competitive success, *Management Development Review*, **8**, No.5, 6–10.

Taylor, L., quoted in Coles, M. (1999). Reappraise the way you develop staff, *Sunday Times*, 14 February.

Thompson, A. A. and Strickland, A. J. (1998). *Strategic Management Concepts and Cases*, New York: Irwin/McGraw-Hill.

Tyson, S. (1995). Human Resource Strategy. *Towards a General Theory of Human Resource Management*, London: Pitman.

Tyson, S. and Witcher, M. (1994). Human Resource strategy: emerging from the recession. *Personnel Management*, August.

Ulrich, D. interviewed by MacLachlan, R. (1998). HR with attitude, *People Management*, 13 August.

Wright, P. M., McMahan, G. C. and McWilliams, A. (1994). Human Resources and sustained competitive advantage – a resource based perspective, *The International Journal of Human Resource Management*, **5** (2), 301–326.

Part 2 Strategies for managing and developing talent

5   *Managing and rewarding for high performance*

The aim of most organizations is to achieve high-quality outputs to standards which are acceptable to customers and with ideally low costs of production. There is assumed to be a link between productivity, individual and team performance and reward. Yet some of the main proponents of the link between performance and reward are now thinking again. Unilever, a consumer goods multinational employing 300,000 people in more than 60 countries, has been an exponent of performance-related pay for almost three decades. But since a board review in 1994, the company has rethought its practice in the context of corporate restructuring and will continue to do so for the foreseeable future (Ashton, 1999).

The changing nature of workplaces

Workplaces are changing. The last few decades have seen organizational vogues come and go. The structures and work practices which were familiar a few years ago are undergoing a serious, longer-term appraisal. Arguably the 1970s was still the period of mass production, reflecting the end of manufacturing on any scale in the UK, and certain characteristics were typical of organizations of the time. They were large concerns with command-and-control management styles. Labour flexibility was limited and there was often vertical integration. Structures were based on the division of labour, a central unity of control, a large pyramid of managers and supervisors, working in remote command chains. In the 1980s, perhaps influenced by the ideas of

Schumacher (1973), large organizations tended to decentralize and created independent business units. These often acted as local fiefdoms and gaining a 'corporate' approach could be difficult. The challenge for HR at the centre was to prove value add. Labour flexibility was still relatively low.

The 1990s have been characterized by smaller, leaner organizations with responsive structures and delayered management. These structures are freer, more flexible and participative. However, one researcher (Wood, 1989) argues that these structures are just another way for managers to gain control over labour through 'attitudinal restructuring'. Core processes have been redesigned and collaborative relations established with suppliers. Teamworking, Total Quality approaches, horizontal integration and medium labour flexibility are also typical of this time. Some pundits describe this as the 'post-modernist' era which represents the end of the large bureaucratic production or 'modernist' era. Hudson (1989) argues that the use of technology, productivity gains and deskilling represents just a reworking of modernist production methods.

The new millennium is said to be the start of the era of nimble or 'agile' production, where labour flexibility will be high and employees will be consciously managing their own careers. Organizations will focus on their core competencies, rather than just their current processes. Rather than being a fixed entity, the organization will be a task-oriented organic structure. It is likely to be characterized by a small core centre and alliances with suppliers and customers. The flexible and the informal will need to co-exist with formal, integration mechanisms. The challenge here will be to create organizations, however decentralized, which are completely unified and coordinated, and where employees experience high levels of participation and commitment. Matrix structures have now become well-established integration devices. Conversely, in sectors where there is intense competition, such as the financial services or the hospitality industry, the trend towards amalgamation, through mergers and acquisitions, prior to dispersal or demerger, seems well-entrenched.

The role of HR in creating integration

If the trend is towards integrated but agile structures, HR has a key role to play in enabling this integration. Shaun Tyson (1995) suggests that the HR department itself will be an integrating device since its remit usually operates across organizational boundaries and often carries responsibility for corporate communications. The internalization of corporate values, through major communication programmes and the organizational culture as a whole, are other major sources of integration.

High-performance work practices

Many studies have shown the substantial economic benefits of adopting high-commitment or high-performance work practices in contrast to conventional 'scientific' management typical of 'modernist' organizations. Often described as 'Japanese' management practices, the case for implementing such approaches is strong. Jeffrey Pfeffer (1996) cites the MIT investigation of the worldwide motor vehicle assembly industry reported in the book *The Machine That Changed The World* by Womack, Jones and Roos (1990). The assembly plants which had adopted flexible or lean manufacturing methods and associated employment-relation practices far outperformed others using mass production methods. Other studies of the textile industry (Dunlop and Weil, 1996) have found that companies which operate team-based work and compensation as well as training for multiple jobs experienced 22 per cent higher growth in gross margins in the 1988–1992 period than other similar companies.

In another US study, Mark Huselid (1995) explored the impact of high-commitment work practices using measures of financial performance. He produced a sophisticated index which showed that a one standard deviation increase of high-commitment work resulted in an annual increase in sales of over $27 000 per employee. What was interesting about this study was that it was found that the effectiveness of these work practices was not contingent on a firm's strategy but consistently led to performance improvements.

These high-commitment work practices are characterized by the following:

- Suggestion schemes, Quality circles, problem-solving groups or other forms of employee participation in idea generation
- Employee participation in decision making
- Freedom of expression

- Extensive teamwork, including self-managing teams
- Reformulation of work to make best use of upgraded skills.

Participation and involvement mean that power shifts from middle managers to those further down the organizational hierarchy – those closest to the customer or the production process. Companies operating such approaches include **Levi-Strauss**, **Motorola** and **Honeywell**. What is common about high-performing companies is their agenda to create relationships with employees which support their business objectives. Employee relations are therefore a priority, to be clear about the kind of relationship the business strategy required, and 'to push the execution of employee relations policies down to the lowest level possible, compatible with the corporation's overall values' (Tyson, 1995). Corporate values are most clearly visible in reward policies which are sometimes used to instil specific values. Profit-related pay and share ownership are obvious manifestations of value statements about the worth of people to an organization. Similarly, formal communications transmit values, though usually more is understood by the behaviour of the people conveying the message than by the words used.

Despite the evidence from organizations which practise Total Quality that these practices work, diffusion seems to be slow. The main barrier appears to be that traditionally the focus of management has been on the financial and strategic aspects of the business, rather than on employee relations. Since high-commitment work practices require major up-front investments, such as in training and higher rates of pay, a willingness to take a risk that these measures will pay off is required; and many management teams are risk averse. Pfeffer points out that managers' own perception of their role and that of other people can interfere with effectiveness. If managers believe that they should be the people leading the organization and coming up with ideas about how things should be done, they are not likely to welcome that idea that the organization's success actually depends on many other people, often more junior, throughout the company.

Political and power barriers can also get in the way of implementing high-commitment work practices. Managers may not wish to accept that previous approaches introduced by them may not have yielded such good results as these methods. Similarly, middle managers whose roles are usually most affected, if not removed by high-performance work practices, often resist their introduction. The relative power of advocates of high-performance work practices (usually Human Resource professionals), measured in part by relative salary levels, is often lower than that of the chief critics of such approaches (often finance directors). Interestingly, one research study found that in Japan, different priorities meant that Human Resources and manufacturing were tied to the highest pay levels of functional heads.

How can HR help to implement high-performance work practices?

By creating a culture which is supportive of high performance

High performance does not occur in a vacuum. The organization's culture must be conducive to productivity and quality improvement. A South African construction company, *Neil Muller (Pty) Ltd*, has managed to improve profitability and the amount of repeat business by instigating a culture change to support improved productivity. Management introduced what became known as Total Company Renovation to address a number of known problem areas, almost all of which related to human resources, i.e.:

- Communication between management and the workforce was fragmented and relations between the management and trade unions were not positive
- There was a lack of trust between management and the workforce
- Measurement and monitoring of productivity on-site was limited
- There was no long-term career planning
- Employees were not involved in any preplanning or decision making
- Supervision on-site was inadequate

Interestingly, the company saw providing job security and a career path as the foundation of the quality-improvement plan. These were considered revolutionary ideas in an industry which has a poor record of providing job security. Another key priority was building trust by improving communication and encouraging interaction between management and the workforce. Ten goals were set, including developing effective participation by all, improving every employee's lot in life, improving profitability and introducing a profit-sharing scheme.

Training played a large part in changing attitudes and skill levels. All company workers attended two-hour sessions covering five days to explain how a company works. Workshops were held for senior managers and supervisors and new ideas were brought into the company by visiting speakers. Workers were not confined to their small piece of a construction. Models were created to allow workers to see how their work was contributing to the whole building. Work targets were introduced as well as daily work measurement systems. These measurement systems are very practical, incorporating data which is already available, such as quantity surveying data, and provide the basic data for costing a job.

The achievement, or otherwise, of daily work targets is discussed by the quality control circle meeting which takes up the first 15 minutes of each day. Problem areas are openly discussed and workers are told what is going on at their site, how the work is progressing financially and why they are doing certain tasks. In addition, each level of supervision has regular meetings to help create effective communication. Social events help create team spirit and the firm's owner and his fellow-directors are actively involved. Good on-site facilities have been provided for workers and site safety is a paramount consideration. The company is no longer unionized but has created an in-house workers' committee known as the Unity Forum. This forum appears to work because of the new levels of trust and communication within the company and a more adult–adult relationship between workers and management (Robinson, 1997).

By influencing attitudes

HR professionals can be effective in bringing about change through their cross-organizational influence, ability to design structures and processes which support the business strategy and helping to create the culture changes through values and communication which support new ways of working. HR can help set up benchmarking visits to organizations which are achieving outstanding results through people. Skilful use of data can stimulate the need for change among executives. One HR team, for example, used data from employee-attitude surveys and turnover statistics and the related costs to make the case for change. Changing the structure to match the proposed work processes should be complemented by corresponding changes in the physical workplace and in the way work is organized.

By designing and implementing HR processes which support the business strategy

At a practical level, to create the conditions for high performance, HR processes such as reward systems need to be aligned to the new ways of working. The following HR processes are typical of 'vanguard' companies described by O'Toole (1985):

- Highly selective recruitment
- Extensive training and skill development
- Contingent or performance-related pay, at high rates
- Employee share ownership
- Benefits tailored to individual needs
- Providing some degree of employment security
- Sharing information about a firm's goals and results so that people know what to accomplish and how they are doing
- Reducing status differentials, if teamworking is to be a reality.

Career processes also need to be aligned to new ways of working. If multi-skilling is a requirement of employees, they need to be given opportunities to develop those skills and forms of knowledge to which they may not have previously been exposed. **Procter and Gamble**, for instance, which is known for its innovative approaches to work teams, tends to put line managers into human resource positions, then rotate them back to line management positions. This ensures that HR is fully integrated with the business, that HR is seen as a credible function and is therefore highly influential.

Performance management

Managing performance is perhaps the key responsibility of line managers and an area where a partnership between line and HR can be most beneficial. HR can help managers to understand how to define roles in the light of business drivers and how to identify the capabilities required to do the job. The key performance indicators for each role should derive from the business drivers and are then built into role processes. This makes each job role more responsive to the changing business environment.

The four key elements of performance management are:

- A common understanding of the organization's goals
- Shared expectations of how individuals can contribute
- Employees with the skill and ability to meet expectations
- Individuals who are fully committed to the aims of the organization.

In managing performance, managers must be able to ensure that employees are appropriately focused into roles, developed and managed.

Job fit and job design – what role can HR play?

HR can develop assessment processes to ensure that the 'right' people are selected for roles. It can also help employees to see for themselves if they have the capabilities for new roles. HR can work with the line to develop self-assessment processes such as are described in the Standard Life case in Chapter 9. The pace of change is so fast that job descriptions, which create boundaries, are inappropriate. Important responsibilities fall between the gaps and most job descriptions are not current for more than a few months. What is needed is a broad role description, with some 'fuzzy' boundaries to allow for growth.

Dealing with poor performance

In some organizations, poor performance is handled by simply passing on the underperformer to another department. Sometimes, managers find difficulty in confronting aspects of poor performance because they lack confidence in their ability to handle the conflict which might arise. Similarly, some managers find it hard to delegate, and others are so thinly stretched that there is no-one to whom they can delegate. Some managers are managing teams of contractors rather than full-time or permanent employees. HR needs to be able to support managers in understanding how they can achieve high standards with slim resources. HR can provide valuable training and other resources to ensure that managers have the skills to coach and develop other people, as well as appraise performance.

Designing effective appraisal and development processes

Appraisal requires excellent interview and counselling skills if the process is to be motivating for those involved. It relies on managers and employees having a relationship in which discussing performance is not seen as a burden or a threat. In many cases, managers do not make the time to appraise people's performance well.

In many organizations the link between personal development and the business strategy is weak, with appraisal being used as an annual administrative chore, which means that employees fail to take personal development seriously. HR can help by designing processes which are simple to use and user-friendly. Mike Spurling, director of internal training at *Oracle*, the software company, sees the need to help people to develop themselves:

> It is crucial that we develop our people. Competitive edge comes from the quality of people; but in many industries, development planning is weak, so people become dissatisfied and leave.

The Roffey Park Management Agenda research suggests that performance appraisals are becoming more complex. The annual review of performance is now generally supplemented by an integrated objective-setting and development planning process. The use of the 360-degree feedback processes is increasing but many of our respondents expressed some distrust of using this in assessing performance. The consensus was that different forms of feedback, such as team-, peer-, or upward-feedback, should not replace the one-to-one discussion with the line manager. Many respondents wanted more regular feedback from their line manager and some would welcome feedback from internal and external customers.

Importantly, there were many comments with regard to how performance was assessed. In particular, it was felt that only results (outputs) are really taken into account and that inputs are taken for granted. There was commonly a lack of the 'soft' measures so useful in bringing about changes in behaviour and culture. Where such measures did exist they appeared to have little bearing on how performance was assessed, with hard measures being the only factors taken into account when bonuses were awarded. Some appraisal schemes in our respondents' organizations therefore appear to be complicated but not necessarily helpful in moving the organization or individual performance forward.

An example of an effective performance management system is the competency-based process at **Bayer Pharma**'s R&D division. The competencies on which the scheme is based were derived from the overall company vision and the strategy for R&D. Performance is managed using clear definitions of the competencies which the company believes will bring success. The performance management scheme is very future oriented, rather than being simply a review of past performance. The new R&D system puts individuals in control of their own performance and development since the individual is expected to take the lead when meeting with their boss to review performance.

The Annual Performance review assesses performance against last year's objectives and a competency assessment identifies areas of development which may have had an impact on performance. The individual prepares examples of work to refer to and is responsible for documenting the discussion. The manager acts as facilitator. Several weeks later a Development Review assesses what might be development priorities from the organization's perspective. The individual identifies their own personal development priorities in the light of their aspirations and a detailed development plan addresses both sets of needs.

A new Web-based appraisal and learning system has been launched by the **Forum Corporation**. Known as the 'Performance Compass', this allows the individual to run the whole process, deciding when and from whom to seek feedback. It links the results of the evaluation with sources of information about training.

In one financial services organization, strategic imperatives to achieve loyal and satisfied customers have been translated into key performance indicators in which all business units and managers are expected to deliver results. Objective areas include leadership, management of process quality, operational results and customer focus and satisfaction. Each of these is supported by behavioural dimensions, together with resources to help people develop effectiveness in these results areas. The HR team has developed a list of ways of developing these behaviours, based on the work of the Center for Creative Leadership. They include suggestions such as:

- Take part in a task force on a pressing business problem
- Plan an off-site meeting, conference, convention
- Integrate systems across units
- Business trip to a foreign country.

Appraisal discussions take place annually, while objective setting and development planning are separate processes which are carried out more frequently.

Helping line managers to set appropriate measures

The old management dictum 'if you can't measure it, you can't manage it' is starting to be turned on its head. Success criteria should be those which make a (positive) difference to the organization. While measures undoubtedly send strong symbolic messages about what is valued, the question of what is being measured and therefore considered important is increasingly being called into question. Targets need to be set for the deliverables which are required but not at the expense of how the deliverables are to be achieved.

Conversely, if measures are set around 'soft' targets such as behaviours, these need to be taken seriously or employees will soon understand that only performance which has a direct impact on the bottom line counts. In many organizations 360-degree feedback processes have been introduced as part of culture change initiatives and senior management development. Some organizations claim that the feedback is incorporated into decisions about pay. In most cases, the link with pay has been almost entirely with bottom line performance with the achievement of other 'soft' behavioural targets being regarded as very secondary.

Reward strategies

The dynamic link between performance and reward has been much debated and the 1990s have been a period of major change in reward management. A CIPD Pay and Benefits survey found, for instance, that many employers are experimenting with merit pay arrangements. The need for revised pay mechanisms reflects the broad shifts in the competitive marketplace. Many organizations have responded to competitive pressures by focusing their business strategies on customer needs and securing customer loyalty by developing more flexible, innovative products and services. The need for flexibility and cost effectiveness has led to organizational restructurings of various kinds, including flatter structures with their focus on teamwork, broader roles and non-traditional work arrangements.

Implementing a flatter structure is meaningless unless there is a degree of consistency between what is expected of employees in terms of working practices and the systems, processes and resources needed to do the job. All human resource systems, especially pay, need to reinforce the forms of skilled performance required of individuals. Yet a large proportion of UK companies have still not developed reward schemes that link pay and benefits to a team's performance and their contribution to corporate values in a flatter structure. Instead, paying market rates remains the preferred model for many organizations alongside schemes that recognize individual short-term performance but not long-term development.

This may be one of the most challenging areas for human resource specialists, since there are many factors to be taken into account when revising a compensation system to make it reflect the diverse aspects of behaviour, skills and experience which lead to the sort of performance organizations require. Typically, problems can occur, for example when work processes are supposed to be underpinned by teamwork, but individual bottom line performance is the only thing that is taken into account when determining pay. Many organizations are experimenting with more flexible packages which include elements of variable pay, linked to job performance, competence, skills development and desired team and leadership behaviours. The new systems include a greater element of discretion for the line manager, feedback processes and a degree of individual choice in benefits.

From the employee perspective, job security and career progression up a clearly defined hierarchy are becoming things of the past. Full-time employment is increasingly being replaced by various forms of flexible work arrangement including fixed-term contract working, part-time and temporary arrangements. Employees whose expectation that material rewards will accrue with experience and seniority are starting to find these assumptions challenged by the way in which reward strategies are being revised to link pay and benefits more closely with the types of performance required by the organization. Reward systems should take into account the needs of employees for whom pay may have replaced promotion as a means of making career progress in today's increasingly diffuse organizations. Reward systems are about more than merely paying people for work done. Increasingly, employees who are looking at strategies to recruit and retain the best people are viewing reward as part of the package – see chapters 8 and 9 for examples of this.

The symbolic power of reward systems

Reward schemes need to meet both the organization's needs for managing its salary bill, for ensuring that it is getting good performance from its employees as well as the employees' needs to be appropriately recompensed for their efforts. Reward schemes carry enormous symbolic significance for employees. They are a powerful means of teaching employees what is actually valued in the organization, as well as what is not. Typically this is achieved by incentivizing particular types of performance, such as increased sales, and by punishing employees who appear to be underperforming. As such, they have a greater impact on employee attitudes and behaviour than corporate rhetoric or values statements which encourage teamworking, for example. So if the organization encourages teamwork but continues to award significant bonuses for individual achievement alone, teamwork is less likely to be taken seriously.

In theory, reward schemes are designed to be motivating, offering appropriate incentives for, and recognition of, desired performance. Whether schemes which focus exclusively on the financial aspects of reward achieve this aim is open to debate. While money is sometimes thought to be a motivator, and it certainly appears to be for some people, at least at some stages of their career, Hertzberg's (1966) well-known motivation theory suggests that money is just as likely to demotivate.

Take the example of someone who is told by their manager that they are going to get a 10 per cent pay rise in recognition of superb performance. The employee will no doubt be very pleased unless he or she finds that other members of the team are going to get a 15 per cent pay rise. Similarly, once the employee has grown used to the level of pay, no matter how large the initial rise, money in itself ceases to be motivating. Losing money, on the other hand, continues to be universally demotivating. There are numerous examples of people whose jobs have been effectively downgraded during delayering, and so have their pay and benefits. The 'running sore' effect of such organizational decisions can cause people to see themselves as victims. Almost inevitably, loyalty to the organization suffers as a result.

The need to revise reward strategies

In times gone by, when organizations had relatively stable hierarchical structures, pay schemes were apparently clear-cut. Job evaluation was used to decide how much each job was worth in terms of its contribution to the organization. Jobs were defined and allocated according to a clear set of job grades, each of which had a salary range. The majority of staff would be on a fixed pay arrangement and pay was often linked with seniority and subject to almost automatic increases regardless of performance. Of course, this made managing the salary pot relatively straightforward.

Arguably, such schemes were acceptable to many employees, especially people working for bureaucratic organizations, since some kind of pay increase could be relied upon, even if the increase was not dramatic. For many HR specialists too, such schemes had advantages since they often appeared to have power in negotiations about pay and promotion. They were the organization's gatekeepers and saying 'no' was part of the job. However, as organizations' needs changed, such schemes seemed to offer fewer advantages, apart from familiarity. A system which reinforced the status quo was increasingly out of step with the need for greater and more flexible outputs from employees. In an attempt to move towards a performance culture, many organizations have introduced pay schemes over the last two decades which are intended to reflect performance in the job more than the job grade itself.

In these changing times, reward schemes quickly become sources of discontent. In flatter structures in particular, there is often considerable pressure for reward strategies to be revised. In more hierarchical structures, being promoted was the only way of gaining status as well as earning more money or breaking though a pay ceiling for a grade. In some organizations, eligibility for promotion was based on age and experience rather than performance. In flatter structures pay should more obviously reflect performance in theory, especially since promotion is less likely.

Indeed, research carried out by Roffey Park found that people who are dissatisfied with their career development are likely to consider that their organization's reward scheme and leadership are inappropriate. It seems that when people are reasonably happy with their jobs and career prospects, the reward scheme is seen as less of an issue. Because organizations can no longer guarantee vertical promotion they are actively looking for ways to promote and introduce the idea of lateral careers. However, fixed grading schemes often deter people from making 'sideways' moves since they will actually lose pay in the bargain. While many HR professionals are keenly aware of the need to reshape reward strategies, the difficulty lies in identifying what needs to change and what the organization wishes to reward. Sadly, introducing revised schemes can raise as many problems as leaving the current system, however inadequate, in place. According to Jeffrey Pfeffer (1998),

> The successful investment in new reward practices involves a great deal of effort, commitment and expertise. And it is probably the most difficult task facing HR managers.

He suggests that there is no such thing as a perfect pay system, but that good systems are about customization and tailoring, rather than off-the-shelf solutions.

Performance-related pay

Incentive schemes and performance-related pay continue to provoke debate. In the USA variable pay systems are growing rapidly. The Management Agenda research (Glynn and Holbeche, 2001) suggests a slight organizational trend in the UK toward extending incentive schemes to a wider group of employees than those who are conventionally offered bonuses. Teachers' unions have been vigorously contesting the government's plans to introduce performance-related pay into the teaching profession.

Yet the trend seems set to stay. **Mercury Communications**, for instance, offers individual contracts to all employees who receive individual performance-related pay awards. The Management Agenda respondents who perceive variable or merit pay to be positive report that they feel that their performance is being clearly recognized through such schemes. Others, however, believe the effects to be damaging since incentive schemes tend to favour exclusively short-term performance, especially with regard to financial targets. Many respondents suggested that incentive schemes also tend to set colleagues against one another and favour individual or departmental targets as opposed to corporate targets.

Research by Scholtes (1995) lists five reasons why performance-based reward, recognition and incentive systems generally do not work:

- There are no data to show long-term benefits
- They set up internal competition
- Reward systems undermine teamwork and cooperation
- They often reward those who are lucky and pass by those who are unlucky
- They create cynics and losers.

In the UK performance-based pay has been relatively well established for a number of years. Such schemes need to be responsive to the business drivers, the changing technology, the new skills needed and the fact that to be successful in a new environment, people need to do different things. Broadly speaking, any reward system needs to reflect the key drivers for future organizational success in the short and medium term. In developing reward strategies which respond to these business drivers some basic questions need to be answered. What, for instance, are the critical roles, tasks, skills which should be rewarded? What are the new working practices that the organization wishes to encourage? Will teamworking be more critical to achieving business goals than individual performance? Is having one system the only way of thinking about a revised system?

The question of what constitutes performance continues to be debated. Organizations are demanding more from their staff, not only in terms of output, in other words, performance against agreed targets, but there is now an increasing emphasis on the input or *how* targets have been accomplished. Inputs include the new skills which people are required to use in their jobs. Many organizations want people to be keen and willing to take on broader responsibilities, learn new skills and develop wider competencies. In addition, technology is bringing about a more fundamental change, switching the nature of the way work is carried out from directive tasks to process-driven activities.

Inputs also include the cultural targets in terms of attitudes and behaviours which the organization wants to encourage. The increased use of technology calls for greater teamworking with broader, more flexible roles and more versatile management styles. In some organizations only outputs are assessed for bonus purposes while in others inputs are also taken into account. Typically, the new areas of incentivization include 'soft' areas such as making creative suggestions, receiving positive feedback from customers, teamworking and demonstrating leadership. To support this approach there is usually an emphasis on competencies and various feedback mechanisms are used.

In some government departments variable pay has met with a mixed response since, for some employees, performance-based pay effectively constitutes a demotion in terms of their pay packet. One of the main consequences of introducing variable pay in place of a wholly fixed pay system is that what is considered as 'core' to the job may assume a lesser importance in the mind of the job holder than any aspect of the job which is singled out for variable pay. Therefore if short-term bottom line performance is the basis of the bonus, employees are likely to put their efforts into this, perhaps at the expense of other things that the organization is trying to achieve in the longer term.

What reward strategies are appropriate in changing organizations?

If organizations require high levels of flexibility of employees, reward systems may also need to be flexible. Job grading, reward and development systems must be linked up with future opportunities. These will still need to evaluate relative contribution but they must also allow assessment of competence and skill progression. At the same time, no system can allow its costs to escalate out of control. The challenge therefore is to find a flexible and tailored alternative, or set of alternatives, which allows for a better match between organizational needs and constraints and employee needs and aspirations.

In organizations which have delayered significantly, traditional job evaluation-based pay structures are beginning to seem outdated and inappropriate. With flatter structures, the reduced number of management levels usually means that people's job responsibilities have grown way beyond the original job description. New skills are called for in a job environment which typically includes large cross-functional teams often managed remotely and pressures to create new and different relationships with a changing customer base. Allocating a 'pricing' value to a job description in such changing circumstances seems restrictive. Above all, reward systems need to be able to provide people with a real sense of progression, or at least not demotivate employees when promotion opportunities are fewer.

The move towards more flexible reward strategies reflects the need to attract and retain key employees.

An increasingly mobile workforce is going to require that there is at least parity in pay and benefits wherever they are working geographically. Expatriate conditions which guarantee a level of secured income are becoming less frequent. A number of organizations are beginning to consider paying the difference between the total compensation in two locations by way of a cash supplement. Given that most European countries are likely to continue to have different approaches to reward, despite the advent of the Euro, the use of total compensation packages is set to increase.

Similarly, the shift away from state benefits in many European countries is likely to put pressure on employers to provide basic benefit programmes including pensions. Employees in years to come will no doubt become adept at comparing the overall value of such packages. Competitiveness in the labour market may well depend on employers thinking ahead about how their compensation package can be used to attract and retain the best talent.

Long-term incentives and share ownership

There seems to be a growing use of long-term incentives (LTIs) and the practice of retaining key people through the use of incentives has long been popular in the USA. In the UK and other parts of Europe where the incidence of such schemes is much lower, there appears to be a trend in multinational companies such as **Shell** and **Total** towards extending these incentive schemes to European senior employees. Employee share ownership appears to be also on the increase. Companies such as **Procter and Gamble** are giving all employees share options to encourage continued commitment to the organization.

Broad banding

Many organizations are introducing broad banding, where a small number of wide salary bands encompasses many varied roles. This should make job enrichment and lateral moves easier, as long as opportunities to make those moves exist. In practice, the process of introducing broad bands is fraught with difficulty. The new bands are often viewed with suspicion by employees, especially if the rationale for grouping together certain roles does not make sense to the job holders. This suspicion is demonstrated in a sketch featuring a well-known cartoon character, in which the boss says to the character: 'We're introducing broad banding...which means that not only will you have the opportunity not to be promoted you will also earn less for more work'.

Other trends

Many organizations are experimenting with competence-based pay (CBP), also known as knowledge- or skills-based pay, which takes the notion of performance-related pay in a particular direction. CBP works on the basis of rewarding the skills an individual possesses and actually uses. Typically, completion of a training unit relating to a particular competency or skills unit usually results in a pay increase. The downside of such schemes is that they tend to be very complex. The emphasis on individual competence can lead to a failure to reflect sought-after cross-organizational business goals such as teamworking and quality.

Many organizations are now trying to encourage teamworking and want to see this reflected in their pay schemes. Team-based pay schemes provide financial rewards to individual employees working within a formally established team. Payments are linked to team performance or the achievement of agreed team objectives. Team pay has not yet been proved to be effective for white-collar workers and research carried out by the CIPD has shown that team pay is often more talked about than practised. One of the drawbacks of the wider spread of team pay is that every scheme is unique. It is not possible to simply adopt some broad recommendations from other organizations, nor are such schemes easy to design or manage. The CIPD found that team pay works best if teams stand alone with agreed targets and standards, have autonomy, are composed of people whose work is interdependent, are stable, are well established and make good use of complementary skills.

Some companies see little need for team incentives while others recognize that flexible working with individuals sharing responsibility implies greater pay equality. The three basic elements of a team-based reward package (assuming that the basic pay is right) are:

- The individual element, i.e. the basic salary but varied in relation to performance or skills/competence
- A team element related to the achievement of team targets
- An organizational element related to business performance measured as profit, or added value.

These may be in the form of cash or shares. Some companies are devising incentives such as coupled team and individual bonuses while others are flattening pay differentials and putting little emphasis on incentives. Hierarchical pay structures are not conducive to teamworking. It is difficult to foster team spirit if individuals are concentrating on promotion. Nor should performance be the sole criterion for rewarding success. According to Danny Chesterman, corporate development advisor at **Kent County Council**, 'individuals should be rewarded for their contribution to teams, and the teams for the way they develop individuals'.

Many organizations are experimenting with 'job families' which allow different professional and business groups to be rewarded differently and reflect market conditions. These have the advantage of reflecting the needs of different groups of key workers, but can be difficult to implement in an organization which has strong centralizing tendencies. Job families are not simply reflected in rewards but also new roles and other HR processes such as recruiting, training, organization, management style and internal communication.

Ideally, for the job family system to work, the required capabilities are established and combined into roles. The key performance measures are then directly cascaded from the measures of business performance. The focus is on 'total pay', which includes both benefits and pay as well as taking into account employees' perception of the package. The notion of individual value and capability is crucial, with increased value reflected in earnings. Since it is recognized that both employee inputs and outputs are different from in the past, the need to create an employment environment which meets employee and business needs is a prime consideration.

Flexible benefits

Given the way the work environment is changing, continuing to offer benefits that are based on the 'job-for-life' assumption is unrealistic. More flexible workforces may not wish to see their deferred benefits accruing in small ways in a variety of employers' schemes. The important thing is to find out how people perceive their benefits and whether these are valued and appropriate to both company and employee needs. In the UK, **Cable and Wireless** has developed a cafeteria-style benefits system. Items in the scheme include pensions, healthcare, childcare vouchers, annual leave, life cover and dental insurance for employees and their partners. Their HR team emphasizes the importance of good communication about the nature of the scheme. Changing social needs are creating the need for more innovative approaches from employers. In the USA, some companies, such as **Lotus Development** and **Apple Computers**, are now extending benefits to domestic partners as well as spouses.

Hoechst Roussel was formed during the 1994 merger of the two pharmaceutical companies and both companies had offered generous and expensive benefits packages. The company took the opportunity to revise, rather than simply integrate the two reward structures. Hoechst Roussel HR team ran a staff attitude survey to find out what people actually wanted in the way of benefits. Ninety per cent of staff said that they wanted more choice over the benefits they received; 80 per cent said that some benefits should be cut back and others expanded; 70 per cent said they would like to swap some benefits for cash; 60 per cent said that they would be prepared to make extra contributions to improve certain benefits. No-one wanted to see benefits abolished in favour of a pure cash equivalent. It was clear that the company needed a flexible benefits system.

The HR team realized that choice is an important benefit in itself. As the HR director, Richard Baker said:

> In the past we'd approached benefits from the company's standpoint, not the employees', but even so there was no link to the company's corporate goals. Now we had an opportunity to use employee benefits to reinforce the culture of the new company, giving employees the same responsibility for determining their benefits that they were being given in other parts of their work.

Benefits clearly have to be relevant if they are to be valued. Managing a flexible benefits scheme is not easy since it is a dynamic situation, people's needs change. Some pundits advise adjusting one or two benefits, rather than revising a complete scheme. Sophisticated software is needed to support a flexible benefits scheme. Introducing a flexible benefits scheme is not a panacea but it should allow for a closer matching of individual needs with the organization's goals.

How do people want to be rewarded?

The last few years has seen the introduction of a range of extrinsic rewards such as:

- Profit (gain) sharing
- Flexible benefits
- Bonuses payable in terms of extra leave rather than pay
- Bonuses payable towards prestigious qualifications
- Long-term incentives (LTIs)
- Deferred incentives
- Extending private health schemes to all employees and their families
- Longer holidays
- Sponsored holidays
- 'Free' family holidays in company-owned cottages
- Enhanced early retirement.

However, our research suggests that intrinsic motivators such as the chance to do something worthwhile, to have a development stretch, to increase job satisfaction are all as important as the financial package and represent 'psychological' rewards. Many people want to feel that their skills and contribution have been recognized by others, especially their boss. Ironically, the more inflexible the formal scheme, the more people appear to rely on other forms of recognition to reward individuals. This highlights a danger with variable pay. With today's increased spans of control, variable pay risks becoming a proxy for performance management. The more performance is rewarded through variable pay, the greater the disappointment of the individual who feels that his or her talents have not been recognized if the bonus is small.

The managing director of a small consultancy decided to introduce a new form of performance-related pay which singled out
the achievement of a number of business goals for special reward.
Junior staff had relatively less access to the resources needed to
achieve these targets. Nevertheless, one junior consultant put in a
major effort to achieve the targets and succeeded in achieving the
performance threshold required for a bonus. Her reward turned
out to be £10, accompanied by a letter from her boss encouraging her to try harder next year! Not surprisingly, the consultant
decided to test her fortunes elsewhere.

Many of the people who took part in the Management Agenda
suggested that some of the best rewards were linked with new
opportunities rather than pay alone. They enjoyed the respect
and recognition of peers and managers. In our different surveys,
very few people appear to have been financially rewarded for
development. If anything, people were rewarded only on outputs
rather than inputs, and in some cases the reward was of the 'up
or out' variety. Some see development as the route to promotion
in the future and that work opportunities come from increased
skills.

Recognition

In many organizations the scope for modifying the reward system
may appear limited. Recognition schemes take on a special significance since they are a symbolic way of reinforcing the 'new'
behaviours and performance needed in the organization.
Research suggests, however, that formal recognition schemes
rarely motivate people in the long term and can be laborious to
administer. However, there are many examples of recognition
schemes which are perceived to be successful since they are
linked to the business strategy, are imaginative and regularly
modified and offer individuals a degree of choice in how they
wish to be recognized.

Supporting culture change through a reward and recognition process

In establishing a TQM process within a company, a transition to
a corporate culture in which there is a continuous improvement
philosophy is a basic requirement. One scheme which has been

well received by employees and includes elements of recognition with financial reward is run by an Australian pharmaceutical company. This annual quality award aims to endorse a culture of continuous improvement by recognising the following types of contribution:

- Exceptional teamwork
- Excellence in normal key tasks
- High achievement in a special project.

Since this company values its role as a community leader, individuals can be nominated for instance for activities which lead to an improvement in the environment.

Nomination forms provide a review of the important attributes of a quality employee. These include:

- Attitude to quality
- Teamwork
- Commitment to their department
- Attitude to company and co-workers
- Consistency with work performance
- Attendance and punctuality
- Enthusiasm
- Accuracy
- Use of initiative and knowledge of customer requirements.

The nominations are reviewed quarterly by the quality committee which consists of eight representatives of each area of the business and includes the general manager as chairperson. Recognition of successful nominations takes place at a company meeting which all employees are invited to attend. Each successful nominee receives a certificate from the quality committee, thanking them for their contribution.

Successful nominations are reviewed and awards made consisting of:

- A monetary component such as a package at a prestigious hotel
- A framed certificate from the company
- An individual and group photograph used for publication in the company newsletter and placed on a noticeboard in the staff canteen.

Quarterly winners of each category also qualify for the Annual Quality Award, the eventual winner of which receives a large cash prize in the form of a travel voucher.

Reward and recognition schemes are obvious areas for active collaboration between Human Resource professionals and the line. In theory, pay structures are really just elaborate ways of recognizing people and providing a fair exchange for their labours an actual income. In practice it is probably unrealistic to expect any pay structure to provide all the answers to the question of how to motivate people.

An arguably more important means of motivating people is often underestimated since it does not lie in one system-wide approach. Research suggests that ongoing recognition by line managers and peers has a greater impact than any company scheme. Recognition by other people of what an individual or team has achieved can be very reinforcing, confidence building and supportive. As such it can form part of an individual's 'psychological' income or what makes coming to work really worth while. Given the need for people to work in new ways, including in teams, formal recognition processes are a means of encouraging people to focus on what the organization really needs, in both the long and the short term.

Conclusion

In producing a high-performance organization, HR has a key role to play. Working with line managers, HR can devise structures and work processes which should enable the organization to achieve its goals. HR processes, including reward systems, need to align with other management practices in moving the organization forward. Pay cannot make up for unpleasant or difficult working conditions or poor management, and addressing some of these sources of frustration is likely to be more rewarding in the long term than simply changing the way people are paid. According to Jeffrey Pfeffer (1998), it is important to recognize that 'pay is just one element in a set of management practices that can either build or reduce commitment, teamwork and performance'.

With reward systems, it seems that the more impersonal and corporate the scheme, the less employees find financial reward motivating. It's as if there are too many external factors which have a bearing on the pay decision, reducing the importance of individual achievement. If excellent performance is required, people need to see the link between what they have achieved and what they are paid. Producing excellent performance then becomes a matter of individual pride and motivation.

Of course, the more 'individual' the package, the more difficult the reward system becomes to administer, but this in itself should not deter the HR strategist who wishes to develop reward systems which are more likely to meet current and future needs. And reward strategies should not focus solely on pay and tangible benefits. No matter how rigid the pay system appears to be, the importance of recognizing the unique contribution of each individual is obvious. This is where line managers and peers have such an important role to play. If an organization is able to revise its reward systems, it may be useful to ask employees what are the important considerations which need to be taken into account. The more employees feel a sense of involvement and ownership of the scheme, the more they are likely to find it motivating. The more choice, flexibility but transparency that can be built in, the better.

The main characteristic of a successful reward scheme is that it motivates, rather than 'turns off'. Some of the more satisfying reward systems from the employee perspective include a large element of collective reward, so that employees are not competing against one another. Reward strategies which take a holistic perspective of what people consider to be rewarding and include a range of rewards in the design of any new system are more likely to motivate and retain skilled employees who are keen to help the organization achieve its short- and longer-term aims. Money is not the main motivator for many people. People need to know that they are valued by their employer and learn to value themselves. When people feel valued and confident, they are more likely than not to release their potential to the benefit of the organization. When this happens, the virtuous cycle of motivation is under way.

Checklist for reward strategies

Managing performance

Is the performance of individuals managed effectively for successful business performance?

- Are strategic and individual objectives aligned?
- How do we define standards in terms of behaviours and out-comes?
- How clear are performance requirements?
- How fair is the distribution of work?
- Do appraisals include a review of past performance, an assessment against agreed standards and targets, as well as feedback?
- How consistently is performance monitored and rated? What scales are used?
- How honest is communication about performance? How are poor performers dealt with? What performance counselling is available?
- How clear are the links between financial/non-financial rewards and performance?

Employee relations

How strong is the commitment between the workforce and the business?

- What degree of employee participation exists?
- How well do employees understand business objectives?
- Is there a sense of acceptance of the organization's philosophies and values?
- Do employees feel a sense of belonging and identification with the organization?
- How well are organizational and employee needs integrated?
- How well is information communicated? Is it two-way? How do managers and employees receive information and how well do they share information?
- What forms of employee representation exist?
- What regulatory issues must be taken into account?

Developing and managing reward strategies

Does the organization's reward strategy achieve the right results?

- Does the reward strategy reflect corporate goals?
- Are the messages sent by the pay system aligned to other management practices?

- Has the organization been sharing its profits in a way which creates a sense of fairness at all levels of the company?
- How do you find out what people value with regard to pay and benefits?
- Are objectives clear and specific? Are performance measures business related?
- Do quantifiable measures help managers to make compensation decisions?
- How competitive are salaries for different groups? Is our reward strategy market-driven? Does it reflect industry 'best practice'?
- How segmented is our pay structure? How transparent is it?
- What are the criteria used in job evaluation, e.g. knowledge, problem solving, accountability?
- What job-evaluation method, if any is used? How do we ensure equity?
- How are hourly paid roles evaluated compared with salaried roles?
- How is reward managed, e.g. performance-related, incentives, benefits?
- Does it include fixed and variable components, as well as short- and long-term incentives?
- What other methods, apart from pay, can be used to build commitment to teamwork and performance?
- How well are these aspects of the reward strategy working? Is it flexible enough to cope with change?
- What innovative approaches might add value?

References

Ashton, C. (1999). Company links HR to business strategy. *Personnel Today*, 1 April.

Chesterman, D. in Coles, M. (1998). Managers pay price of life in the fast lane, *Sunday Times*, 1 March.

Coles, M. (1999). Reappraise the way you develop your staff, *Sunday Times*, 14 February.

Crabb, S. (1995). Adding value with better benefits, *People Management*, 13 July.

Evans, T. (1996). Recognising and rewarding individual roles and competencies. Paper presented at the Business Intelligence Conference: Developing Your Company's Human Capital. June.

Dunlop, J. T. and Weil, D. (1996). Diffusion and performance of human resource innovations in the US apparel industry, *Industrial Relations*.

Glynn, C. and Holbeche, L. (1999). *The Management Agenda*. Roffey Park Management Institute.

Herzberg, F. (1966). *Work and the Nature of Man*. New York: World Publishing Co.

Hewitt Associates (1999). *Inside Human Resources*, Issue 2.

Holbeche, L. (1997). *Career Development: The Impact of Flatter Structures on Careers*, Oxford: Butterworth-Heinemann.

Holbeche, L. (1997). *Motivating People in Lean Organizations*, Oxford: Butterworth-Heinemann.

Hudson, R. (1989). Labour market changes and new forms of work in old industrial regions, *Environment and Planning Society and Space*, 7, 5–30.

Huselid, M. (1995). The impact of human resource management practices on turnover, productivity, and corporate financial performance, *Academy of Management Journal*, **38**.

IPD (1998). *The IPD Guide on Team Reward*. London.

IRS Employment Trends: Pay and Benefits Bulletin (1996). *Team Reward Part One*. No.604, PABB 2–5.

London, C. and Higgot, K. (1997). An employee reward and recognition process, *The TQM magazine*, **9**, No.5, 328–335.

Mason, J. C. (1996). Extending benefits to domestic partners, *HR Focus*, February.

O'Toole, J. (1985). Employee practices in the best managed companies, *California Management Review*, **XXVIII**, 35–66.

Pfeffer, J. (1996). When it comes to Best Practices, why do smart organizations occasionally do dumb things? *Organizational Dynamics*, Summer.

Pfeffer, J. (1998). Rethinking reward practices: myth and reality, *Reward*, July.

Robinson, J. (1997). Productivity: A case study, *Management Services*, March.

Scholtes, P. R. (1995). Do reward and recognition systems work? *Quality Magazine*, December, 27–29

Schumacher, E. F. (1973). *Small is Beautiful*, London: Blond and Briggs.

Tyson, S. (1995). *Human Resource Strategy*, London: Pitman publishing.

Womack, L. P., Jones, D. and Roos, D. (1990). *The Machine That Changed the World*. New York: Simon & Schuster.

Wood, S. (1989). *The Transformation of Work*, London: Unwin.

6   *Working across organizational boundaries*

Working across boundaries is here to stay, or so the pundits would have us believe. Flatter organization structures, globalization and the desire to bring the right people together to work on the right projects are just some of the reasons why people are increasingly likely to be required to work beyond their own departmental or organizational boundaries. In this chapter we will be focusing on what it means for employees to interact with people who are not part of their traditional 'functional' work team. In chapters 10 and 13 we look specifically at the international implications of working across boundaries. For many people, cross-boundary working may seem unfamiliar or even potentially threatening. The business press regularly features aspects of cross-boundary working, such as joint ventures or strategic alliances which appear to have gone wrong, often thanks to the 'human factor'. After all, cross-boundary working involves working with people whose culture, the 'way they do things', may be different from your own. It means working outside your own boundaries, whether these be knowledge-based, experience-based or habit-based and potentially outside comfort zones.

Forms of cross-boundary working

Typically, in international organizations, people are working together across the boundaries of different national cultures. After all, in these days of the global marketplace, in which manufacturing, purchasing, customer service and other aspects of a single organization's operation may be carried out anywhere round the world, organizations are increasingly requiring employees to interact with fellow employees across geographical regions. Whether the organization's focus in European, transnational or truly global, the boundaries which many of its employees will encounter are national and linguistic and for some people, working in a multi-cultural environment presents real challenges. These challenges can be exacerbated when colleagues rarely or never get the chance to meet each other and have to rely on communicating by e-mail and other means of virtual working.

Another prevalent form of cross-boundary working is where employees of different corporate cultures are required to work closely together. Widespread competition from a range of sources is leading to greater corporate amalgamation within the marketplace. The ongoing trend for organizations to merge or at least work in some form of strategic alliance with erstwhile competitors, customers or suppliers means that increasing numbers of employees are having to develop new allegiances and be prepared to work effectively with people whose working practices may be very different. While a merger may be publicly celebrated as a 'marriage' as was the 1998 merger of jewellers Asprey and Garrard, employees may see the relationship more in terms of a divorce from all that is familiar. Nor is the public sector immune to cross-boundary working. In the UK, government pressures for greater responsiveness and efficiency are leading to cross-cutting initiatives between civil service departments and to 'Best Value' regimes in local government.

An increasingly familiar form of cross-boundary working is evident in flatter organizational structures. This is where people who may be at very different levels in the hierarchy are required to work together in ways which would be unusual in a more conventional hierarchical structure. So a first-line supervisor might be expected to understand the strategic implications of some aspect of the company's operation for which he or she is responsible when producing relevant reports for an executive. The boundaries which employees have to cross then become intellectual. They are being required to bridge different levels of attention – from an operational/technical focus to an implementational/strategic one.

In leaner organizations, the thin staffing levels often cause employees to have to cooperate effectively with other departments in order to produce work to the required standards. Sometimes, especially when work is organized along process lines, horizontal working involves working in teams of various sorts. These may be *ad hoc* and temporary, or more permanent. Indeed, some organizations, particularly those involved in high-tech industries, are increasingly organized along project lines with teams drawn from people with the relevant skills and expertise for the team's task. Working in such teams often requires people to work with others who have different functional specialisms and to be able to cross departmental boundaries for the good of the joint project. The case study featured later in this chapter focuses on this kind of cross-boundary working.

The challenges of working across boundaries

So if working across boundaries is on the increase, what are the challenges for employees? For many people, working in this way for the first time requires them to develop a specific mindset, one in which flexibility and responsiveness to others form the basis for collaboration. One of the key features of cross-boundary working is that some employees experience mixed loyalties. This is particularly the case when project teams are seen as a 'bolt-on' to the team members' ordinary work.

In a matrix structure, this often means that team members continue to have a clear reporting line back to their functional manager, with only a dotted line to the person responsible for the team. In practice this can mean that people lack commitment to the team or that they are withdrawn from the project team before their work is done. Some employees consider that they have to become guardians of their functional specialism within the multi-functional team, putting their own functional standards ahead of the need for collaboration.

Lack of trust

When a major change, such as a merger between two organizations, brings about the need for cross-boundary working, the differences in culture soon become apparent. When there are obvious 'winners' and 'losers' in the process, a lack of trust between the employees of the acquiring and the acquired companies may be inevitable. People become highly sensitive to signals about whether they are on the winning or losing side. In the early days of a merger these signals can include senior appointments, redundancies and whose working practices and brand dominate.

Depending on the business rationale for the merger, there are sometimes benefits in keeping operations largely separate, with collaboration at senior management level only. In other cases, the best course may be to develop a new combined culture similar to the 'third way' proposed by UK Labour politicians. Of course, this should ideally consist of the best practices and aspects of culture from both organizations contributing to the achievement of clear business goals.

Unfortunately, this is hard to achieve in practice, especially when lack of employee trust can lead to a loss of commitment. Roffey Park's research into the human aspects of mergers (Devine, Hirsh and Holbeche, 1998) is littered with anecdotes which illustrate the dangers to the organization of this lack of trust. In a merger between two major pharmaceutical companies, some employees in the acquired company simply hid the outputs of research projects until they felt that their position was secure and that they could work in the new combined organization. This phenomenon was called 'burying our babies'.

What is particularly striking about our merger research is that many executives of organizations on the acquisition trail appear to be unaware of, or prepared to ignore, the importance of understanding the differences in culture before the damage is done. We found several examples of relatively large and bureaucratic organizations which had acquired smaller, more entrepreneurial companies. Within months, even though the acquirers were keen to retain the services of more entrepreneurial employees, the creeping introduction of the acquirer's detailed procedures caused 'star' employees to seek their fortunes elsewhere.

Turf issues

Working across boundaries can also appear to threaten employees' sense of their own territory. This can then lead to political behaviour in which power games can be unproductive. At one level, this can appear quite trivial, but unless 'turf' issues are sorted out, cross-boundary working can be jeopardized. In a financial services organization, a new senior manager in charge of a large data-processing plant wanted to introduce new cross-departmental processes to improve efficiency and raise standards. He could not understand why various previous attempts to introduce new working practices had foundered. He gradually realized that, although the work being carried out across the plant was essentially the same, employees in one department saw themselves as being superior to the rest. They were, after all, allowed to have the radio on during the day while other departments were not. It was only after these differences were aired in an 'open space' meeting in which the employees generated the agenda that there was a gradual willingness to move towards cross-departmental working.

Territorial issues tend to be well disguised. They may emerge sounding like strong business arguments, but the underlying issues may actually be more related to the exercise of power. In cross-functional teams there can be a tendency for technical experts to pull rank, with the financial expert always having the last word. Organizational systems may well be at odds with cross-boundary working even though this may be unintentional. Working across boundaries requires people to bring their particular skills and knowledge to the achievement of a joint task for which no individual is likely to take the credit. If the reward processes reinforce the importance of individual rather than team performance, employees may consider that doing their 'day job' is what will be taken seriously when performance is being assessed and may lack commitment to cross-boundary work.

Knowledge management

A more fundamental barrier to cross-functional working may have its roots in the ongoing uncertainty of the employment market. In the information age, there is the potential clash of employee and employer needs with respect to how information is developed and distributed. This is embodied in two apparently contradictory edicts. One is 'knowledge is power' and the other is 'knowledge is to be shared'. From the organizational perspective there are clear benefits in the pooling of information, about clients for example, and the generation of shared knowledge, thus preventing the organization from becoming dependent on any single employee's knowledge.

From the individual point of view, however, there can be little incentive to share information if by so doing you render yourself dispensable. After all, a person's expertise has traditionally been regarded as their key asset in the employment market. In these uncertain times, valuable experience and expertise are also seen to be a means of keeping your job when those about you are losing theirs. For some people, career uncertainty is not the issue. They may simply not want to share their expertise beyond their own boundaries if it means reducing their power base as 'the expert'.

Clearly there has to be a shared platform of trust and the opportunity for employees to develop valuable new skills through the team process if people are to see benefits in collaboration. For while there is plenty of anecdotal evidence that people who develop effective knowledge management processes derive development and personal satisfaction from the new forms of learning they acquire, the barriers to being willing to collaborate can be strong. HR has a role to play in ensuring that team processes and use of information can address both organizational and individual needs. Training and appropriate rewards may be part of the answer.

Cultural differences

Perhaps the biggest obstacles to cross-boundary working lie in cultural differences which become apparent as people work together, whether the cultures in question are for instance national, departmental, functional, age or gender related. In his extensive study of joint ventures in China, my colleague Professor Peter Smith (1997) has identified a number of key areas where cultural differences become apparent. To name but a few, these include the ways in which decisions are taken and tasks are allocated, attitudes to time, including the keeping of deadlines and punctuality, the ways in which meetings are conducted, poor performance is evaluated and in which work is coordinated. There can be fundamental differences in what two groups believe to be important, and significant variations in how they expect staff and customers to be treated.

Any of these cultural differences can cause division without team members being able to identify the reason. Language problems can also lead to communication difficulties. It is essential for effective cross-boundary working to be successful, for the key differences in culture to be identified and taken into account when people are expected to collaborate. Peter Smith's work has led to a detailed understanding of ways in which people from different national backgrounds seem to experience cross-cultural working and helps to identify some of the areas where specific help, such as training, may be necessary.

Us and them

Cultural differences of any sort can lead to an 'us and them' approach which is unhelpful in cross-boundary working. The perception of who is 'us' can change almost overnight. A few years ago a merger between two major manufacturing companies, one French, the other British, resulted in managers from each of the two national groups reverting to national stereotypes and perceiving the other as 'them'. However, when the company was later acquired by an American company, the French and British managers realized that they had more in common jointly than with the American management team. British managers found themselves acting as a bridge between the more hierarchical, long-term focus French and the more democratic, 'do it now' Americans. From our merger research, it seems that 'us and them', 'winner and loser' behaviour is more likely when people feel threatened or are acting in unfamiliar settings. This suggests that some forum, whether training, teambuilding or other means of getting people talking with each other and better understanding each others' needs and strengths, is important.

Cross-boundary working – a manufacturing case study

A major international engineering company, whose UK base has a number of sites throughout the south and west of England, has introduced some aspects of cross-boundary working in recent years through various quality initiatives. The company wants to increase the amount of project working which brings together the talents of key individuals from different sites for extended periods. Roffey Park was called in to help the company's management better understand the nature of cross-boundary team working so that learning could be applied to other parts of the organization. The Roffey Park researchers, Caroline Glynn and the author, were supplemented by a number of in-house researchers whom we trained in the approach used.

Our task involved studying the workings of two teams, one of which was established some three years ago and the other was formed more recently. The longer-established team (team A) is essentially working on a single major project with a very long-term deadline, while the other (team B) has a range of projects whose deadlines are shorter term. While team A, consisting of a central team of thirty people, was based at one site, team B was split between two sites approximately 40 miles apart. The immediate teams consisted entirely of men. Both teams were considered by managers to be highly successful, though team A was felt to have greater potential than had yet been realized, and the two sub-teams within team B operated almost independently of each other. Team members also considered the teams successful. They reported a sense of pride at being part of their team and were clearly motivated by being able to contribute to their team's success.

Our research method included interviews and a survey of team members. Our aim was to draw on the experiences of team members in order to gain an understanding of the features of cross-boundary working which have contributed to its success and also to learn from those aspects which have emerged as obstacles to effective performance. We also wanted to gain an understanding of how cross-boundary team working differed from other forms of teamworking – if indeed it did.

The characteristics of successful cross-boundary teamworking

Clearly it would be dangerous to generalize on the basis of studying two teams and the research base has since widened considerably. However, certain factors did become apparent for both teams. These form the basis for our ongoing study of cross-boundary working. We start with the people considerations and then look at other relevant factors.

An effective team leader

One of the key features of both teams was the critical role of the team leader. This was highlighted over and over again, with one interviewee commenting 'ranked 10 on a scale of 1–10 in importance'. In this context, the team leader was the person who not only set the direction for the team but also negotiated and obtained resources, including people for the team. As such it was felt important that the leader should be sufficiently competent technically that he or she could appreciate all the functions encompassed within the team. Similarly, the leader was expected to manage the diversity inherent in the team and enhance the performance of the team as a whole by building on individual strengths.

In these two teams the leader was a senior manager who effectively acted as sponsor of the team at senior levels. An essential aspect of the role was clarifying the roles of individual team members and managing the conflicts which arise across functional boundaries. As such, having an effective leader becomes perhaps more critical for a cross-boundary team than for a conventional functional team. The leader has to manage the political interface and act as a shield for the team from the rest of the organization. In finding its own 'third way', the team may need to have the freedom to experiment and be genuinely 'empowered' to discover the best ways of working. This is usually not a problem as long as the team is seen to be successful. In the early stages, though, the team leader may find his or her credibility under strain as the team learns from its mistakes. The leader needs to be prepared to create an environment where experimentation is encouraged and team members are supported for doing so.

Given the diverse backgrounds of team members, and that there may not initially be a lot of common ground between them, the role of the leader in providing a tangible focus and direction for the team becomes all the more important. Being able to be both strategic and operational is important. They must be seen as someone who 'leads from the front', setting a strong vision and objectives for the team. They perform the important role of providing drive and determination in the face of difficulties. Within the two teams this was an aspect of leadership which seemed to be going well at the level of broad objectives, in that everybody was aware of the longer-term goals and quality/cost objectives. What was going less well was the setting of shorter-term objectives which gave people real focus in the context of a lengthy project.

The leader's role was both internal and external to the team. Both leaders were reported to be 'sold on teamworking' and were effectively acting as coach and mentor to different team members. It was widely recognized that they needed to have excellent interpersonal skills not just for communicating with the team but also for helping the team communicate effectively with each other. In terms of style, both teams felt that decision making should be the ultimate responsibility of the leader, to avoid functional experts pulling rank, but that decision making should be carried out in a participative way. The team leader was also seen as being responsible for communicating the team's successes to the wider organization and building up a strong profile for the team throughout the business. The team leader therefore needs to be visible, both to the team itself and within the organization as a whole.

The team builder

It was recognized by both groups that there was a need for someone within the team who could act as the 'spur to team excellence'. On some occasions this was carried out by the team leader, but not always. In both teams, an individual was identified as a model for good team behaviour, proving that the team can change for the better. They were seen as natural leaders who are self-motivated, confident and charismatic. They were also seen as supportive of failure and willing to try new things. As such, even without formal authority, the team builders were seen as the internal motivator of the team to better things, providing continuity, whereas the leader has to maintain both an internal and an external perspective.

More so than in a conventional team, the Belbin team role of team builder is called for. This aspect of the role is managing conflict within the team. This is an area where problems are more likely, given the complexities within a cross-boundary team. Interviewees noted that the team builder acts as the oil on troubled waters, diffusing conflict through clarifying roles and creating a 'union of individuals around common objectives'.

Facilitators

Team B used facilitators from the outset to help establish effective functioning of the team, especially in the early stages. The key functions of facilitators were described as enabling open communication, mediation and breaking down hostilities within the team. Opinions were divided as to whether facilitators would be needed over the long term and therefore whether the facilitator should be internal to the team or an external person. There was strong agreement, however, that in the early stages it was important for the facilitator to be external. It was felt that internal facilitators would not be considered impartial and would be likely to suffer from role conflict. It was also felt that an external facilitator would be more professional and expert in this role.

Team A had not used facilitators. However, the team leader recognized the importance of reviewing how the team was working and Roffey Park were invited to facilitate a team review which provided the team with some processes which could be used for ongoing purposes.

Team members

Team members noted that there were a number of characteristics which were essential to working successfully within a cross-boundary team. Individuals must be committed to the team, with a real desire to achieve team goals. This means that team members must be able to balance their focus on team goals alongside functional goals. Individuals must also be willing to share success and failure with the rest of the team. Accepting their share of responsibility for both means that team members must be also prepared to confront others who fail to deliver things for which they are accountable.

Team members must be willing to help each other but they should also be able to learn from others and explore new areas outside their own environment. Simply relying on one's own functional knowledge is not enough. After all, a cross-boundary team is likely to consist of a number of people who are expert in their own field, but may not know much about other areas. It is important that members understand the broader business context within which the project is being conducted and appreciate the different elements of the project being carried out by others. This does not entail having a detailed understanding of other people's technical specialisms, but enough of a sense of their priorities and requirements to ensure that the project plan can work smoothly, without people making unnecessary demands on others through ignorance. Members therefore have to be able to liaise across boundaries within their team and between the team and the rest of the organization, including their boss.

Adjusting to cross-boundary working involves being able to work effectively without hierarchical structures, since cross-boundary working often cuts across hierarchical levels, with senior people reporting to a more junior project leader. It was also seen as important that team members were experienced within their functional field and were not in the position of having everything to learn before they could contribute. As such, people in our case study felt that a cross-boundary team was inappropriate for someone who needed coaching or training on their functional specialism. This is one area which further research will explore.

For both teams, interpersonal relationships within the team were felt to be a strong feature of team success. In team B, strong relationships were built up within each of the subteams but working relationships between the two sites were not built up due to the geographical divide. There was a clear sense that team members respected each other and that the environment was one of trust and confidence. These relationships were aided to some extent by social activities outside the work environment. Although these social events were considered beneficial for team-working, the relationships within the team seemed to be developed mainly at work.

Role clarity

Team members need to be clear not only about their own role, but also about the roles of other team members. Role boundaries and team responsibilities need to be understood to minimize the potential for conflict through role overlap, or gaps in provision which will threaten the success of the team. This is an area which is ideally addressed by the team leader in the 'forming' stage of team development when group members begin the shift from independence to interdependence. Time must be spent communicating the vision for the team and clarifying individual and team responsibilities and objectives. The research has highlighted the importance of setting a clear focus for cross boundary teams, uniting activity around a common purpose. This is particularly important given the individual's functional ties outside the team and the danger that, without clarity of cross-boundary team objectives, individuals will fall back on functional links.

Communication and co-location

The key difference between the two teams was about communication, which seemed to be largely due to the fact that one team (A) was co-located, while the other was not. Team A were very positive about the level of communication within the team. They were able to hold frequent informal discussions as well as regular review meetings. The dissemination of information was felt to happen on a regular basis which meant that information received was timely and relevant.

This was in contrast to team B, who felt that there were clear divisions between the two sites. They were united in blaming the poor communication between the two halves of the team on the geographical divide. Members in each of the sub-teams felt that they were well informed about their part of the team, but had very little knowledge of what was happening at the other site. The fact that there were very few face-to-face encounters between the two sub-teams seemed to lead to conflict which then took time to resolve.

Clearly, co-location, though ideal may not be practicable, especially in global organizations in which virtual teams become the norm. However, this case highlights the importance of at least an occasional opportunity to 'personalize' the relationship through meetings, visits, video conferencing, the use of electronic 'team rooms' and other means of helping people to establish a relationship with one another. This is in addition to the need for regular briefings and updates so that people can feel part of the larger whole.

Measures

Within the teams there was agreement that measures were important, but that what was currently measured were the 'hard' measures relating to project targets, resource usage etc. These measures were set on an individual basis. There was no conscious monitoring of 'soft' measures relating to team processes and learning; consequently there was a sense that the effectiveness of the team was judged entirely on results rather than taking into account how those results had been achieved. In a cross-boundary team where there is potential for teamworking to be seen as peripheral to individuals' main role, the use of soft measures may help keep the team focused on learning and gaining more transferable skills.

Team learning

Although there was general agreement that team learning did occur within both teams, it was also apparent that this was very much at an informal, unconscious level than through any formal learning process. One of the problems with the informal learning was that there was no retrieval system so that the team as a whole could learn from its mistakes and successes. Team A sought to kick-start a more formal approach to reviewing learning through an off-site facilitated process while team B undertook deliberate teambuilding at an early stage.

More formal processes are now being considered and introduced. These include regular debriefing of learning events, general learning reviews of team processes as well as technical learning reviews and harnessing the expertise of more experienced team members. Where these processes have been introduced, team members have commented on the way in which trust has been built through the open approach to learning and that this is an important element of team 'bonding'. They have also remarked on the increase in job satisfaction they have felt when time has been allocated to understanding how an effective end result has been achieved.

Benefits of cross-boundary working

Clearly, when cross-boundary teams work well, they bring benefits to both the organization and to individuals. One of the key characteristics of both cross-boundary teams studied was that the people in the teams were very enthusiastic about this form of teamwork and proud to be part of teams which they recognized as successful. This success was a powerful motivating factor itself, but interviewees also valued the personal growth gained from the experience. They felt stretched within the team, commented favourably on the new insights they had gained into other aspects of the business, and appreciated their relative freedom from organizational constraints.

The only real demotivators were linked with recognition; in particular, team members resented the lack of recognition of success outside the team. They recognized that working across boundaries involves a great deal of complexity, whereas they had the sense that 'the organization does not accord enough importance to the concept of cross-boundary teamworking'. Clearly, as cross-boundary working becomes the norm, rather than the exception, the challenge for organizations will be to ensure that these sophisticated team skills are nurtured, developed widely and rewarded. If not, people with these eminently transferable skills are likely to find a ready market for them elsewhere.

In this organization, these 'building blocks' of cross-boundary teamworking have now been applied to other teams beyond the original two. In a real sense, enabling these teams to work effectively was a joint responsibility between the line and HR. After all, line managers were responsible for the performance and outputs of the teams, while HR were able to help find ways of getting the teams working even more effectively. HR provided the teams with a mechanism for monitoring some of the important 'soft' issues which were affecting performance. With the minimum of training or other conventional interventions, HR were able to help the teams to continue to help themselves. In this next example, the cross-boundary working is across national cultures.

International teamworking at Ericsson

International teamworking is on the increase in **Ericsson**, the Swedish communications multinational. This reflects the increasingly international nature of the business, with locations chosen according to their particular benefits within the global economy. In line with many companies, the drive for growth and increased margins means that Ericsson is moving its production closer to the main points of sale and where there is a lower cost base. Units exist in the USA and other global centres. In China alone there are five production centres.

On the other hand, though European countries such as France, Holland, Spain, Sweden and the UK are main markets, the cost of labour means that production is being phased out of the UK. The supply business is closely monitored so that change can be implemented, if need be, within a six-month period. Growth rates are driven by the global financial markets. Investors are now more sophisticated than in times gone by; so too are customers.

Sales are carried out by region, mainly to multinational customers. The importance of meeting the differing needs of an internationally diverse customer base means that the composition of sales teams must reflect the cultures of the customers. With widely varying customer perceptions of what constitutes value and quality service, international sales teams need to be competent in the 'soft' issues of customer care and be able to marry perceptions with reality. Sales teams tend to be based in the lead country of their major international clients, whether this is the operating centre or headquarters. The important thing is to be close to where the power of the customer is so that the team can fruitfully spend time applying their understanding of cultural issues.

Tony Booth, UK chairman of Ericsson, believes that these sales teams need to be empowered to negotiate the sales pitch and any trade-offs within a broad negotiation margin. The desire to give sales teams ownership of the sales process has to be balanced against the need for pricing consistency across Europe. The advent of the Euro means that customers can compare prices across Europe instantly. The separate teams therefore need to operate as a higher level corporate team to avoid undercutting one another while improving their own sales figures.

The teams report to both local managers and the corporate centre. They are supported, rather than controlled, by the centre. Tony Booth believes that there is no one model of reporting which works in every circumstance. The key thing is to put people with the appropriate skills and ability close to the customer. Team members need to be credible to the customer. Credibility is often based on what the individual has achieved in their career to date, and, in some countries, their perceived power within Ericsson. The team needs to be made up of self-starting, experienced individuals who have made their mistakes elsewhere before becoming responsible for a major account.

In addition, team members have to work together as a real team, supporting each other on issues where in the past they might have expected help from HQ echelons which no longer exist. They have to work together physically and virtually and to act as their own team catalysts. Increasingly customers want to see that the whole team is credible, not just the individual sales person. The team also has to dovetail resources and skills in tough marketplaces.

The team leader, an international account manager, can be based with the team or operate in a 'virtual' way. The leader is expected to win the business and help the team deal with the challenges of delivering the business. The influencing skills of the leader therefore need to be of a high order as there are in effect two types of cultural negotiation taking place. First, the sales negotiation has to reflect the complexities of local requirements and styles. Second, bringing the business back into the corporate culture requires the leader to win support from production and other parts of the centre in order to succeed.

It is often assumed that sales people are primarily individual performers rather than team players. In Ericsson, the team aspect is taken seriously and is reflected in the bonus scheme. There is a potential team bonus of 20–30 per cent which reflects team effort, as well as achievement. Teams would have to demonstrate, for instance, how they have taken the whole team's needs into account when bidding for resources. As a multinational supplier, teams also need to be able to negotiate with other teams when bidding for resources. This can result in conflict which has to be dealt with internally and not be evident to the customer.

Conclusion

HR can assist groups and individuals to develop effective cross-boundary working. This may mean providing team building support when new teams are established. It can also mean enabling teams to communicate effectively both within the team and beyond the team itself. This requires some understanding of the cultural differences represented and the ability to help teams make the most of their diversity. In particular, HR has a key role to play in enabling line managers to overcome some of the barriers to cross-boundary working and to make the most of the positive power of conflict. This will involve helping all concerned to identify what is different in the way they are required to work, to gain clarity about their own role and to appreciate the benefits which they will gain from this increasingly common form of working.

Checklist for cross-boundary teams

Are we using teamworking effectively to meet organizational goals?

*   Does the team function effectively?
*   Has it a common vision and synergy?
*   How clearly are roles defined? Do people understand their own and other people's roles?
*   Are there complex interdependent tasks and a clear plan?
*   How effective are the team dynamics?

- Does the team generate new ideas?
- If the team members are not co-located, how do they create 'human' links?
- How do liaison and coordination work?
- What training does the team need? What learning processes does it apply?
- How does the team analyse its own effectiveness?
- How does the team ensure maintained commitment to the task?
- Is there an effective team facilitator? Team champion? Team leader?

References

Devine, M., Hirsh, W., Garrow, V. and Holbeche, L. (1998). *Mergers and Acquisitions: Getting the People Bit Right*, Roffey Park Management Institute, November.

Smith, P. B., Wang, Z. M. and Leung, K. (1997). Leadership, decision-making and cultural context; event management within Chinese joint ventures, *Leadership Quarterly*, Winter.

7

Recruitment and retention strategies

> Ask leaders what their biggest challenge is, and you get the same
> answer : finding, attracting and keeping talented people. Ask tal-
> ented people what their biggest career challenge is and you will
> hear the same refrain: finding good people to work with – and to
> work for.

Attracting new talent to the organization is a key task, especially
when the talent in question is in short supply. Retaining talent is
another set of challenges. Though recruitment and retention are
often spoken of in the same breath, as here, the factors driving
them are not necessarily the same. In this chapter we shall
explore some of the issues related to the process of recruitment
and look at some of the reasons why people leave their organizations. A strategic approach to recruitment and retention needs to
incorporate a wider set of policies, such as reward, development
and job design. None of these factors are enough in isolation. We
focus specifically on the inter-related stategies of developing people in Chapter 8, and the creation of effective career paths in
Chapter 9. These must reflect an understanding of employee
motivation and be closely linked to trends in the changing labour
market, as well as to the organization's needs. The days when it
was sufficient for a company to be a household name in order to
attract candidates may soon be over.

In parts of the labour market there is still some buoyancy and
there are skills shortages in certain areas, such as COBAL or
EMU specialists. Turnover is also increasing. In the CIPD
Labour Turnover survey it was estimated that average staff
turnover in the UK is between 18 per cent and 20 per cent.
Organizations are aspiring to become the 'employer of choice'
and job advertisements increasingly hint at employer branding.

Typically, advertisements now make clear how employers envisage the employment relationship between themselves and employees. One example from a job advertisement for a commercial manager acknowledges that employees are attracted by more than pay and the work itself:

> What does success mean to you? It could mean having a major say in a FTSE 100 company, a truly global organization where you enjoy real influence. That is what you will get here without question. But you will also gain so much more. You will find an atmosphere of change, growth and innovation; where the IS department is recognized and rewarded as a key driver in our business development; and your ideas will be heard throughout the entire organization....

Strategic recruitment

Recruitment needs to take its place within the HR cycle, as one strategy among others, in building the organization's capability in a changing marketplace. Other strategies, such as developing current staff, should not be neglected in favour of external recruitment. Recruitment should ideally not be simply a question of filling gaps but be focused proactively on bringing into the organization the kind of skills and experience which cannot easily be built from within. With too little external recruitment an organization's processes and staff can start to stagnate. Conversely, if recruitment from outside is the only means by which senior positions are filled, internal candidates soon realize that they must leave the organization if they want to be promoted. Having some sort of balance which is appropriate for the time is perhaps the pragmatic solution.

Recruitment is a strategic opportunity but strategic approaches to recruitment are rare. Most are tactical or short-term. It helps if there is a clear purpose behind recruitment rather than simply replacement. When **Thresher**, the UK drinks retailer (now part of First Quench), for instance, were aiming to transform attitudes and behaviours among staff in their operations, a number of ways were found to involve staff. As a result, many employees became energized and revitalized by the change. The operations director, Brian Wisdom, and HR controller, Chris Johnson, however, recognized that change needed to be embedded at all levels and that relying on the goodwill generated would not be sufficient. They deliberately recruited external 'architects of change' who would bring a different perspective into the workforce. These were people in line management roles whose experience of other change processes caused them to act as the 'grit in the oyster'.

Recognizing that these people would be under pressure to conform to the status quo rather than pursue the change required, Brian and Chris acted as mentors to the newcomers, offering a 'hotline' service when the going became difficult. The result was that the majority of newcomers stayed and had the desired effect of bringing about change from within. Many have since moved through the organization, their change agent skills recognized and valued. For more details of the change project in question, see Chapter 14.

Recruitment should be part of an overall career management strategy which is driven by the business strategy. The key elements of such a strategy are as follows:

1   *Understand the implications of the business strategy*
    Where is the organization going? How are needs changing? Is growth anticipated?
    Are we becoming international/global?
    How much change and innovation do we wish to inject into the system?
    What costs are we expecting?
    How much flexibility will be needed in servicing customer needs (e.g. 24-hour retailing)?
2   *Work out what is required to support the business strategy*
    'Stocktake' current staff
*   How many people do we have? What are their skills, knowledge, experience, attitudes to change?
*   What do our current staff want in terms of career development? Are these expectations realistic?
Assess future needs
    *   How many people will we need in the short-term future (e.g. 2–3 years)? What will their skills be?
Identify gaps
    *   Who has particular talents which we wish to nurture?
    *   Who do we especially want to retain?
    *   Who is at risk of leaving?
    *   What key skills areas are we likely to be short of?
    *   Where have we too many of the 'wrong' skills?
    *   How much will people be willing to retrain?

3 *Develop an integrated set of processes to sit alongside development plans*
- External – develop hiring plans
- Internal – develop retention strategies, removal plans
- Set measures of effectiveness and identify costs

4 *Create an infrastructure for development*
- Develop HR policies which support development and learning
- Ensure that organizational values, feedback processes, senior management behaviour, reward mechanisms and development all align
- Create mechanisms for self-development such as 360-degree feedback, development reviews, development centres, learning resources, career workshops etc.
- Ensure that line managers are trained to help others with their development.

The recruitment process

The days when employers could pick and choose among a wide selection of excellent candidates may be becoming a thing of the past. According to headhunters, there is a much wider calibre of people applying for jobs than in years gone by. As employees develop their marketability and 'knowledge-based' skills are a prized asset, employers are having to compete for the best candidates.

Industries and sectors whose image may seem less attractive to candidates are struggling to find new recruits. The construction industry, for instance, which once had a steady flow of candidates for jobs that involved difficult working conditions now experiences competition for candidates from employers who can provide office-based roles using computers. Similarly, the insurance industry suffers from a sedentary image which may not appeal to young candidates. Where employers are looking for specific skills and experience, especially where these have a high market value, such as in the IT sector, competition can be intense.

Increasingly, employers are recognizing that the process of recruitment may be as powerful an incentive to candidates to join as generous pay and conditions. David Hope, formerly director of human resource systems and personnel relations at **CGU**, believes that the interview process, put together with a firm of business psychologists, helped graduates to understand the brand, culture and the company's commitment to graduate recruitment. Above all, 'it created a sense of excitement about CGU and an eagerness to get involved'.

A well-designed recruitment process can attract good candidates and give the employer useful indications of future performance. Candidates are usually more positive about the organization if they can see a clear link between the recruitment process and the job. Structured interviews, using behavioural and critical incident interviewing, can be helpful as they allow specific job-related areas such as team leadership and customer service to be explored. Psychometrics which are relevant to the work content and realistic simulations can also be useful. Simulations in particular allow managers to see a candidate's performance at first hand. They also provide the candidate with a chance to assess the role and to gather information about the company's approach to doing business.

Flexibility is also important in ensuring that excellent candidates can be seen at times which are possible for them, rather than to a fixed interview schedule. This conveys the message to candidates that they are considered an important part of the organization's future. Decisions should be conveyed early and feedback offered so that even an unsuccessful application becomes a development opportunity. Disappointed candidates can still become advocates of the company if they feel that they have had a useful experience and been treated with respect. The professional image created by the recruitment process can therefore be an important part of attracting quality candidates in the future.

For senior management and other key positions, search agencies are often used, though it is thought that 40–50 per cent of top appointments are filled by contacts. Increasingly, search agencies are adding a suite of activities to their portfolio which should ensure that the successful candidate becomes effective in their new role. Typically, services for the candidate include the usual follow-up counselling sessions with the search consultant. In addition, several agencies are offering one-to-one coaching and specific accelerated skills training.

Recruitment and search agencies are themselves undergoing something of a transition thanks to the impact of technology. Whereas search consultants have made their money by identifying candidates for posts, the growing use of the Internet is starting to make this information freely available to employers. Search organizations such as Korn/Ferry are now starting to provide new website-based recruitment services such as *Future Step*, where the value added by the consultancy is in the quality of candidate assessment and in their systematic closing procedures. Candidates, typically mid-level professionals, are encouraged to complete a set of questionnaires and instruments which produce a profile. They can place their CV on the web which means that they become available through the search consultant's website to employers around the world. Internet-based recruitment is a major trend for junior/middle management posts.

In essence, the successful attracting and recruiting of new talent means that the needs and offers of both the organization and the individual need to marry up. The 'fit' has to be right – in terms of skills and experience as well as values and needs. It is therefore important that both parties are as open as possible throughout the recruitment process. There will inevitably be a process of negotiation around those respective needs, usually over pay or the type and level of work on offer. Increasingly, individuals wish to ensure that the organizations which they are thinking of joining can offer some form of ongoing development and CV enhancement.

Organizations which recognize this and put concrete plans in place to enable development are more likely not only to attract but also to retain good candidates. When the successful candidate joins the organization, each side will be monitoring the situation to ensure that the other party is living up to their promises. There is plenty of anecdotal evidence that the more help and support provided to candidates in the first few months, the more likely it is that the candidate will be able to perform satisfactorily. Similarly, candidates often feel more inclined to stay in an organization where support and interest has been offered. After all, recruitment is an expensive business. With up to 30 per cent of jobs vacated again within months of recruitment due to disappointment on either side, ineffective recruitment is the source of unnecessary expense.

Generation X

During the 1980s many employers were concerned at what was seen as the demographic timebomb – that there would not be enough 18-year-olds and graduates entering the workplace in the 1990s. As things have turned out, the nature of the problem is not so much the shortage of individuals as the mismatch between what young employees expect and what organizations deliver. A great deal of research both in the USA and the UK has been carried out into the needs of the so-called 'Generation X' – or people under the age of thirty. Research carried out by Demos in the UK examined how lifestyle aspirations affect the attitudes of these young people to life and careers (Cannon, 1998).

One of the characteristics of people in this age group is their high educational attainment. The numbers of young people entering further or higher education have increased dramatically in recent years. In the UK, more than 340 000 students entered university in 1998 which was more than double the numbers entering in 1990. During the 1970s only 5 per cent of 18-year-olds had the opportunity to gain a university degree. By 1988 the figure had risen to 15 per cent and today more than 30 per cent of young people are pursuing further or higher education. This brings young people in the UK more in line with their counterparts in other European countries, especially Germany, where higher qualifications have traditionally been valued.

There are some important differences, however. In Germany there has been a tradition of making good use of skills and higher education when the individual enters the job market (and indeed many qualifications are vocationally oriented). In the UK, by way of contrast, many of the jobs on offer to graduates have not changed from those which might formerly have been offered to school leavers. Employers who might once have recruited A-level students for management trainee positions are now becoming graduate recruiters. Job literature produced for university 'milk rounds' continues to imply early opportunities and the rapid promotion of yesteryear. In practice, graduate recruitment is followed by quiet streaming as genuine high-flyers are selected from the rest. Unrealized expectations about exciting careers can lead to disillusionment and cynicism among young employees.

The Demos research suggests that people within this age group have been exposed to a range of experiences to which previous generations did not have access. These experiences may have shaped their expectations and values in ways which are hard to grasp from other vantage points. While there are dangers in generalizing about generations, various research projects indicate that Generation X has been exposed to more information than its predecessors through TV and other media and are used to receiving information in simple form at a fast rate. They expect things to happen at high speed. They are also accustomed to travel and are considered the first truly 'global' generation, even if the links are only through a common currency of consumer products. They are heavy users of technology, including the Internet, and are able to see some of the potential applications of transformational technology.

These experiences have potentially shaped their attitudes in a number of ways. There is a perceived lack of trust, especially in employers since they do not provide secure employment, and there is a wariness about commitment to anything long term. Loyalty to an employer is not an appropriate concept. They expect honesty from employers, especially with regard to career opportunities and dislike feeling manipulated. Organizations which promise international assignments, for instance, and then fail to deliver may produce cynical employees who leave when they are at their most valuable to their current employer.

Young people value their freedom and appear to look for control over their worklife so as to be able to enjoy other aspects of their lives. This generation appears to learn and absorb information quickly, particularly about areas of interest to them such as consumer products and services. The Demos research suggests that young people want money, greater control of their time and the chance to use some of their intellectual potential.

Recruiting and getting the best out of Generation X

Given that many young people defer their entry into the job market, graduate recruitment may need to be seen as an ongoing activity rather than one linked purely with the 'milk round'. This may mean devising graduate development schemes along flexible lines to accommodate people with different levels of experience. The Demos research suggests that young people are attracted to join 'winner' organizations in which they can look good in the eyes of their peers. These are organizations which are future-oriented and developing and using new technologies. They are places of work where people apply their minds to adding value, such as consultancies, and where employees are involved in exciting projects. 'Loser' organizations are those where people's intelligence and individual contribution are perceived to be of only limited value, such as primary manufacturing.

Employers can engage the potential commitment of young people by redefining work in terms of projects which offer variety and learning. More flexible working patterns may be attractive and this may involve restructuring work processes. Organizations can also benefit from making good use of young people's ability to develop specialized forms of knowledge. Young people want their ideas to be taken seriously and need speedy and appropriate feedback about their performance. This can be difficult to achieve in lean organizations where managers and supervisors are often thinly spread, but is essential if young people are to feel that their contribution has been noticed and valued. Managers need to take on the role of enabler and project leader and may need training and other support if this is not their 'natural' style.

They also want the chance to build marketable expertise. Some organizations assign young people a mentor who is experienced in the company's approaches if not at a higher level in the hierarchy. Where the mentor and young employee are involved in a community-based project, for instance, there are opportunities for the young person to experience being an organizational representative. Organizations which invest in training young people but also put them into project roles where their expertise can be used to good effect may benefit from making good use not only of available talents but also from increased employee commitment.

Motivation and retention

Many managers are grappling with the issue of how to build, maintain and retain intellectual capital. Recruitment may be one way of building intellectual capital but it is of little use if an organization cannot retain key employees. After all, unlike many other assets, human ability is extremely volatile and capable of being harmed by a range of factors. Typically these are factors which have a bearing on employee security needs, motivation, morale and sense of worth. Roffey Park research into the impact of mergers on employees, for instance, suggests that in times of major change, many employees simply 'hide' their best ideas until they sense that the time is right to market those ideas. While this may be a sensible stratagem for the employee in the short term, organizations which are looking for innovative solutions may fail to capitalize on the potential of employees.

Loyalty

Some of the biggest changes in the increasingly fragmented job landscape are the shifts in employee attitudes. Loyalty to the employer is becoming a thing of the past and many organizations are urgently reviewing ways of securing the commitment of people whom they do not want to lose. A main contributory factor to the reduction in employee loyalty is the way many employees feel that their career prospects have been damaged by organizational restructurings. Perhaps understandably, in the changing economic climate of the 1990s, many organizations abandoned career planning initiatives, continued to shed jobs and told employees that they should take on responsibility for managing their own career. Arguably this could be interpreted as a sensible approach and a shift away from the paternalistic employment practices of many large organizations. After all, the idea that an organization, even a large one, is a static entity has been seriously challenged as companies which are household names merge, reshape or disappear.

However, at a time when all the power in the employment relationship appears to be with the employer, such a change of stance towards employees seems to be open to other interpretations. Interestingly, many employees we have interviewed perceive messages about 'manage your own career' to be an abdication of responsibility on the part of the employer and they no longer trust in the mutual benefits of the employment relationship. Judging from Roffey Park's earlier research findings, few employees continue to believe that the organization will manage their career. For people who have amassed a great deal of experience in one organization but whose skills are not transferable elsewhere, the possibilities of managing their own career may actually be limited and may lead to some frustration.

The implications of career self-management are rather different for employees who have transferable skills, who know their own worth and now lack trust in their employers. Knowing that they are employable increases employee choice and confidence. This means that employers are no longer having things their own way. There have been a number of well-publicized examples of employees refusing to comply with their employer's bidding even though they effectively close the door on major career opportunities.

This more adult–adult relationship between employer and employees is based on the increasing power of the knowledge worker to make demands of the organization which go beyond pay and rations. This is particularly clear in the IT sector where the success of several organizations relies on the product development skills of a few key individuals. It is also marked in the oil industry where filling overseas assignments as part of a broad career route for high-calibre employees is becoming increasingly difficult. This is partly explained by the rise in the number of dual-career families as well as by the increasing unwillingness of employees to make sacrifices if they are not guaranteed promotion on return from the assignment.

The truth of corporate value-speak such as 'our people are our greatest assets' is a lesson which has been painfully learned in some cases when individuals move on. There is already a good deal of anecdotal evidence that employees with transferable skills and experience are more confident of being employable and less tolerant of the frustrations of poor management, inappropriate reward and few growth opportunities. Ironically, the very skills which many employers are looking for – such as the ability to get things done, be innovative, customer oriented etc. – are precisely the skills which will help people get jobs elsewhere.

Why do people leave?

Retention problems are usually a symptom of other things going wrong in an organization, such as ongoing change or poor management. In many cases, the main reason for people leaving is that they do not like the way they are managed. In retention strategies, it is important to identify why people tend to go, using exit interviews and other information as valuable hints as to what needs to be done. Exit interviews conducted some six months after someone leaves, often by a third party, can yield very rich, and more objective data. Analysing turnover statistics by business unit, department, or team can add further insights. In some organizations, careful research is carried out to answer the question *'why do people turn us down?'* at the recruitment stage. This, linked with the exit interview data, provides a useful steer as to where improvements need to be made. Then, HR and line managers need to work on those problems and delay people from leaving for a while at least.

In 1994 and 1996 Roffey Park carried out two surveys in organizations which had delayered their management structures. The same people were surveyed and, naturally, some of those people were no longer there. Indeed, up to 27 per cent of the previous group were no longer with those organizations. Most of these people were redundancy casualties and were mainly in junior and middle management roles, a disproportionate number of whom were junior HR specialists. The survivors, all of whom claimed that they had more work to do than just two years previously, fell into three groups:

- People who had been promoted in the previous eighteen months (21 per cent). These were mainly senior people and included a number of HR directors who were now in the second tier of their organization's hierarchy. Some of these people were considering leaving as they did not feel well equipped to cope with the exposure of a job at this senior level
- People whose jobs were at the same level but which had grown in some way (45 per cent). These people spoke of having career development, job satisfaction and variety and mostly intended to stay with their company
- People who were essentially in the same job as before (34 per cent). Almost all these people lacked job satisfaction and were actively looking for other jobs.

This latter group was the most explicit about their reasons for wanting to leave. They complained about having no opportunities for career progression and, at the same time, criticized management as incompetent and felt that they were not paid appropriately. This explosive combination of ingredients were typical of the 'push' factors which appear to drive people out of organizations. Interestingly, none of the people in the group whose jobs had grown complained about how they were paid. Perhaps, complaining about pay is a more socially acceptable way of pinpointing frustrations than discussing career disappointments. Giving money as the reason for departure therefore may not be the real cause of people leaving; it is more the result of a decision to leave.

In the Management Agenda, major sources of dissatisfaction include the increased workloads and lack of work/personal life balance alluded to earlier. Other sources of frustration include the **slow** pace of change within some organizations and the increase in organizational politics. These were seen by many as regrettable facts of life, leading to job dissatisfaction but essentially to be endured. If these factors are common sources of dissatisfaction to many people, as our findings suggest, there may be some merit in organizations tackling at least one of these factors through revised policies and practices. Enlightened leadership may well be called for to address these sources of dissatisfaction.

Findings from other research projects such as the Roffey Park study of Work/Personal Life Balance reinforce the importance of management being seen to do something to address employee concerns such as the issue of long working hours. Another important social shift needs to be taken into account when planning employee-friendly policies – that is, the growing implications of eldercare. The changing pressures on employees throughout their working lives can be relieved somewhat by the sensitive provision of appropriate flexible conditions. Staff turnover at US-based retailers **Eddie Bauer Inc.** has dropped significantly since a range of work/life programmes were introduced which recognized the changing priorities of employees at different stages of life (see Chapter 2). Management needs to set a clear priority on introducing effective policies and practices which are more than just window dressing.

However, what many people said would cause them to leave their organization was poor management and a lack of appreciation and recognition. This points once again to the importance of training line managers in the skills of feedback and coaching. Other triggers for people to leave their organization include a lack of opportunity for promotion. The vast majority of respondents recognize that they are responsible for managing their career and 57 per cent of respondents are currently grappling with the dilemma of whether to stay or leave their organization.

This is where career management becomes a key priority for HR professionals. Simply telling people that they are responsible for managing their career is not enough. The irony is that the people most capable of doing this do not need help from the organization. If they become too frustrated, they simply go elsewhere. Effective career management can offer hope that development is possible, which in turn may encourage people to stay.

Career management is critical too for the majority of employees who are likely to stay. Unless there are regular opportunities for personal or professional growth, people's performance is likely to peak and decline.

Why do people stay?

In the Management Agenda survey, money appears to be considered the main way in which people expect to be rewarded, in addition to recognition from the line manager. However, the main motivator for the majority appears to be a challenging job, rather than money alone. This is backed up by a recent CBI Employment Trends survey (1999) of 830 participating UK companies which found that what contributed to employee satisfaction were pay (84 per cent) and interesting work (78 per cent). So while paying well may help an organization to recruit, on its own, money will not help retain people. This corresponds strongly to Roffey Park research into the motivations of 'High Flyers' (Holbeche, 1998) where only 4 per cent of respondents reported being motivated by money.

For this group, personal achievement and challenge were primary motivators (Figure 7.1). Other motivators include variety, autonomy and good interpersonal relationships within teams. The opportunity to use personal drive to good effect seems to be an important motivator for many respondents. A key source of satisfaction appears to be gaining influence at strategic level,

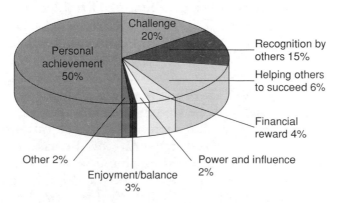

Figure 7.1 *The top motivators*

regardless of one's position in the hierarchy. Enriched roles and the opportunity for significant personal development appear to be important retention factors.

Towards a strategic approach to retention

Under devolution of HR responsibilities, responsibility for retention is shared between line managers and HR. Specifically, the line should be responsible for recruitment and retention, with facilitation by HR. There are often tensions around this issue due to a common paradox – retention, though critical to business success, is not treated as a strategic issue. Line managers often want a 'quick fix' when a key employee threatens to leave or is about to be poached by another company. HR, on the other hand, has to consider the integrity of the pay system – doing a 'deal' in one case could set a dangerous precedent. Line managers then accuse HR of going back on the 'empowerment' idea with which they were sold devolved HR responsibilities. All too often, HR then reverts to type.

Elements of a retention strategy

A more strategic approach is to put efforts into prevention, rather than crisis management. This involves doing a risk analysis on the target group. What is the likelihood of them leaving and what would be the impact of their departure? HR and line management can then have an informed dialogue about the priority areas for action. Employees can be ranked to identify who falls into the 'danger zone'. These can be given special attention. Planned actions can be put in place for other groups.

- *Do not oversell the organization in the first place.* Many people in our surveys felt that the job or the organization had been oversold to them at recruitment. They had been led to believe, for instance, that there were opportunities for rapid promotion, which turned out not to be the case. Graduates who were most disillusioned on this front were people who had been recruited after being wined and dined during the university 'milk round'. Many of these employees were actively looking to leave their organizations by their mid-twenties. Of course, recruitment is a mutual selling opportunity, but it should be honest.

- *Help people to become aware of their own career 'derailers'.* Research suggests that there are a number of common causes of career derailment which include changes in technology, personal life or one's boss. HR can provide career workshops which can help people become more aware of what these factors are for them, so that they can do something about them. Many organizations now use 360-degree feedback for this purpose. When the instrument is available on-line, the whole process is easier to manage. Helping people to become aware of their own strengths and development needs can spur them on to further development.

- *Manage down employers' expectations about how long they can keep people.* It is unrealistic to expect a complete career lifetime commitment from any employee, yet employers continue to act as if this is what they expect. Employers must expect to see the new employment relationship as one of ongoing negotiation as needs change. This means that retaining key employees is both a strategic and a tactical issue in which the day-to-day interactions between managers and employees can undercut the best-laid retention plans or, conversely, retain an employee because of the strength of the relationship.

- *Consider paying retention bonuses.* This is very much a short-term measure and should be considered a pre-emptive strike. Various City firms specialize in offering 'golden handcuffs' to key employees especially during mergers and other major change situations. It is important to recognize that not everyone is motivated by pay and that, in most cases, you can't buy loyalty. It is also important to be realistic about what pay can do with regard to retention – at best it is a hygiene factor. Perhaps more effective is the 'lock-in' effect of generous share options and other benefits. One high technology company was concerned at the numbers of key employees who were going to work for the opposition. The main reason given was that competitors paid more. Some fact-finding by HR revealed that although competitors did appear to pay more, their company had a better overall benefits package. By producing and communicating this 'benchmark' data to the target groups, people in the 'danger zone' were able to make a more informed decision and many who had been contemplating leaving chose to stay. Moreover, some of the people who had left did not enjoy their new work environment and returned within a matter of months. The company wisely chose to welcome them back.

- *Give people a chance to have variety.* This can take many forms, including attending conferences, representing their company as members of consortia etc. Ideally all employees should have the chance to learn new things, meet new people and be stimulated by external input.
- *Consider supporting people to update their qualifications.* In the High Flyers Survey, over half of those interviewed have updated their qualifications since joining their present employer. Proportionately slightly more women than men have done this (62 per cent compared with 56 per cent). Most of the people who have updated have gained an MBA. Of these, half had a degree when joining and just over a quarter had professional qualifications, 40 per cent have obtained a professional qualification and 20 per cent have gained a job-related qualification. Indeed, many of the respondents who joined their organization in the last two years had already achieved postgraduate or professional qualifications before joining.

Interestingly very few employers seem to consider supporting qualifications as part of a retention strategy. Employees, in contrast, seem to value highly the opportunity to do an MBA, for instance. Given that the average part-time course lasts two years, and that if the course is chosen so that the individual can work on projects for their employer as part of their coursework, this seems a sensible way of retaining experienced staff for the duration of their course at least. The peak age for gaining an MBA and a professional qualification appears to be during the thirties in the Roffey Park respondent group. Gaining a first degree seems less age-specific with small numbers taking degrees in their early thirties and another small group in their early fifties. As one managing director who recently completed an Open University degree said, 'I just wanted to see if I had it in me'. People with first degrees alone were most likely to take an MBA, a postgraduate or professional qualification or to seek professional membership. Those who joined with a professional qualification are most likely to have upgraded their qualifications with a first degree, HND, professional membership, other job-related qualifications or an MBA.

Why do people update their qualifications?

People were asked why they had updated their qualifications and nearly half stated that they wanted to be more effective in their current job. Verbatim comments include:

'Better financial skills'
'Lack of management qualifications'
'To cement experience'
'To keep myself up to date'
'To bring together current skills and perfect new ones'
'To gain a greater understanding of the business'.

Only one person stated that they wanted to earn more money as a result. Another main motivation for updating qualifications seems linked with career development: 47 per cent of those who updated said that they could see their qualifications would be useful to them in the future. Several respondents from the public sector in particular where there is ongoing restructuring stated that they want to improve their CV and marketability. Comments include:

'I've reached the ceiling'
'To prepare for the next career step'
'To remain competitive, widen knowledge'.

In other cases, especially in the more regulated financial services industry, professional qualifications have become a requirement. Many respondents were extremely cynical about continuing professional development (CPD) and the requirement to document development. Others were not interested in pursuing training and education courses because they were accredited to a degree or other qualification. Largely the key considerations in choosing a course were relevance and interest.

For other people, especially by their mid-thirties, pursuing a qualification course seems to be in response to a need for a developmental stretch which they may feel they are not getting from their current job. With promotion opportunities more restricted than in the past in organizations with flatter structures, many people see gaining an MBA, for instance, as a means of developing their ability to operate strategically. Over a third (39 per cent) say that they have updated their qualifications for personal interest reasons. One person specifically turned down the opportunity to do an MBA at a well-known business school because the interviewer had insisted on assuming that the candidate's motives for taking the course were to get himself promoted, which was not the case. Typical reasons given include:

'To develop myself'
'Academic interest'
'I wanted to experience self-managed learning'
'Hands-off challenge'
'I wanted a different experience'
'To gain an understanding of management theory'
'Part of my own philosophy of lifelong learning'.

Several respondents were in the fortunate position of having so much money as owners of their own companies that they need to take a tax break. 'Broadening the mind' seems to be preferable to spending a couple of years in some tax haven.

Company support for qualifications

The survey asked respondents who had obtained further qualifications (58 per cent of the total) if their company had supported them to do this. A significant majority (92 per cent) said that they did receive support. This was primarily (86 per cent) in the form of financial sponsorship and two thirds also obtained time off for study. Few people reported receiving support or encouragement from their boss or an internal mentor.

Other support included job placements and the provision of an external mentor. Only 8 per cent believe that they did not receive any form of support whether in terms of finance, time off to study or simply encouragement. For all the people who took qualifications, the biggest obstacles appear to be lack of time to study and a sense that the learning was not valued by their employer since it was usually not directly used in the business. What therefore appears to be particularly valued is the combination of time to study, financial support, moral support from the boss, recognition of achievement and the chance to apply the learning.

Getting people to want to be members of your organization

Professor Robert B. Reich has identified what he calls the six 'social glues' of the company of the future:

1   *Create a sense of ownership through financial rewards, in particularly stock options.* In the UK the Chancellor's 'Shares for All' scheme announced during his 1999 Budget Statement should encourage more businesses to extend the benefits of share ownership to their employees. Under the new scheme, employees can receive a tax-free gift of shares of up to £3000 per year. Companies can also allow employees to buy up to £1500 worth of shares a year out of pre-tax earnings. With other concessions, employees will be able to receive up to £7500 worth of shares per year on tax-advantageous terms.

2   *Give individuals an opportunity to work on projects which make a real difference and where the goal aligns with personal goals and values.* Ensure that people have interesting, challenging work to do. If challenging work is a motivating factor for many people, it follows that most people will gain satisfaction from having some sort of 'stretch' in their job. Sadly, in many organizations which have shrunk their workforce to the core, some of the most interesting projects do not get offered to internal staff but to contractors. In addition, contractors tend to be paid more than existing staff, which can rub salt into the wound.

3   *Create a culture that values learning. This links with the first 'social glue' – money – learn more now and earn more in the future.* Creating a learning culture is explored in Chapter 16.

4   *Make work fun; if it isn't fun it won't attract the best talent.* Increasingly people choose to work for a company on the basis of the image portrayed of what the workgroup and working atmosphere will be like. Good people want to work with good people. In many cases, the long hours' culture means that people will not always have the time or energy for a social life. Particularly in stressful situations, having a light-hearted but professional atmosphere can be conducive to good teamwork and to people being prepared to 'go the extra mile'. When work can also be fun, the fact that one is working long hours becomes less of a problem.

5   *Create a sense of pride in the organization.* One high-flying City broker was offered the chance to double his salary if he were to join a start-up firm in the USA. The broker decided against the move on the basis that he still had plenty of work challenges where he was, and he enjoyed these. Furthermore,

he was proud to work for the long-established firm with its unblemished reputation. He was pleased to say which company he worked for at social gatherings.

In some organizations the sense of community is strong. This is engendered in many ways by little things can make a difference. In one organization, the chief executive makes a point of remembering the birthdays of staff and their partners. The CEO reflected on what had happened over time : 'it's just been a collection of things over the years which I thought were important and we've ended up with a strategy.'

6 *Value and facilitate balance with the organization.* Issues concerning balance are explored in Chapter 2. Where flexible working would be valued by employees, it should ideally be introduced. This could include establishing core time and developing contracts which include working from home or on shifts.

Helping managers to make the difference

Many surveys suggest that managers make the biggest difference to people wanting to stay. The euphoria attached to pay increases usually lasts only a few weeks, whereas the impact of a manager on the morale and motivation of his or her team can be long-lasting. HR can help by using attitude surveys to find out the facts. These can identify what the problems are, where they are and how deep they are. Some managers may need help in developing their management style to be more appropriate to the needs of their teams.

Every manager is likely to be involved in setting targets and making improvements. It is possible that some managers, especially if they have been promoted from a technical role, may lack the skills required to manage people. They may need help in understanding how to set stretch targets which keep people motivated. Guidelines can be produced to make performance appraisals a positive experience for all concerned. Continuous improvement and learning targets should be features of the process of managing for high performance. Teamwork should be encouraged and team targets set which encourage cross-departmental cooperation. In particular, managers should be encouraged to identify and get rid of the daily frustrations which sap the morale of their teams, making it easier for everyone to do a good job.

Conclusion

Many organizations are now grappling with the need to recruit and retain fresh talent. Finding good people is becoming so difficult that one HR director of a rapidly growing telecommunications company said: 'losing people should be a criminal offence'. Measuring the impact on the bottom line of retaining talent is always difficult, even with climate surveys and other forms of feedback. That same director has calculated that the cost of not retaining, and therefore having to recruit a new employee, is equivalent to two and a half times the person's salary, not to mention the loss of morale and money apparently wasted on training the departing individual. His company has invested heavily in management development from the top down. As he says, 'people don't leave organizations where they get good development'.

There is no one panacea for retaining people. Seeking to use reward as the main means of motivating people is a waste of time. Blanket solutions to individual needs tend to backfire. A more tailored yet strategic approach is most appropriate to the management of recruitment and retention.

Recruitment and retention checklist

Making excellent appointments

- Is our job analysis underpinned by the organization context, our resourcing strategy and a candidate specification?
- What would make our organization attractive/unattractive to the candidates we want to reach?
- In our recruitment strategy do we have adequate sources of candidates, effective recruiters, appropriate methods of recruitment and selection, a budget and action plan?
- Do we use the most appropriate methods of attracting candidates, e.g advertising, search, word-of-mouth, etc.?
- In managing the candidate relationship do we manage or raise expectations with regard to the job, career prospects, etc.?
- In assessing candidates do we use relevant and effective methods, e.g. assessment centres, behavioural interviews, psychometric testing, references?

- In making the decision, how do we handle the process internally?
- In integrating the new recruit into the organization, what support do we provide, e.g. induction, mentor, 'buddy'?
- In following up with the candidate after several weeks, how do we assess how well they are integrating and what their needs might be?
- In evaluating our recruitment strategies, do we take into account cost, time, effectiveness and longer-term value add?

Managing for motivation – what motivates people in our business?

- In assessing the needs and expectations of employees do we focus on the individual, the group, the department, the organization as a whole?
- How do we measure morale and satisfaction?
- What kind of management style dominates – one which restricts or shares communication or one where decision making is top-down versus participative?
- What kinds of reward systems are in use – formal (e.g. pay, benefits, bonus, promotion, other incentives), psychological – status, the nature of the job (e.g. interest, challenge)?
- What kind of work environment do we provide – physical, community, etc.? Do we provide challenging and satisfying roles?
- Is there a sense of community in this organization – and are people pleased to belong?
- How well do managers provide recognition?
- What help can HR provide to help managers with their role in retention?
- Which groups of employees are 'at risk?'
- What do we know about what motivates them?

References

Cannon, D. (1998). *Generation X and the new work ethic*, Working Paper, Demos, London.

Holbeche, L. (1998). *High Flyers and Succession Planning.* Roffey Park Management Institute.

Hope, D. (1999). Quoted in Yapp, M. and Myatt, R., How to buy staff in a seller's market, *Sunday Times*, 28 March.

Reich, R. B. (1998): The company of the future, *Fast Company*, November.

8

Strategies for developing people

The workplace is being radically reshaped in a number of ways. People are now expected to have a wide range of skills in areas such as customer relations, business awareness and leadership. The impact of technology on people's jobs is becoming ever more apparent, leading to a growing importance attached to the 'soft' skills as well as the 'hard'. Peter Cochrane, Head of Research for **BT** and a well-known futurologist, suggests that 'the future belongs to highly skilled professionals working long hours on short contracts who won't have time for the routine of daily life, which will create opportunities for others' (1998).

In this period of rapid change, the need for employees to continuously update their skills, and develop new ones, has never been greater. Few young people entering the job market these days would expect to have finished learning when they complete their formal education. Paradoxically, the pace of change and the demanding workloads of most employees act as a deterrent to conscious development. Employees will often claim that they are too busy to attend training courses and too exhausted to carry out part-time education in out of work hours. Development strategies need to take into account the reality of most people's working lives and the fact that conventional training is only one way in which people can develop, as the Roffey Park research data suggests. Development solutions can take many forms, not least using technology, and strategies should ideally be as innovative as employees are now required to be.

In creating a development strategy, it is important as ever to start with where the business is going and what that suggests in terms of the skills which will be needed. So often HR teams are criticized for developing training and development strategies which do not match business priorities. Sometimes the problem lies within the HR team itself. If the person who attends board meetings is the HR director and he or she fails to discuss strategic imperatives with the professionals charged with Human Resource Development, it is not surprising that the HRD team will do what they think is appropriate.

The development strategy should be guided by a vision and set of values. What is the philosophy which will underpin development – do you want people to be self-sufficient or do you see development as a partnership between the individual and the organization? This, of course, might vary according to the groups of employees in question, but having a broad philosophy which can be communicated to employees and provides the rationale for the choice of elements in the strategy is important.

The question which development strategies need to answer is *how do we ensure that people are developed to their full potential and maximum effectiveness?* Development needs to be focused on areas which are relevant to the individual and the organization. One employee, for instance, might need a rapid injection of job-related skills due to a change in technology. Another may have reached the stage in his or her career when a development stretch, such as a major new responsibility or an MBA programme might provide, is required. While a development strategy should be sufficiently flexible that it can adapt to individual needs, organizational priorities may take precedence. This is where having a guiding framework and criteria for decision making can be helpful.

In any development strategy there are likely to be three areas of focus:

- Organizational level, where corporate requirements such as Induction, Quality Improvement, Leadership, Customer Care and Culture Change Programmes are addressed
- Departmental/Business Unit level, where job-related training and development is likely to take place
- Individual level, where people are usually motivated to close the gap between their current and desired capabilities

Some areas of development, such as the identification of talent, high-flyer schemes and succession planning, usually involve all three levels.

It follows then that to ensure an optimum return on the time and other resources invested in development, that those activities are well targeted. This means ensuring that development activities address real needs, that appropriate solutions are offered and that these make a positive difference. Making a difference can be measured at a number of levels. Donald Kirkpatrick's (1996) evaluation framework suggests four levels:

1 Reaction – what do participants think about the activity at the time?
2 Learning – how have skills, knowledge or attitudes improved as a result of the activity?
3 Behaviour – how does participants' changed behaviour affect their constituents, e.g. their workgroup?
4 Results – how do these improved behaviours, skills and knowledge translate into bottom line impact?

Needs analysis

One way of finding out what is needed is to carry out some form of development needs analysis based on the existing workforce. There are many ways of doing this which include surveys, using existing data such as appraisal information, sampling of specific groups, benchmarking with 'world-class' organizations to identify obvious gaps etc. Clearly since development activities, especially job-related skills acquisition, should lead to enhanced performance, managers need to be involved in the process of identifying needs and providing follow-up. The analysis should provide answers to the questions:

- What is needed and why?
- Where is this needed?
- By whom?
- How will this best be provided?
- How much will this cost?
- What will the expected return look like?

Evaluation

This last point is perhaps the most critical from the business perspective. Increasingly 'hard' measures of the impact of

development activities are required. These are always notoriously difficult to distinguish from a host of other variables.
Kirkpatrick suggests the following guidelines to implementation
when trying to assess the impact of training on business results:

- Use a control group, if possible
- Allow enough time for results to be achieved
- Measure both before and after training, if feasible
- Repeat the measurement at appropriate times
- Consider the cost of evaluation versus the potential benefits
- Be satisfied with the evidence if absolute proof isn't possible
  to attain.

The link between the objectives of the individual, the development activity and the individual's performance needs to be
strong if level-four evaluation is to be credible. In one financial
services organization in the early 1990s, poor business results
meant that there was a freeze on promotions. There was also a
squeeze on management development and any spend needed to
be justified. The HRD team, in partnership with some of the
business heads, argued that the company would lose some of its
'star' employees unless some form of development was offered.
The question was, where should limited investment be focused?

The HRD team had been engaged in the identification of leadership competencies and it was decided that these could be used as the
basis of a development centre for an identified group of 'at-risk' high
flyers. The outputs of the centre were to be information which individuals could use to drive their personal development plans with
their managers. To ensure that these plans could be relevant, managers were involved before and after the event in identifying individual objectives and in providing on-the-job coaching. Managers
clearly needed, and received, careful briefing about their role.

Individuals and managers needed to discuss and agree, prior
to the event, what the individual's main development needs were
relative to the competencies. Various tools were provided,
including 360-degree feedback, to help them to prioritize objectives. They had to be quite specific about how addressing that
need would help. So they had to answer questions such as:

- If you were to learn to deal better with that situation, what
  difference would that make to you, to other people and the
  business?

- How will you know that you are making progress on that objective? How will you deal differently with the situation? How will people respond differently to you? What difference will that make to you, to others and to the business?

Participants came with very clear objectives and measures of success in mind. They were therefore active partners with the HRD and Management team who were delivering the activities to ensure that the centre met their needs.

Immediately following the centre, individuals met with their manager and agreed a practical action plan to build on the outputs of the centre. The participants were followed up over the next eighteen months at three- and six-monthly intervals. The results were impressive. In addition to the 'soft' targets of the centre, such as making people feel valued, boosting morale etc., there were many examples of the impact on the bottom line of improved performance as a result of people taking part in the centre. One participant was able to pinpoint how, by changing his own leadership style as a result of the feedback and coaching he had received, he had managed his own team more effectively (and the team agreed). Nothing else had changed – it was the same team, and the market conditions were just as tough. However, within a year of the centre, that team had outperformed all other comparable teams, producing millions of pounds' worth of extra sales revenue.

Pressure to prove that development activities add value is usually at its worst when business results mean that every item of expenditure needs to be justified. However, carrying out evaluations on this scale can be time consuming and costly too, except that the costs are likely to be hidden. Indeed, a CIPD survey (1999) found that employers significantly underestimate how much they are spending on training and development. This is partly because salaries of trainers and trainees are usually excluded when costs are calculated except in sectors such as local government where the purchaser/provider accountability split still focuses minds on true costs. The survey revealed that 25 per cent of organizations did not have training budgets and nearly 35 per cent have budgets which cover only the costs of external courses.

Marilyn McDougall and Angela Mulvie (1997) carried out a study of how companies measure the impact of HRM to the bottom line. They found that currently many organizations make access to management knowledge and skills available on a general basis to employees as part of a philosophy of continuous learning. Participants are therefore not expected to produce improved bottom line results thanks to the training in the short term, though the researchers predict that this situation might change.

Prioritizing development needs using competencies

The need to ensure that training and other forms of development are tailored to the business requirements as well as to those of individuals is evident in the widespread use of competency-based development processes. These should ensure that development opportunities are targeted to meet specific objectives for the relevant individuals. Some organizations are offering managers 360-degree feedback based on a range of competencies. One software company, for instance, provides feedback from skilled facilitators followed by a range of optional workshops which managers can choose according to the needs identified through the feedback.

Competencies can be used to develop self-assessment questionnaires and other feedback processes to ensure that individual needs are understood. Ensuring that development opportunities are appropriately targeted may prove more difficult. It is useful to identify shortlists of priority areas of management development for the short, medium and long term. In the medium term there may be significant merits in standardizing role descriptions using competencies to define the skilled components of each role. In the short term, management development effort may perhaps produce best effect when applied to specific business objectives and particular groups or individuals according to relevant criteria for prioritizing such as:

Business needs
- The current short- to medium-term business strategy. If, for example, the current main business priority is maintaining quality standards, it may seem inappropriate to put effort into *change management* and *leadership*. Conversely, if the management team wishes to prepare the organization for ongoing change, these competencies become priorities
- The biggest obstacles in terms of management skills or behaviour to achieving the overall business goals, i.e. does the

lack of certain competencies prevent the organization from maximizing opportunities or actually cause operating problems?

- The specific priorities of different business groups
- What managers would like to develop
- Cultural priorities.

Typically, it may be helpful to focus on areas which are broadly perceived to be key competencies and which are also seen as development needs.

Building to strengths

Focusing development on areas which people consider strengths may seem contradictory. However, there is a reasonable amount of research evidence to suggest that people are usually motivated to even higher levels of performance when they are working on areas in which they feel they are effective.

Cultural needs

In one UK local authority, there was common agreement among senior managers that employees within the borough would increasingly be required to work corporately, as the effect of various local and central government initiatives work their way through. However, a management review revealed that employees generally did not attach much importance to developing corporate working practice, other than to recognize this as an area of weakness. Similarly, while many employees acknowledged the need for change they were well aware of a 'blame culture' in which mistakes are punished. The management approach appeared to emphasize tight management of current systems, at the expense of encouraging experimentation and learning.

Leadership training was recommended in which change management and developing a learning culture were key themes. In this organization it is particularly important that chief officers and directors take the lead in attending the training to demonstrate the importance attached to the issues. Given the inevitable role modelling implicit in senior roles, senior managers need to reinforce the leadership messages through their behaviour.

Prioritizing resource allocation according to different development needs

How do the strengths and development needs of managers, high flyers and directors differ? Roffey Park has carried out research into the effects of the changing workplace on employees for a number of years. Two surveys carried out in 1998 highlight the needs employees perceive with regard to the skills required to do their jobs. One survey, the Management Agenda was completed by a cross-sector population of managers mainly based in the UK. The sample was a good mix of junior, middle and senior managers as well as people who were running their own companies. The other survey was a focused look at the needs of high flyers in 400 organizations.

The surveys asked both groups about their current skills and strengths. In both surveys, the information supplied was a self-assessment and may be viewed differently by people reporting to the individuals surveyed. The top skills of the 'Agenda' group reflected the broadly 'people management' aspects of their role and were as follows:

- Interpersonal
- Communication
- Flexibility
- People management
- Organization/planning
- Analytical
- Presentation
- Motivational
- Leadership
- Coaching

The high flyers had a similar range of skills and strengths but there were some different priorities in terms of job focus. For nearly half of this group, developing strategy is their key priority with other responsibilities for managing a team, building and maintaining relationships with clients and managing the financial side of the business. These priorities reflect the business focus and direction setting so often associated with high flyers. Similarly, the emphasis given to managing a team and managing relationships with clients suggests that people-related activities are important. However, the high flyer group as a whole placed little priority on issues relating to customer satisfaction and quality management or training and development.

Not surprisingly, the current skills and strengths of the high flyers reflected their priorities to a large extent as follows:

- Communication
- Managing people
- Strategic thinking
- Interpersonal
- Business
- Financial
- Political/influencing

Organization/planning skills, analytical and leadership skills were seen as strengths by a small percentage of the high flyer sample. Interestingly, although almost half the group saw strategy as their key priority, a rather smaller percentage of the group (35 per cent) considered strategic thinking to be a strength. Many more people reported that they knew they should be operating strategically, but that day-to-day work pressures and the 'comfort factor' attached to doing an operational role meant that in reality many senior managers were failing to take a leadership role with regard to developing the organization. The probability that these individuals were failing to delegate appropriately was high.

The survey asked both groups what they believed were the skills they needed to develop to equip them for their current role (i.e. short term). The Agenda group's needs were as follows:

- Political/influencing skills
- Strategic thinking skills
- IT skills
- Financial
- Entrepreneurial
- Leadership
- Business
- Change management

This group appears to be mainly in implementation roles, with an emphasis on raising or maintaining quality. Ideally, these managers should have opportunities to improve processes across their organization. Without making this overly complex, senior managers can improve the efficiency of services while developing themselves at the same time. They may need help in project management skills, including dealing with third parties as work is increasingly put out to tender. The art of managing a flexible workforce is somewhat more challenging than managing a directly managed staff.

Development needs of high flyers

The high flyer group perceived some short-term development needs in IT although 17 per cent of the total sample felt that they needed no more skills to do their current job. People saying this tended to be older and/or to have been in their current role for some time. While this is no reason to assume that people are stagnating, there is the possibility that people are in roles which have become too 'easy' for them. New business skills may also be needed to continue to be successful in today's changing organizations. Peter Cochrane suggests that in the new millennium

> ...the big bucks will be earned by 'data gurus' – specialists who can navigate their way through the information overload with ease and tell you what you need to know. At the very least, you're going to have to be computer literate to earn a living – or even get in your front door. But you don't have to become a nerd.

The skills people felt would equip them for future success were diverse. The main areas were as follows:

- Business
- Political/influencing
- Managing people
- Communication
- Leadership
- Interpersonal

Interestingly, rather at odds with current management trends, this group does not see the ability to coach and develop others as crucial to future success. This may reflect the pragmatic reality that in many organizations promotion to senior positions has not depended on a manager being an effective 'people person'. However, as many organizations are attempting to integrate culture change objectives with succession planning, this may change. A number of the organizations referred to in Chapter 11 are now screening candidates for senior roles on the basis of how they demonstrate leadership behaviours.

How do high flyers learn best?

The majority of high flyers in our survey considered their biggest learning experience to be having been 'thrown in at the deep end'. This was backed up by remarks about needing to 'achieve against all the difficulties'. In many cases, their learning had occurred by being given special projects, often without fully adequate resources and being left to get on with it. This suggests that some of the best forms of development for high flyers are to give them specific responsibility for challenging projects, especially if they need to negotiate for some of the resources required. However, what also came across strongly was that people only considered the effort worthwhile if their achievement was recognized by others. Lack of recognition of a major achievement can be disheartening for anyone but is particularly damaging to a high flyer.

Other ways of learning involved one or a combination of the following:

- Studying, especially MBAs
- Training, though mainly linked with other interests than work
- Dealing with office politics
- Dealing with people generally, but managing a team in particular
- Doing the job, as long as the job has plenty of challenge and variety
- Learning about yourself, often through personal development groups or simply reflecting
- Risk-taking, often involving a change of personal direction
- Learning from hardships
- International experience
- Family/life experiences

People who were studying for MBAs seemed to find most value in the kinds of courses where their studies related directly to their own work. MBAs are particularly useful for developing strategic thinking ability as well as general management knowledge, but the real challenge for the HRD team is to ensure that the learning is transferred to the workplace. One of the main causes of disillusionment in fact was where people felt that there was no opportunity to put their enhanced skills to good use in the workplace.

Supporting the development of high flyers

For the majority of high flyers in the survey, having the chance to achieve was of paramount importance. This suggests that job roles should provide opportunities for significant challenge, but that managers of high flyers and others need to be able to give effective recognition to keep the high flyer feeling valued. Qualifications were seen to offer a useful 'stretch' by many people and they are a means of retaining people while they are studying.

The challenge for organizations, especially HR professionals, is to understand how better use can be made of higher-level skills. To some extent, the choice of qualification or course programme can make a difference as to whether the skills are seen to be useful to the organization. Some MBA programmes focus more obviously on applied project work based on participants' own work rather than relying largely on case studies. Organizations are likely to benefit from this approach during and beyond the period of study and individuals are also likely to gain the opportunities to apply their skills. Indeed, some companies such as British Airways sponsor their own MBA programmes to ensure that outputs are geared to the business and that assignments are work-based. Managers who have been through the programme form a network providing support to new cohorts of students.

Although most of the high flyers in the survey considered that they were 'self-starters', many acknowledged that other people had been influential in their development. One of the biggest forms of help was supportive (senior) management. This often took the form of senior management involvement in young high flyer schemes as well as the attention paid by senior management to project work being carried out by high flyers.

Almost a third said that supportive colleagues had helped them. There were many examples of networks of individuals who have developed a collegial relationship, despite individual differences and rivalries. One group of (female) chief executives of **NHS** trusts formed such a network following a leadership development programme. The group provides mutual support and encouragement as well as practical sharing of ideas. However, what several members of such groups suggested was that it was important that such networks be exclusive in terms of level, so that people of roughly the same seniority would be sharing ideas.

Some people acknowledge help from a mentor other than their line manager, but for the majority, recognition by the line manager was crucial. Younger high flyers particularly valued the coaching and feedback provided by helpful line managers. In short, the most effective organizational support appears to be provided by people who are interested in the high flyer's development.

Similarly, the biggest blocks to development appear to be other people, especially unhelpful management. When compounded by an atmosphere of rampant organizational politics, many high flyers felt unable to achieve. In some organizations, a blame culture acted as a disincentive to risk-taking, one of the main sources of learning for high flyers.

Ideally human resource managers should have a conversation with each of the high flyers in their organization to find out what really motivates them and to see to what extent their needs can be accommodated. Through such individual attention it may be possible to give people at different stages of their career the chance to move into more challenging roles which do not necessarily involve promotion. In some cases this may require the organization to display greater flexibility. More details of approaches to developing high flyers can be found in Chapter 11.

Directors

Many of the high flyers, if they are not already directors, aspire to 'high level positions'. In a separate and ongoing study of the development needs of directors, known as *The Strategic Leader as Learner* (Holbeche, 1994), a number of chief executives, managing directors and directors have been interviewed since 1994. In this brief extract from one interview, the Chief Executive of an arts organization was asked about his current skills, as well as those required for the future:

Q   *What skills, knowledge, experience etc. are required in your current role?*

A

- A thorough understanding of the processes of the (business) at all levels.
- Wide management experience covering a range of activities.
- Experience of dealing with unions, human resources, health and safety.
- Knowledge and understanding of profit-making activities, e.g. catering and bookshops.
- Good negotiating skills, communication skills and the ability to persuade and influence people at all levels.

Q   *What areas of skill would you like to develop beyond their current levels?*

A

- The ability to think really creatively about the problems which present themselves and then achieve a logical and systematic resolution to those problems. Very often these are not new problems and I would like to be able to think creatively about the best long-term solutions. This will prevent what happens at the moment which very often feels like firefighting.
- The need for more detailed future planning particularly in the area of communication will also become increasingly important. As strategies/policies change, people need to understand why.

This survey suggests that many directors need an:

- Injection of creative thinking into their current work
- Understanding of how other organizations deal with similar issues
- Ability to take a longer-term view of situations and problems that are going to arise
- Ability to provide improved leadership
- Ability to help managers develop

Interestingly, on the last point, management trainers had been called in to assist a large PLC to train managers in coaching skills. The last group to go through the workshop were the most senior. The trainers reported the experience of working with this group as 'odd'. Of all the groups who had been through the programme, this was the least skilled at helping others to develop.

They needed plenty of coaching before they were able to drop their 'arrogantly fearful' mask of not taking the issues too seriously. The HR director who took part in this workshop found the process illuminating and worrying: 'it's given me an interesting insight into how our senior managers work – they don't bring people on.'

Innovation

Arguably one of the key priorities for directors should be to provide a strategic direction for the organization. This is likely to require them to be innovative or at least to recognise and nurture innovative ideas in others. In *Innovation at the Top* (1999) a survey of 120 CEOs, main board directors and senior managers was supplemented with focus groups and interviews with directors who were known for their innovative approaches. The research focused on two issues: what informs decisions of senior managers and directors and what inspires creative decisions.

The findings revealed that for many directors the pace of change can drive out the ability to innovate. For the majority, their flashes of inspiration occur outside work on the whole, while carrying out innocuous and seemingly unrelated activities such as listening to Radio 4 or taking the dog for a walk. In addition to the amount of work and the pace of change, it seems that the weight of Western tradition with its preference for structured, analytical thinking can militate against the more radical and innovative thinking so often required in the development of strategy, new products etc. According to Jean Lammimann and Michel Syrett (1999), authors of the report:

> Right brain thinking, which exists on a metaphorical and spatial plane, is the stuff of which new ideas are made. It sits uneasily in the context of a management culture founded on a rational process of thought that is presumed to result in informed and effective business decisions.

How can directors be developed?

Directors have a primary leadership role and represent role models to other senior managers. It is therefore essential that they are seen to take the lead in any development. Some of the most effective development takes place when directors have the opportunity to meet informally for off-site sessions to address strategic issues. These are likely to be most effective when directors focus on major topics to the exclusion of mundane tasks. Sometimes short, issue-based events such as conferences are a means of exposing directors to ideas from outside the organization. Some companies have formed consortia who create an agenda for a series of 'masterclasses' provided by a management guru or leading business figure. These are often supplemented by visits to consortia members' sites so that directors can come to understand other companies' issues and ways of handling them.

Given the importance of directors developing fresh ideas for their organization, the relationship between time and creativity appears to be a key issue according to the *Innovation at the Top* research. The workplace is likely to be the main forum for idea development and a routine which encourages creative thinking would be an asset. Many directors are keen teamworkers and prefer to develop strategy with a colleague and speak regularly with NEDs about broad business issues. Similarly, while the research suggests that directors tend to shy away from formal programmes like a benchmarking group, it may be helpful for directors to join or establish an informal development network with groups of peers from other organizations. It may be possible for visits to other companies to take place which can be used both as informal benchmarking and as a means of bringing back different approaches to management and leadership.

Key skills for directors – leadership, strategic thinking and change management

The problems in developing senior managers often lie in getting them to sign up to the need for some development. This may be because they consider development of any sort as remedial, or that they believe they should be 'good' at everything because they are senior. It may be the case that they have not received direct feedback from constituents and are therefore unaware of how they affect the organization. In numerous surveys, these competencies appear to be areas of relative weakness within the senior management across all sectors. Senior managers need to be willing to open themselves up to new learning and to own the output of development programmes.

Ideally, these related competencies can be addressed through a strategic leadership programme of some sort. Given the learning preferences of directors, this is likely to be a relatively short e.g. a three-day training programme which introduces some key ideas, followed by a number of follow-on meetings on specific themes. These meetings could take the form of seminars or 'content-free' learning groups where the emphasis is on managers' own learning objectives. Ideally, such a process should be linked to an actual change initiative or set of activities to provide a context and rationale.

Ideally, all senior managers within an organization should experience a similar programme so that the benefits of shared messages and experiences build up in a way which reinforces good practice. Typically, some of the most effective ways of developing leaders involve the use of feedback processes, such as upward or 360-degree feedback. The design of such a programme should have a practical focus and lead to action. Ideally, senior managers should work in teams to undertake real organizational or business projects after the training programme which allow them to transfer the benefits of their shared learning directly to the business.

Supporting managers' development

Creating a self-development culture

Development should be seen as primarily the individual's responsibility but encouraged and supported by the organization. A newsletter which regularly focuses on development achievements will convey the message that development is taken seriously, especially when directors contribute. Similarly, where people set themselves development targets they should be encouraged to identify the organizational benefits (including bottom line) of what they are planning to do. That way, people's development can be more clearly understood and celebrated in terms of its contribution to organizational effectiveness.

In the medium term, reward systems should be enhanced to reflect people development. Managers should be rewarded on the achievement of people development targets and individuals should ideally be offered a small bonus, or a slightly higher salary if their improved skills enhance their contribution. The appraisal scheme can be supplemented, if this has not yet happened, with a development planning process. This again calls upon line managers to be willing and able to hold development discussions with individuals.

Enabling development through competencies

People should be encouraged to move jobs around the organization, acquiring different forms of experience. Competencies can be helpful in facilitating this process in that job requirements can be defined in ways which enable people to undertake a realistic self-assessment. Job profiles can be updated and specific technical competencies defined. This way, a data bank of people requiring specific forms of development can be matched against available options. There may also be opportunities for job swaps and secondments if resourcing is a problem. The increased mobility of staff can also be supported by greater awareness of the roles of different business groups. This can be encouraged by briefings hosted by different business groups at their place of work.

Methods of learning

On the job

It seems that most senior managers learn best by experience. On-the-job learning is therefore likely to be the primary source of development. Given the importance of this form of learning, it is essential that managers arc able to support people with their development as well as their current performance.

- One of the key sources of development on the job is having some challenge, without being 'stretched' to breaking point. Challenges come in various forms and have greater or lesser motivational effect depending on the individual. Typically, a rewarding form of development occurs when someone is given responsibility for a venture whose outcome is not guaranteed, where the outcome is important and noted by others. It is important that achievements should be recognized by others, especially managers, and appropriate rewards (even if only a show of esteem) be given.
- Another key source of learning is variety. This can also take many forms, including the chance to try new things, meet

new people, develop new work interests. Again, imaginative problem solving between manager and direct report can assist in identifying opportunities for variety in any job, however mundane. Having the opportunity to represent your employer at a conference, for instance, can be useful.

- Ironically, hardships are apparently a major source of development, providing that people are able to recover some learning from the experience. Some people may find the ongoing cost-cutting approach represents a form of hardship. Focusing on how to overcome difficulties can generate positive and creative solutions. Having a (peer) mentor can help in this process.
- Other people, especially bosses, are a major source of development. The role-modelling effect is strong and emphasizes the importance of training senior managers to act consistently with organizational values.

A few major corporations have trained directors to be career counsellors for other people. This is an organization-wide responsibility, rather than being restricted to direct reporting relationships. Each director takes on a small 'caseload' of people who are regarded as key to the future, but for whom there may be no immediate prospect of promotion. The benefits in the form of improved morale and retention of key people can be great.

Training

Many of the managers in the Roffey Park survey referred to various types of training as the main form of organizational support for development. The CIPD survey also found that traditional classroom-based training is still popular and is expected to grow. This survey found that the main strategic business objectives for investing in training were:

- Organizational development (89 per cent)
- Increasing returns on investment (77 per cent)
- Improving market share and increasing the levels of product innovation (66 per cent).

Training can be helpful for both awareness raising and skills development. There are clear benefits, for instance, in raising senior managers' awareness of the strategic issues for their organization through briefings and networks. The majority of respondents, however, considered that most of their development took place on the job, or outside work. A number of criticisms of training provision can be summed up in the following typical comment:

> I'm concerned about the lack of structure in my development (which has led to poor timing in some events), a lack of personal involvement in decisions and I feel that some of the formal training was too general in character and therefore did not relate specifically to my needs.

This lack of tailoring to individual needs is perhaps inevitable if a 'sheepdip' approach to training is still taken. There is also the danger that managers will resort to training as a remedial solution to a 'people problem' rather than thinking more creatively about how a person might be developed. Ideally, any training solution should allow people to come up with solutions themselves, rather than simply forcing them through hoops. There is often little awareness about how people can be developed on the job. In many organizations, cultural and staff surveys highlight the same issue with monotonous regularity: line managers do not know how to help other people to develop. They are often perceived to be too busy, unsupportive, have inappropriate management styles or simply do not see developing others as part of their role.

Mentoring and coaching

In many organizations, tools are now provided to encourage self-development, including the use of development centres and learning resource centres. Some were assisted in areas such as people management by a mentor, though in very few cases were mentoring relationships established as part of a formal scheme. Coaching and mentoring can be helpful but line managers generally need training in relevant approaches. One manager described the benefits she had gained from skilled coaching:

> When I first joined the **NHS** I expected that success meant promotion every eighteen months. One-to-one coaching from my manager cured me of this blinkered, black and white approach.

Many organizations such as **British-American Tobacco**, have trained managers in coaching skills and the trend towards the 'line manager as developer' is well established. In some companies, managers' ability to help others to develop is now taken into account when bonuses are being allocated. Learning groups are increasingly being used in a number of organizations such as **ICL** and the former **Glaxo-Wellcome**. These can enable individual needs to be met in the work context.

Some organizations are introducing peer mentoring to address both organizational needs for teamwork and greater collaboration and individual needs for support. Peer mentoring involves two, three or more individuals agreeing to have a development relationship with one another. This is primarily a development relationship with the clear purpose of supporting individuals to achieve their job objectives. HR can help such relationships to be established through creating a mechanism whereby peers can identify likely peer 'resources'. Often this is through the use of a database on which information is stored about people who have specific expertise and are willing to act as peer mentors. These can be matched against people who express specific needs.

Sometimes people are looking for a mentoring relationship with someone from another part of the business simply so that they can increase their understanding of how that part of the business operates. Other people wish to link up with individuals who have developed their careers in particular ways within organizations. HR can help people to think through their objectives and give some guidance on how to approach peers with a view to forming a formal mentoring relationship.

Ideally the relationship should offer reciprocal benefits for it to work. One example is a training manager and a human resources manager from the same organization who were called on to work on the same major project for a period of several months. There was a history of some hostility between the two departments which they represented, and, as individuals, they did not warm to each other's styles. However, they took the decision to go through a formal contracting process to see if they could help each other. The project proved to have benefits for both individuals and their departments. The individuals concerned now have a much greater understanding of one another's needs and what they can offer.

Learning opportunities using computers

Many pundits predict a huge growth in on-line learning in the next few years. This is driven by shortage of time to attend training and the increasingly global spread of organizations which makes training solutions costly. Research by the Chartered Institute of Personnel and Development (1999) found that only one quarter of organizations used the Internet or intranets for training and development, but forecast that there would be a 70 per cent increase in the early years of the new millennium. Similarly, CD-ROM usage is expected to grow by 60 per cent of respondents in the CIPD survey.

Prudential Portfolio Managers is the investment–management arm of the Prudential Corporation which employs 1000 people in various global locations. The challenge is to provide development opportunities without requiring employees to be constantly travelling. Nick Holley, director of Prudential Portfolio Managers UK says:

'The biggest issue is time. Personal development is seen as important but not urgent, so it is easy to put off.' A new on-line system which allows for just-in-time training has been launched called 'I'. This is described informally as a global virtual university and covers eleven technical areas such as portfolio management, and generic skills such as delegation and performance management.

Knowledge management has been built into the system. When an employee enters a particular learning area, the first page supplies the names and contact details of other employees with expertise in the area who are willing to provide support. Each learning area provides information on training courses including a wide range of externally run courses and lists other development resources available from the company's open learning centres. There is also a list of recommended reading which was created through a deal with a bookshop which supplied a list of the best books on a given topic.

The system gives employees on-line access via the intranet to a management training system operated by a UK management centre. This gives people the resources they need to manage their own learning following an assessment of their skill needs. The system covers topics such as teamworking, strategic awareness, leadership and financial awareness. Various toolkits allow people to apply management models to their own circumstances.

Conclusion

The need for employees at all levels to be involved in ongoing development – of new skills, exposure to new experiences and learning to learn – is apparent. HR can work towards creating a culture in which learning is valued and supported, and where the enhanced skills of the individual are put to good use. In such a development culture the pressure to measure a return on every development activity may be less strong than in a culture which believes that any off-line activity is a cost. Individuals can take responsibility for managing their development. After all, it is in their interest to do so, but the organization can help 'kick-start' the process by providing people with the opportunity to understand what to develop and how.

Ironically, pressure of work in some cases is so strong or the company ethos so 'macho' that people are not always prepared to learn, especially through training. Various innovative approaches such as 'just-in-time' training, using on-line resources, can help, but sometimes the best form of development is when individuals take themselves to a residential training programme and make time to reflect. Senior managers in particular are important role models in both learning and valuing learning. They set the tone and need to be willing to exercise some old fashioned command and control with regard to development. Encouraging people to prioritize development, whose returns to the business may not be immediate, over short-term business demands, at least occasionally, may well produce larger returns in the long run.

Checklist for development needs

The changing nature of work and implications for development

- Will there continue to be a demand for the types of service or product we currently offer?
- What will this mean for the kinds of skills and competencies which will be required of those providing the service or product, e.g. will they need more/less specialist knowledge, greater flexibility etc.?
- How buoyant is the employment market for these kinds of skills? What will these mean in terms of ease of recruitment?
- How many alliances or joint ventures does the organization currently operate? How well are they working? Are there some alliances which the organization should be forming to deliver a better service to clients?

- Will people be required to work in various forms of alliance in the future? What will this mean in terms of training needs, working practices and HR policies?
- How often do we review the nature of people's work tasks?
- What proportion of employees are working on areas where their knowledge and competencies are best used?
- How will work be distributed? What will HR's role be in redistributing staff rather than recruiting additional staff?
- How are the roles of specialists changing? Will they need to function at a higher level in several areas, rather than one? What will be the priority areas for professional/technical training and development? How will people be counselled about possible role change?
- How will 'knowledge workers' work with 'service providers'?
- To what extent does the organization's current structure work well? What could be done to improve it?
- With which management systems is our organization most comfortable?
- Are these still effective, or do they need to be changed?

Development

Is this organization developing its staff and securing employee commitment?

- What are the current top development priorities for the organization?
- How will addressing these help the organization to move forward?
- How will we resource the top priorities ? Will we use external support?
- What costs will be involved in addressing the top priorities?
- What should we focus on in training and development?
- How wide a choice of development methods do we currently use?
- How do people in our organization prefer to learn?
- How flexible is learning design to meet different learning needs?
- How much do we/should we use technology to help people to develop?
- Are people encouraged to attend training and other forms of development in work time?

- How well selected and trained are people who act as mentors on formal programmes?
- What mechanisms are in place to encourage peer mentoring?
- What practical tools are provided to ensure that people can manage their own development?
- How easy is it for people to access information about development opportunities?
- Who are the best role models of line managers as coach? How can they help their peers to improve their skills?
- What help can be given to ensure that line managers provide effective follow-up after training to help transfer learning to the workplace?
- What cost/benefit analysis is carried out on development opportunities?
- How effective are our evaluation methods?

References

Cochrane, P. (1998). Quoted in Parrish, J., Just the job. *Evening Standard*, 20 April.

Holbeche, L. (1994). *The Strategic Leader as Learner*. Roffey Park Management Institute.

Institute of Personnel and Development (1999). *Training and development in Britain, 1999: The First IPD Annual Report*, April.

Kirkpatrick, D. (1996). Revisiting Kirkpatrick's four-level model, *Training and Development*, January.

Lammiman, J. and Syrett, M. (1999). *Innovation at the Top: Where do Directors Get their Ideas from?* Roffey Park Management Institute.

McDougall, M. and Mulvie, A. (1997). HRM's contribution to strategic change: measuring impact on the bottom line, *Strategic Change*.

Rogers, A. (1999). Desktop menus offer quick training snacks, *Sunday Times*, Financial Appointments, 30 May.

Seven out of ten German employees, despite their involvement in the running of their enterprises, would change jobs for better prospects, more flexible hours or better pay, according to a survey carried out by Gemini Consulting. Similar findings were reported from thirteen other developed nations. Insecurity is a major factor behind the findings, with two-thirds of those polled having been directly affected by downsizing or restructuring (Whiteley, 1998).

Back in 1994 the author began to investigate what was happening to people's careers in organizations that were changing their structures, in particular flattening them by removing management layers. At that time, delayering was often linked with downsizing to produce a leaner, meaner organization which could meet the challenges of the recent recession and the impact of technology and come out on top. The research involved organizations across the sectors both internationally and in the UK and found some interesting trends which the author has been following up with the same organizations and individuals over the past three years (see Holbeche 1995, 1997a).

The changing psychological contract

The last few years have seen some of the old 'truths' about the nature of employment in the West being fundamentally shaken. These 'truths' or expectations have been described as the 'psychological contract' between employer and employee. It used to go something like this: as long as the employee was doing a good job they might expect continuing employment and be able to contemplate promotion up the career ladder. In return, the employer expected high levels of performance and loyalty from employees.

However much the reality of working life differed from this, when flatter structures came along they challenged the expectation about career development being 'onwards and upwards'. Organizations were simultaneously telling employees that they were responsible for managing their own career, while shedding jobs and abandoning previous career management practices which maintained the myth that careers could be planned. Linked with continuing organizational change and uncertainty, jobs for life have become a thing of the past. In their place organizations talked of offering employability to employees in return for versatility and multi-skilled outputs, plus a willingness to find other employment gracefully when they were no longer needed. The author's recent research set out to explore how much of this was actually happening and whether the shape of the career landscape has really altered. The changing psychological contract has various implications for HR. In this chapter we focus on its effect on career strategies. We have already looked at balance issues in Chapter 2, and return to issues of organizational learning in Chapter 16.

The effect of flatter structures on employees

So how have flatter structures affected people? In the first stages of the Roffey Park research (1994–96) an overwhelmingly negative picture emerged. People complained of continuing uncertainty, lack of career development, overwork, long hours, stress and increased political behaviour. The effect on roles was dramatic: many people were unclear what their role was or how to succeed and managers were frequently described as not walking the talk of empowerment. Senior managers, on the other hand, complained that people were not willing to become accountable, that there was little innovation and risk-taking, and that 'plateaued performers' were unwilling to rise to the challenges of developing the new skills and attitudes required.

The growth of flatter structures

In the 1997 research phase and the return of growth in many countries, the author was interested to find that talk of flatter structures was as widespread as ever, even in organizations which appear to retain up to fourteen organization layers from the bottom to the top of the hierarchy. Why should this be? It's almost as if organizations are expecting employees to adopt the mindset which goes hand in hand with flatter structures. In other words, to be flexible, willing to learn new things and to develop at the same organizational level even though many of the structures, processes, management styles and rewards are firmly rooted in the old hierarchy.

It is easy to understand why organizations should want to have their cake and eat it. Flatter structures seem to offer the potential of a wide range of benefits since they should make possible greater teamworking, customer-driven processes and the elimination of waste. After all, who needs checkers checking checkers? Flatter structures should also make it possible for 'more' to be truly achieved by 'less' if people are able to work to their potential in an 'empowered' environment. The theory also suggests that employees can also have more rewarding and fulfilling jobs in such an environment. Yet it seems that the extent to which these potential benefits are actually being achieved is very patchy indeed. On the one hand, businesses are finding that flatter structures are helping them to be more profitable and that there is increased teamworking. Much of the increased profitability is essentially short-term since it relies on savings achieved on headcount and accommodation. On the other hand, how much people are experiencing job satisfaction and developing new forms of career is debatable.

New forms of career development?

The research found, for instance, that, contrary to the rhetoric of flatter structures, promotions are still happening but perhaps for a different group of people than in the past. In the research sample, one fifth had been promoted in the past two years, but these tended to be people who were already relatively senior. An interesting group of young high-flyers also appears to be zooming through the ranks. Several examples were found of managing directors below or about the age of thirty. One of the biggest challenges for this super-elite involves leading management teams who are significantly older than themselves. Interestingly, many of the people who had been promoted had no intention of staying with their organization for very long, suggesting perhaps that promotion can no longer secure loyalty.

For other people, remaining at the same level appears to be becoming a reality, with ever-widening gaps appearing between levels. The people who appear to be most dissatisfied are those whose jobs have remained the same as two years ago, but demands on them have grown. These people spoke of lack of career development, continuing uncertainty, poor leadership and inappropriate rewards. It was almost as if frustrated career hopes caused people to be extremely dissatisfied with the organization and its systems, although many people still claimed to be relatively loyal to their employer. Nevertheless, this group were mostly looking for other jobs outside their current organization.

In contrast, people whose jobs have grown in some way, albeit at the same level, seem generally happy to stay with their current employer. It was this group who reported most of the benefits of flatter structures, such as having greater autonomy, teamwork, more challenging and satisfying roles. Though still at the same level, many of these people spoke of having opportunities for career development. One woman, for instance, works for an electricity company where she was previously responsible for facilities management at one plant. As the company has grown, her role has expanded to include responsibility for all plant facilities, becoming consequently more strategic, rather than purely operational. These people tended to be less concerned about pay issues or the competence of leaders, though it is arguable that it may be only a matter of time before these energized performers also become dissatisfied if their enhanced skills are not appropriately recognized and rewarded.

The paradoxical effects of flatter structures on roles

There are many contradictory effects on people's roles. On the one hand, there appears to be a widespread trend towards generalist roles, with people being encouraged to become multiskilled project team members. In many organizations specialist roles are still being outsourced. On the other hand, there appears to be an increasing requirement for new kinds of specialists, who can simultaneously be experts in their fields but also think and act as business people. For many IT and Human Resource professionals, for instance, this means being able to provide credible, value-added services in a consultancy capacity.

Some of the most paradoxical effects are to be found in managerial roles. Many of the people whose jobs have disappeared during the period of the research were in junior line management roles. Arguably, increased use of technology is likely to see this trend continue. Some senior managers considered their roles to have narrowed in organizations where staff at more junior levels are 'empowered' to do things which would previously have been within the remit of the boss. Yet in other ways there seems to be more demand for management roles than ever. With continuing trends towards outsourcing and the growth of the flexible or contract workforce, many managers find themselves these days coordinating the work of people who have no formal links with the organization other than through temporary contracts. As such, managers become the 'glue' which holds teams and projects together.

Similarly, many managers have seen their spans of control expand considerably, and fashionable trends towards the line manager as developer have simultaneously applied pressure on managers to provide appropriate support to their teams, while preventing them from having the time to do this. In British government departments, for instance, many senior civil servants whose previous role was to supply policy advice now find themselves being encouraged to take on a much more obvious people-development role, enabling those lower down the hierarchy to provide advice to ministers. Ironically, many ministers, and indeed customers of other organizations, are out of step with the 'empowered' environment since they still expect to be in contact only with the person 'in charge'.

How much people are really adjusting their career expectations is questionable, which is hardly surprising given the mass of conflicting messages at large in many organizations. 'Manage your own career' sits uneasily alongside the more obvious ways in which high-flyer and 'fast-track' schemes are returning, providing rapid advancement for the privileged few. Nevertheless, some people do appear to have successfully managed to make their mark in these changing organization structures. One piece of the research involved interviewing individuals who were considered by their organizations to be indispensable, to see if these individuals had anything in common which might provide a 'success template' for careers in flatter structures.

A 'success template'?

The things which these people had in common were broadly that they all viewed change as inevitable and generally had a positive and even opportunistic approach towards it, being able to take some risks. None of them thought or acted like victims and they all seemed able to learn from mistakes without reproaching themselves. They were good at making things happen and skilled at interpersonal relations. They were visible and good at networking inside and outside the organization. They all had a strong sense of what was important to them. Ironically, two thirds of this group had left their organizations two years later, mostly because they were frustrated at the slow rate of change. Loyalty to themselves was a higher priority than loyalty to the organization. These were people truly able to manage their career. The very skills which made them valuable also made them employable and able to exercise choice.

It will be interesting to see what happens over the next few years. Although organizational trends do seem to have a built-in pendulum effect, the shift to lean but effective structures which allow for organizational effectiveness and individual growth seems set to continue. As long as there is a good balance between both sets of needs, flatter structures may provide the longer-term keys to survival and success for organizations. To bring about that balance may require major shifts of thinking, management style and investment strategies on the part of organizations and a willingness to learn and develop new ways of thinking about careers on the part of employees. While few employees seem to be considering the kind of portfolio, freewheeling careers predicted by many pundits, flatter organization structures may yet provide the means of developing the skills and experiences which should ensure employability and job satisfaction in years to come.

The role of HR professionals

Among those organizations that are restructuring, human resource and training professionals can help to enrich jobs and

keep people motivated. One crucial element in this role is helping employees to develop a positive approach to lateral career
development. Often there is considerable stigma attached to the
idea of a sideways move and many people who have experienced
such moves report a lack of support or understanding of their
development needs in order to help them function effectively in
their new role as quickly as possible. In some cases, Human
Resource professionals have worked with line managers to create
a tailored development package for the individuals concerned.

In some organizations, there is a deliberate attempt to reposition sideways moves as developmental. Examples include individuals on lateral transfers being featured positively in company
newsletters and the payment of a one-off bonus in recognition of
the effort and learning curve involved. Care has to be taken to
ensure that the benefits of sideways moves do not seem biased in
the organization's favour, since they often release bottlenecks
and create opportunities for others. This is where a well-thought-
out policy on lateral moves and the provision of help where necessary can be useful to make it possible for individuals to develop new skills.

Changing structures often lead to confusion over roles which
can lead to stress, overwork or poorly targeted effort. Training
can help, especially in providing employees with the 'new tools
of their trade'. There seems to be a decided upturn in the
amount of training taking place especially on job knowledge,
assertiveness, decision making and quality processes. In some
organizations, competencies are being used to help employees
gain a clear picture of what skills and behaviours are required in
the changing organizations, and also for job-profiling purposes.
This can lead to greater clarity about the role for the current job
holder as well as facilitating cross-functional moves in a way
which may have been rare in the previous structure. Where this
is combined with an open job posting scheme, 'surprising' moves
can prove very successful for all concerned. Again, Human
Resource professionals can facilitate this process to ensure that
human capital is being maximized.

A common shift in role is that of line managers being expected to take on a more developmental responsibility towards their
staff. Some managers find this a relatively unfamiliar role and
one for which they feel ill equipped. Training for managers can
help them to develop the skills and willingness to see people
development as a business priority among others. Often training

in coaching skills is offered to managers in tandem with new appraisal schemes. The trend in many organizations seems to be to separate out job review processes from development discussions.

Despite the difficulties that the Roffey Park research uncovered, the most encouraging message for Human Resource and training professionals is that, with their help, flatter organizations are working. With work practices that position lateral moves as career opportunities, honest appraisal and support for team-working (including a reward strategy that reinforces team development), human and organizational needs can converge and lead to an energizing new working environment. It seems that flatter structures can produce benefits for employees if they are willing to adjust their expectations about career development. They have to develop new perspectives on their careers, and to appreciate the value of forms of status other than traditional promotion. Most importantly, employees need to adopt an enterprising approach to their own career development.

Towards a new psychological contract – helping people to help themselves

Employees who successfully adapt to flatter structures have accepted responsibility for managing their own career. Such employees are architects of change, thriving in the flatter structure by constantly looking for new ways to improve their practices and challenge the status quo. These self-empowered individuals are motivated by teamwork and developing broader skills rather than simply achieving conventional status. Such new-style employees actively negotiate development opportunities as part of their recruitment package and take responsibility for their own learning. These employees seem to have a clear sense of what is important to them, and indeed this is a common characteristic of individuals identified by their employers as key contributors.

Some organizations are providing self-development processes to help people to manage their own careers. The **National Health Service** has encouraged personal responsibility through a process that helps employees to recognize the need for self-management. The Roffey Park Management Institute designed a three-day event for the National Health Service called a PEER (Personal Exploration and Evaluation Review) Centre. This is partly a development centre and partly a development planning process where the participants are trained to observe and coach each other.

The PEER process allows individuals to explore the issues relating to structural change. They can also get feedback on their effectiveness measured against the organization's own expectations. This type of exercise is going to become more common and more crucial as a vehicle for development in flatter structures that encompasses all employees, not just those on the management fast-track programme.

A key feature of this process is the emphasis on helping individuals to clarify their personal values and to use this enhanced awareness to help them find ways of increasing their job satisfaction in the here and now. This twin emphasis on the needs of the organization and those of the individual allows people to develop a pragmatic approach to development planning.

Companies in the fast-moving technology sector seem to be among the first to develop new forms of career development. For example, **Sun Microsystems Europe** is a computer company in a state of continuous growth. To maintain stability while restructuring, the company clarified its employees' career objectives through sponsoring the development of a tailored programme. Called *Managing Your Career in Sun*, the programme provided a forum for people to discuss their concerns about career opportunities. Trained Human Resource professionals were able to show individuals the alternatives to vertical promotion by expanding their current job function.

Organizations in other sectors are looking to implement similar training and evaluation schemes in which people are responsible for maintaining and taking responsibility for their own employability. In return, organizations provide the resources to assist the employee and a variety of growth opportunities. For example, work shadowing, secondments and project teams give junior employees the chance to work more intimately with others at a more senior level, while the development of community roles, such as sitting on educational governing bodies, provides an outlet for an individual's skills as well as communicating positive messages about the organization.

At another computer manufacturer, **Tektronix**, employees play a key part in managing their employability by monitoring their own performance. Performance management at Tektronix has been developed under the Results Management System

(RMS). RMS is a competencies-based appraisal system, designed to assess individual performance in a variety of areas varying from actual 'hard' results to 'soft' ones such as communication skills and relationship development. Goals and objectives are decided through negotiation and Human Resources use job descriptions only for recruitment purposes. The personal growth process at Tektronix has ensured that long- and short-term development needs are noted and that this becomes a live document which is reviewed quarterly.

At **PricewaterhouseCoopers** (PWC), the career management service helps employees to write their own job description and create a more satisfying working life. This independent career counselling service helps people to recognize their development needs and work out what they must do to achieve them. People are helped to focus on their career preferences and to talk through the options, both within the company and outside. The service is self-referred and confidential. Most of the work is done in one-to-one sessions during which people can discuss career issues which concern them. Individuals are then helped to set objectives which help people develop performance in the context of matching their needs to those of the business.

One scientific-based organization has drawn up possible elements of a career framework as shown in Figure 9.1. The company has developed the tools for the individual, in response to low career satisfaction ratings in a staff survey and after extensive consultation with employees. It is up to individuals whether or not

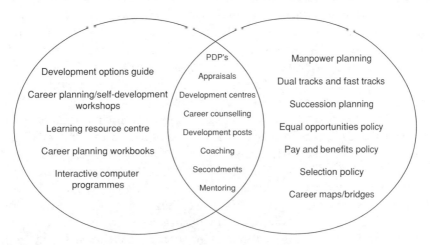

Figure 9.1 *The possible elements of a career framework*

they use them. Initially, take-up of some of the tools was low. It was only when line managers were helped to take on a coaching role that the self-development tools became more widely used. Currently the organization is focusing on the 'overlap' areas such as personal development planning processes and appraisals. Training in the new processes has been provided for both managers and individuals. Currently the focus is on creating a self-development culture. Plans are in place to develop complementary organizational processes such as succession planning, pay and benefits which will add 'muscle' to the policies.

Helping people to help themselves is not simply a question of leaving people to it. Career management and development should be a partnership between the organization and individuals, since it is in both parties' interests to collaborate.

Career Development at Standard Life – an update

In *Motivating People in Lean Organizations* (Holbeche, 1997b), I described the initiatives under way within **Standard Life** to enable employees to manage their careers. The principle on which this was based involves a partnership between the company, individual employees and line managers, with different responsibilities for each party. Under this 'triarchal' partnership, individuals are expected to take responsibility for their own career and the organization is expected to provide the framework and resources to enable them to do this. An example of one such organizational resource, the Open Access Development Centre, is described in Chapter15. Managers are expected to reconcile individual and organizational needs, including being able to say 'no' if the organization's needs are not judged to be well served by an employee's request for development .

One of the processes introduced to enable individuals to take responsibility for their career is known as Horizons. This is a PC-based self-analysis tool, designed on DOS to enable employees to use it at home rather than having to use corporate computers. An active decision was taken not to network the data since the Career Management team believed that employees owned the information. Horizons allows individuals to explore their work values and understand what is important to them. They can compare their transferable skills and occupational interests with national tables compiled by the Department for Employment and Education. Horizons also offers a number of self-insight instruments such as learning styles and a range of psychometrics to provide individuals with indications of their personality type. The tool helps people to identify their strengths and limitations, what they enjoy about their job and possible training and development needs. It also helps people to prepare a development plan and encourages them to share the plan with their manager, a coach, colleagues so as to have a 'reality check'. Horizons has currently been taken up by 3000 staff.

To support individuals and their managers further, a pilot scheme – supporting workshop has been developed to enable Contribution (line) managers to understand the tool and provide more help to individuals. Individuals are also encouraged to organize their feedback, self-assessments, current curriculum and contribution plans in a Personal Recognition Portfolio. This provides additional information on how individuals can market themselves internally.

Developing innovative career tracks in a scientific environment

In recent years, especially in organizations with flatter structures, the trend for career development to take place through a generalist route has become well established. 'Core' employees have by implication been encouraged to become multi-skilled, business-oriented individuals while specialist services have often been outsourced. Many specialists, including training and development professionals, have often therefore become business-focused external contractors. Interestingly, this trend appears to be currently somewhat in reverse in UK organizations.

In some companies, the nature of the business is specialist and technical skills remain in-house. One such organization operating as part of a government agency directly employs large numbers of scientific and engineering staff, almost all of whom are highly qualified. On the whole, the workforce has a relatively young age profile with 44 per cent of employees being between the ages of twenty and thirty. The organization is attractive to many potential recruits because of the high-powered scientific nature of the work carried out. However, many recruits join with high expectations about rapid pay progression. Given the constraints on public sector pay awards, shrinking incomes and the ongoing uncertainty of the sector within which the organization operates, these expectations are somewhat doomed to disappointment.

The organization operates a matrix structure, with pressure to reduce bureaucracy and fixed overheads. The business requires that customer requirements are captured quickly and that a more flexible service is offered to a wider range of clients. The majority of the work carried out is project based. To achieve these objectives, the organization needs to continue to attract but also retain high-calibre staff. On the plus side, the work is challenging and rewarding but on its own this is not enough to attract and retain high-calibre staff. There are good levels of investment in training although some of this is unfocused. Technical training is widely available and there is some management training. The organization has a 'sink or swim' environment, which appeals to some of the high flyers, although some people quickly 'go stale'. However, on the whole, staff are highly educated and articulate, with high expectations. Retention is becoming an issue since many employees can see no obvious career progression.

Career issues

Prior to reforms of UK central government, including the development of agencies, most of the civil service operated a similar pay and grading system which allowed for a degree of mobility for employees through a well-established system of promotion boards. Individuals could ask for and receive career counselling from senior civil servants. Promotion was often achieved by migrating between government departments and smaller entities, such as the organization in question. Career ladders for both management and scientific grades co-existed up to certain senior levels. Despite the many limitations of the previous system, it did have the benefit of offering clarity.

In the current set-up, obvious career ladders have disappeared. Formal progression systems such as through gradings, job titles and pay have also been disaggregated. In theory, this separation should make progression on merit easier. However, in real terms the system offers drawbacks as far as employees are concerned and indeed in terms of meeting the needs of the internal job market. Where once a person's job grade made project managers who were choosing staff for new projects aware of a person's likely competence, the complexity of the new system means that staffing projects is very much a matter for the resource manager (who knows the population's skills) and project managers. This means that employees need to maintain good relations with resource managers if they wish to have their interests promoted for interesting projects.

Other problems are linked with employee needs for recognition. There can be inconsistencies in pay levels for similar jobs. Professional standing is no longer evident from employee titles which are meant to reflect qualifications, experience and competencies, rather than seniority. While in theory the new employee title system includes six stages, in practice most employees recognize only two: technician and professional. Employee titles are not yet widely perceived by all as a mark of status and recognition, nor are they used publicly. Civil service grades continue to exist as 'shadow grades', i.e. not formally part of the structure but referred to by individuals when describing where their own and other roles fit in the hierarchy in terms of status.

In terms of career progression, while technical and managerial careers do exist, there are no formal definitions. Most employees soon learn that what amounts to career advancement is through customer-facing roles such as project management. The current structure offers some limited scope for other forms of advancement. A few posts exist for technical leaders who are role models and quality monitors. Similarly, a few resource managers are responsible for allocating individuals to projects. Apart from these roles, progression to business area manager is what most employees are likely to aspire to and qualifications for these roles are largely based on having taken responsibility for managing projects of increasing size and complexity.

This leads to the problem that employees perceive that the only way to progress is through management and that the organization does not value technical work. Whereas in the past, employees would have been encouraged, and expected, to spend several years in purely scientific roles, now it is not uncommon for employees to be managing projects within their first year of employment. For people who join the organization with a strong desire to carry out scientific work, the current options are disappointing since they are obliged to leave behind the detailed scientific work if they want to be promoted. Some simply leave the organization after a few years to carry out more highly paid project management roles in industry. They reason that since they are not doing what they wanted to do, namely scientific work, they might as well be more highly paid for managerial work elsewhere. Another problem is that early access to project management roles, and the relatively quick progression this makes possible for some, means that promotion opportunities run out by the time people are in their early thirties. Again, this is a critical age for turnover.

Career tracks, not ladders

To address the problem the HR team, in partnership with management, has adopted a five-phase strategy for career development. Much of this strategy is in the plan/consultation phase and remains to be implemented. However, the plans appear to have met with a favourable reaction from the staff consulted (who represent at least half the workforce). The phases are as follows:

1   Research into staff aspirations and gaining ownership
2   Competency profiling
3   Developing a training framework
4   Developing a coaching culture
5   Defining career stages and developing a range of career tracks which are clear, feasible and desirable to employees.

The aims of the proposed system are as follows:

• To meet individual needs and aspirations
• To create a system which is manageable and affordable
• To provide public recognition of status
• To ensure that the new system is fully integrated with HR processes
• To be flexible and enable individuals to switch between career tracks
• To be consistent with the parent organization's systems and processes.

Similar issues and options exist in many organizations. The following case study highlights some of the challenges of career management and career development within a professional service firm. I am indebted to Christina Evans of Roffey Park Management Institute and John Bailey in the Human Resources Development team of **KPMG** for the development of this case study. Thanks also extend to the individuals who contributed to the research by talking about their own career experiences within the firm.

Career management within KPMG UK

Organizational background

> KPMG is the global advisory firm whose purpose is to turn knowledge into value for the benefit of its clients, its people and its communities (1998 Annual Report).

To achieve this purpose KPMG has an extensive and complex structure, consisting of three core disciplines: Assurance Services (Audit and Accounting, Transaction Services and Forensic Accounting), Tax and Consulting and eight lines of business. These include, for example, Corporate Finance, Corporate Recovery, Risk Management, Consulting. The firm prides itself on its reputation for being a respected professional service provider; something which it acknowledges can only be achieved through the quality and commitment of its people and through the delivery of a professional service.

The firm has recently revised its values and has introduced a Values Charter which sets out how these values apply when conducting business. Several of the statements in the Values Charter relate to the topic of career management, for example:

- We will respect all our people and the contribution they make to the firm.
- We will listen to and aim to understand alternative perspectives,
- We will openly and proactively share knowledge,
- We will respect our own and our people's need to balance personal and business lives,
- We will support our leaders, encourage our peers and develop our people.

KPMG has achieved continued growth in its business despite the recent difficulties in the global economy. However, it has found it difficult to resource this growth due to the highly competitive market for skilled professionals. Thus in addition to recruiting more high-calibre professionals the firm has continued to invest in developing and retaining its existing people. Some of the new initiatives in this area are highlighted in this case study.

The information presented in this case study was gathered from one-to-one discussions with a number of individuals working in Audit, Corporate Recovery and Consulting. The individuals were performing different roles and at different stages in their career. Several had moved between business areas within the firm. Some had moved from a business support role into a fee-earning role. Others had chosen to combine a fee-earning role with a business-support role. Additional information was gathered from discussions with the Human Resource Development team, the latest Annual Report and the firm's corporate website.

Perspectives on the term 'career' and what career success looks like

While gaining promotion, either to a higher grade or further up the management hierarchy, is clearly important to individuals, promotion alone does not seem to be an overriding success criterion. Several other themes emerged from the research regarding how individuals perceive career success. Some spoke of career success in terms of personal challenge. These individuals stressed the importance of having opportunities to work on challenging and stretching assignments.

Others spoke of career success in terms of having a balance. Balance was referred to in a number of ways. First, having a balance between work and home: here the need for work–life balance to be recognized and respected by others within the firm was stressed as being important. Second, balance in terms of being able to develop a broad skills set would lead to more opportunities in the future. Some individuals spoke of how in this type of environment it is easy to get stuck in the 'expert role', which can be restrictive in terms of career development. Others spoke of career success as relating to enjoyment and job satisfaction. For these individuals having the opportunity to work on a variety of assignments and roles was stressed as being important to them. The general view from the discussions was that the firm is currently able to meet these needs.

To be successful in managing your own career in this type of environment it seems that individuals need to have highly developed skills in: networking and influencing, self-management, self-awareness, as well as the ability to manage risk at a personal level.

Career paths and options within the firm

Although there is a fairly traditional career path for fee-earning staff within the firm, the research highlighted that for those who want to have a protean or more individualistic career the firm offers a wealth of opportunities. The general picture gained from the research was that the firm provides 'a land of countless opportunities, but that sometimes it is difficult to work out the terrain and best route to get to where you want to be, because of its size'. However, there was a great sense of optimism in that if an individual is interested in something, be it a particular piece of work or the opportunity to work with a particular type of client, all he or she needs to do is put their hand up and the opportunity is usually made possible. One individual commented that 'If you want something and you want it enough, then pursue it. There is usually a way to get there.'

A typical career path for individuals who have chosen a career as an accountant, for example, is that they join KPMG from university and then follow a three-year training process to qualify. This route is perceived to be a good grounding even for those who do not necessarily see their longer-term career within accountancy. There is an assumption that, once qualified, individuals will be promoted to manager position within two to three years. Thereafter, the career path is promotion to senior management, followed by partner, assuming that the individual meets the firm's performance and assessment criteria. Individuals also need to establish several sponsors who can support them with their case for becoming a partner.

The time period between qualifying and reaching manager position is perceived to be key in terms of creating opportunities for broadening one's skills and gaining exposure to different roles and projects within the firm. There is a perception that once an individual has reached manager position there is less opportunity for working in a different discipline, because of the need to keep one's professional knowledge and expertise up to date. Unlike in other organizations, managers in the firm are expected to remain technical experts, so that they can build credibility with clients and manage client projects. The perception is that time spent in another part of the business, where the manager's technical knowledge is not kept up to date, would make it difficult to return to their former role.

However, those already working at manager level do not perceive out-of-date technical specific knowledge to be such a barrier to mobility as those aspiring to manager position. Managers feel that in some cases it may simply be a case of scheduling time for individuals to get back up to speed when they return to their former role.

For those working in a business support role, i.e. a non-fee-earning one, the career paths are less clearly defined. For these individuals career development occurs more through development within the current job role, or through movement to a similar role in a different part of the firm. However, it is possible for business support staff to pursue a fee-earning career path should they choose. One way of achieving this is to study part-time to gain a professional qualification, and this would then enable the individual to move into a fee-earning role. This is something which the firm encourages and supports, both at a practical level as well as financially. Another option is to move, in a business support role, to another business area, and having developed the relevant skills become more involved in fee-earning activities. The growth in the consulting side of the business has opened up opportunities for individuals from different disciplines and with a varied business sector knowledge and/or experience to transfer into a more broad-based consulting role. Some of the individuals who contributed to the research had made this type of career move. Again this is a positive example of how individuals are developing their careers in both a lateral as well as vertical, way.

Responsibilities for career management

The firm does not have a formal career management system as such. It recognizes the need to identify and develop talented people, but there are no separate programmes or processes for individuals who are considered high potential. The partners are responsible for managing succession planning and 'talent reviews' within their own areas. This approach means that the promotion process is perceived by some as not being as open as it could be.

Individuals are expected to manage their own careers. This is something which is made clear to them when they join the firm.

At one level there is an acceptance that this is how it should be, since this is a professional community who have the capabilities to manage their own career development. However, in practice, identifying and facilitating development needs is more of a partnership between the individual and his or her counselling partner/manager.

There are two formal processes which enable individuals to receive feedback on their performance and discuss their more immediate development needs, as well as future career options. One is the appraisal system which focuses on achievements over the past year, objectives for the coming year, as well identifying development needs. The appraisal system is values and competency based; thus it is perceived to be an equitable system as individuals know what is expected of them. The appraisal discussion is a key forum for individuals to discuss their development needs and the types of assignments which could help satisfy these, with their counselling partner/manager. Appraisals are usually conducted annually, with some areas holding them biannually.

To ensure that they get the most out of the appraisal discussion individuals need to spend time gathering feedback and information from others beforehand to feed into the process, for example from other managers with whom they have worked over the year, peers and, in some cases, clients. This gathering of evidence for oneself seems to be particularly important where an individual may not have worked directly for the counselling partner/manager over the year.

A second process for discussing performance and development needs occurs through the Engagement Review system where specific feedback on individual contributions to a client project are gathered. When conducted in a timely way individuals feel that the Engagement Review system provides another useful source of personal feedback. Again individuals need to take responsibility for ensuring that they receive the feedback from this process and that they have an opportunity to discuss it with their counselling partner/manager.

The managers who participated in the research feel that it is important for them to listen to the needs of individuals and to watch for signs to indicate that an individual is not being fully challenged, or indeed that an individual is under too much pressure. They also see it as their responsibility to act as an information source in terms of job opportunities currently available within the firm, or on the horizon, which may fit with an individual's development plans. The manager's role in supporting individuals with their development plans, even where this means transfers to different parts of the firm, is crucial for maintaining the credibility of this open career management system.

While this open and less structured approach to career management has worked well in the past, most individuals who participated in the research expressed the view that a more structured approach would be more helpful to individuals, particularly at different phases in their career. In part, this need has been recognized by the firm and several new support initiatives have recently been introduced in response to these concerns and are detailed in the next section. These initiatives have been the result of a partnership approach between Human Resources and individuals in the business.

The role of HR in facilitating career development

The Human Resources role in facilitating career development is increasingly becoming more strategic, focusing on the longer-term human resource needs of the firm. Increasingly HR is involved in discussions at the top table through the European HR director's role within the UK management team. In practice, the more recent career management support systems have been introduced through a partnership approach between Human Resources and individuals in the firm. The Career Broker role and the Career Ownership Workshops are examples of this successful partnership approach.

Support for career development

There are several support mechanisms in place to help individuals manage their career. Some of these operate at a corporate-wide level and some are more specific to a particular business area, unit, or department.

Corporate-wide support mechanisms

Development and assessment centres

All individuals who are appointed to senior manager position attend a Development Centre where their skills and behaviour, in relation to a known set of values and competencies, are observed. As part of the Development Centre process individuals receive one-to-one feedback on their performance from an observer. Following the Development Centre individuals may also have one-to-one coaching sessions with a Human Resources Advisor to help them take forward development needs identified during the Development Centre. Individuals who participated in the research and who had been through the Development Centre process spoke of how they had found this to be a very useful experience. In particular, they valued the support made available to them after the Development Centre, for example having access to a personal coach to help them work through their identified development needs.

Individuals who are being considered for partner position attend an Assessment Centre, which is also values and competency based. They also have a one-to-one session with one of the Human Resources Advisors to discuss the individual's motives for wanting to become a partner. Questions like 'Why do you want to be a partner?' and 'What will it mean to you to be partner?', are raised and discussed during this session.

The Human Resources Advisor who works most closely with individuals aiming for partner explained how initially existing partners were sceptical about this approach. However, over time they have begun to realize that it is acceptable to discuss these types of questions and that it is important to consider what the individual wants, as well as what the firm wants. Going forward, this questioning process is perceived to be crucial for individuals too, particularly as the role and demands on partners are changing. Increasingly, partners are being expected to demonstrate excellent people-management, business management and relationship management skills.

As well as the support provided for those aspiring to be partner, individuals can help their own case by identifying several sponsors who are willing to guide and support them with their case. Through experience individuals learn that it is important to have an eye for building relationships with sponsors from different business areas. In this way they maintain visibility and support in an organization which is constantly evolving and restructuring.

Individuals aspiring to partner position are also expected to have an 'out of the box experience' which is expected to last for a period of at least six months. The objective of this approach is to broaden an individual's experience prior to moving into a partner role. Individuals are involved in the discussion regarding which 'out of the box experience' would be most appropriate. It can be an international assignment, a project in a another part of the business, or working within a client organization.

The concept of an 'out of the box experience' is new to the firm and inevitably there have been several tensions. First, there is a concern that six months is not really enough time to get to grips with a new area and make a significant impact. Second, individuals can find it difficult at times to identify which 'out of the box experience' would be most appropriate for them given their longer-term career goals. Third, these experiences can cause personal tensions, particularly for those in a dual-career family situation.

Career Ownership Workshops

Career Ownership Workshops, introduced around a couple of years ago, were a direct response to a concern regarding the need to retain more individuals who had undergone their professional training within the firm, particularly those in Tax and Audit. Individuals who are about to qualify have several choices to make regarding their future career at this particular time. In the past individuals have found it difficult to identify what these options are and where to go for support and information, because of the sheer size of the firm. As a result many newly qualified professionals have left the firm just at the point when they qualify. This was perceived by many as a lost opportunity, as well as a drain on resources.

The decision to run Career Ownership Workshops was taken following a consultation process between partners and those newly qualified in Audit. The workshops enable individuals who are about to qualify, or have recently qualified, to find out what their future career options are. They may be half-day or full-day events. The firm has adopted an open approach to these workshops, recognizing that they are in competition with other organizations for newly qualified professionals. The rationale behind the workshop is to provide a forum where individuals can stand back and review their career options, both within the firm and outside, as well as identify people who can help them think through their decisions. Individuals who participated in the research commented on how much they valued the open attitude adopted by the firm.

During the workshop there are presentations from different parts of the business on the type of work and range of clients they work with. Individuals may also hear from external speakers who can give them insights into opportunities outside the firm. There is the opportunity for individuals to gain advice on preparing their CV from recruitment consultants. There is also an opportunity to have informal one-to-one discussions with a number of people about possible career routes within the firm. On some workshops individuals who have worked for the firm in the past have been invited back to give a presentation on how they have developed their career outside the firm.

Career Broker role

Following on from the success of the Career Ownership Workshops a Career Broker role has been introduced in some business units. The Career Broker acts as an independent advisor, as well as an information source, for individuals who are unsure about how or where to develop their career. Career Brokers network with managers and other Career Brokers in other parts of the firm so that they can put individuals in touch with the right people with whom they can have informal discussions about possible job roles and career opportunities. The intention is that this role will complement the advice provided by counselling partners/managers during the appraisal process, not replace it.

Individuals who perform the role of Career Broker are selected from the firm. Some may combine the Career Broker role with their other responsibilities. In this way Career Brokers have direct experience of working in a particular business unit and are thus in a better position to help others decide whether working in a particular area will meet their career goals. Although the Career Broker role is still in its early stages the response thus far has been positive. For individuals it has provided the independent source of advice which some have voiced as being an important additional support tool.

Performing the Career Broker role is a developmental experience in its own right. Individuals performing the role find it challenging and stretching. It is a way of developing some of the softer skills too, for example relationship building and questioning skills, as well as building up one's knowledge of the firm. Some individuals have found that the role provides them with an opportunity to work more closely with Human Resources, thus also helping to meet a personal career development goal.

Other resources and development routes

The firm has an intranet site called 'An Ocean of Opportunity' which provides information about current job vacancies within the firm. This is linked to other parts of the intranet which contains information regarding the range of projects being undertaken by different parts of the firm, as well as contact details. Each of these sources provide key information for individuals to help them manage their career. Individuals can also gain sponsorship for external training, particularly qualifications such as masters programmes, provided they can demonstrate how this will add value to the firm.

The firm also provides an extensive range of development activities covering technical and personal skills. Development opportunities can also occur through the firm's Community Broking Service. An example is the head-teacher mentoring programme which operates in forty schools throughout London. The programme involves KPMG staff mentoring head teachers in order to help them develop their financial management and organizational development skills. Secondments to other parts of the business and/or teams are another accepted way for individuals to develop their career. The opportunities seem plentiful and they can extend to any part of the firm, including internationally.

Some local initiatives

Several of those interviewed spoke of local departmental initiatives which have been introduced to help individuals with their development needs. These are initiatives which have been introduced following discussions within the department on what additional support would be of value to individuals to help them manage their career development. In Consulting, for example, a coaching role has been introduced. This role was introduced in response to a direct request from consultants, particularly those new to the role, as a way of helping them settle into their new role and develop their consulting skills through learning from the experience of others.

In Corporate Recovery, a manager has been assigned the role of more closely matching personal development needs with the skills needed on client project work. The perception from individuals within this part of the firm was that development needs were not always given sufficient priority when allocating staff to client projects. Individuals felt that resources were being assigned to projects on the basis of known past experience, which meant that they felt that they were being pigeon-holed in a particular role; something which was felt to be limiting in personal development terms. This appointment arose as a way of addressing these concerns. This particular manager is now involved in the appraisal process so that she has a better understanding of each individual's development needs. In this way greater alignment is being achieved between the skills required for a particular client project and the development needs of individuals.

Tensions relating to achieving career success

A number of tensions relating to career development within the firm were uncovered during the research. The key tensions and how these are currently being managed are discussed below.

Gaining access to information

Individuals who participated in the research spoke of how much they valued the openness and lack of formality of the internal transfer process. As mentioned earlier, known job vacancies are made public on the intranet site 'An Ocean of Opportunity'. While there is a formal job application process, individuals have an opportunity for an informal discussion with the relevant partner/manager. Assuming that there is a match between the needs of department and the individual the transfer usually goes ahead. The support of the current manager is vital in terms of making this open job posting system work.

However, not all jobs and client assignments are posted on the intranet. Thus given the size of the firm and the range of client projects it undertakes, individuals can find it difficult to gain up-to-date information upon which to make career decisions. Individuals who participated in the research commented that to manage your own career within the firm you have to be pushy and spend time networking. This is felt to be the only way of finding out what project work and opportunities are coming up and for getting your name in the frame. Several of the individuals who contributed to the research had engineered roles on projects which mapped directly onto their development goals, through personal networking. Some of these roles were on fee-earning projects, others were on business support projects, such as working on Human Resources projects. Networking with people at all levels and in different business areas is perceived as being key in terms of getting to where you want to be. However, individuals spoke of how networking can be difficult at times, particularly when working for long periods of time at a client site.

The Human Resources Development team are currently developing an on-line Career Management System which will act as an additional resource bank for individuals to draw on when exploring career options. The system will contain information such as: how to get from A to B in terms of the competencies required; profiles of individuals showing how they got to where they are within the firm, as well as a list of resources which individuals can draw on to help them manage their career. The system is expected to be completed later on in the year.

Balancing a career with other commitments

The nature of the work within the firm can make it difficult for individuals to gain a balance between work and their non-work commitments. Fee-earning work often involves working long hours and sometimes requires working away from home for extended periods of time. This can create tensions for individuals and their families. Although one of the firm's values is to demonstrate respect for an individual's need to balance their personal and business lives, there is a sense that the firm does not always pick up the signs that an individual is under stress as quickly as it could. It was felt that more could be done to support individuals who want to achieve greater balance in their lives.

For women wishing to develop their career within the firm the tension of achieving work–life balance is felt to be more problematic. Family commitments mean that some fee-earning roles are not feasible, which can create tensions in terms of building up the necessary experience for more senior roles. Moving to a business support role, where the opportunities for working in a more flexible way seem more feasible, is an alternative career option. However, this is perceived as taking a backward step. The research highlighted different perceptions regarding the extent to which achieving work–life balance impacts upon career progression within the firm. Those already in more senior positions feel that achieving balance is less of a problem once one's credibility within the firm has been established. In this case it is more likely that personal preferences and commitments are taken into account when projects and workloads are being assigned. Thus should an individual ask not to be assigned to a particular project, and they have a good reason for this, this is not usually a problem and it does not create a black mark in terms of future career development. However, those who are just starting their career and are not currently in a management role were less certain of this.

While there are many existing policies relating to flexible working practices, many individuals are not necessarily aware of what these all are. In addition, there many informal flexible working arrangements operating within the firm; as these are not widely publicized this again makes it difficult for individuals to know what is currently feasible. For women, in particular, this is perceived as a barrier in terms of future career options. This is a view echoed by Ruth Anderson who was appointed to the KPMG board in 1998. In a news item in *The Guardian* at the time of Ruth Anderson's appointment she was quoted as expressing the view that more effort needs to be invested in helping women balance their work and family commitments so that they can reach senior positions within the firm.

Careers in the future – opportunities and challenges

In response to the question 'What do you see as some of the future challenges facing the firm with regard to career development?' the following thoughts were expressed:

* Helping individuals (in particular women) develop meaningful careers while respecting their need for work–life balance. It was felt that there was an opportunity for exploring different forms of flexible career options/working practices which would ensure the continued delivery of a respected profes-

sional service, but enable individuals to have a more balanced lifestyle.

One team is already championing a new working approach to help address the issue of work–life balance and have introduced the idea of a *'Quality of life week'*. Individuals in this particular team take it in turn to have their quality of life week, which means making a conscious effort not to work long hours. Making this approach work in practice requires a partnership approach between team members. Each team members need to demonstrate sensitivity to the pressures others are experiencing, as well as offering support to the individual who is having their *'Quality of life week'*. This has to be a reciprocal arrangement to work effectively.

- Enhancing and promoting the career development opportunities for those pursuing a career in a business support role, thus ensuring that individuals in these roles feel more valued.
- Balancing the tension between an individual's 'in demand factor' and the danger of burn-out. Here it was felt that there was an opportunity to improve the process of matching skills to assignments/situations, thus not placing individuals in untenable situations. In addition, the option of some scheduled time away from fee-earning activities was raised as a way of minimizing the risk of burn-out, as well as creating the space for individuals to work on projects which are more closely aligned to their longer-term career goals.
- Given that career success for many individuals is aligned to their need for interesting and challenging work, the continued availability of this type of work was raised as a major challenge for the firm.
- Develop a more open succession planning system so that individuals can base their own career decisions on relevant and complete data.
- More forums for individuals to gain firsthand information about the firm's future plans. Again this was felt to be a key source of data for personal career planning.

Conclusion

Careers remain a number-one agenda item for many employees. The idea of managing your own career has caught on, but many employees lack the time and know-how to do this. Helping people to come to terms with what careers look like in the new economy involves helping them recognize that jobs as we knew them may cease to exist. The skills of career self-management can be learnt, and the wise employer makes resources available for people to do this. Increasingly, the challenge for employers will be to retain those employees who are highly employable – and helping people develop themselves and their careers has been proved to do this. It is therefore a business imperative that organizations attract and retain talent by providing people with opportunities for growth.

In today's changing organizations this may not mean conventional promotion. Career management will need to be much more individually tailored than the provision of blanket training opportunities. Imagination and flexibility will be needed on the part of both employees and employers if a satisfactory development route is to be found. Some of the genuine attempts described in this chapter to break out of the career straightjackets through which people have been channelled deserve success.

Checklist for the new career structures

- How do we help individuals to utilize their strengths, as well as help them to broaden their skills and experience?
- How can we help people to manage their own careers? What help do people want?
- What development tools can we provide?
- How can individuals be helped to develop their careers in different areas to broaden their experience?
- How can we reposition lateral development so that it is seen as a positive?
- How can we encourage individuals at all levels to become comfortable with giving and receiving feedback?
- How can we facilitate career development while at the same time managing expectations?
- What career routes can be created to stop people from being 'boxed in' to either technical or managerial roles?
- How can we help managers act as career enablers?
- How can we help people develop the skills which will enhance their employability – such as teamworking and knowledge skills?

References

Armstrong, H. and Gattegno, G. (1993). How are you going to manage if the good old days don't come back? *Management*, May.

Church, J. A. (1993). Change begins at square zero, *Directors and Boards*, Spring.

Holbeche, L. (1995). *Career Development in Flatter Structures: Organizational Practices*, Roffey Park Management Institute.

Holbeche, L. (1997a). *The Impact of Flatter Structures on Careers*. Oxford: Butterworth-Heinemann.

Holbeche, L. (1997b). *Motivating People in Lean Organizations*. Oxford: Butterworth-Heinemann.

Kiechel, W. (1994). A manager's career in the new economy, *Fortune*, April.

McCall, M., Morgan W. J. R., Lombards, M. and Morrison, A. M. (1988). *The Lessons of Experience*, Lexington, MA: Lexington Books.

Waitley, D. (1995). *Empires of the Mind*, London: Nicholas Brealey Publishing.

As many as 25 per cent of employees who come back from an overseas posting resign within a year, according to a survey by the Centre for International Briefing. After two years the figure rises to a staggering 40 per cent. Some find that no new role has been defined for them and look in vain for appreciation of their new skills which often includes a second language (McLuhan, 1999).

This chapter looks at some of the challenges of developing international high flyers. It highlights some of the changing organizational requirements of people in international roles and some of the dilemmas facing both companies and their employees. The skills of international high flyers are discussed and a number of approaches to development are outlined. One of the biggest challenges is ensuring that the skills of international high flyers are put to good use beyond their immediate project or assignment.

The growth of international business

As we enter the third millenium, the trend towards globalization in both the marketplace and production has caused many organizations to push back their operating boundaries and become 'international' players. Though a survey carried out by Roffey Park Institute in 1999 found that 39 per cent of respondents' organizations were trading in Europe, other parts of the world were also well represented, with 16 per cent of companies trading in Asia, for example. The shift to emerging markets such as the Pacific Rim, Central and Eastern Europe, South America and India is evident across most sectors.

How well organizations are able to succeed in commercial and cultural situations which may be unfamiliar depends to some extent on the skills and attitudes of staff and of managers in particular. The growing interest in identifying and developing international high flyers reflects these shifts. Now the centre of attention is international, if not global. In a survey carried out in 1995, 70 per cent of UK based multinationals anticipated future shortages of international managers.

What is an international organization?

What is required of international managers is to some extent determined by the degree of 'internationalism' of the company. Many organizations which claim to be international are in fact predominantly national companies which export overseas. Their main international effort may lie in the sales, marketing and customer service arenas. Management teams are likely to be largely made up of nationals and opportunities for an international career may be rather limited. The 1999 Roffey Park survey found that, while the majority of participating organizations are conducting business internationally, only 56 per cent of respondents agreed that their organization provides the opportunity for international careers.

Other companies are more truly international in that they may be owned by parent organizations whose nationality differs from the countries in which they mainly operate. They may be based in Europe or other regions where there is a clear market for their product but the parent company could well be Japanese, American, etc. They may operate as multi-domestic organizations. Management teams are likely to be made up of a blend of nationals from the operating countries, with direction and control coming from the parent company. The national characteristics of the parent headquarters often have a strong bearing on the management styles, working practices and trading approaches which are considered appropriate.

The degree of centralization or decentralization of organizational decision making can have a major bearing on what is required of international high flyers. Multinationals operate with relatively autonomous units, each focused on maximizing results within its territory. Local management teams may have a reasonable degree of autonomy within a clear management framework. Truly global transnational companies seek to weave their units into more flexible, web-like structures with a dual focus which is both global and local. It is argued that managers in the global corporation have to be able to work at much greater levels of complexity – in terms of geographic scope and cultural diversity and of balancing global and local agendas.

With the creation of a single currency zone in Europe, multinational companies are increasingly moving towards pan-European structures, developing centralized service centres which group together support processes such as customer services, sales or marketing. These are a way of reducing duplication, such as in IT systems, and cutting the numbers of staff and therefore cost. Specialist staff will be expected to relocate or at least seriously commute to the country in which their service centre is based. In other cases, the 'Euromanager', who lives in one country but is peripatetic and operates across national boundaries, is a reality.

Joint ventures are increasingly replacing wholly owned subsidiaries as the dominant form of overseas investment. Typically, the main problem areas are likely to lie in relations between the overseas company and the local company, especially on issues concerning communication and decision-making. Child's (1990) study of joint ventures in China found distinctive differences of approach of parent companies from different countries. In US-owned joint ventures, there was a strong tendency for the procedures and approaches of the parent company to be introduced into the joint venture partner, despite the problems this caused in the fields of informal communication, decision making and training. By contrast, Japanese companies were found to be less likely to impose home-based Japanese management styles onto their partners, preferring instead to adapt to local circumstances. For an international manager working in a joint venture, the challenges may reach a higher level of complexity than those experienced when working for the parent company.

The role of the international manager

The role of the international manager seems to be changing. No longer is it sufficient for an international high flyer to have technical skills and to be a troubleshooting manager who can go from country to country. With barriers coming down and organizations trying new forms of international coordination and integration, the international manager is someone who can exercise leadership across a number of countries and cultures simultaneously, perhaps on a global or regional basis. Increasingly, personality factors and the ability to manage local operations are seen to be critical to effectiveness.

What does an 'international' role look like?

The ways in which international managers are developed will to some extent reflect their organization's preferred way of conducting international business. Typically, organizations are unclear about their strategy for internationalizing managers. For decades, the dominant model has been that of the expatriate assignment. Particularly common in multinationals, this has usually meant a mobile group of high-flying executives enjoying special financial and other benefits. For some employees, an expatriate assignment has been an essential part of their career development, prior to returning to a 'home' base. For others, expatriate working has become a lifestyle of postings to different parts of the world. As we will explore later in this chapter, the expatriate model of international assignment appears to be on the decrease, with organizations and employees less happy to commit to this form of assignment.

An alternative model is the development of local managers who can understand and work with the corporate culture, but whose career is likely to be based in their home country or region. In the past, local managers have been often relegated at best to 'second in command' positions, reporting to an expatriate manager. The shift away from colonial-style relationships is evident in many parts of the world such as China and South Africa. Governments are requiring international organizations who wish to trade in their country to 'upskill' local talent who can take over the management of the enterprise over time. The challenges of this form of development include enabling the 'local' manager to develop insights into the corporate culture and to be able to influence corporate strategy in an adult–adult way.

A third 'hybrid' model consists of being primarily home based, but with international assignments of varying lengths. These may range from a six-month technical assignment to a short business meeting with clients or team members in different locations. The Roffey Park research suggests that this is by far the most popular form of international career from the employee perspective, though organizations are slow to find new ways of carrying out their international business in ways which make sense to shareholders and their employees. Indeed, with the advent of virtual teams it is possible that an international high flyer may have no need to travel at all since technology makes possible many forms of communication, except for 'in the flesh'. However, leaders of global teams would no doubt resist the notion that all team work can be carried out by teleconference or e-mail.

How willing are managers to accept an international assignment?

Increasingly there are signs that expatriate and longer-term overseas assignments are becoming harder to fill. An Ashridge Management College survey (Panter, 1995) found that shortages of international managers were particularly acute for British multinational companies. Two-thirds of the companies surveyed said that they had experienced shortages of international managers and over 70 per cent indicated that future shortages were anticipated. Reasons suggested for this shortfall are that UK salary levels are uncompetitive and also that managers are becoming less mobile.

This lack of mobility can be explained by a number of factors. In a large expatriate survey conducted by **Shell International**, 'Shell expatriate outlook' (1996), several demographic trends affecting mobility are charted:

- The increasing number of women in the workforce
- The increasing percentage of women with their own careers and who are not willing to abandon their own career in order to follow their partner to an overseas assignment. The so-called 'dual career' issue is keenly affecting industries such as oil and the utilities. Similarly, many male partners are unwilling to be parted from their families for extended periods of time
- More aged dependents
- Greater travel opportunities and chances to experience other cultures without the need to expatriate
- Reluctance to send children to boarding school.

Other factors relate to some of the major shifts in the employment relationship which have taken place mainly in the West over the last decade. The widespread reshaping of organizations to cope with competitive pressures has had a profound impact on the so-called 'psychological contract' between employer and employee. Few organizations these days promise a lifetime's employment and, with flatter management structures, the opportunities for conventional vertical promotion have become restricted for many people. Ironically, organizations which have sought to pass responsibility for career development to employees and have told them to manage their own careers are starting to see the impact of employee choice if the employee's skills are marketable and in short supply.

The impact of ongoing uncertainty and lack of career progression has been a lessening of employee commitment in many cases. Whereas at one time employees would have been prepared to take one or two lengthy assignments in less popular locations in order to advance their careers, the link between employee sacrifice and career reward appears less clear. For some employees who have accepted overseas assignments, there seems to be a negative link with promotion, especially if they believe that they have been forgotten while overseas. Similarly, there are signs that the long-hours regime evident in many organizations is finally taking its toll. In some cases employees are refusing assignments which would upset the balance between home and work life even if they pay the price in terms of missing out on promotion.

Organizational versus individual expectations

While demand for international employees seems to be increasing, the desire to accept international assignments has flattened at best. Some organizations simply do not have enough people with the skills, experience and motivation to live and work in another country. The Roffey Park International Leadership survey (1999), of 160 UK-based managers found that there was a clear mismatch between what employers were expecting of employees and what employees considered to be their needs and aspirations. There still appears to be a strong expectation from employers that if an international assignment is offered, the employee should not refuse it.

The survey found that while two thirds of respondents were willing to accept an international assignment, 79 per cent did not consider having an international management role as part of their individual career plan. For those people who were interested in an international assignment, the main attractions were the challenge it offered, the chance to experience another culture and the opportunities it would open up in the future. However, only 3.5 per cent saw such an international assignment as a necessary career move.

Of those managers not willing to accept an international assignment, 52 per cent said that this was because of a reluctance to uproot the family, and 62 per cent of managers surveyed preferred to be given an international assignment which did not involve expatriation, even though many acknowledged that not as much experience would be gained as from an expatriate role. Over a third of the sample stated that a home-based international role involving travel is most appealing. The most popular destination was North America, which may reflect a concern over language difficulties and cultural issues. For managers who had experienced international assignments, the biggest problems they faced were cross-cultural working and language barriers.

Nevertheless, there are signs that, from the company perspective, attitudes towards international assignments are changing. The response of many organizations to the shortfall in numbers of international managers is to recruit international-minded graduates and send them on overseas assignments in the early years before other commitments make such assignments seem less attractive. Rather than being a corporate afterthought, international assignments are moving to the forefront of management and organizational dynamics. Companies are slowly realizing that well-managed international assignments are a key element in developing global corporate competencies. Expatriate postings, where they exist, are becoming interconnected with executive and leadership development as well as with succession planning. They are also being increasingly regarded as logical and required steps in career paths – and not only for those on fast tracks.

The role of HR in managing assignments

Managing assignments is therefore a key responsibility and opportunity for global HR to grow talent within the company. These responsibilities include:

- Finding employees with the appropriate skills
- Providing cross-cultural and language training for employees and their partners
- Creating career management strategies which support employee interests during and on return from assignments
- Supporting partners of employees when on assignment.

International mobility at Ericsson

In common with many international companies, **Ericsson** has to address the challenge of people working abroad for extended periods. Overall, it has a remarkable number; some 3500 long-term ex-pats living and working around the world. Team members typically have three- to four-year assignments and for some people with families this may cause considerable disruption. The shift away from the old paternalistic culture in which employees would be guaranteed a career enhancement on return from assignment means that people are now more aware that they too are responsible for managing their careers.

Ericsson is addressing the issue of employee mobility by a two-pronged strategy. On the one hand, more local managers are used wherever it makes business sense, such as in Asia-Pacific where ex-pats can be less acceptable to customers. On the other hand, the company is becoming increasingly selective about who goes on an overseas assignment. Ericsson is choosing people who are more independent and self-starting where possible. This is in addition to the high technical knowledge and the culturally sensitive customer skills they need as a member of an international sales team. Not surprisingly, finding the right people can be difficult. Internal candidates are sought and employees are asked if they would like an international career. HR also pinpoints individuals whose skills profile matches requirements.

For people who are on assignment, the challenge of reintegrating into the home base when they return is somewhat eased by the information flow from parent companies. Typically, while on assignment, employees receive all local press releases and highlights of the 'home' business so that they are up to date with key issues. The company intranet is another useful way of maintaining contact. In addition, people are encouraged to be proactive in maintaining regular contact with their home base although, typically, they become consumed by current relationships and events.

Naturally, in a global business, international exposure is seen as an essential part of preparation for senior management. Typically, people move on from leading an international team to running a large division with profit-and-loss responsibility. Sometimes they are given the chance to work for a major subsidiary to gain additional experience. Ericsson has a wealth of experience in international teamworking developed over more than 100 years of worldwide operations – UK chairman, Tony Booth says it's in their bloodstream!

Selecting international managers

The development of international managers often takes place through assignments or postings abroad of differing lengths of time. Interestingly, few organizations appear to use a specific list of international competencies when selecting people for international roles. In the Roffey Park research it was found that the criteria used to select international leaders are often unclear. In many organizations, functional expertise appears to be the most important criterion in selecting and preparing employees for international work. Often the selection process focuses on the person's willingness to go abroad, rather than on other factors. International assignments are often used to address a particular business problem or opportunity and their potential use as an excellent training ground for refining the core skills of future organizational leaders is often missed. Yet arguably, the skills and competencies involved in performing effectively in an international context are of a high order and should not be left to chance.

Research (Tung, 1988) has found that the greater the consideration paid during the selection process to adaptability and the ability to communicate, the higher the success rate in the assignment. Other research suggests that several factors which should be included in the selection criteria for international leaders are:

- Conflict-resolution skills
- Leadership style
- Effective communication
- Social orientation
- Flexibility and open-mindedness
- Interest in and willingness to try new things
- Ability to cope with stress.

Given the growing shortage of international managers a number of companies are seeking to recruit employees, especially graduates, who are willing to manage abroad, rather than trying to persuade reluctant existing employees. They market the international nature of their activities and emphasize the prospects of early international experience to attract graduates who are specifically seeking an international career. The recruitment of foreign students is becoming easier and cheaper through the use of technology. Accessing on-line CVs of overseas university students over the Internet is becoming a common feature of sourcing for graduate entry. Mobility and the willingness to move across borders are seen as prerequisites to future success.

Recruiting and developing international managers in BP Amoco

BP Amoco is committed to developing an internationally diverse leadership. One of the most direct ways of achieving an international management cadre is by deliberately recruiting people with an international perspective. BP Amoco has consciously attempted to develop a more multi-cultural management workforce in recent years and recruitment takes place through the worldwide recruitment network. A common set of recruitment competencies is used and these are as culturally 'neutral' as possible so as not to disadvantage candidates whose first language is other than English and whose experience of life does not include the UK, the USA or Europe. A genuine attempt has been made to devise culturally neutral selection procedures, with candidates tested and interviewed in their native language.

In addition, approximately 15 'Eurograds' are recruited each year. These are expected to be internationally mobile, to speak a minimum of three languages and be typically high potential. There are currently 60 alumni in the scheme and over time it is anticipated that this more culturally diverse graduate intake should percolate through to senior management.

In addition to recruiting international talent, BP Amoco is committed to internationalizing the current leadership. Typically this is achieved by sending senior managers to international business schools, through training and through group meetings and networks which take place in different global venues. International experience outside work is well utilized, but the primary means of internationalizing managers is still by sending them on expatriate assignments. Given the nature of the business, expatriation is likely to be a significant part of an international manager's experience for some time to come. However, this is proving increasingly difficult for employees who have dual-career families or who are not keen for the disruption to family personal life caused by such relocations.

BP Amoco is working hard to eliminate barriers to successful expatriation. The company has devised a Partner Assistance policy to help alleviate some of the financial hardships experienced when the accompanying partner has to give up his or her job. Support is provided to help the accompanying partner to understand their career choices in the destination. Where possible, the process of finding work for the partner in the destination country is facilitated by the company. If having a job proves impractical for various reasons, partners are assisted in remaining current in their own career field. This may mean being provided with relevant trade literature, doing a distance-learning course or attending a professional conference in another location. Vocational or educational training is provided locally if possible and child-care supplied.

Help is provided to both partners prior to, during and after the assignment. Before the assignment, partners receive as appropriate a mini-severance payment to compensate to some extent for the loss of income. Career counselling is available and language lessons are offered to both partners, as is cultural training related to the destination country. During the assignment, partners are given help with CV preparation, job-search counselling, visas and work permits. Further language training is provided as well as IT support. Partner groups are established who become an active network. Partners are also assisted in re-entering the job market upon repatriation, and are offered job counselling for the UK market and help in preparing their CVs. They are given support in updating their job skills such as learning new technical or IT systems which may have changed significantly in their absence from their home country.

A number of other international companies are struggling to find creative solutions to the dual-career issue. Motorola, for instance, actually pays a percentage of their annual domestic salaries to spouses of employees on international assignments. Motorola believes that this helps partners to adjust better while overseas and to prepare for repatriation and employment on their return to their home country.

The skills of international high flyers

Clearly the scope of the organization's international activities will have a bearing on the skills required of international high flyers. However, there are certain skills and characteristics which most international careers have in common. According to Professor Peter Smith (1992):

> Working effectively across cultures is not therefore simply a matter of applying skills found to be effective within the culture of one's own country or organization. It requires also that one can understand and cope with the processes of communication and decision-making in settings where these are achieved in a different manner.

International leaders need to change their frame of reference from a local or national orientation to a truly international perspective. This involves understanding influences, trends, practices, political and cultural influences and international economics. They will need to understand and develop competitive strategies, plans and tactics which operate outside the confines of a domestic marketplace orientation.

Maury Peiperl of the Centre for Organizational Research at London Business School has carried out a survey in fifteen countries looking at the skills of international managers. He states that:

> The skills needed and the ones where chief executives see a gap are adaptability in new situations, international strategic awareness, ability to motivate cross-border teams, sensitivity to different cultures and international experience. They have less to do with the traditional talents of achieving targets (though that's always important); vision and change management are the needs of today.

Peiperl's (1998) survey found that British and German managers had the same two gaps in their skills portfolio: being able to motivate cross-border teams and to integrate people from other countries.

Being able to understand and lead multinational teams is critical. Leaders need to be able to deal with issues of collaboration and cross-cultural variances. Merely recognizing that cultural differences exist is not enough. International managers need to be able to manage those differences if the team is to operate successfully. They need to develop processes for coaching, mentoring and assessing performance across a variety of attitudes, beliefs and standards. At the US semiconductor company Intel, the company does not try to impose a company culture on the national culture; rather, it takes for granted that these differences exist. The preferred approach to team meetings at Intel, wherever they are run, is to ensure that the meetings are structured and run in a particular way. This approach is based on the belief that having a common framework and routine provides a stability which helps overcome potential difficulties which may arise from cross-cultural differences.

Language skills are also clearly important as is being willing to continue to learn new languages if, for example, your specialist service centre is in a different location. These skills are an essential gateway to understanding and working effectively within the culture of the country in question. Being limited in language ability therefore runs the risk of missing out on the subtleties which can make the difference between business success or failure.

According to a report published by the Economist Intelligence Unit (Krempel, 1998), businesses are looking for graduates who are multi-lingual and able to understand business practice and how it differs between countries. The Peiperl study found that when it comes to language skills, British managers compare unfavourably, speaking on average, 1.7 languages in contrast to their counterparts in fourteen other countries who speak an average of 2.8 languages each. In the Roffey Park study, 35 per cent of the sample recognized language skills as being the main skills required, closely followed by cultural awareness and understanding.

Some leading industrialists suggest that even these skills are not enough to ensure that future international leaders are able to lead effectively over time. According to Michel de Zeeuw, General Manager of **Unisys**, graduate recruits ideally have specific skills such as computing ability, as well as good communication and teamworking skills since they will be required to work with people from different countries. This is in addition to specific technical skills such as accountancy if they are moving, for instance, into a finance function. Yves Nanot, chief executive officer of **Cimentz Français** in Paris, suggests that, given the ongoing pace of change, managers will need a more rapid rate of thinking and making decisions and an ability to anticipate and prepare for changes. It will be important for managers to be able to 'cut through all those barriers of narrow, nationalistic thinking that for us were insurmountable'.

The traditional role of making order out of chaos will shift to one of continually managing change and chaos in ways which are responsive to customers and competitive conditions. International leaders will need to be effective well beyond traditional management practices to reflect sensitivity to cultural diversity and perspective. They need to understand different – and sometimes conflicting – social forces without prejudice. They need to speed up business development where possible by exploiting and adapting learning between countries and markets. They also need to be able to manage their personal effectiveness and achieve a satisfactory balance between work and home.

Developing international managers

Many organizations appear to lack a clear strategy for developing international high flyers. So while many employees appear to want home-based short-term assignments, the dominant method of internationalizing managers appears still to be through expatriate or longer-term assignments, except where organizations have been encouraged or forced to adopt more flexible approaches. For many international companies most of the focus on training and development is based around the expatriation process. The development and training needs of host country nationals tend to take a back seat.

Development through expatriation

Using appropriate selection processes for specific postings or assignments is only one part of the equation. Another important ingredient is the identification of individuals with international potential long before they might be expected to take on an international role. That way, effective screening, training and familiarization can take place to ensure that individuals are ready for an international leadership task. **Honeywell Inc.** believe in identifying and developing potential candidates usually years before a posting. Each employee is made aware, via routine testing with specialists and consultants, of cross-cultural strengths and weaknesses.

Managers use these tests as pools to identify potential expatriates, discussing career paths with them. The aim is for them to develop a cross-cultural intellect, or what they call 'strategic accountability'. A manager may suggest that an employee begin studying a language or informally explore areas where he or she may be flexible and inflexible in a foreign culture. Honeywell managers are encouraged to pick US employees for international task teams for one- or two-day meetings abroad. Some are sent on six-month foreign assignments with no home leave to see how they will adjust to an overseas posting. Expatriates need to be aware that they will experience cultural differences in problem solving, motivation, leadership, use of power, consensus building and decision making.

While effective preparation is known to be a key ingredient in ensuring the success of an international assignment, organizational support is often surprisingly minimal. A few companies have begun to use expatriated employees to coach other employees who are about to be posted abroad. The briefing works well if the returnee has recent experience in the host country. However, just the interaction with someone who has lived and worked in another country is invaluable for the soon-to-be expatriate, especially if it is their first posting.

Shell has 5000 expatriates worldwide and puts great effort into cross-cultural coaching. Those being sent to countries whose cultures are very different from the UK (about 35 per cent) undergo a week's residential training course in the UK or the Netherlands to give them the knowledge and understanding of the social and business mores which they will encounter. At least 95 per cent receive individual attention from one of the 'area desks' specializing in facts on every region of the world. About 1300 people receive briefings of one kind or another every year. Significantly, Shell intends that all graduate entrants will in future receive compulsory cross-cultural training, whether or not they have been earmarked for a foreign assignment.

ICI and **NatWest** conduct extensive international in-house seminars. These courses cover national cultural differences, local politics and laws when conducting business abroad, family adaptation and international finance. When training is provided it should ideally focus on three aspects of development: pre-departure, on-site and repatriation. Language training should be geared to cultural understanding rather than total fluency. Even a modest knowledge of a language can create some 'equilibrium of power' in transactions. Some European companies take a front-end approach by selective recruitment. They look harder for young men and women who already possess fluency in at least two languages, can demonstrate cross-cultural ability and have a serious interest in working globally.

Developing international managers at Standard Chartered Bank

Until the late 1980s, most senior positions at **Standard Chartered Bank** (SCB) were filled by British managers on expatriate assignments. Though a British company by virtue of its majority shareholding, SCB has over 500 branches in forty countries worldwide, but does not have a high street presence in the UK. British directors were in the majority on the board and British managers tended to be offered most of the opportunities for significant career advancement. However, business difficulties in the mid-1980s caused management to overhaul the way the business was being run. As the business's main competitive advantage was its multi-country customer base and trading heritage, it became apparent that a new global business strategy which was also responsive to the local market was needed. SCB would have to transform itself from being a multiple domestic operation to a more transnational bank. It was recognized that it is the local managers who know the environment and are probably best placed to be at the forefront of the business. But it was also seen that, as the business is very international, local managers also need to develop a more global perspective.

One of the first changes was to the management structure, transforming it from a federal approach to one based on functional reporting lines. Other changes were specifically to address the dominant management culture which was better suited to a more colonial and federal organization with high levels of local autonomy. In the early 1990s, a management development programme called Focus 300 for the top 300 people in the organization was followed by Focus 2000, a similar scheme for middle managers. This helped to start a significant shift in attitudes and willingness to change in the management population. A next step was to shift focus away from managing through expatriates. Not only was managing an expat workforce becoming increasingly inappropriate for the business, it was also very expensive.

Similarly, many of the host countries in which SCB operates have quotas on the numbers of local managers that foreign firms must employ.

Moving away from the expatriate management model

A new policy on international mobility was introduced to enable a shift away from the dominant expatriate model to one in which mobile staff are 'assigned'. Under this policy there are a number of options. One is for short-term assignments of three to twelve months. The home and host country share responsibility for managing the individual who is not required to relocate his or her family. Individuals are paid a per diem allowance and this form of assignment is commonly used for projects and to expand mobility and product or market knowledge, especially for high-potential employees. A 'boomerang' overseas assignment, lasting between one and five years, is where the individual is still on their home-based salary but with international benefits which reflect the medium-term temporary nature of the assignment.

A 'global' assignment is for a smaller group of employees whom SCB consider permanently mobile. Typically they work in a second 'host' country and may have the potential to reach the most senior levels in the bank. A fourth option is a permanent international transfer. This is where the employee has spent five years or more in a second country. Under a transition scheme their expat package becomes a local one. As a result of these changes, the number of staff on permanent expatriate terms has fallen from 800 to fewer than 100. Over 500 staff are currently on different types of international assignments. As a mode of gaining international experience, more use will be made of short-term assignments, particularly between the major centres such as Singapore, Hong Kong and London.

Developing a cadre of internationalized 'local' managers

Of course, one of the quickest ways of changing a culture is to bring in people with new ideas and relevant approaches. Recruitment from other companies with leading global practices brings a rapid injection of new ideas into SCB. Seventy per cent of the top 500 managers have joined the bank in the last seven years. As Geoff Rogers, global Head of Human Resources for Treasury, puts it, 'the performance benchmark (i.e. standards) is rising all the time'. In addition to shifting away from expatriate working, SCB has sought to grow potential managers for local operations through an extensive programme of targeted graduate recruitment. The idea is that developing international mindsets will be partly planned and partly 'organic'. Since 1993 the bank has carried out targeted recruitment of graduates from fifteen countries, of Asians and Africans in particular who have been educated at universities and business schools in the UK, Australia or the USA. International graduates are not necessarily required to be mobile. They are hired on 'home base' contracts and it is recognized that they have strong family and cultural ties. However, with their international education, graduates will more readily be able to 'think global, act local'.

Around 60 people a year have been recruited via the International Management Trainee programme. Potential recruits attend an assessment centre through which 'world-class people' are identified. For the first six months the successful candidates attend a global training programme which is held in London and Singapore. This provides an in-depth induction into the business and a professional foundation programme. Topics addressed include the core skills of banking as well as some of the 'soft' skill areas such as multi-cultural awareness. International competencies underpin the programme. Previous international recruits attend each programme to share experiences and to assist the development of networks. Global briefings are held to introduce graduates to the SCB culture, systems and business strategy. The briefings are facilitated by company executives. Recent developments include providing the same training opportunities to locally recruited graduates on this international programme. This adaptation reflects the fact that the original approach was probably too global and did not have enough 'local' ownership.

The overall aim of the training is to help the graduates to develop a 'group' mindset, rather than seeing no further than the specific division to which they have been assigned. As such they are very much a global resource, even though they may eventually be living and working in their own home country. The training and policy of developing a cadre of local managers appears to be paying off. Not only has business profitability improved dramatically but there are now many more 'local' or non-British CEOs and senior managers. They in turn are influencing the people who come after them.

For more senior employees a framework of management skills training which is the same everywhere is available. The more senior the employee, the more international is the nature of the training. So global induction introduces all new employees to the need to apply global templates to local issues. Middle to senior level management briefings are run in London by a multi-cultural team every three months. Briefings enable managers to meet directors and to feel part of the SCB 'family'. Employees, wherever they are based, can apply to obtain an MBA via distance learning. Some senior managers attend an international management programme at Insead. People with board level potential take part in a Global Consortium which includes organizations such as **ABB** and **Lufthansa** and is organized by the London Business School. The consortium members visit each others' companies and operating bases.

Supporting international high flyers

For managers who are about to go on an international assignment, help in preparing for the experience can make the difference between an effective start to the assignment or a dismal failure. Preparatory help includes training in cross-cultural issues, setting up procedures to maintain contact with the home office and help in finding employment for spouses. Once on assignment, employees look for help in adjusting on a practical level. A mentor can be useful here: not only someone who is familiar with the local customs and who can ease the process of integration but also someone at the home office who can be a vital link for the assignee on career issues. Support networks involving communication through travel and company newsletters can also be useful.

Perhaps the main area where employees look for support from the home office is on preparing for their return on repatriation. Typically this is an area of shortfall and relocation research has shown that many employees are dissatisfied with the quality of the communication, support and advice they receive prior to, and following, repatriation. Practical help and moral support are often needed to enable families to adapt to the change. There is evidence that many returning employees suffer 'reverse culture shock' and other problems of adaptation. This often happens because of a significant mismatch between people's expectations prior to their repatriation and what they actually encounter when they return home. The greater the clarity about possible return roles before the assignment begins, the better.

Conclusion – benefiting from international leadership

One of the greatest challenges for both organizations and their high-flying international employees is making the most of the enhanced skills and knowledge gained by individuals through their international role. The problem is perhaps most acute on repatriation when typically the employee is expected to slot into any available role. If the individual's knowledge is not used to good effect, the employee typically leaves the organization within a short time. The phenomenon is not simply that of a bruised ego and the individual finding him- or herself to be a small fish in a big pond. It is more that there are potential business benefits in enabling the individual's enhanced skills, and knowledge of the local market with its challenges and opportunities, to be put to good use. In many cases there is not even a formal debriefing of the individual after the assignment. Frustration at having no outlet for these skills, together with dissatisfaction about career prospects, are the common reasons given for individuals leaving after an international assignment.

So this chapter suggests a potential paradox: the demand for international high flyers is likely to increase at a time when there is a growing reluctance on the part of both employers and employees to continue down the expatriate route of development. Organizations are going to have to be more creative in the ways they attract, motivate and retain people. Clearly much can be done at recruitment to ensure that people are really interested in an international career, and that travel periods are concentrated.

Better use of technology will help in the management of international teams but will not replace need for people to work together face to face. More skilful support to employees and their families who are on assignment may reduce the number of expensive assignment failures. Better use of enhanced skills may retain valued employees for longer. Giving people the chance to develop and apply the high-level skills required of international leaders is only one part of the equation. Recognizing and using these enhanced skills to the mutual benefit of the organization and the employee is the surest way to tap into the motivation and commitment of international high flyers.

Checklist for international management strategies

- What are the main ways in which international employees are deployed, e.g. on short-term assignments, expatriate postings etc.?
- How much does your organization consider 'local' managers as part of the international management cadre?
- To what extent is telecommuting replacing the need for international assignments?
- How much does your organization consider 'local' managers as part of the international management cadre?
- To what extent is telecommuting replacing the need for international assignments?
- What are the implications for managers of enabling 'high touch' continuous interaction in support of international team members?
- How are employee motivation, reward and recognition currently aligned to the changing business and organizational priorities?
- How are terms and conditions for international employees currently defined? Are special terms required for expatriation, or simply reward arrangements which reflect flexibility and mobility?

References

Child, J. (1990). *The Management of Equity Joint Ventures in China*. Beijing: China – EC Management Institute.

Glynn, C. and Holbeche, L. (1999). *International Leadership*, Roffey Park Management Institute.

Ettore, B. (1993). A brave new world – managing international careers, *Management Review*, April.

Krempel, M. (1998). *Shared Services: a New Business Architecture for Europe*, The Economist Intelligence Unit.

Loose, A. (1998). Jobs sans frontières', *The Times*, 12 November.

McLuhan, R. (1999). The homecoming. *Personnel Today*, 4 March.

Panter, S. (1995). *Summary Report of a Qualitative International Research Survey*, Ashridge Management College.

Peiperl, M. in Coles, M. (1998). Global managers despair at heirs. *Sunday Times* 8 November.

Sansom, J. (1993). *Survey of Repatriation Assistance*, University of Westminster and CBI Relocation Council.

Smith, P. B. (1992). Organizational behaviour and national cultures, *British Journal of Management*, **3**, 39–51.

Solomon, C. (1996). 'expats say: Help make us mobile', *Personnel Journal*, July.

Tung, R. (1998). *Selection and Training of Personnel for Overseas Assignments*, Cambridge, MA: Ballinger.

11   *High-potential assessment and*
        succession planning

Jack Welch Jr is 'possibly the most admired business leader in the world and probably the most successful'. He has been placed among the top 40 power players in HR by *Personnel Today* because he places people issues at the top of his, and GE's priorities. GE is believed to have the best executive talent in the US because of Welch's development programme. Graduates flock to apply to the company, despite unattractive interests such as power generation. There are few better companies to benchmark against (Beagrie, 1999).

Senior management development programmes, graduate entry, accelerated development, high-flyer schemes, MBA recruits...the return of fast tracking appears to be underway in the UK. After a period in the 1990s when most large organizations gave up attempts to plan for executive resourcing and succession, the return of growth in the economy has brought with it renewed confidence in the future. The promise of speedy advancement up the corporate ladder is being resurrected as a means of attracting and retaining the 'best' candidates the job market can supply. The return of the graduate milk round, increased headhunter activity and job adverts which describe development packages alongside the usual benefits are just some of the indicators of such buoyancy.

The changing shape of succession

One expects achievement (performance) to be directly translated into climbing the organizational ladder: upward mobility is not only an achievement in its own right, but doubly so, since it is a negation of the alternative options: immobility (getting 'stuck' on the career ladder) or even demotion, if not dismobility (sacking) altogether. (Altman, 1997).

'High-potential' or 'high-flyer' employees have long been thought of as people who are likely to move rapidly up the corporate ladder. The assumption is that 'high-potential' people will carry on moving up the organization when those who are less able cease to progress. Most 'high flyers' are identified as such early in their careers, often at graduate entry. Other high-potential employees join organizations having obtained an MBA or professional qualification or having begun a fast-track career elsewhere.

Until relatively recently, most organizations of any size have developed succession plans for key individuals and posts in order to ensure that there is a ready supply of individuals prepared for the top jobs in the future. Typically, succession planning for the top executives in many organizations is based on:

- Contingency (emergency replacement)
- Replacement (of one person by another at a certain time)
- Succession (employees who may be groomed for a post over a number of years)
- Development (of employees with high potential).

Often, certain key competencies, such as strategic vision and the ability to manage change, are regarded as differentiators for top jobs. The development of the candidates for those jobs is often carried out on an individual basis and is usually focused on remedying weaknesses and pursuing individual aspirations.

The assumption implicit in succession planning is that most senior management roles can be filled from within and that growing internal talent is preferable to riskier options. Fast-track programmes described by Altman (1997) as 'the conscious, purposeful process of grooming that individuals go through on their way to the top' have been a common feature of such corporate career management. Indeed the term 'fast track' is attractive to many potential recruits to an organization and is designed to appeal to 'the best' candidates in the job market. As John Fuller, former Head of Fast Stream and European Staffing Division in the **Cabinet Office** put it:

We did review the logic behind it (the fast stream) in 1994, and the report concluded that there was still a need. If nobody had fast-track entry, then perhaps nobody would need one, but as long as (other) employer are making these offers, we need one that is competitive'. (*Management Today*, March 1997)

In recent years the fast rate of organizational change has meant that many succession plans have come unstuck and become unworkable. Even so, some organizations have attempted to keep succession planning going and the trend appears to be that other organizations are actively reinstating succession planning. Indeed, several have made a virtue out of maintaining a consistent approach to high-flyer recruitment and development during the turbulent years of the early 1990s. The focus of this chapter is to identify some of the difficulties relating to 'conventional' succession planning in the context of changing organizations and to identify some possible approaches from a range of organizations. Note that although conventional fast-track and succession planning schemes are generally referred to in the past tense, I am conscious that such approaches are still very much with us.

Conventional fast-track schemes and succession planning

In the days before the recent recession and consequent economic turbulence, most organizations were structured hierarchically with as many as twelve management levels between the first-line supervisor and top management. For most employees, advancement up the career ladder was gradual. Promotion opportunities were often via the management rather than the specialist route, even in companies where 'dual tracks' had been developed. Conventional 'fast tracks' were available to the very small minority of employees, perhaps no more than 2 or 3 per cent of the workforce, who were deemed to have potential for taking on general management or other executive roles. A slightly broader group, perhaps up to 10 per cent of the population would be developed for senior management roles.

The aim was, of course, to ensure that the organization had a small pool of potential successors for key roles, especially the top jobs, in the future. Promotion was from within. Typically, the chosen few would be offered a series of 'broadening' moves, sometimes at the same level, before being moved into a position of real influence. Senior post vacancies would be checked with the succession plan first. Sometimes individuals were told about their perceived potential. However, such assessments often remained confidential to the Human Resources professionals and senior line managers responsible for making such career judgements.

Conventional succession planning was not without drawbacks. A critical issue was how potential was assessed and whether the performance of 'high flyers' was seriously monitored. Such judgements were often made early in a person's career, often at entry. Early assessment was no guarantee that people could really cope with more serious responsibilities over time. More often than not, once an individual was labelled 'high flyer' it was unlikely that such opinions would be reviewed unless he or she seriously failed at some important activity. Similarly, people who were not classed as fast-track material early in their careers were often denied the opportunity for real advancement even if their talents later proved to be highly relevant to a significant role. If you missed the early opportunity for rapid advancement, you did not usually have a second chance.

Another common issue was the unworkability of succession plans in practice. Even in relatively stable times, roles with several identified 'successors' were frequently filled by people from outside the organization or the successors themselves were not available when the post became vacant. This became all the more apparent during the late 1980s and early 1990s with the ongoing downsizing and delayering of organizations. In many companies succession planning revolved around roles which it was assumed were critical to the organization and which were subsequently reengineered out of existence.

During mergers many roles simply ceased to exist, or individuals from the acquired company who had previously been judged to have potential were not given opportunities for political reasons. With the trend to flatter, leaner structures, many organizations gave up the attempt to plan for succession. Typically the function responsible for managing the fast-track processes, Human Resources, was itself downsized and devolved to the line. Fast tracking became increasingly an anomaly. After all, in a 'flat' structure, where was a 'high flyer' to 'fast track' to? With such issues unresolved, succession planning in many organizations simply stopped.

Changing career messages

Implicit in the notion of fast-track and succession planning schemes is the idea that the organization will make career possibilities available to individuals. To a large extent, this 'parent – child' relationship to career development works well if the individual's needs are satisfied by the opportunities on offer. Typically, the implied promise is that the organization will offer continuous employment and promotion opportunities in return for loyal and committed performance from individuals. However, the evidence of the recent past has seriously challenged key aspects of this 'psychological contract' between employers and employees. The balance of interests being served appears to have swung in favour of the employer, at the apparent expense of the employee. Job security is no longer a given in exchange for good performance and flatter structures have reduced the career options for many employees. Employability is supposed to have replaced job security as part of the new deal. As far as promotion goes, the common message given by many employers has been 'manage your own career'.

Interestingly, many employees perceive messages about 'manage your own career' to be abdication on the part of the employer and they no longer trust in the mutual benefits of the employment relationship. Judging by the Roffey Park research findings, few employees now believe that the organization will manage their career. On the one hand the idea that an organization, even a large one, is a static entity has been seriously challenged as companies which are household names merge, reshape or disappear. On the other, the increase of confidence in employees who know their own worth and who no longer trust in their employers has led to some well publicized examples of employees refusing to comply with their employer's bidding even though they effectively close the door on major career opportunities.

The extent to which employees have adjusted their ideas about careers is open to question. The Roffey Park research has looked at whether people are adjusting their career aspirations to consider lateral growth a viable alternative to the vertical progression implied by fast tracking. We have certainly found that for some people the opportunity to broaden their job role, albeit at the same level, has represented a form of career development since they have had greater challenge, visibility and a chance to learn new things.

However, this has been in the absence of high-flyer schemes. The return of such schemes is causing some frustration for people who have accepted the idea of lateral career growth over the last few years. In one major UK retailer, for example, graduate entry schemes were abandoned in 1991. The people who were in the last intake and who are now in their late twenties have found themselves on the same level and offered fewer growth opportunities than the people recruited with the return of graduate entry in 1995. Understandably, several of the earlier group have taken their skills and aspirations elsewhere.

On the whole we have found few people who seem prepared to abandon ideas of conventional career progression in favour of lateral growth. In our recent survey of high flyers we asked people what their ultimate career goal was and the most frequent response (38 per cent) was a 'high-level position'. On the face of it, employers who are offering fast-track development may well be able to tap this market of ambitious individuals. At the same time employers are becoming more demanding and are upping the entry level stakes. The increasing requirement for most roles is a first degree at least and usually a professional qualification as well. But while it is obvious that there is increased competition for the 'best' candidates, what happens to new recruits whose expectations have been raised by the recruitment process is less clear. One government department hired a number of people with PhDs for relatively junior executive officer jobs. Not surprisingly, several of these expensively hired new recruits left months later when the reality of their employment conditions and prospects hit home.

A more adult–adult relationship between employers and employees is based on the increasing power of the knowledge worker to make demands of the organization which go beyond pay and rations. This is particularly marked in some of the oil companies where overseas assignments as part of a broad career route for high-calibre employees are becoming increasingly difficult to fill. This is partly explained by the rise in the number of dual-career families but also by the increasing unwillingness of employees to make sacrifices if they are not guaranteed promotion on return from the assignment. There is already a good deal of anecdotal evidence that employees with transferable skills and experience are more confident of being employable and less tolerant of the frustrations of poor management, inappropriate reward and few growth opportunities. Ironically, the very skills which many employers crave – such as the ability to get things done, be innovative, customer oriented etc. – are precisely the skills which will help people get jobs elsewhere.

The recruitment and development of leadership talent

A traditional objective of succession planning, the development of future leaders, has often taken place around specific roles. In some companies there are only succession plans and planned development for the top-level jobs and for people identified as having high potential. **IBM, Rank Xerox** are examples. The trend currently is to develop leaders with a broad range of leadership competence in addition to any specific business experience they may offer. Leadership is highlighted as an area of competence in itself because of the changing requirements of business leaders to be able to provide focus and bring people with them in times of change. If the identification and growth of leadership talent is a primary objective, related objectives include the retention of talent and continuity of leadership.

Many organizations including **BP, Glaxo SmithKline** and **Texaco**, have developed generic leadership 'competencies' which are used to define leadership potential and as the focus for executive development. **Unilever** uses competencies for the assessment of potential, for graduate recruitment, executive recruitment, leadership training, appraisal (performance development planning) and rewards. Texaco's Core Leadership Competencies emphasize behaviour-based leadership in addition to specifically business-related skills.

Campbell's Soups identify talent at departmental, country and global levels. This is based on an assessment of potential, not only performance. Assignments are planned to develop skills and leverage strengths. Many organizations now use assessment centres routinely to select candidates for fast-track development and competency models, together with 360-degree feedback processes are increasingly used not only for individual development but also for talent identification. This is particularly the case in organizations which consider leadership development and succession planning as key tools in changing the organization's culture.

Developing and updating success profiles

Leadership competencies are also being used to create 'success' profiles for executives, though some organizations, such as **ICL**, have recognized the importance of encouraging a range of diverse talents within the organization through their 'professional community' approaches. Many organizations such as **Nationsbank** and **ICI** are using competencies as the means of developing executive success profiles for spotting potential and for development purposes. Increasingly, in organizations as diverse as **Texaco, Unilever** and **Philips**, success profiles are built on generic 'leadership' competencies as a means of bringing about culture change.

As ever, a warning note needs to be sounded: if leaders are to be capable of performing in today's and tomorrow's constantly changing environment, beware the limited shelf life of success profiles when business requirements change. Competencies must be integrated into the business planning process.

The assessment and development of high potential at BP Amoco

The information included in this case study is based on research carried out in BP shortly before the merger between BP and Amoco. However, numbers have been updated to reflect BP Amoco. The early indications suggest that **BP Amoco** is likely to adopt the former BP model and incorporate best practice from Amoco.

In a company with the size and reputation for development of BP Amoco it is hardly surprising that the assessment and development of people perceived to have high potential should be taken seriously. Indeed, at a time (in the early to mid-1990s) when other organizations were giving up the notion of succession planning because the volatile economic climate seemed to make such exercises fruitless, BP Amoco stepped up the quality and quantity of effort spent on the identification of employees considered to have high potential. BP Amoco has long enjoyed a relatively stable workforce, with many employees still expecting to complete their whole career in the company. As such, BP Amoco has the opportunity for relatively long-range planning with regard to succession.

The person largely responsible for stepping up BP Amoco's assessment and high-potential activities at Group level was Dr Candy Albertsson, an American whose experience including

Profile: Dr Candy Albertsson

Candy's role in this process was to act as an objective and neutral third party. Her objective was to achieve the best development of the individual for the organization and she therefore occasionally had to challenge some senior players. Her success relied on the trust which she had built up among managers and high potentials and her reputation for integrity and confidentiality.

Candy Albertsson is an industrial/organizational psychologist with ten years of experience in the strategic, design and operational phases of various management development systems including competencies 360-degree feedback, assessment centres, high-potential development programmes, executive succession planning and survey processes in BP Amoco. She has been based in London since 1992. Previously she worked for American Telephone and Telegraph in their Selection and Assessment Center Division in Basking Ridge, New Jersey.

Her last role with BP Amoco was Manager, High Potential Development, where she provided the managing director with strategic support on a variety of issues including a review of BP's leadership talent pool, supply and demand for top 25 succession and the supporting infrastructure to develop world-class leadership. During the latter part of 1999, Candy established an independent management consultancy based in London.

working for AT&T stood her in good stead for her role in management development.

Within BP Amoco, 'high potential' refers to the perceived ability to reach one of the top 100 jobs out of a workforce of 94 000. The majority of people who are thought likely to reach such roles are among the 25 000 professional and middle management employees. Before 1992, high-potential employees were principally the responsibility of a group level committee with representatives from the three businesses (i.e. Oil, Exploration and Chemicals), the Regions and Corporate and focused primarily on deployment. Career development often took the form of a series of moves around the main businesses, acquiring different levels of responsibility and experience.

The limitations of this relatively basic way of developing future leaders were recognized but attempts to improve the process were not without challenge. One initiative was the introduction of Personal Development Planning to supplement the company-driven deployment approach to development. This introduced more of a partnership between individuals and the organization. People were given the opportunity to reflect on their career aspirations and short-, medium- and long-term goals. In some cases, people aspired to strategic, rather than operational roles and there was a 'reality check' against performance feedback to suggest whether an individual's aspirations were realistic.

The identification of high-potential employees needed special attention. Though graduate recruitment was, and remains, the main entry point for high-flying employees, formal assessment of high potential tends to take place at a relatively junior level, some four to ten years after joining the company. While talent can be spotted at this stage in a person's career, lack of line management or cross-functional experience may make it difficult to recognize undeveloped management talent. However, for employees who were not perceived at this early career stage to have high potential, the route to the top jobs was much more difficult. Candy Albertsson felt that only a junior level programme for identifying potential was wasteful of late-blooming talent. She introduced the idea and gained support for developing a senior-level assessment that would enable the identification of potential later in one's career.

Improving the processes

Candy's objective was to ensure that the group as a whole would benefit from the effective identification and development of high-potential talent. Clearly, the challenges of winning the support of the top twenty business heads for changing processes which appear to be working well from a local business perspective required high-level influencing skills and credibility. Working with a small team of management development specialists, Candy set about creating the infrastructure for improved processes, including winning senior-level support. Key moves included the globalization of the junior level Assessment of Leadership Potential (ALP) assessment programme to create one standard Group programme. This replaced four established regional junior level assessment programmes. Other key moves were the introduction of a senior-level assessment programme – the Leadership Enhancement through Assessment and Development (i.e. LEAD) – and the introduction of a cohort review process for high potentials at Group level.

Following Project 1990 (i.e. culture change programme), an 18-month study generated a set of nine leadership competencies which were used as a means of providing a consistent approach to high-flyer development at group level. These competencies were measured in a 360-degree feedback process. However, while 360 provided good individual development data, it could not be used to compare between different people. Further data from the 360-degree process cannot be aggregated and therefore it is not possible to assess the aggregate strengths and development needs of the organization. It was important to build on the early success of the new tools by building a standardized process and means of measurement across the group.

Candy believed in making these processes as transparent as possible, and the competencies were a good start in showing people what successful performance looks like: 'It is important to communicate to people what skills are required, and what the expectations of performance are in the organization. You need to provide a user-friendly way for people to measure. 360 is a powerful development tool, but it has its limitations.' A limitation of the use of 360 was that while each leadership competency can be examined through a questionnaire, different raters, such as the individual's line manager, peers or direct reports, may not have had the opportunity to observe a particular competency. Similarly, certain jobs may not provide the opportunity for the job-holder to demonstrate that particular competency. When views about development are being made based on incomplete or potentially unrepresentative information, the drawbacks of the process need to be recognized. The LEAD programme addressed these limitations.

The LEAD programme

Candy Albertsson set about introducing the concept for a new process for the later identification of talent to supplement the junior-level assessment process and to provide the standardized objective yardstick needed across the group. She led the project team which started developing the LEAD Programme in early 1993. A key strategic objective of the programme was to gain quality data on the main organizational training and development needs as well as an overview of the talent pool within BP Amoco. Candy worked in partnership with a consultant, Joel Moses, in the design phase and the first programme was piloted in June 1994. It has been managed in-house since the first programme and is run once per quarter. The programme is championed by the Deputy Chief Executive and high-potential committee. Participants in this process include employees of long standing, often with twenty years' experience, many of whom may not have aspired to a senior level role earlier in their career. The participant pool of about 1000 managers are drawn from the top 1500 managers.

The LEAD programme is essentially an assessment centre in which all nine leadership competencies are assessed. It is intended to complement existing performance data rather than being seen as a pass/fail or ranking exercise rendering all other data redundant. However, the data which come from the centre in the form of a LEAD report are widely used and important. Development Groups including a line manager, a mentor and HR specialist 'reality check' the assessment report. The report addresses each of the nine leadership competencies, plus feedback on style and approach. An important element is the in-depth feedback to individuals which goes beyond the feedback typically covered in a performance review. LEAD provides participants with one and a half hours of development feedback from a line manager and there is a process in place to link feedback to action plans – the Development Group which is described later in this chapter.

An important benefit of the LEAD programme is the development opportunity it provides for observers. It is critical that observers are able to assess behaviours as objectively as possible and to translate their observations into feedback. The observers, who are very senior line managers (i.e. the top 300), are trained in coaching and feedback skills and are required to fully understand the leadership competencies which they will be observing and evaluating. Key benefits of senior managers taking part in this skilled process are the positive impact on their own approaches to management and the further bedding down of the competencies from the top of the organization. Observers generally value taking part in the process and this has strengthened the base of support for the programme. This common approach to understanding what is required of future leaders has provided a powerful tool which generates 'developmental blueprints' used by individuals, line managers and development committees.

How the LEAD programme works

Each LEAD programme is run over four and a half days in two parallel teams of six participants and three observers. Delegates take part in a business simulation which reflects the environment BP Amoco leaders face in complex global markets. However, to ensure that there is a level playing field and that the simulation does not favour people with specific forms of knowledge or experience, the exercise is set outside the oil industry. The simulation contains a number of written and verbal exercises, including an in-tray. Actors are used for a situation in which participants are required to coach their 'direct report'. The simulation also contains a number of team problem solving challenges on business, regional and group issues.

The programme is designed to measure leadership at strategic and operational levels by examining an individual's approach to decisions and problems, rather than using psychometric tests. Observers are trained for one day before the start of the simulation and then have a day's integration meeting in which they aggregate and review their observations on each individual. The output of these discussions is an agreement of whether each of the nine competencies demonstrated by a participant is a strength, development need or weakness. Strengths are defined as where the individual demonstrates 'real power' in the competency; the 'development zone' is where the level of competence is 'probably sufficient for the individual's current level of responsibility but will need to be strengthened for higher levels of responsibility'; potential weaknesses are areas of limitation which could have 'significant impact' on their performance at higher level and are a priority for development. Participants receive on-site feedback on Friday morning from one of the managers who has observed the process.

The written report which follows the programme consists of a leadership competency profile and three to four written pages elaborating on each of the nine competencies, on development priorities and options. An individual's leadership competency profile can be compared against a number of development profiles identified for critical business situations such as start-ups, business expansions and alliance building. These profiles were developed from interviews with forty senior line managers and can be used to determine 'development moves' or 'ideal fits'.

Validating the findings

One of the common criticisms of assessment or development centres is that there is a lack of follow-through when participants are back at work. Does anyone care or notice if someone has started to improve on an area of weakness? Is the information from the programme valid in the work context? Will information about strengths and weaknesses be taken into account when decisions are made about jobs? The LEAD programme attempts to provide a comprehensive follow-through from the centre, integrating with other existing processes and performance information to ensure that the data are used.

Following LEAD, all participants are strongly encouraged to establish a Development Group consisting of their line manager, an HR development specialist and a mentor. A minimum of two meetings is recommended and the aim is to enable participants to link their feedback to a written action plan back in the workplace. It is very easy for findings from a development process to be discredited or ignored if participants can say 'well, I'm not like that at work'. The development group's function is to provide the reality check for the data emerging from the LEAD programme. Ninety per cent of the Development Groups validate LEAD reports in this way, which is very powerful in strengthening the metric.

Once the findings have been validated, the reality check and action plan are permanently attached to all copies of the individual's LEAD report. The report is now available to Group and business development committees and is used for selection and development moves. The action plan is incorporated into performance appraisal objectives and personal development plans. Multiple comments can be added over time as development needs are addressed. As such it is a living report (see Figure 11.1).

Identifying organizational strengths and development needs

Data on individual strengths, development needs and weaknesses are aggregated to provide a composite picture of the competency areas which need special attention. This allows trends to be identified and information which can be used to determine organizational training and development needs. It also highlights areas within the talent pool where there may be issues or gaps. Candy Albertsson believes that no other tool can provide an organization with data of this quality and strategic significance, particularly since the top 300 generated the data in the first

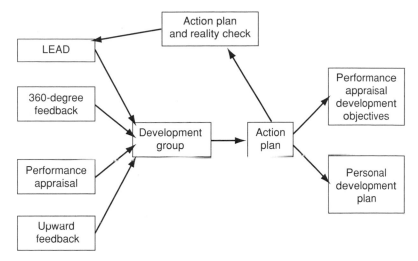

Figure 11.1 *Linking competency assessment to development*

place. This information can then be used to proactively identify appropriate training and development solutions.

Succession planning for the top jobs in BP Amoco – a strategic approach

An interesting approach to succession planning for the top jobs in BP Amoco is based on a structured, long-term assessment and development format. The 200 high-potential candidates viewed to have the capability to reach the top 100 jobs in the company are mainly drawn from the top 2500. A broader group of achievers are expected to reach the top 500 roles (i.e. Group Leadership), but development of these people takes place largely within their own businesses, i.e. Oil, Exploration, Chemicals or Global Business Centre. The supporting infrastructure for succession planning consists of a set of functional development committees within each of the businesses. These link into HR committees within each business which in turn link to the group-level HR committee (Figure 11.2).

Draft plans are initially generated by a combination of current incumbents' knowledge of direct reports and others and the HR secretariat for each committee. The committees then work to finalize the plans based on personal knowledge of potential

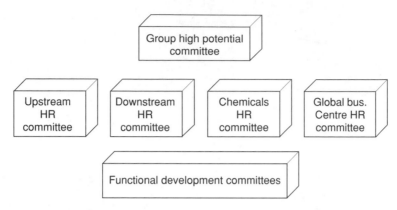

Figure 11.2   *The supporting committee infrastructure in BP Amoco*

successors and high potentials. This personal knowledge is developed through an on-going annual review of all high-potential individuals. Each committee focuses on a different group of high potentials. Succession planning is taken very seriously by the business.

The high potential population is divided into four groupings or 'cohorts' and these are based on:

- Stage of their development, e.g. their grade at the time
- Historical rate of progression, e.g. moving through the grades every eighteen months as opposed to the norm of two years
- Longer-term potential, i.e. perceived ability to reach the top hundred or even top twenty jobs.

The four cohorts are grouped according to the approximate number of years required for individuals to reach the top jobs. Progress within cohorts is reviewed using a Development Checklist which summarizes whether a person has acquired all the key experiences for their stage of development. The checklist, prepared by the Group HR Executive support team, is easy for senior managers to understand and helps the review process to work smoothly (Figure 11.3).

The cohort analysis is done annually, with one cohort being reviewed per quarter. Only half a cohort will be reviewed at a time, with special attention being paid to those who will move in the next twelve months. Cohort membership is not static. Feedback about individuals is provided by committee members or by Dr Candy Albertsson, Manager, High Potential Development (for

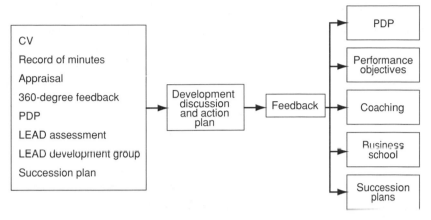

Figure 11.3   *The cohort review process in BP Amoco*

profile, see above). Nor is the information concerning the review kept secret. Feedback on development and gaps has an impact on personal development plans and individual performance objectives. Typically, 20 per cent move up in a cohort annually. There is not necessarily an even distribution between the cohorts. On a few occasions, a relative shortage of identified junior talent has prompted the high-potential committees to actively seek out potential lower down the organization. It is also recognized that telling people that they are part of the high-potential programme tends to encourage and motivate them.

However, the primary purpose behind grouping individuals into cohorts is that it enables more closely targeted development opportunities to be made available according to the individuals' stage of development. To reach the top 100 jobs it is essential that individuals are able to work across boundaries. They must have some international experience and have built up international exposure to reach the most senior roles. So for people in cohort four, i.e. fifteen to twenty years away from a top job, it is considered important that they acquire some cross-functional experience. During their tenure in this cohort, individuals will be likely to attend a junior version of the LEAD programme, known as ALP and take part in the 'Stage 1' management development programme. Stage I offers a strategic overview of the business – the issues and deliverables within the regions. Participants meet with members of the most senior management tiers and gain a better understanding of their region.

People in cohort three, ten to fifteen years away from the top jobs, have the opportunity to acquire international experience and cross-business exposure. They are likely to have people management and bottom line responsibilities. They will also be invited to take part in the 'Stage II' management development programme which has a clear group focus on business strategy and people management. For people in cohort two, five to ten years away from a top job, there are opportunities to attend an international business school and the LEAD programme.

In cohort one, with only five years before individuals are considered ready for a top 100 job, development is very individually focused. It is also expected that these senior managers will take a lead role in the development of others – by acting as mentor or an observer on the LEAD or ALP programmes. They will be invited to Group Leadership meetings and contribute to group-level initiatives. They are able to state their aspirations through the personal development planning process and their names start to appear on candidate lists. Candy Albertsson acts as an internal job/people broker where she networks their names with line managers and committee members, coaches high potentials on their development and builds momentum for a role change. Top 500 roles each have a candidate list of potential successors, categorized as 'possible', 'emergency' and 'preferred'.

The changing employment context

The employment landscape into which fast-track schemes are being reintroduced is changing in a number of ways. The increasingly international or global nature of many organizations' operations has cross-cultural implications for resourcing strategies for key positions. Another trend – the emphasis on continuing professional development which predates the government's lifelong learning initiative – is now well established. This reflects the increasing recognition that the competitive advantage of organizations depends on the calibre and motivation of its 'knowledge workers'. Even as recently as five years ago the impact of the knowledge revolution and its resourcing implications had hardly been felt.

Employers are no longer having things their own way. This is particularly clear in the IT sector where the success of several organizations relies on the product development skills of a few key individuals. The truth of corporate value-speak such as 'Our people are our greatest asset' is a lesson which has been painfully learned in some cases when individuals move on. The definition of who is a 'key' employee is widening beyond those perceived to have high potential. Some of the biggest changes are to be found in employee attitudes. In the increasingly fragmented job landscape, loyalty to the employer is becoming a thing of the past and many organizations are urgently reviewing ways of securing the commitment of people whom they do not want to lose.

What's happening to fast tracking?

Of course, every organization has a responsibility to attempt to secure its future and many now recognize that developing people who will supply present and future success is key. The degree to which fast tracking should be seen as the main means of achieving this remains open to question. After all, conventional succession planning generally works best when an organization's environment, market conditions and structures are relatively stable and predictable. Understandably, in times of change, the basic parameters of planning, such as knowing where the organization is going, the skills needed for the future and the resources the organization currently has, are difficult to establish. Planning exclusively around roles seems shortsighted in such circumstances. Perhaps a more helpful model is based on identifying the skills and experiences which the broad business direction suggests will be required in the future and planning around developing talent at different levels in the organization.

An important question to answer when taking stock of current employees is who is key now and in the short- to medium-term future? The answer to that question may be different now from what it might have been several years ago. Similarly, organizations need to think through what they mean by potential and how to assess it. Some organizations insist that potential can only exist outside and hence rely heavily on external recruitment to resource key management positions. Often the tendency to rely on external recruitment is due to a combination of factors, including a widespread ignorance of the current skills of the existing workforce. However, such policies seem to have a largely negative effect on the morale of existing employees. A more useful approach might be to widen access to such schemes to include internal people who might have missed the fast track first time round if they appear to have the skills and attitudes which the organization needs as it moves forward.

This is not a purely philanthropic approach. Both the cost of external recruitment, especially if the new recruit does not 'fit' and soon leaves, and the value of the often irreplaceable knowledge of existing employees suggests that fast tracking should be a continuous, wide-based process rather than a scheme.

Building the talent 'pool'

Increasingly, succession planning activities in some sectors are being extended beyond a small privileged group of 'key employees' to include a much wider group. In such organizations, succession planning is not restricted to the top jobs. The question being asked in such organizations is 'who is key?' in this era of knowledge workers and intellectual capital. This is largely driven by the recognition that, in many cases, the real assets of an organization are its employees.

Of course organizational value statements have implied this for a number of years, but in knowledge- or skills-based industries such as IT the truth of such statements is apparent when highly skilled individuals who may not be considered top management material leave. This model of succession planning, focusing on people rather than specific jobs, is increasingly being adopted by **British Airways**. Other companies following a similar route include **United Airlines** and **ICI**. John Lee of ICI said 'a major issue for the 1990s will be the need to develop every member of the organization to his or her potential, and not just a cadre of senior people. Companies simply cannot afford to have under-utilized resources, or to make out-of-date assumptions about what individuals can and can't do'.

Campbell's Soups also recruits for talent rather than position. At a major insurance company, procedures vary according to level. All director-level jobs, for instance, are backed up with possible successors. Below director level, the process includes a wider population and allows for changes in roles. The aim is to build up a 'pool' of candidates who are being developed to fill positions at a given level in the organization. **United Airlines** has broadened the management levels included in succession planning by lowering the administrative burden through the use of client/server technology. This has enabled individual career planning and organizational succession planning to be better integrated. The **British Post Office** has developed a succession planning system which aims to develop a broad group of people with senior management potential. This approach breaks away from the conventional elitist mould which it replaces.

One model of succession planning concentrates on identifying a discrete list of candidates who are 'ready now' to step into open positions. **ICI** considers those who are 'ready now', those who will 'probably' succeed and those who will 'possibly' succeed. The **Dow Chemical Company** is employing an approach which uses competencies for global leadership to blend these two models in order to have the 'best of both worlds'. The process is based on the identification of competency profiles for the top positions. The type of succession planning model used depends on the number of roles which share a common profile. The 'both/and' approach allows for both a more targeted approach to talent identification and development as well as the assurance of appropriate succession in critical roles.

Sun Microsystems UK is one company which has focused on building up a broad cadre of individuals with a range of current and potential contributions to the business alongside providing accelerated development for a few. Sun offers all employees the opportunity to carry out career self-assessments and access to a range of development opportunities. One of these, a career development workshop called 'Manage your career within Sun', helps people to gain a realistic view of their strengths and development needs, an understanding of the career options within Sun and, most importantly, a greater insight into their own values and motivations. This runs alongside high-flyer development in a conventional sense. The success of this approach in retaining employees in a highly competitive job market is evident in much-reduced staff turnover rates. HR director Paul Harrison calls this 'providing career development opportunities for the top 80 per cent'. This range of integrated activities and processes make it practically possible for employees to manage their own career, including making internal moves.

This emphasis on individuals' values and choices is very much in line with the current climate in which employees are becoming more selective about who they want to work for. Career development is increasingly becoming a more obvious arena for negotiation between organizations and employees. Fast tracks which seem to offer rapid career development in a harsh and competitive organizational climate may be less attractive than they may at first appear. Far from seeking to whizz up a corporate ladder and take on yet more responsibility, some skilled and valued employees are now considering opting out of employment. Several major consultancies and at least one bank are now offering senior employees various forms of flexible working arrangement in order to retain them. Increasingly some knowledge workers are looking for more congenial working arrangements in organizations whose ethos they can espouse. As one 'high flyer' said as she joined her new employer, 'at last I'm working for a company whose product I believe in'.

Fast tracking then should become almost a state of mind as well as a development route. The 'fast' element should include opportunities to acquire the skills and experience needed by the organization in the short and medium term. One UK financial services organization has introduced a three-year structured development programme for a large group of existing and new employees of different levels and ages. The short-term payback to the organization is high morale among programme participants and widely applied learning. An international bank is introducing fast tracking to accelerate the development of an international management cadre. HR staff are aware of the danger of setting up an elite and work is underway to develop career tracks for employees at all levels.

All fast-track processes need managing and individuals on such tracks need ongoing monitoring and support to ensure that they are delivering what was intended and able to make the progress implied. Some organizations make extensive use of mentors for this purpose. In **Thresher**, a change initiative known as the Operations Development Project, brought about shifts in working practices and job roles. New staff were seeded into the organization with the skills and experience to maintain and develop the momentum for change. Recognizing that such employees might be subject to pressure and frustrations, the Operations Director and Human Resources Controller took charge of the recruitment processes and continued to act as mentors and support to these individuals for two years or more. The individuals were not on a fast track as such, but having the support they needed no doubt allowed them to contribute to the full. Most have now been promoted or internally head-hunted.

Towards a new form of succession planning

In the days of conventional succession planning, the purpose of the process was to supply successors for key posts in the organization in the future. Often succession planning was seen as a 'stand-alone' activity which was generally considered the responsibility of a specialist Human Resource unit. The tendency was to recruit and develop high flyers in the image of existing senior managers, rather than identifying the skills and behaviours required of future leaders in line with the general business direction. In one financial services organization, the process of identifying potential through management development reviews was known as 'cloning'!

As succession planning is reintroduced, there are opportunities to learn from the past as well as to examine from scratch how to maximize the potential of such processes. It will be important to consider what is really required in future business leaders over the next three to five years and beyond, which may not be quite the same as in the past. Similarly, in the current climate of ongoing economic and organizational change, succession planning should sit within a coherent, flexible and integrated set of organizational development strategies. Just as Human Resource strategies should support the business strategy, so succession planning should be a key means of building organizational capability. Conversely, if a holistic approach to succession planning is adopted, it is very easy to 'take one's eye off the ball' and lose sight of whether the processes are meeting the requirements. So with that warning note, an integrated approach, focused on building organizational capability to meet current and future business objectives, is the starting point for succession planning.

Recommendation one: Integrate succession planning with other initiatives

Link succession planning and corporate strategy

Among the limitations of conventional succession planning is the tendency for the planning process to be divorced from the corporate strategy and from what the organization is trying to achieve longer term. If succession planning takes place in isolation from the way the organization is going, 'successors' are unlikely to have the relevant skills and behaviours for leadership roles in the future. In devising new approaches to succession planning it is important to have a clear business imperative and be able to identify how the process must impact on the business. Of course, in times of change, developing a longer-term corporate strategy with clearly defined goals and management requirements is not always possible. Even a well-defined corporate strategy will need to flex with changing circumstances and succession planning processes will need to do the same. The **Corestates Financial Corporation** addresses this issue by focusing on its corporate vision, principles and core values rather than detailed corporate and business plans and so provides a focus for the development of leaders during a period of rapid change in the banking industry.

Link succession planning with management development, leadership performance and assessment

So if what is required in changing industries are innovative, proactive succession strategies aimed at strengthening business success, it is important to tie together succession planning, employee development and the use of assessment instruments to enhance leadership performance. In **Hershey Foods Corporation**, assessment instruments can be used to assist in the candidate/job matching process. In the **Post Office**, career planning, talent review and succession planning are linked. **AlliedSignal Aerospace** integrates performance management, development, succession planning and reward processes. **Texaco** combines the use of competencies, the development of the 'talent pool', culture change and succession planning. For senior management positions in Texaco, the key to differentiating candidate readiness for advancement is through the demonstration of Texaco's Core Leadership Competencies. In **Philips**, leadership competencies are at the heart of an integrated set of processes which include selection, performance appraisal, development, education and training and succession planning.

BP Amoco succession planning is part of an integrated set of initiatives which include an internal audit of talent, an understanding of gaps to be filled, senior-level assessment and management development. Individuals with potential are identified, join the LEAD programme and form 'cohorts' who are at different stages of their leadership development. Information from appraisals, 360-degree feedback, Personal Development Plans,

Leadership assessment (LEAD) and succession plans feeds into tailored development discussions and action planning. Feedback is then given on the individual's personal development targets. Depending on the individual's need, further development may take place through performance objectives, coaching or business school attendance.

Schering-Plough Pharmaceuticals review successor and high-potential talent within a three-year framework for management and organization development. Of course, in a short-term results-oriented organization, the benefits of an integrated approach to succession planning may need selling to the senior management team. Senior management attention is usually focused on matters financial, technological or concerned with market share. In a decentralized organization this task can be even more difficult, especially if the regional operations see no reason to 'share' information about high-potential individuals with the centre. In **BP Amoco**, the most senior levels of management are directly involved in the management of high-potential programmes, with the High Potential Committee chaired by the Deputy Chief Executive.

Recommendation two: Be clear about what else you want to achieve though succession planning

It is therefore important to be clear what objectives are being served by the succession planning process and for measures to be set to ensure that those objectives are being achieved. A few key objectives which appear to be complementary and achievable follow.

Workforce planning and development

A key objective of succession planning is the identification of candidate 'pools' from among existing employees who are ready for advancement. For this to happen systematically, a meaningful and effective system for talent pool review and development needs to be created. This will involve management development assessment and planning. For the process to be systematic, it will need to be against agreed criteria which are clearly understood and stem from business requirements. Data will need to be collected, analysed; decisions taken and plans made. The process will need to be monitored to ensure that the 'talent' identified is being developed and demonstrated in practice.

For the data gathering to be effective, line managers across the organization will need to be involved, trained and taking responsibility for identifying and nurturing the organization's potential. Of course, this is easier said than achieved, especially in a decentralized organization where the benefits of business unit autonomy have to be weighed against the longer-term benefits to the organization as a whole of developing people potential as a corporate rather than local resource. As has already been stated, any planning system of this sort needs to be reviewed to ensure that it is meeting needs and moving in line with the business. It also needs to be as simple and transparent as possible. This does of course suggest an automated process to some extent but the decisions about the process should in every case precede automation considerations.

Workforce planning should highlight gaps in the organization's capability to deliver its longer term strategies. Typically these gaps should be filled by judicious recruitment, both for specific roles and to build up the supply of new talent within the organization. Gaps in the organization's current capability can also be filled through management development. The danger in a rapidly changing environment is to assume that gaps can only be filled by recruitment rather than development, because development takes too long. This contingency approach to planning can backfire in several ways. Not only do new people usually need time to become effective in their roles, but if their 'fit' with the organization does not work, expensive mistakes can be made.

Similarly, a policy of external appointments for key roles can demotivate internal candidates, especially if they have developed the relevant skills for a key role. The challenge is to strike a balance by developing processes which aim to identify organizational and individual needs and gaps while creating short and medium term solutions which include both development and recruitment. A happy compromise between external and internal recruitment to high-flyer schemes appears to have been struck in a UK retail bank. Their leadership development programme lasts for two years and the programme's aim is to develop the perceived potential of high flyers by exposing them to a range of learning and business opportunities. Recruits to this programme include a number of individuals in their forties, who have been with the company for a number of years and whose potential for senior roles has only recently been recognized.

Create a lever for critical cultural change

Of course, if businesses are going through change, they are likely to require different skills and behaviours of employees in general and of leaders in particular. Given the generally recognized importance of leaders 'walking the talk', succession planning can have an important role in developing leaders whose skills and values are in tune with the changing culture of the organization. One financial services organization highlighted the problems caused by senior managers failing to practise the teamworking values which they advocated for others. The company in question attempted to bring about behaviour change by training senior management in leadership skills and using upward feedback processes. When that failed to produce significant changes in behaviour, feedback results were fed into decision making about bonuses. Management behaviour soon shifted in the desired direction.

In **Rhône-Poulenc Canada** succession planning is linked to management development, organizational strategy and culture. In making these connections it is important to identify both starting points – by carrying out an audit of the current culture – and 'destination' points in the targeted culture. These should be described in terms of competencies or behaviours. The leadership competency models should be built around around the targeted culture and assessment and development tools developed for 'high-potential' candidates in the succession planning pool. In Rhône-Poulenc, 360-degree models and psychometric tests are used, together with performance measurement data. The information gathered is fed into the succession planning system.

In **SmithKline Beecham**, leadership planning is considered as important as succession planning. Through the Leadership and Development Review, managers are judged not simply on what they produce but on how they perform against the values of the organization. As such, the leadership planning process becomes transformational in supporting the business, not just a transactional exercise. Leadership development is considered to take place mainly on the job and feedback from management teams is an important part of fine tuning leadership ability. For leadership development to become a process, not an event, line

managers need to be engaged in assessing potential and supporting development.

Federal Express has created a Leadership Institute which
conducts week-long courses where attendance is required as
managers move into the various levels. Courses are also run on
improving leadership effectiveness with a special emphasis on
developing the 'soft' skills of leadership. A parallel process
known as the Leadership Evaluation and Awareness Process
(LEAP) is used to assess and prepare individuals for their roles
as managers. The process allows people who are interested in
formal leadership roles to put themselves forward and receive
self-development tools and personalized coaching. FedEx leaders and performers are directly involved in helping other people
to develop. This has produced twin benefits by increasing the
readiness of managers for leadership responsibilities as well as
reducing the turnover of front-line management.

Recommendation three: Create the processes, then assess and monitor performance

The basic questions to ask when developing succession plans are
relatively straightforward and stem from the Human Resource
planning cycle. They are:

- *Selection* Who are the right people to meet our business
  needs?
- *Performance appraisal* How have they performed against their
  objectives?
- *Development planning* What is their potential? What steps do
  they need to take to realise that potential?
- *Education, training and learning* What learning opportunities
  are required to support their development?
- *Succession planning* Who will fill our key positions now and in
  the future?

Ideally, a succession planning policy should take into account a
number of key factors:

- The organization's external business environment and the
  market trends which suggest new commercial requirements
  and skills in the employee base

- Current and future business strategies and resourcing requirements
- Current and changing culture and values
- Defining key roles within the organization, together with the skills and competencies required to carry them out
- An assessment of the current employee base in terms of skills and competencies
- An assessment of the organization's future needs in relation to the number of employees required, their skills, training and overall makeup of the workforce in terms of background etc.
- Plans for bridging gaps.

The core processes are also relatively simple in theory, but more difficult to implement in practice for a variety of reasons. Typically these include succession planning being seen as a 'stand-alone' activity or as a responsibility of Personnel alone, processes becoming outdated or inappropriate and inadequate data flow. At the very least, succession planning processes should be developed to cover:

- Ongoing planning activity which assesses how well the organization is placed to meet replacement requirements etc.
- Individual performance and potential assessment
- Individual development planning.

Interconnected processes include:

Selection
- College recruiting – the 'milk round'
- Experienced new hire selection, including MBA recruitment
- Internal job movement

Performance appraisal
- Appraisal of job responsibilities and accomplishments
- Reviewing personal and team effectiveness
- Assessing the balance between what has been achieved and how

Development planning
- Assessment of potential
- Identification of development needs
- Career development planning
- Development action planning and review

Education, learning and training
- On-the-job development
- Educational and training programmes
- Learning groups
- Peer coaching
- Learning 'logs' and development portfolios
- Programmes to support organizational and individual development needs

Succession planning
- Identification of successors and potential successors for key roles
- Creation of development opportunities for potential successors

Effective collation of information

It is important to create a process infrastructure which enables succession planning to work effectively. There need to be simple and direct methods of assessing employee potential, for spotting opportunities to help individuals to develop and which allow for the integration of information from a range of sources including different forms of feedback. Increasingly organizations are using competencies as a means of providing a common language about performance. Information needs to be tracked and data kept up to date. Individual and job profiles must also be kept up to date so that effective opportunity matching can occur. A coherent set of processes is evident in **Wendy's International**. A suite of activities takes place which include ongoing disciplined job analysis, screening tools for success, assessment centres, Human Resource planning, individual development planning and outcome-based evaluation.

In **United Airlines**, the process of pushing succession planning down the management ranks is assisted by developing automated processes which overcome some of the limitations of paper flow logistics. This has enabled individual career planning and organizational succession planning needs to be married up more efficiently. Internal resumés are used to ensure that relevant skills are captured, together with candidates' internal/external history, future assignment and relocation interests. These can then be matched against selected management positions. Having access to the information online has resulted in streamlined reporting and improved staffing for vacancies.

Many companies have a central function with a role in succession planning. In decentralized companies, the central functions typically attempt to collect information on key employees. In decentralized succession planning systems such as at ICI, a series of management committees takes an overview of the processes of development and succession planning within an international business group or location. These committees review the succession plans of each business unit within the international business. The usefulness of any review process depends to a large extent on the quality of information provided by line management. Often, divisions are asked to supply the following:

- The strategic plan
- A review of the previous year
- Information about each individual, their performance, promotion potential and functions to which they are perceived to be best suited
- Details of past job and training history including current performance ratings
- Future career development plans, especially of high flyers
- Individual career ambitions
- Information on individual's cross-functional moves, including international experience.
- Information on an individual's training and skill levels.

In the **BOC** group additional data gathered includes what new jobs may be created in the future and who might fill them. The process is regulated by standard forms. Each business is also required to report on the strengths and weaknesses of its management, professional and technical workforce and produce an action plan to address problem areas. Companies such as **ICI** and **Rank Xerox** use a computerized succession planning system for storing information on both staff and positions.

Succession planning systems should ideally be incorporated into human resource planning systems so that detailed planning exercises can be undertaken for any part of an organization. Employee information such as:

- Skills and performance profiles linked to overall business criteria
- Training and development profiles
- Individual succession plans with alternative career/succession plans

can be supplemented by data modelling to facilitate:

- Resourcing and job/skills matching
- Tracking of expertise and experience in key project areas
- Successor identification
- Identification of 'what if?' scenarios.

Using development planning and interventions to achieve organizational success

In a few of the organizations involved in the Roffey Park study, training and development planning for individuals are now more closely tied to important areas for the business. Assignments and project work arising from education and training are being taken seriously by senior management as a means of both developing high flyers and addressing real business problems.

In decentralized organizations people responsible for management development and succession planning face a number of challenges. One of these is how to identify and develop 'high-potential' employees in different regions without harming the autonomy of regional management. One of the ways of doing this is by balancing the short-term needs of individual business-es with the long-term needs of the organization. In some organizations, generic competencies are used for the identification of potential while the development opportunities are made relevant to the local business in which the individual is operating. When the benefits to the region's business become apparent, regional managers usually develop a cooperative approach towards taking part in 'central' succession planning.

Managing assignments as well as development in place

ICL now offers longer assignments so that people have a chance to really achieve major objectives and see them through. In the case of international assignments, support may be required prior, during and after the assignment to reintegrate the individual and their learning. A number of organizations are now using mentors for this purpose, even when there is no overseas element to the assignment.

For most high flyers, development in place is likely to be the norm. Providing challenges and assignments to develop skills and leverage strengths should lead to retention. Development will involve continually 'raising the bar' and some organizations in our survey are identifying multi-sourced executive development opportunities. In some cases, organizations are collaborating on providing shared development opportunities for their high flyers. Such opportunities include secondments to other organizations in the network and joint working groups on industry-related issues.

Creating key management ownership of the process

Of course, relying on Human Resource processes alone for the identification of potential is not necessarily the best policy. It is important that line managers consider that they have a responsibility to spot and nurture talent as an organizational resource. Line managers are also ideally placed to assess actual performance and are a key partner in the objective-setting process. Some organizations such as **Schering-Plough Pharmaceuticals** are now measuring and rewarding managers for their part in developing others. Training and feedback processes can be helpful in enabling senior managers to take on this role. Involving senior managers in assessing potential through assessment centres, for instance, can be helpful in building up awareness and ownership of the process.

It is important that there is line ownership and senior management support for succession planning. Without this ownership, the day-to-day identification, development and management of high flyers may be confined to the occasional training or assessment intervention. It may be necessary to sell the importance of this to senior management and to garner support from critical constituencies.

A partnership – balancing the needs of the organization with those of the individual

Succession planning has long been seen as an organizationally owned process aimed at securing the organization's future. Often planning processes have been held in 'secret' with the organization's judgement on employees' potential, readiness for a move and current abilities withheld from the individual. Development moves have been offered to the individual who has been expected to fall in with these plans. Indeed, failure to keep moving has been seen as evidence of falling off the fast track, or 'derailing'. On the other hand, our survey suggests that high flyers are becoming more discriminating about what they require from their employer and less compliant with organizational 'offers' unless these meet the individual's needs.

If the 'empowered' employee has his or her own plans, can succession planning hope to incorporate these? A number of organizations are attempting to meet a number needs through their succession planning approaches. **AlliedSignal Aerospace** aims to meet the needs of individual employees, teams of employees and the organization through its integrated approach to performance management, development processes and succession planning. The **Post Office** aims to develop a coherent architecture of learning, experience and personal development at all stages of a manager's career, up to and including the boardroom. Some organizations are developing 'maps' of managerial careers to enable people to spot opportunities for themselves as well as gear their development to areas of interest to them.

In the **Springfield ReManufacturing Corporation**, employees are provided with a list of all jobs available in the organization and are asked to identify the next position they would like to hold. Training and development programmes are then built around qualification for the next position. Supervisors and managers track employees' progress and feed back results through individual annual reports. Similarly, managers are asked to provide a list of people whom they believe could fill their position. The management team then assesses whether potential candidates require further training before thcy are 'ready' for their specified jobs. This approach has led to the development of a pool of committed potential successors at every level in the organization.

The question of how open should an organization be about how a person's potential is perceived is often asked. The fears are that people may have expectations raised which may not be fulfilled, or that 'high potentials' will become more demanding if they know how they are perceived. These fears may be justified. On the other hand, if people are also made aware that while opportunities for promotion may be limited, other opportunities can be made available, the expected exodus may not be as large as anticipated. One FMCG company, for instance, trains its executive group in career counselling techniques. Each executive has a number of high-flying 'clients'. The objective here is not to promise rapid progression up the hierarchy but to convey the message that the organization values these individuals and is interested in their development. Being open with these individuals has not proved a problem, quite the reverse.

Conclusion

Increasingly, the processes used in succession planning and management development generally – such as individual development planning and 360-degree feedback – provide people with insights and information which inevitably help them to self-assess their potential. Involving employees in the succession planning process in an open and honest way may allow for more detailed, realistic career planning and lead to better retention. Adopting a 'partnership' approach with the individual should also turn succession planning into a validated process rather than a fortune-telling exercise.

Succession planning needs to be a continuous process, rather than an annual event. It should be focused on longer-term development and retention, rather than short-term replacements or emergencies. It should centre on what is needed, rather than on who is in place. It should consist of processes which overcome some of the inevitable inconsistencies in the assessment of potential. It should facilitate the removal of blockages and enable a healthy turnover in key positions. It should involve staff and create a pool of available talent at all levels in the organization. It should also lead to talent being positioned in the best place to meet both individual and organizational needs.

HR will need to take on a facilitative, coordinating role as well as being able to design and monitor processes to ensure that they continue to meet business needs. This is a significant responsibility given that the link between the quality of leadership and business success is evident in many organizations. In a real sense, the future success of the organization can depend on the way in which its leaders have been selected and developed.

While conventional succession planning and fast-track schemes may satisfy the desire for conventional career development for a few, any organization which 'puts all its eggs in one basket' is potentially leaving itself exposed longer term. Employee loyalty can no longer be taken for granted and our research suggests that promotion does not guarantee a desire to remain with an employer.

Fast tracks can happily co-exist alongside other development routes but any organization which ignores the need for some form of development for the bulk of its employees may be doing itself a disservice. If succession planning activities are restricted to the senior jobs, there should be career development for all. What the high flyers we interviewed, and many others who were not so described, call for is the opportunity to really achieve. Career processes which provide people with increased challenge and personal growth do seem to satisfy people and increase their commitment to the organization, for a time at least.

Checklist for succession planning

Does the organization have the leadership for the future required to move it forward?

- How do we define leadership? How do we assess and select for it? How do we define the difference between managers and leaders?
- How do we define potential?
- What is our philosophy with regard to high-potential development – small or large group, or both?
- How can we develop people in such a way that they gain meaningful experience?
- What gaps do we have in our top management succession?
- How can we ensure that people with potential have a real development challenge and appropriate recognition?
- How can we ensure that the organizational needs and those of the individual are met?

References

Altman, Y. (1997). The high-potential fast-flying achiever: themes from the English language literature 1976–1995. *Career Development International, MCB*, 2 July, 324–330.

Baruch, Y. and Peiperi, M. (1997). High flyers: glorious past, gloomy present, any future? *Career Development International, MCB*, 2 July, 354–358.

Beagrie, S. (1999). Top 40 power players in personnel. *Personnel Today*, 15 April.

Bird, A. (1994). Careers as repositories of knowledge: a new perspective on boundary-less careers. *Journal of Organisational Behaviour*, **15** 325–344.

Cox, C. J. and Cooper, C. L. (1988). *High-Flyers*, Oxford: Basil Blackwell.

Doherty, N., Viney, C. and Adamson, S. (1997). Rhetoric or reality: shifts in graduate career management. *Career Development International*, 2 April, 173–179.

Duller, J. (1997). In: Jo Oliver, The new-look fast track. *Management Today*, March.

Grundy, T. (1997). Human resource management – a strategic approach, *Long Range Planning*, **30**, No.4, 507–517.

Holbeche, L. (1997). *The Impact of Flatter Structures on Careers*. Oxford: Butterworth-Heinemann.

Holbeche, L. and Glynn, C. (1998). *The Roffey Park Management Agenda*, Roffey Park Management Institute.

Kaplan, R. M. (1990). The expansive executive, *Human Resource Management*, **29**, No.3, 236–247.

Kotter, J. (1995). *The new rules: how to succeed in today's post corporate world*. New York: Free Press.

Larsen, H. H. (1997). Do high-flyer programmes facilitate organizational learning? *Journal of Managerial Psychology*, **JZ**, 48–59.

Lewis, G. B. (1992). Men and women towards the top: backgrounds, careers and potential of federal middle managers. *Public Personnel Management*, **21**, No.4, 473–491.

Marsh, C. B. (1992). Fatal flaws. *Executive Excellence*, **9**, No.1, 18.

Oliver, J. (1997). The new look fast track. *Management Today*, March.

Phillips Petroleum recruitment advertisement, *Sunday Times*, 15 February, 1998.

Van Gennep, A. (1960) *The Rites of Passage*, Chicago, IL: University of Chicago Press. Referred to in Altman (1997).

Wallum, P. (1993). A broader view of succession planning, *Personnel Management*, September.

Some organizational references drawn from conference inputs as follows:

IQPC Conferences on Succession Planning, 5 March, 1997 and 21–22 October, 1997.

International Competencies Conference 15 October, 1997.

Part 3   HR as a strategic function

How can HR be more strategic? While there is no simple answer to this, I suggest that delivering results within an increasingly strategic agenda is part of the answer. Having the skills, knowledge and courage to act strategically is another. Dave Ulrich (1995) describes an effective senior manager who took the risk of introducing cooperative work practices at the factory he managed, in the face of opposition from head office. The gamble paid off and performance was enhanced. When asked why he was willing to take such a risk, the manager replied 'I've worked in other places before, and I may have to again'. This manager was willing to take a calculated risk, and take action, even though there were plenty of reasons to leave things as they were. The challenge for HR professionals is to decide where they are going to focus, and bring about change which is in line with what the business needs, even if there may be some short-term costs to the function.

Developing a strategic HR agenda

The impact of environmental changes on employees and organizations cannot be over-estimated. If organizations are to achieve their business strategies, they will need skilled and motivated employees who are committed to achieving these goals. HR is at the heart of building a competitive culture. HR professionals need to know which of the major environmental shifts – through technology, globalization, etc. – are likely to have the biggest impact on the business strategy and then put actions in place to equip the organization for change. This will require using data effectively – such as an inventory of current skill levels against future requirements. Technology will drive changes in working practices, including empowerment of skilled workers and the need for new skills in utilizing information in decision making. Spans of control are likely to remain large and employees will need help in becoming self-managing.

Cost pressures due to increased competition, largely as a result of globalization, are driving the need for greater speed, innovation and quality. If employees are to be expected to 'go the extra mile', their commitment must be reciprocated. The organization must find ways of helping people to develop new and satisfying careers and reward them appropriately. The development of global leaders is likely to become a key priority in many organizations; ways will need to be found to help managers function effectively on a global scale but also act effectively at the local level. HR too must find ways to mirror local conditions in policies and practices while at the same time raising the overall standard of skills amongst local employees. Obtaining organizational synergy through effective HR processes which improve organizational functioning will be major contributions.

A strategic agenda for HR is likely to be long term and set the criteria for HR practices which are more short-term and may need adjusting as conditions change. While meeting short-term needs is important, HR can help to create a 'broadly and powerfully defined culture which is (1) strongly customer focused and (2) capable of leap-frogging the competition through continual and radical innovation' (Brockbank, 1997).

What do HR professionals see as priorities for the future?

In the Roffey Park *Personnel Today* 1999 survey of personnel professionals, the following priorities were considered to be 'top of the list' by respondents from all sectors:

* Training and development
* Communication
* Performance management
* Aligning HR and business strategies
* Reward and recognition.

At the bottom of the list of future priorities were:

- Ethics
- Welfare issues.

Interestingly, some of the areas known to have an impact on employee satisfaction such as career management were considered only medium priorities. The development of leaders too, especially the top team, was not considered especially important yet arguably such is the importance of leaders to culture change that focusing attention on developing the management cadre may well achieve several strategic objectives simultaneously.

Repositioning HR – from transactional to value added

If HR strategy is going to be taken seriously within an organization, HR has to 'earn a place at the table' (Brockbank, 1997). Rightly or wrongly, HR suffers from a bad press. An article about HR in *Fortune* magazine asked 'why not blow the sucker up?' For Neil Hayward, formerly HR Director for **Booker PLC**, 'it is not enough to redesign, restructure or reposition HR. A re-invention is necessary'. Reengineering involves improving the effectiveness of HR while reducing cost. It requires assessing how work is performed and how processes can be improved. Then processes which have the greatest potential for improvement and cost savings need to be identified. Internal customers' needs must be clearly defined and the people rearrangements for improving business fundamentals determined. The basics involve asking:

- Why is an activity done?
- Why is it done when it is done?
- Why is it done where it is done?
- Why is it done the way it is done?
- Who does it and why?

HR programme delivery can then be revamped accordingly. In Neil's experience, simply reengineering HR in order to redesign HR processes in a dramatic rather than incremental way is less effective than recreating the HR function to help an organization build and maintain the capabilities needed to execute business strategy better than competitors. Benchmarking, though useful in some ways, is not enough. For a start, what works in one organization may not work elsewhere. Second, following what others are doing is not a way to build capabilities which are unique and difficult to imitate. What is needed is a detailed understanding of competitive dynamics and being able to translate these into the people and culture implications.

HR professionals need to be aware of how the nature of their business is changing and make an honest assessment of the business challenges. They need to involve the line in understanding the implications of those changes for people. What should drive HR decisions are the unique people needs of the business, which may or may not be in line with an HR professional's ideal scenario. It's about building credibility by understanding what's happening at top level, then working with the business to translate strategy into action. HR professionals need to be able to say:

- What's the business problem?
- Where can we add value?
- Here's what we'll do.

They also need to stay flexible and nimble, being prepared to continually adapt structures, processes, roles and activities to the company's changing situation.

Developing this business knowledge may not be easy, especially if your career has been exclusively in the human resources arena. There are many ways of expanding awareness of how businesses operate such as:

- Having an internal job swap
- Carrying out a secondment in another organization (public/private sector partnerships for mutual benefit are encouraged by the government)
- Taking an MBA
- Attending management meetings or briefings
- Attending conferences
- Taking part in /leading a cross-business business initiative
- Taking part in business process benchmarking visits
- Reading industry and other trade press.

Above all, listening to the priorities and issues in different parts of the business should help to deepen the HR professional's understanding of his or her own business as it stands currently, and where people believe it is going in the future.

Reinventing HR means looking at new ways to deliver services and answering the question 'What is the purpose of HR in this organization?' HR has to balance short-term skills and long-term development needs, local activities and corporate integration. Increasingly this involves working in business unit partnerships, supporting managers as the local face of HR. In some cases, HR centres of excellence are established made up of experts who focus on specialized consulting services providing mission-critical HR disciplines. Administration service centres, providing shared services that deliver low-cost, highly automated transaction processing to employees (internally or externally) are replacing junior personnel officer and administrator roles. Rapid response teams are *ad hoc* groupings formed to provide services for specific needs such as a major acquisition or divestiture. The important thing is to gain a track record of keeping basic HR processes in order. For Wayne Brockbank, (1997) this means that

HR must ensure that:
1 The right people are being hired, promoted, transferred and fired
2 Measures and rewards are aligned with short-term business results
3 Individual employees have the technical knowledge to achieve short-term results.

HR competencies

In addition to developing a strategic agenda, HR professionals must implement the strategy. This is far less simple, since organizations as we know can have complex political dynamics which may make the implementation of what makes sound sense very difficult. One of the core challenges for professionals is to build their ability to effectively influence others. One of the key elements of influence is personal and professional credibility.

Developing credibility

Credibility is HR's most precious asset, and it is hard to acquire though easily lost. It is based on the ways in which HR professionals deliver organizational change – through systems and cultural initiatives – which support the business in its goals.

Another ingredient of developing credibility is making sure that short-term business needs and HR processes are effectively managed. HR is expected to deliver in their 'unique area of expertise', as Dave Ulrich (1995) puts it. An important test of credibility is the perceived professionalism with which the HR team operates. All too often HR is out of step with the rest of the organization, especially with regard to the use of IT. HR systems have often been developed in a piecemeal way over the years and very often different systems do not speak to each other, leading to duplication of effort. This potential Achilles' heel can lead to a loss of credibility within the organization, leaving the HR team open to accusations of not being able to organize the proverbial party in a brewery.

Another important test of credibility is in the nature of relationships established with line managers. Ulrich details credibility as:

* Having a track record of success
* Having earned trust
* Instilling confidence in others
* Having 'chemistry' with key constituents
* Asking important questions
* Framing complex questions in useful ways
* Taking appropriate risks
* Providing candid observations
* Providing alternative insights on business issues.

Credibility is achieved through knowing what your own values and beliefs are and being prepared to challenge and make a stand if need be. It's about managing paradoxes and ambiguity, with integrity. It involves knowing the business and thinking and acting as a business person first, an HR professional second. This means that the messages you are giving are more likely to be listened to and being able to use data and theories to make a case. It means being clear about how the business can build its competitive advantage through people. This can be achieved if new technology is quickly and effectively adopted, operating technologies improved and strategies constantly adjusted to customer needs. Employees must be equipped with the required technical and the cultural skills, such as team working and flexibility, in order to realize this form of competitive advantage.

Communicating with the line

To some extent, the Churchillian statement about the British and Americans being 'two nations divided by a common language' could be said to reflect relationships between line managers and HR. Line managers' preoccupations are likely to be short-term, productivity focused, and mainly centre on their part of the business. HR, on the other hand, may be rather more concerned about longer-term or cross-organizational issues. Line managers' perceptions of the value added by HR may be influenced positively or negatively by company history as well as by the popular jokes made at the expense of HR e.g. 'the department of Human Remains'. The different priorities are usually reflected in the language used and the amount of time spent on issues considered to be important. These different languages can get in the way of effective communication, unless a way is found to bridge the gap.

HR needs to be able to communicate the value of people using business language which ties directly in to business strategy and results. If people really are the critical source of competitive advantage, line managers may need to be challenged to think through the implications of what they are asking of HR. HR can initiate debate about some of the implications of environmental change on parts of the business:

HR: *The nature of the business is changing. Government welfare reform means that the cost base will be heavily regulated. We will have to do things differently, probably by reengineering processes. What do you think the impact on people will be?*

Line manager: *We're not at that stage yet. Let's talk further down the line when things are a bit clearer and we're definitely going to do something.*

HR: *I'd rather talk early so that I can influence the decision. It may be cheaper, for instance, to use labour based in India – do you understand the cost base and HR implications of using labour there?*

Getting other people to think strategically can prevent the trap of always working to short-term agendas.

Influencing

In addition to using the right language, HR needs to be fully in tune with the informal system where the power and political dynamics of the organization are in evidence. In the Roffey Park/*Personnel Today* survey of Personnel professionals (1999) the ability to influence key decision makers was recognized as important by 91 per cent of respondents. However, only 62 per cent of respondents felt that this was an area of strength for them. One of the most effective ways of influencing senior managers appears to be to play them at their own (rational) game. Using data effectively can be the most powerful means of persuading managers to a course of action, especially if you let them draw out some of the inferences from the data themselves. So, for example, when they see that there is a numerical short fall of certain types of skills needed to implement a key strategic initiative in the short-medium term, they are much more likely to support the need for recruitment, development and succession-planning.

Gaining cooperation

Professionals need to build good working relationships with different kinds of people and maintain these despite physical separation and lack of time. They must assess which are the key relationships which must be nurtured or started. They need to build a wide range of influencing skills in order to gain cooperation without having to use formal authority. An active business partnership between equals relies on there being mutual respect and roughly equal, if different, sources of power. Gareth Morgan (1986) has identified many sources of power and influence within organizations, some of which are very pertinent to HR. These include:

• Formal authority
• Control of scarce resources
• Organizational structures and procedures
• Boundary management
• Control of knowledge management
• Ability to manage uncertainty
• Symbolism and the management of meaning.

Where HR may lack power is in the control of decision processes and this area above all is where HR needs to work collaboratively with the line to ensure that decisions made concerning people do not favour a solely short-term agenda. One of the ways of achieving this is by being able to facilitate and participate in senior management discussions. Knowing what is important, using political judgement and having the confidence to say what needs to be said are all elements of building credibility.

Kotter (1985) suggest four basic steps for dealing with the political dimensions in managerial work:

1 Identify the relevant relationships
2 Assess who might resist cooperation, why and how strongly
3 Develop, wherever possible, relationships with those people to facilitate communication, education, or negotiation processes needed to deal with resistance
4 When step 3 fails, carefully select and implement more subtle or more forceful methods.

The political frame emphasizes that no strategy will work without a power base. Managers always have a 'power gap'; managerial jobs never come with enough power to get the work done. HR work can only be undertaken with the cooperation of other people, often large numbers of other people. Moving up the ladder brings more authority, but it also leads to more dependence because the manager's success relies on the effort of large and diverse groups of people. Rarely will those people provide their best efforts and greatest cooperation merely because they have been told to. If you want their assistance, it helps a great deal if they know you, like you, and see you as credible and competent.

The first task in building networks and coalitions is figuring out whose help you need. The second is to develop relationships with these people. Kanter (1983) found that middle managers seeking to promote change or innovation in a corporation typically began by getting preliminary agreement for an initiative from their boss. They then moved into a phase of 'pre-selling' or 'making cheerleaders':

> Peers, managers of related functions, stakeholders in the issue, potential collaborators, and sometimes even customers would be approached individually, in one-to-one meetings that gave people a chance to influence the project and the innovator the maximum opportunity to sell it. Seeing them alone and on their territory was important; the rule was to act as if each person were the most important one for the project's success.

Once you have the 'cheerleaders', you can move on to 'horse trading', that is, promising rewards in exchange for resources and support. This builds the resource base that lets you go to the next step of 'securing blessings' – getting the necessary approvals and mandates from higher management. Kanter found that the usual route to success at that stage was to identify the senior managers who had most to say about the issue at hand, and develop a polished, formal presentation to get their support. The best presentations responded to both substantive and political concerns, because senior managers typically cared about two questions:

*   Is it a good idea?
*   How will my constituents react to it?

With the blessing of higher management, innovators could go back to their boss to formalize the coalition and make specific plans for pursuing the project.

The basic point is simple: as a Human Resources professional, you need friends and allies to get things done. If you are trying to build relationships and get support from those allies, you need to cultivate them. Like it or not, political dynamics are inevitable under conditions of ambiguity, diversity and scarcity.

Diagnosing needs

HR professionals need to be able to use cognitive diagnostic and problem-solving skills to help them assess correctly the perceptions, goals and stakes of different people. They must be capable of seeing the subtle interdependencies in each situation and identifying the implications of this diagnosis and then making decisions and implement solutions effectively. In the Roffey Park/*Personnel Today* survey of personnel professionals, only 53 per cent of respondents felt that this was an area of strength.

Diagnosis is an essentially good interpersonal and business skill, combined with solution-centred problem solving. A range of analytical techniques such as fishbone diagrams, Pareto analysis and cause-and-effect diagrams are widely used. These can be used mechanistically, but with good effect in facilitated quality team meetings etc. Some internal consultants increasingly use systems analysis tools to help make sense of the complex interdependencies within problem areas. Once the system has been identified, the problem solution is usually straightforward. Brainstorming and other creative techniques are used to generate possible solutions.

The classic consultancy cycle consists of :

- Gaining entry – relationship building and establishing rapport, deciding to become involved, determining who is the primary client
- Contracting – sharing expectations, defining roles and responsibilities, setting ground rules, creating trust
- Diagnosing the need – identifying the perceived requirement, collecting data, determining the client group and exploring limits
- Identifying options – determining resources and time scales, identifying a range of options and possible outcomes
- Implementing strategy – deciding on the strategy and methods, taking action, measuring, monitoring and being open to change
- Evaluating the outcome(s) – learning from experience, disengaging

The ability to work effectively within this cycle depends to a large extent on the consultant's expertise, experience, ability to influence, and willingness to influence. In managing strategic change, the HR consultant has to be receptive to the organization's outer context, leadership behaviour and imprecise visions. The HR professional has to be skilled in the art of clarifying those fuzzy visions and providing feedback to top managers and others.

Roles people play

In different situations, HR's role in a client situation may be that of a counsellor, coach, facilitator or reflective observer. Very often, the opening relationship with an internal client is where the client looks to HR as technical advisor or expert for a problem which the client has identified. This form of relationship, if it continues, can carry some risks. Known as a 'doctor–patient' relationship, this kind of role can be tempting since there seems to be an acknowledgement by the client of HR's expertise. One danger is that HR consultants can be lulled into complacency and assume they know all the answers. If the client has identified the wrong problem, the consultant must convince the client that their diagnosis is wrong. The client is in charge and may choose not to accept the 'prescribed medicine', causing a loss of consultant credibility. The solution itself may be implemented by the client group without further intervention from HR – occasionally, without further involvement, the solution may cause more problems than it solves. Worse still, the client blames the 'doctor' if things go wrong.

Another less than satisfactory relationship is the so-called 'purchase-sale' or 'pair of hands' where HR is used as an in-house contractor to deliver a service. In this kind of relationship the client has both defined the problem and the solution. Negotiating for a different solution may be very difficult if this is the modus operandi. Typically, in this kind of relationship, HR is treated by the client as a junior, non-strategic function.

Perhaps the most fruitful of all relationship types is the so-called 'business partner' or 'process' model. This is where both client and consultant recognize each other's skills and needs for mutual learning. Both the nature of the problem and the solutions are likely to be jointly identified. The HR partner will probably be involved in some way with the implementation of the solution. The benefits of the solution are likely to be both short and long term, not least in the nature of relationships and the trust established through partnership working.

To work effectively in this way requires good process skills and confidence to ask the kinds of questions which bring out the real needs. While there is a greater likelihood of meeting 'real needs' there may also be high risk and the process will need to be 'managed' with integrity. Such process relationships take a lot of time and commitment and, because of the 'fuzziness' of the kinds of problems to be solved, they may be harder to budget. For clients, the process may be uncomfortable at times and will require real objectivity to recognize where the problem exist. However, clients will usually achieve a workable solution from process consultancy, as well as new skills for themselves.

Making things happen

Identifying needs and solutions is not enough. Implementing solutions needs good planning and project management skills. Above all, it needs good organization of time and resources and a sense of urgency to get things done. As HR professionals who took part in the Roffey Park/*Personnel Today* survey suggest, implementation is hampered by the following:

> *HR is spread too thinly*   Agree strongly or slightly – 63 per cent
> *HR is too reactive*   Agree strongly or slightly – 61 per cent
> *HR spends too much time on trivial matters*
> Agree strongly or slightly – 60 per cent

HR professionals therefore need to be excellent time managers, who are able to prioritize and reprioritize as need be.

Change management, especially with regard to culture change is the art of intervening within the formal and informal systems, integrating change initiatives, measuring progress etc. This is perhaps the most important element of the strategic HR role and will be the subject of Chapter 14. In the Roffey Park/*Personnel Today* survey of Personnel professionals, managing change and culture change ability were regarded as key by 83 per cent of respondents. However, they were also the area of greatest perceived weakness, with only 41 per cent feeling that they had strengths in managing cultural change.

Structuring HR

If HR is spread too thinly, it is important to consider the options. Assuming that HR reaches the point of being seen to add value by top management, how should HR ideally be structured to deliver the type of service which is right for your organization? There is no ideal blueprint, but the structure should reflect the short-term deliverables which have to be right, as well as the longer-term value added. This may mean separating strategic HR structurally from service delivery. Some companies' HR teams are providing a strategic service, looking after corporate needs such as succession planning and culture change, and a consultancy-based service delivery tailored to business unit needs. In addition, companies are increasingly providing operational HR help desks or service centres. **Boots the Chemist** (*Personnel Today*, 29 April 1999) downsized its HR provision so that between 150 and 200 HR staff will cover 31 000 staff. A new level of personnel advisors has been created to carry out more administrative tasks, and a new group of area personnel managers will be in charge of about eight stores of varying sizes.

The issues to consider when restructuring include:

- What sort of service do clients need as opposed to want?
- What do you believe are the strategic priorities?
- How can these be delivered, and by whom?
- What are the relative costs and benefits of different structures?
- If parts of the service are to be outsourced, how will you maintain service quality?
- If HR services are separated in this way, how can HR professionals develop the experience and skills to make transitions between different types of HR role?

If parts of service delivery, such as training and development are outsourced, a key skill lies in the diagnosis of business needs, the selection of providers, the monitoring of quality and thorough evaluation. HR professionals need to be skilled in the managing of relationships with suppliers such as consultants and contractors and at the same time must be fully in touch with the needs of the clients and consumers of these services to ensure that needs are being met.

If the team at the strategic centre is small, it needs to be influential, well connected with the business and the rest of the HR community. HR throughout an organization needs to operate as a team and be a role model community for good communications and personal development. All team members need to be aware of the business agenda and how the HR strategy and their role contributes to achieving this. In a global HR team, tact and compromise are likely to be hallmarks of effective teams who find ways of collaborating on global and local issues. In many global companies the real challenge is not only the development of global leaders but also the raising of standards of the global HR team. It seems that there is no substitute for tough/tender team building to ensure that the global HR group welds into a team, and helping to create the global HR agenda is one way of focusing team building on an issue of real importance.

Adding value at Standard Life

Stephen McCafferty's role as Assistant General Manager Resourcing and Development is to lead the HR team in Standard

Profile: Stephen McCafferty
Stephen McCafferty joined **Standard Life** from Safeway Stores
PLC as Assistant General Manager, Resourcing and Development.
His was a new role, created because the Group Head of Human
Resources saw the need for someone who could help reinforce the
culture change programme to reflect the strategic ambitions of the
company under a change programme called Total Customer
Satisfaction (TCS).

Life to focus on 'value added' activities such as consultancy,
development and management style. Other facets of the traditional personnel function, such as payroll, are clearly important,
but in Stephen's view should not be a key focus. His aim is to
bring about culture change in a paternalistic organization, to
enable it to continue to reap some of the benefits of paternalism
while at the same time equipping the organization with the skills
and talents which will form the basis of continuing success. The
Total Customer Satisfaction change programme is described in
Chapter 13. The following account of how Stephen McCafferty
approaches his role is based on a number of conversations with
Stephen and members of the Standard Life HR team.

Q. What do you consider to be strategic HR?
'I don't believe I've seen strategic HR – only bits. I can think of
some excellent practice, here and there, but it seems rather a move-
able feast to me'. Stephen's view is that while it is generally
acknowledged that humans are an important asset, it does not necessarily follow that HR is considered important. The challenge is
how we change that, which in his view means being customer
focused but also confident in your own contribution. It's about:

- Understanding your business
- Understanding your customers
- Delivering solutions
- Being innovative.

Stephen suggests that HR has a responsibility to educate and
enlighten customers if 'they don't know what they don't know'.
The only way you win the licence to do this is by having 'your foot
in the door' and have the confidence to challenge.

continued

Q. What do you consider the most effective way for HR to add value?
In Stephen's view, the best way to educate the business about how
HR can add value is by demonstrating what can be done. In his
experience what works well is to come up with practical initiatives
and take a pragmatic approach to carrying them out. What counts
is successfully carrying out what you have started. He suggests that
you have to start from the top of the organization and find the 'big
hitters' – the issues which really matter to the executive group.
Typically, these issues include succession planning and leadership.
Given the changing nature of the business, it is important to be
identifying and developing the people who will be leading the business into the twenty-first century. In the case of Standard Life,
diversification and business growth have meant that the styles of
management familiar in the business to date will need to change.
There is a need for strong values and a guiding philosophy on what
is important.

Standard Life's UK workforce has grown by 40 per cent in
three years and currently numbers 9700 employees. The skill
mix required for the newly developed telephone banking and
investment company businesses are different from those required
in the core Life and Pensions business. The local labour market
for these skills is highly competitive and retention is always a
challenge. The HR team is putting retention strategies in place
and is experimenting with various forms of flexible working to
ensure that Standard Life attracts the right mix of staff to meet
both its business needs for extended working and individual
work preferences.

Stephen works directly with the business heads on the issues
which concern them. The consistent message he sends out is
that HR is there to help line managers cope with the implications on people of changes in their environment. For one manager in customer services for example, this may mean helping
with the problems of retaining young people. In this case, the
introduction of an 'apprentice' scheme and a two-week induction are helping. Another example is where a manager is struggling with a department of fifty people characterized by low
morale and a siege mentality. Helping the manager turn the

situation around is not only satisfying but also significantly helps the business. The effect of providing a high-quality solution to people problems which are getting in the way of the business is increased credibility and management support for HR.

Another key concern is to change the culture of the organization to bring it in line with the changing business. Characteristic of the culture are a very traditional, conservative and cautious approach to change. This is hardly surprising given that Standard Life is a complex business which has operated successfully for over 175 years. Attitudes tend to be entrenched which may cause difficulties when the business wishes to seize new opportunities. Setting up a new banking operation from scratch in less than 18 months meant the need to put old ways of working to one side and utilize a more entrepreneurial style.

Similarly, management styles are predominantly characterized as inflexible but these are changing. The majority of managers tend to be middle-aged men whose main career experience has been with Standard Life in which there is a very strong work ethic. Some of these managers find it hard to understand the attitudes and motivations of an eighteen-year-old recruit. These young recruits may arrive with high expectations of rapid career advancement and become impatient if they are not promoted within a year. Bridging this attitude gap is important if Standard Life is going to be able to develop effective new employees for the future.

Research carried out by Gallup suggests that the most important person from the point of view of people development is a person's immediate line supervisor. There is now a lot of support for developing managers as leaders and coaches and a critical mass of good practice is being built. A number of important initiatives to enable managers to take on a more facilitative and coaching role are under way. These are aimed at building better relationships between managers and their teams. Some involve using line role models to inspire their peers. All are focused on managing performance robustly and building trust. A consistency of message is important and managers are now more aware of the many ways in which people can develop. On-the-job development, linked with what managers are dealing with anyway, is now a key focus.

Perceptions about the value of HR

Q. How do you believe HR generally is perceived?
A major concern is the quality of people entering HR as a profession. Stephen questions whether the profession is attracting the best people. He believes that the HR community needs to attract high-calibre people who can bring about significant change in their own organizations and help shape the employment agenda more broadly. This will become a major challenge in the next two decades. A shift from HR being seen as a low-credibility, service, transactional partner to a more strategic business partner needs to take place.

Currently there is little evidence of this in boardrooms. A vicious circle seems to be at work: Human Resources specialists often seem to be passive and lack confidence, perhaps because they have not been perceived as adding value in the past. Ironically, this might have been because they were too closely associated with employees, rather than with the business decision makers. At a time when employees have been seen as dispensable, the image of HR may also have suffered. Then, perhaps due to a lack of confidence, HR professionals are often accused of being too hesitant, checking for consensus at a time when this is difficult to achieve. When 'checking' behaviour leads to decision-making paralysis, the impression of poor value-added is compounded.

Stephen's recipe for breaking out of the impasse is straightforward and he believes reflects his background in the highly competitive retail sector: 'If you see a decision needs to be made, just do it; don't wait to be asked. You'll be told if you go too far. Obviously, you've got to have worked out a sensible approach but you should go with what you feel is the right thing.' He suggests that HR professionals can be too apologetic, seeking permission and approval of senior colleagues for their strategies. Stephen agrees with the Vice President of Human Resources of a major international manufacturing company who asked 'when was the last time a financial director was called on to account for his strategy and actions?' He does not advocate going as far as the HR director of a major insurance company whose function is held in high esteem because of perceived added value, especially in bottom line terms. In this case, the HR director simply makes up a plausible ROI which nobody questions. In real terms, being called upon to justify decisions more than any other function would symbolize a lack of respect for the function.

Another way in which HR teams can help themselves is by recruiting fewer people but these must be people of high ability. The business must also be prepared to accept that continuing to provide the conventional HR service may not be making the best use of this asset. Currently, this message may be a little too challenging and may not be acceptable in many organizations.

Q. What's important to you in building your HR team?
As with any team, the important thing is to build on strengths and compensate for weaknesses. The acid test as to whether you have the right people in the right roles is to ask 'if I had to lose five people from the team, would I notice? Part of my role is making sure that people have a sense of purpose and clarity about what's important and what's not.' An example would be telling the team not to waste time on ongoing but low-level issues in terms of value added, such as one-off team-building courses, when the major challenges are around making tangible new career opportunities for employees. 'I also believe that what's important is what you say, your thoughts, as well as what you do. If you have a good idea, share it. My job is to create the environment where it is safe for people to share ideas.'

Stephen is keen to ensure that Standard Life attracts and retains the 'best' and is therefore wrestling with the dilemma of whether to recruit people at the beginning of their career and sponsor them through their CIPD qualification or take people who are two or three years into their career. Similarly, while at one time having a degree was considered a bonus, a two:one grade is now considered standard. He is considering therefore targeting people with first-class degrees of any sort. For him the issue is how to attract the best candidates to HR as a career. Part of the problem he perceives is that the image which the profession currently enjoys may not be appealing to the most ambitious recruits. Stephen is willing to pay more for the best and upskill people working in the HR area.

Stephen is working to a three-year plan through which he hopes to have a team with all the right people in place to continue delivering high-quality solutions to the business. He has made clear what his vision and values are to which he wishes the team to work. In some cases this has meant moving some people out because they did not subscribe to what Stephen was trying to do or because their skill set did not match what was required. He has been careful in the way he has moved people to other parts of the business to which their skills are more suited or has helped them move successfully out of the business. Where there have been gaps in the existing team, new posts have been created.

One of these posts is that of an ergonomist. The post-holder is responsible for designing work environments so that the organization gets maximum value from employees who in turn feel valued by their organization. Typical socio-cultural issues dealt with by the ergonomist are the impact of the arrival of new technology on the way teams are working. A specialist in call centres has also been recruited to support an important and growing aspect of Standard Life's work, namely dealing with customers over the phone. Members of the team were given specific responsibilities linked to functional parts of the business such as the customer service division or the bank. The HR consultants work with the management teams to link their operational functional plans with their strategic plans and help managers to understand the implications of these for people. The internal consultants help managers understand how to manage their people, how to get the best out of staff, how to develop employees as well as recruit and train them. Consultants are aware that their role is to offer best practice and help but also to step aside if they are not needed.

Q. What is your approach to management development?
One of Stephen's first key deliverables was getting management development off the ground. Prior to his arrival, management development had mainly been provided through the Open University Business School. Stephen changed the policy on study as he wanted to address the balance between the investment made by the organization and that made by the employee. Unusually, the balance had swung too much in favour of the employee with little return sought or achieved for the organization. There were many examples in which there were abuses of the organization's generosity, for instance over study leave.

The new policy clarifies criteria and offers employees three levels of organizational support. If an employee wishes to obtain the professional qualifications needed for their job, the organization pays. Similarly, if the qualification is not essential but adds 'profile' to an employee's role, such as a CIPD qualification, the organization pays. However, while Stephen believes that the organization has a key role to play in supporting individual development, he also believes that individuals should be prepared to contribute to development which benefits them. If an individual wishes to have an MBA or other optional management qualification, the organization will pay three-quarters of the fees up front and reimburse the employee for the remaining quarter on successful completion.

Stephen's three-year plan is nearly complete. His next key challenge is to help the team build on their success and motivate them to make the next step. A key priority is developing the skills of team members and enabling them to become the best in their field. He points out that HR teams are usually the 'cobbler's children' when it comes to development and he feels that ongoing professional upskilling is an essential element of being strategic. He takes a day out with the whole team twice a year to review progress and discuss next steps. The Standard Life team now has a relationship with a professional management development consultancy who are called on to facilitate these days. The facilitators have worked hard to understand the team and the issues they are facing. The same company works on a retainer to provide a

---

Q. How do you win support from the business?
Stephen's approach to winning support is very pragmatic and politically astute: he knows when to 'roll with the punches' and when to choose the right moment and method for introducing initiatives In his first few months with Standard Life he made a presentation to senior management on the subject of strengthening the role of training managers in the functional areas. He felt that, rather than these roles being filled with people who had little in the way of training skills, they should be staffed by professional training managers, perhaps CIPD qualified and with a career history of successful, business-focused training. At the time, Stephen believes that he was unsuccessful in persuading senior managers of the need for professional trainers and was willing to work with a less preferred option which was for Quality managers to take responsibility for managing functional training. It was the Quality managers who influenced their business head bosses to address the issue when the business could see the need for itself. Within twelve months, Stephen was asked to set up the new professional training manager system.

'clinic' for the development of internal consultants. This means that Standard Life trainers can use the local training facilities of the consultancy, can talk through sensitive issues with external trainers and reflect on good ideas. The consultancy has been helpful in diagnosing where the team's skills need strengthening.

Stephen believes that it is vital to try to understand the key decision makers and their priorities. However, he is painfully aware of how difficult this can be. When he first joined the company he was used to a fast-paced retailing environment. His early attempts to achieve this highlighted the significant differences in approach and fit between Standard Life and what he was used to. Senior colleagues would appear to agree with what Stephen was proposing but in fact nothing would happen following the decision. There was little real support for these initiatives. When the chief executive asked him how he was getting on at the end of the first year, Stephen's frustrations came through: 'I can't understand why I can't get anything done. There are lots of things which I thought were agreed but I see that there are plenty of things left unsaid.' The chief executive encouraged him to continue and Stephen gradually learnt to adjust to the more introverted culture, to set clear expectations and check his assumptions. Nine months later, when he delivered the strategic module on the Executive Learning programme, his senior colleagues were able to confirm that he was adding significant value to the company.

Winning support very much depends on whether you are in tune with the needs of the business or not. You need to understand the changes which are affecting your organization and its sector. In the financial services sector, for instance, changing regulations and more discriminating customers mean that there has to be a fundamental shift in employee behaviour and standards of customer service in many organizations. HR needs to help managers think through the implications for people of those required changes. So, for example, it is one thing for a business strategy to set targets for doubling the number of claims processed within a set period. HR can help managers think through:

- How do you know people will manage that change?
- How is it physically possible to process twice the number of claims?
- What capacity do people have to work that quickly?

Stephen suggests that if you wish to influence senior decision makers you need to take time and win people round by the strength of the intellectual argument. While Stephen subscribes to the ideas of Daniel Goleman and others who have described how emotional intelligence underpins effectiveness, he is wary of using 'buzz' terms which might alienate managers who may not have been exposed to these ideas. He prefers to convince managers by talking about people's drives and motivations. The challenge for HR professionals is to be an importer and generator of good ideas on people issues, but to do this in a way which makes the ideas acceptable to the organization. According to Stephen,

Strategy's the easy bit – the intellectual challenges seem fairly straightforward – it becomes intuitive. You need a good grounding in theory but you need to overlay common sense. This is where many management books seem to fall down and unsophisticated HR professionals use theory ineptly. What's hard is bringing other people with you. When you're working with line managers, you have to get inside their heads. They won't pay attention to a functional expert because you are an expert. They just want to know how you can help. You have to establish credibility, say things that make sense. You have to find out where you can help and drop ideas in. You have to learn the language of the business not the language of HR. If you can talk about cost, productivity, efficiency they'll listen to you.

Q. Standard Life won the HR Excellence Award in 1998, due to the fit between the HR and business strategies. How do you achieve this integration?
'We work hard to achieve integration. The HR strategic intent, the range of HR initiatives and the bottom up drivers all stem from the changing needs of the business in its economic context. The main way of ensuring integration is by measuring what's happening. What makes a difference is how you measure. The HR scorecard was designed to match up with the business scorecard. We engaged the business by saying "staff costs make up two-thirds of overall operating costs. Help us develop measures which will show whether the people management initiatives are making a difference". Where they rubbished any measure which the HR team had suggested, we challenged them to come up with a better measure.' The HR scorecard stands alone but fits into the Corporate scorecard. So measures such as the People Satisfaction Index are assessed through a full staff survey every two years, with sampling at more frequent intervals.

continued

Q. How do you know whether you are winning or losing?

'It's about backing the message about the importance of people issues into the heart of the business. It's based on relationships and it takes time. Relationships are not linked to the big-hitting issues – it's more a constant chipping away at resistance. You know when you're getting somewhere when you are asked back, or by the nature of the conversations you get invited to take part in. It's when senior managers and directors start to ask your view on key strategic activities, such as recruiting for an important position when in the past they would have done their own thing and possibly seen their decisions backfire. It's when people make it clear that they value your opinion that you know you're getting somewhere. It's also when you start to see senior line managers taking part in learning events voluntarily, when in the past they would not have dreamt of taking part.'

Proof that HR is now being seen as central to the business is abundant. One measure of this is the relative ease with which Stephen can gain time with the chief executive. Stephen was invited to accompany board members on a US study tour. The prompt for the tour was the need to regain focus and clarity following diversification. The purpose of the trip was to benchmark Standard Life against various world-class companies such as **Sun Microsystems**, **Rank Xerox**, **Harley Davidson** and **Microsoft**. The European Foundation for Quality management (EFQM) model was used as the framework for the benchmarking exercise. The Board were able to compare and validate practices on the different aspects of EFQM such as:

- Focus and prioritization
- Measurement
- People management
- Leadership.

One idea which is likely to be adopted is a one and a half day 're-energizing programme' for all staff, similar to the programme run by **Rank Xerox**. Stephen, acting as the board's scribe, was able to pull together the key messages for a strategy review in May. By October, much of the learning was being implemented in the business.

Many of the new ideas for moving the organization forward are still being worked through. Stephen believes that the time is right to win a clear mandate for HR. Stephen helped to prepare a presentation delivered by his boss, the General Manager for Personnel, to his board colleagues. The mandate has been won through a review of the value which has been added through HR. There is now greater clarity on who owns what, on where there is flexibility and where responsibility for different aspects of HR lie. Consistency based on common values is important. Staff values and operating principles have been clearly laid out and are being integrated into all staff management processes as well as being used as recruitment tools.

A strategic HR network

Stephen was a prime mover in establishing an HR network between six of the leading employers in Scotland. The network is targeted on senior HR executives and attendance at meetings is regarded as a business priority for network members. The emphasis is on the practical, on sharing and collaboration. Examples of joint activities include job swaps with employees having the opportunity to do real jobs in other member organizations for six months. Events are organized which expose network members to leading thinkers such as Manfred Kets de Vries and other practitioners. The benefits to both secondees and host companies can be enormous. A senior civil servant seconded from the **Scottish Office** to Standard Life's corporate affairs department was helpful with respect to political lobbying. Similarly, Standard Life employees seconded to **Scottish and Newcastle Breweries** shared useful approaches to business planning.

Other joint activities include learning groups or 'sets'. These are established between people at different levels in the member organizations. Meetings tend to focus around specific issues relevant to the group in question such as cost control or how to book into a new distribution network. Exchanges also take place where experienced contacts are placed in member organizations which share common needs, such as revamping a company secretariat. Members of the network act as brokers to their own management in getting the best out of such opportunities. At graduate level, the joint Graduate Forum is both a network training programme and an exchange scheme.

Of course, to derive benefit from such a network requires a degree of trust among participating organizations and a willingness to share good practice. It also requires top management support, without which there would be a risk of good ideas from the network being rejected by senior managers who were not part of the process. Stephen recognizes that risk but believes the network has found appropriate means of dealing with issues which could undermine trust: 'we talk about issues and deal with them.' One example is where a headhunter working on behalf of one of the member organizations was attempting to 'poach' employees from Standard Life. Stephen was able to get on the phone to the network member (who knew nothing about the headhunter's activities) and was able to stop the poaching. Strong relations based on openness have helped maintain the credibility of the network but also mean that absorbing new members becomes a well-thought-out process. All members have to feel comfortable with new partners.

The network is managed by a working committee who arrange the events and activities in which members take part. A board-level 'gin and tonic' group, consisting of the bosses of individual members, meets in Edinburgh annually and is able to inject ideas into the network. This is also an important cross-check that the network is adding value to each of the member organizations and not simply a social outlet for individuals. Stephen and fellow members update their boards during the year on relevant network achievements and opportunities. These include relatively straightforward sharing of learning on subjects such as who is the most effective consultant to use for a particular purpose. The network members are aware that, as the six biggest employers in Scotland and having formed these bonds of mutual trust, they are now in a position to shape the employment agenda in the business community. They hope to exert greater influence on introducing practices linked with lifelong learning, for instance. They are also able to make deals with suppliers which benefit different network members. For Stephen, the most effective professional groupings are those which individuals initiate for themselves.

> We've come a long way but this is a journey – you never arrive, or as someone once said, this is a race with no finishing line. Total Customer Satisfaction is integral to what we do; it forms the philosophy and the basis for the way we run the business. HR has made a big impact in influencing senior managers on the need for commonality of HR processes, underpinning the employee brand. It was great, for instance, when the Group Managing Director,

Scott Bell committed his thoughts to paper for the benefit of top managers across the different businesses on the subject of the importance of good people management practices.

The main thing is making the values real and reinforcing good practice. When you look at what some of the most admired companies such as **Merck, Coca Cola** and **Johnson & Johnson** have in common, there appear to be strong values and good people management practices which in turn create employee loyalty. The challenge for us is to operationalise espoused values and measure our journey to achieve this so that the impact on the business can be made obvious. People in all parts of the business should experience the same employee brand, and that sets the agenda for HR. It's about closing the loop. We've worked hard to get to a place where people processes are considered important.

Conclusion

At the current time, one measure of success for HR is whether line mangers are working in tandem with HR and turning to HR for support and input when crafting business strategy. This only happens if HR as a function has established credibility through delivering operational excellence, managing change and in developing a strategic HR agenda.

Looking ahead, the challenge for HR is to balance both long- and short-term agendas. Shaun Tyson has analysed several features of HR in the future which suggest that there will still be a need for the operational, largely technical role which is 'financially adequate and apolitical' He believes that a range of specialists whose affinity is to a network rather than to an employer will emerge, leaving the client line manager as the policy interpreter. He predicts that 'there will be a considerable number of HR seats at top tables' but that their occupants will increasingly be drawn from a variety of backgrounds. This means that HR professionals will need to be rigorous in raising the standards of delivery by the HR function.

They will also need to take their own development seriously and avoid the 'cobbler's child' syndrome. They will need to broaden their experience – of other parts of business and other organizations – if they are to gain the necessary experience for more strategic roles. Above all, HR professionals will need the skills of conceptualizing and delivering on the agenda for the human side of the business which will build their organization's competitive advantage. For Jeffrey Pfeffer (1992)

> Innovation and change in almost any arena requires the skill to develop power, and the willingness to employ it to get things accomplished. Or, in the words of a local radio newscaster, 'If you don't like the news, go out and make some of your own'.

Checklist for strategic HR practitioners

*   Do we have the right HR structure for this organization's short- and medium-term needs?
*   Is the HR team aligned to the business strategy?
*   How well are HR strategies integrated with the work of other functions?
*   Are HR team members measured and rewarded for their contribution to the delivery of strategic initiatives?
*   Do we have a clear mandate from the management group?
*   What is the quality and calibre of HR staff, both individually and collectively?
*   What skills does the team need to develop?
*   Do team members think, act and speak like business people?
*   How good are we at process consultancy?
*   What parts of the HR agenda do we need to get under control?
*   Have we established a set of internal service standards, performance guarantees and ongoing satisfaction measurement programmes?
*   Do we operate to total quality practices?
*   With whom does the HR team need to develop relationships?
*   How good are the relationships the team has developed within the business?
*   How much do we involve line managers from other departments in the development of HR plans?
*   How much is the HR team involved in the development of strategic HR plans?
*   Do we have a regular schedule of meetings between the senior HR professionals and business heads?
*   Are we able to use data in a concise form to show each senior manager how HR's efforts can benefit their business units?
*   Do we have plans to educate employees about the role of HR?

References

Brockbank, W. (1997). HR's future on the way to a presence, *Human Resource Management*, Spring, **36**, No.1, 65–69.

Galford, R. (1998). Why doesn't this HR department get any respect? *Harvard Business Review*.

Kanter, R. M. (1983). *The Change masters: Corporate entrepreneurs at work*. London: Routledge.

Kotter, J. (1985). *Power and Influence – Beyond Formal Authority*, New York: Macmillan.

Kotter J. (1988). *The Leadership Factor*, New York: Free Press (Macmillan).

Lee, J. (1990). Cited in Growing your own – succession planning in decentralized organizations, *Recruitment & Development*, Report 2, February.

Morgan, G. (1986). *Creative Organizational Theory: A Resource Book*, Beverly Hills, CA: Sage Publications.

Pfeffer, J. (1992). *Managing Power*, Cambridge, MA: Harvard Business School Press.

Tyson, S. and Fell, A. (1995). A focus on skills, not organizations, *People Management*, 19 October.

Ulrich, D., Brockbank, W., Yeung, A. K. and Lake D. G. (1995). Human resource competencies: an empirical assessment, *Human Resource Management*, Winter, **34**, 473–495.

The key to the great global success of the 21st century is the development and management of creative talent capable of operating across borders and cultures. IT can facilitate knowledge transfer around a worldwide business, but the critical advantage will be the human ability to manage diversity; to create the genuinely multicultural, as well as multinational organization (Kennedy, 1998).

The days of the global marketplace are here. Global alliances are proliferating and according to John Naisbitt in his 1994 book *Global Paradox*, small businesses are better able to achieve success in the global economy because they are nimbler. Few large organizations appear able to achieve a truly global culture in which local businesses achieve a high level of global integration. Typically, part of the problem is that the focus of senior management is on understanding the key elements of the business strategy which they believe will make the organization successful in the global marketplace. Executives tend to forget that their organization must be capable of adapting to changing circumstances, which means managing and developing people who can adapt and deliver the business results. Yet potentially, developing the international expertise of staff and deploying talent appropriately is an effective way of growing the business. Equally, the lack of an effective multi-cultural HR strategy can potentially undermine the organization's ability to achieve those results. Chris Brewster, Professor of European HRM at Cranfield School of Management, who has conducted research into many international organizations, points out that

Although HR forms a very substantial part of their operating costs, so far there has been very little serious attention paid to thinking strategically about it. (Quoted in Kennedy, 1998)

The universal dictum 'think global, act local' (or 'glocal') is difficult to implement in reality, especially when the issue under debate is an aspect of Human Resource management. In decentralized organizations the need for a centrally driven HR strategy may be challenged by local business and HR teams. According to Fons Trompenaars (1997), even the notion of HR management is an Anglo-Saxon approach and is difficult to translate to other cultures. Yet arguably certain HR matters deserve a level of collective attention which ensures that action is taken on key issues. The major question is not on which approach to HR policy making and implementation – centralized or decentralized – is 'right' but on whether anything is happening at all to strategically further the needs of the organization and its employees.

A global HR agenda

The debate rages about which HR policies should be standardized in multinational companies and which should be left to local autonomy. HR strategy development may need to be managed so that all professionals develop a shared understanding of the overall strategic goals and direction. HR services at the 'centre' should focus on adding value through, for instance, the design of corporate processes or change programmes. Other 'corporate' needs might include top team recruitment and high-flyer development. Similarly, many companies consider that a key responsibility of global HR is sourcing talent within the company from around the world. In decentralized and federated organizations this can be difficult to achieve globally. The **BP Amoco** approach described in Chapter 11 shows one company's approach to integrating regional and global sourcing of talent. A key enabler of global sourcing of talent is having an effective international Human Resource Information System (HRIS) which can make a more strategic deployment of staff possible globally.

Global HR can be responsible for determining how learning can best take place in different locations and enabling the process. A number of multinationals, such as **Coca-Cola**, have created a position called Chief Learning Officer who is responsible on a global scale for ensuring that the company's human capital is put to good use. The challenge is to decide how learning can best take place in each country and develop appropriate processes. This requires a flexible approach by Global HR in implementing policies worldwide. Similar approaches have been taken on issues concerning employee rights. Companies such as **American Express** and many others now have designated 'Company Ombudsmen/women' who have the responsibility of ensuring that company and employee interests are appropriately served.

Conversely, corporate approaches which generally come unstuck at local level are in areas such as management by objectives, pay for performance, terms and conditions. Western-style appraisal schemes and training programmes which encourage frank face-to-face dialogue can be very inappropriate in some cultures. Corporate values, especially with regard to diversity, when rigidly imposed may run counter to local norms. One American company has an inflexible approach to maintaining core values, such as insisting that discrimination will not be tolerated. They have, however, allowed some flexibility in the manner in which this value is imparted in different locations. Consistency of intention is balanced by flexible pragmatism in delivery.

The danger of too much centralization is that inappropriate policies are imposed and fail to be implemented. Equally, too much localization can mean that delivery becomes fragmented and resources are wasted with endless reinvention of wheels. Decision making can become bogged down. HR managers need to operate as a worldwide team, take into account the culture of different countries and decide which aspects of policies and systems need to be addressed locally and which are truly global. The global HR team needs to be able to share information and power with one another and with other people which requires a degree of flexibility in both behaviour and policies. Undoubtedly, the task of global HR at the centre is more complex and demanding than in the days when multinationals simply issued edicts from HQ which had to be implemented locally. In the global marketplace, however, such centralist approaches seem to be inappropriate at the current time.

A global HR team needs to have the skills and credibility to carry out a global agenda which will further the organization's strategic mission. If, for instance, an organization is contemplating a joint venture with another company in another culture, HR should be involved in identifying and eliminating as far as possible potential 'hotspots'. This will involve analysing the differences in working practices, leadership styles, organizational cultures etc. which are likely to cause problems. Acting on this information can be vital in ensuring that the joint venture stands the best chance of succeeding. Similarly, if an organization plans to open a facility in a 'new' country, HR needs to carry out a comprehensive and early analysis of the HR system in the country, including the education level of potential workers, employment laws and national cultural norms relating to work practices. Recommendations can be made which reflect the realities of the political, economic and labour context.

HR needs to be seen to add value by supporting the strategic objectives of the organization. However, research carried out in multinational companies for the International Personnel Association (1998) suggests that HR is typically not involved as business partner because management is not interested in involving HR and because HR professionals lack the expertise to address key issues on a global scale. So often HR is not considered aligned with the strategic goals of the organization. According to researchers Linda Stroh and Paula Caligiuri (1998) 'the biggest barrier to HR units becoming strategic is their own lack of expertise of international business-related issues'. Global HR teams need to anticipate the HR needs of their organizations while coping with a range of operational issues such as staffing foreign subsidiaries and establishing compensation rates. Getting the right balance will ensure that the HR contribution is strategic rather than reactive.

The research found that the three critical aspects of people management to the success of multinational companies in the global arena are as follows:

- The adoption of flexible management policies and practices worldwide
- The inclusion of the HR function as a strategic business partner in global business
- The development of global leaders.

Developing global leaders

Stroh and Caligiuri suggest that 'successful multinational corporations recognize the value in having global managers with the expertise to anticipate the organization's markets and to respond proactively. These organizations have learned that leaders who are flexible and open to the demands of the global market have made possible the organization's international business success'. Most successful global companies recognize the importance of having senior managers with an international orientation. An essential part of a strategic HR agenda is enabling managers to develop global leadership skills. This may require sending managers on overseas assignments as developmental experiences, not simply because there is a technical need for their skills. Global HR should also be involved in developing a global orientation in 'local' or host country managers, as described in Chapter 11. Typically, 'local' managers can be introduced to global leadership through visits to the corporate headquarters and other company centres around the world.

Supporting transnational teams

Another vital area for HR activity is supporting transnational teams to achieve business success. Transnational teams as defined by Bartlett and Ghoshal (1989) bring together individuals of different cultures working on activities which cross national borders. Team development involves the full range of HR activities such as selecting staff for teams, clarifying roles, developing appropriate appraisal mechanisms, enabling performance, building reward processes and career planning.

Research carried out by Snell *et al.* (1998) for the International Consortium for Executive Development Research (ICEDR), however, suggests that HR teams in many multinationals are not yet in a position to fully support transnational teams. In many cases HR policies perpetuate traditional organization structures rather than the more 'web-like' structures of transnational operations. More flexible approaches to team development are needed and HR strategies need to be aligned to the business needs if effective transnational teams are to be appropriately supported. The ICEDR research indicates that most transnational teams need to balance three concerns relating to worldwide competition. These key strategic drivers are local responsiveness, global efficiency and organizational learning. In successful international organizations, HR strategies and policies support these drivers.

Local responsiveness is critical as teams need to make allowances for the specific demands of different cultures and market conditions. Variety therefore needs to be a feature of a transnational team, especially since members of transnational teams are often dispersed geographically and need to be able to deal with local issues appropriately. Some companies take a poly-centric approach to staffing, with new members added only if they add value.

Training programmes can improve a team's responsiveness to local issues, but those which seem most helpful are programmes which emphasize the company's strategies and processes so that team members can understand the big picture within which they are operating. Typically, transnational teams work as virtual teams which not only need all the training and development usually made available to co-located teams but also have the added dimension of communicating mainly through technology rather than face to face. Managers of such teams may also need help from HR in understanding the implications of managing a multi-site operation.

Conversely, the demand for global efficiency means that a high degree of coordination and integration are required. HR practices need to ensure that global concerns are not neglected. In some companies this is achieved by deliberately understaffing teams in order to ensure that team members collaborate in order to make up for the shortfall. Cross-cultural awareness training can be helpful as can deliberate teambuilding activities when a team is first formed. Teams can be trained in conflict resolution as well as being able to establish ground rules which can lead to integrated teamwork. Some companies emphasize the corporate values as a means of blending together teams in a way which transcends national and functional boundaries. To aid integration further, team leaders can be trained to achieve decisions by consensus and individuals can be given responsibility for carrying out a task on behalf of the whole team. If the HR function is to support transnational teams it is important that the HR group itself operates as a transnational team. This may require the team to be involved in its own team development process before being able to work effectively on supporting other teams.

Teams also need to leverage knowledge continuously around the world and be able to institutionalize the learning within the organization as a whole. **IBM**'s International Airlines Solutions Centre has developed an intelligence network which enables the knowledge generated by transnational teams to be shared. Formalized communications can be a helpful spur to organizational learning. In one company, the business planning process involves team members in researching and reporting back to the rest of the team on the needs of a range of external constituents. Improved use of technology also means that teams can gain access to talent elsewhere in the organization which might otherwise have been 'hidden' in the hierarchy. HR information systems need to operate on an international level to include data on potential team candidates wherever they are based. Ideally such systems should allow for the storage of data which also includes individuals' preferences about where they would like to work.

Clearly, reward schemes should ideally reflect these needs. However, formal reward systems are often problematic with regard to international teamwork. An international software provider achieved considerable business growth throughout the 1990s and is now operating globally. In the early days of establishing the international business, each 'local' business fought for its own business and supplied customer service locally. Rewards were heavily geared to business winning. When the business had achieved a critical mass, the sales operation was restructured so that sales were carried out by the UK team only, leaving all the 'local' operations to supply customer service only. Since rewards continued to be based on sales, rather than customer service, this change was understandably unpopular with the local teams.

The ICEDR team found that where individual goals and incentives were used, they appeared to encourage local responsiveness. Surprisingly few companies in their survey used formal team-based incentives. Similarly, few appraisal and reward schemes appeared to recognize learning even though executives achnowledged the value of organizational learning through transnational teamwork.

Building a global culture in Standard Chartered Bank

At the time of writing **Standard Chartered Bank** (SCB) employs 26,200 staff in over forty countries. This extensive network is a source of competitive advantage since many customers need cross-border, international products. Though a British company by virtue of its major shareholdings, there is no large home domestic base of operations, with 90 per cent of staff being employed outside the UK. Head office functions are based in both London and Singapore. SCB is a medium-sized bank in global terms. It was a multiple-domestic operation but it is now building a 'transnational' organization with businesses in international, corporate, global financial markets, trade finance and retail banking. The aim is to move to a position where the SCB operates internationally instead of having a domestic market and seeing international business as something different. Profits have nearly trebled in four years, with 60 per cent of profits coming from Asia-Pacific, despite the Asian economic crisis. Ironically, the 'local' nature of the business in the different countries in which it operates has helped SCB respond and adapt rather better than some of its competitors. The turnaround of SCB fortunes is all the more remarkable considering that in the mid-1980s it was making significant losses and facing hostile takeover bids.

Part of the reason for that success lies in the change in management thinking from being a dated colonial culture to one which encourages local development within a corporate framework. Part of the shift included moving away from long-term expatriate assignments for mainly British managers to the development of an internationalized cadre of local managers. As a result of these changes, the number of expats on long-term assignments has fallen from 800 to 98 during the 1990s. A more egalitarian approach has replaced the old culture, where everyone has opportunities regardless of gender or ethnic background. SCB has long exported expertise to its overseas operations. If people leave from the UK they cannot always be guaranteed career entry back home. Graduates and other managers who become internationally assigned are no longer expected to move regularly from one posting to another; they will tend to return to their 'home' countries after one or two international assignments. They do, however, need a global perspective through either their background, experience or education. Many live and work in their home countries but become part of an international network.

The 'One Bank' philosophy is expressed in the catchphrase 'Global as you can, local as you must'. Geoff Rogers, global Head of Human Resources for Treasury, stresses that SCB believes itself to be a 'transnational network' organization, rather than a global one and that a key element of competitive advantage lies in the bank's ability to sell its unique network. The organization's strategy, such as working on a cross-border basis, its structure, culture and systems all aim to be transnational. Typically this means having a local customer focus and global product management. The idea is that good practices shall be invented once in centres of excellence and then migrated globally. The global template must then allow enough latitude for systems which need to be local. Given that SCB is still emerging from a heritage of being a 'federation of local fiefdoms', it is hardly surprising that implementing 'One Bank' can prove challenging.

Profile : Geoff Rogers

Geoff Rogers, formerly Regional Head of Human Resources for UK/US, is now in a corporate role within Treasury. As an HR leader and part of a global business stream, Geoff's is an advisory role. HR specialists reporting to him are based in Singapore and London. He sits on the Treasury Management Team as a general manager providing HR expertise. His particular focus is on developing HR strategies with regard to the:

- Capabilities required in the business
- 'Top team' succession plans and 'talent pipeline' management
- International assignments
- Business-specific reward policy – core policy is 'One Bank'
- Business-specific training and development.

The role of the global HR function

In moving from a multiple local to a transnational bank, SCB needs to globalize many of its processes. In particular, people processes need to be re-engineered. In HR development terms, this means creating a framework for management skills training which is broadly the same everywhere. The intention is that as people move up the organizational hierarchy they are exposed to more international programmes. At junior levels, training will be provided locally; at senior levels, training will be at international business schools; in middle management, people will be exposed to both local and global programmes.

The need to create common systems for managing HR data highlights the importance of striking a balance between the local and the global. One example is the introduction of People Soft, a global Human Resource Information System (HRIS), which is proving a challenge to implement because it has sought to establish a more global approach. People Soft was piloted at the UK Service Centre and has initially delivered 80 per cent of the functionality of the previous local system. This is one instance where it was necessary to give up a local template to achieve global benefits. The complexities of trying to standardize processes in a multi-cultural environment are demonstrated in issues such as how names are recorded on HR systems. In many cultures, people can be called by a variety of 'family', 'known' and 'given' names which have local cultural significance. Nevertheless, in common with other organizations which operate internationally, SCB is attempting to provide enough common systems and processes to facilitate the business and its personnel, without invading the autonomy of local units.

The changing HR role and organization are driven by a need to be aligned with the business organization. With echoes of Bartlett and Ghoshal (1989), the structure of HR mimics that of the business as a whole with roles built around:

- Relationship management services (known as Business HR and offering an advisory and internal consultancy service)
- Global/local product management
- 'Regional' HR Service Operations Centres (where mainly transactional, data operations (e.g. pay) are carried out).

The aim is that only those HR contributions which are considered critical should remain in-house. Some early experiments with outsourcing, including global communications and data processing, have met with mixed success. Line managers, rather than HR professionals, are seen as the HR champions. Part of the difficulty with this approach is the current lack of common hard systems to support managing at a distance. Databases in different parts of the world do not contain the same information and are not operated in the same way everywhere. A major investment in technology should assist line managers with their devolved HR responsibilities. Lotus Notes will enable line managers to have access to HR and management information, regardless of different time zones, within the next one to two years. A future in which line managers will be able to directly access most of their HR and management information and complete many of the basic personnel administration task themselves will require a significant shift in role and thinking by HR professionals, not just in the UK but across the SCB network.

The HR global team structure

The challenge for those charged with introducing standard approaches is overcoming resistance. For while there is plenty of verbal support for the 'One Bank' philosophy, there is a degree of 'not in my backyard' or 'not invented here' rejection of common practices. In planning a change programme for HR, Geoff Rogers and his team are aware that despite a superficial acceptance of the need for change, there is a lack of real consensus. Clearly, if HR is going to be able to contribute significantly to the globalization process, it will be necessary for the creative tension between different approaches to lead to breakthroughs. Debate and opportunities to contribute to the development of strategy are starting to create the consensus which will be so important if HR is to work in genuine partnership with line management.

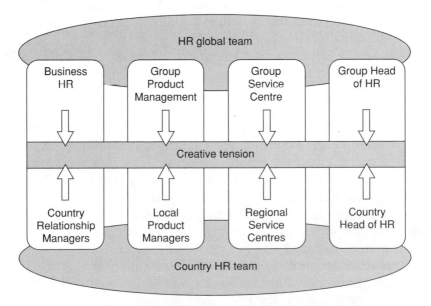

Figure 13.1   *The HR global team at Standard Chartered Bank*

So, for example, Geoff Rogers, working in Business HR, drives initiatives which are important to Treasury through a line relationship with Country HR Relationship managers whose perspective is likely to be more 'local'. When HR was restructured along Business Partner lines, this meant a significant shift in role and focus for the majority of HR professionals. The global HR team had been involved in developing the changed structure and were therefore bought into the need for change. However, the relationship managers had not and in some cases had neither the skills nor understanding to support the changes at a local level. Similarly, the HR service was now divided by both business segments and geography requiring matrix reporting lines for most HR professionals. Specialist groups reporting to the Group Head of HR look after resourcing, training and development and reward strategies.

A great deal of integration was needed before professionals could see the potential benefits of the new organization. This was mainly achieved through conferences – a global conference for the top HR team, a meeting for relationship managers on a global business issue – and the establishment of formal networks, such as one for HR relationship managers. It is critical that HR models good management practice. A programme intended to upgrade the skills of the HR community and to develop a cohesive approach to international HR was under way at the time of writing.

- *Relationship Management* At global level small teams work with global business heads to define the strategic cross-border HR priorities. At country level this works through business division HR relationship managers who are located with local business heads focusing upon 'value-added' services. As ever, the tension lies in balancing global versus local needs and priorities.
- *Product management* The role of the HR team at the centre used to be to invent everything and export new processes to HR business heads and line managers. Now corporate product specialists agree global priorities. The corporate centre is focusing on making the 'One Bank' philosophy tangible through its talent management strategies. Rather than directing strategy, the centre's role is now to facilitate the senior 'HR business community' in aligning business and people policies. This involves helping HR colleagues think through

what the organization needs to develop in order to achieve the one- to three-year plan. It also means designing and communicating critical global HR systems and defining what needs to be global and of equal importance compared with what needs to be local. This can be a difficult balance between global quality/efficiency and local ownership and adaptation.

Global HR practices emerge from centres of professional excellence. Part of the challenge for the centre is identifying and growing these centres of excellence and facilitating knowledge transfer. Though the group at the centre see themselves as leading the 'HR professional community' from a 'One Bank' perspective, this is through leadership of the local HR network, rather than through formal dictat.

Global HR priorities

Inevitably priorities change over time. Geoff Rogers would be the first to admit that while many of the stages of HR activity were planned, some evolved naturally and others emerged from previous initiatives. This very much echoes the evolution in thinking within the business at that time and should be seen as embedding HR strategy into global business priorities, rather than having a separate HR strategy, however far-reaching. The change programme introduced in the early 1990s, known as 'Focus', brought about a significant culture shift at senior levels. The

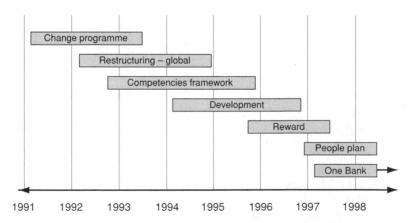

Figure 13.2 *Global HR priorities at Standard Chartered Bank*

programme was run globally and focused on how the business needed to change to cope with the demands of the then business environment. When the change programme was cascaded down to middle level it became local. It was at that point that the need to restructure became apparent since changed mindsets were not enough to overcome the limitations of the way the structure operated. A matrix was introduced, with some difficulty because of the power of some business heads who felt that their influence was being eroded. Three global business streams were established, dominated by local businesses. Corporate governance became an issue.

During the mid-1990s, an international competencies framework was developed to provide a common template for understanding effective performance. This started with a project which created the competencies to be used for senior-level recruitment and development. An international project team was then established to review the initial competency work and adapt it for use across the group at all levels. For Geoff Rogers, trying to impose a rigid centrally driven system is a mistake:

> You have to get processes interpreted locally. You progressively take the organization in a particular way, working steadily and consistently. You have to recognize that it takes time to work things through in a global organization.

The competencies are based on the organization's values and have become a shared language for identifying strengths and development needs at individual and organizational levels. The values expressed as behaviours are readily understood and accepted by line managers who might otherwise dismiss the notion of values statements as 'airy-fairy'. A number of applications of the competencies highlight the importance of recognizing local cultural differences. Upward feedback, for instance, although developed five years ago, is only now proving acceptable in some countries. In a more traditional Chinese culture, for example, the notion of giving feedback to someone older or more senior may seem disrespectful. The competencies are also used to design targeted development programmes. One of these programmes (The International Management Programme, designed by INSEAD for SCB) was devised to enable local managers to develop global mindsets and business skills.

The reward strategy focused on global performance management and appraisal. A common bonus for the top 600 employees was introduced, symbolizing that they were all part of one global team. By the late 1990s it became apparent that better communications with staff as a whole were needed. Briefings and workshops were rolled out globally under the banner of 'Plan for People'. These briefings helped to embed what had already taken place with regard to performance management, reward, resourcing and international development. The 'One Bank' concept will provide further impetus to reconcile the challenges of global and local initiatives and ownership.

Key achievements

Some of the highest-impact HR interventions have been achieved by mobilizing global focus on a few key priorities. In particular, changing cultures and mindsets was a major challenge. The Focus programme was pivotal in the change. While painful and high risk at times the programme provided the opportunity for people to challenge and come to terms with the way the business was going. Another key initiative was the development of cross-border performance management and measurement systems. Again, the global template and local application means that implementation may not be entirely even, but in Geoff Rogers' view, it is important not to be too prescriptive when creating a transnational process. He suggests that this adaptive approach to developing HR strategy is a more typically UK or North European view of management, rather than of some US companies which tend to prefer a more globally standard approach.

Remaining challenges

International development and careers

One of the main challenges for HR is the development of effective career development processes. Despite the development of local managers, high-potential employees are still expected to be mobile and lack of mobility is a limiting factor in career terms. To some extent it is hoped that the recruitment of international graduates, many of whom are mobile for a time at least, will ensure that people acquire the requisite experience at an early stage in their career. Middle managers who may need some hard management experience are increasingly being offered opportunities for short-term assignments through the Group Management development programme.

Increasingly people see their careers developing through the global business streams rather than the bank as a whole but this places even more importance on the need to develop 'One Bank' general managers. While this gives the business streams a strong role in developing people, it also tends to mean that organizations are reluctant to release people for roles in other parts of the business. A senior-level management development committee looks at the high-potential and senior populations and encourages heads of business streams to make sacrifices for the good of individuals and the group as a whole. This is achieved by influencing hearts and minds rather than mandating.

Pressure on costs

Managing and learning at a distance is costly. SCB has invested heavily in the distance-learning MBA at Henley, for instance, with over 150 people having gone through the programme. Certificate and diploma programmes have also been developed with the Open University. The HR team wants to measure and track how the learning is applied. They are planning to use the intranet to encourage people to take more responsibility for their learning and to find out how learning could be more cost-effective.

However, Geoff Rogers is very clear that skills development must have some interactive element and that the inevitable travel costs are expensive. Video conferencing, though increasingly used, is no substitute for bringing people together. Geoff is keen to ensure that the most appropriate way of achieving a need is found and that a transnational company is likely to have high communication costs. He has found that there are dangers in giving people difficult messages via Lotus Notes, for example. Far better to pick up the phone and have some 'personal' contact than relying on an impersonal medium which happens to operate in all time zones.

When is a local focus appropriate?

In SCB's experience, there is a relatively clear split of responsibilities between the global and the local HR delivery. At global level, issues related to senior managers' share scheme and group bonus are key priorities. Executive recruitment and development is also a global responsibility. At local level, responsibilities include employee relations, market benefits and general recruitment. Responsibilities which are both global and local are shared through the HR network. These include management training, reward planning and graduate recruitment.

Key lessons

In developing an integrated global business, an HR strategy which is fully integrated with the business strategy is essential. This means not running before you can walk. Geoff Rogers suggests that it is important to identify and focus on a few critical HR practices rather than attempt a large number of initiatives which do not deliver. He considers that globalizing the key players in the HR community is an essential first step, along with helping the whole team to understand the importance of achieving an effective global/local balance. Finally, it is worth recognizing that global network cultures are more complex than those in 'conventional' single country organizations and require much coordination and persistence.

Checklists on globalizing and supporting the international business

Supporting the international business

Research by ICEDR indicates that most transnational teams need to balance three concerns relating to worldwide competition. These key strategic drivers are local responsiveness, global efficiency and organizational learning. In successful international organizations, HR strategies and policies support these drivers.

- How well is HR currently supporting transnational teams?
- To what extent is a polycentric approach to staffing taken?
- How are managers helped to develop a global perspective?
- What approaches are used to develop international teams and leaders?
- What are the selection criteria for leaders of international teams?
- How flexible are the HR practices in use?
- Which HR practices need to be global and which local?

- How do HR practices ensure that global concerns are not ignored?
- How do global 'hard' systems support HR and global management?
- How is resistance to global approaches overcome?
- How effectively does the global HR team operate? How does it achieve a global/local balance?
- How is knowledge generated in one region leveraged within the business as a whole?

Globalization

Research carried out for the International Personnel Association (1998) suggests that the three critical aspects of people management to the success of multinational companies in the global arena are as follows:

1 The adoption of flexible management policies and practices worldwide
2 The inclusion of the HR function as a strategic business partner in global business
3 The development of global leaders.

Researchers Linda Stroh and Paula Caligiuri (1998) suggest that 'successful multinational corporations recognize the value in having global managers with the expertise to anticipate the organization's markets and to respond proactively. These organizations have learned that leaders who are flexible and open to the demands of the global market have made possible the organiza tion's international business success'.

- How does your organization manage across borders, i.e. is your organization predominantly
  - Domestic
  - Multi-domestic
  - A simple export organization
  - Using local agents
  - International
  - Truly globalized with a complex web of businesses, joint ventures and alliances across most of the world's economies?
- What is the impact of globalization, i.e. should HR be centralized, decentralized or a combination?

- What are the main ways in which international employees are deployed, e.g. on short-term assignments, expatriate postings etc.?
- How much does your organization consider 'local' managers as part of the international management cadre?
- To what extent is telecommuting replacing the need for international assignments?
- What are the implications for managers of enabling 'high-touch' continuous interaction in support of international team members?
- How are employee motivation, reward and recognition currently aligned to the changing business and organizational priorities?
- How are terms and conditions for international employees currently defined? Are special terms required for expatriation, or simply reward arrangements which reflect flexibility and mobility?
- To what extent do current reward initiatives encourage sustained commitment, flexibility, innovation and quality among transnational workforces?
- Despite a common governance initiative of sustained shareholder value creation, can common approaches, e.g. on cost minimization and commodity pricing really work in a global company?
- Can Western-style pay structures and systems be successfully adopted internationally?
- What scope or expectation exists across international boundaries to develop flexible 'total compensation' initiatives?
- How do international employees achieve a work/personal life balance and is it the organization's responsibility to do anything to assist this? If so, what can be done?

References

Bartlett, C. A. and Ghoshal, S. (1989). *Managing across Borders: The Transnational Solution*. Cambridge MA: Harvard Business School Press.

Kennedy, C. (1998). Global dreams, local realities, *Human Resources*. March/April.

Naisbitt, J. (1994). *Global Paradox*. New York: Avon Books.

Radford, A. (1995). *Managing People in Professional Practices*. London: Institute of Personnel and Development.

Snell, S. A., Snow, C. C., Canney Davison, S. and Hambrick, D. C. (1998). Designing and supporting transnational teams: the Human Resource agenda. *Human Resources Management*, Summer, 37, No.2, 147–158.

Stroh, L. K. and Caligiuri, P. M. (1998). Increasing global competitiveness through effective people management. *Journal of World Business*, 33, No.1.

Trompenaars, F. (1997). *Riding the Waves of Culture*. London: Nicholas Brealey.

Part 1   Implementing strategic change

Facing an increasingly competitive market in the financial services industry, Brighton-based Family Assurance introduced a change programme through staff focus groups in 1997. But as well as this 'bottom-up' approach it became clear that 'top-down' changes were also needed. Leadership became a key issue. Time and again the message from the focus groups was that the management approach was too project focused and was seen as not being interested in the people issues. To address these issues, directors took part in a transformational leadership workshop, using 360-degree feedback which led the directors to place greater priority on the people issues (McCurry, 1998).

Change is an inevitable consequence of strategic decisions. Planned strategy involves inventing the future and bringing about desired choices. If the strategy is to be successful, employees have to be energized and committed to the change and able to achieve their part. So many of the 'brakes' on strategy lie in the way the organization's culture operates and the lack of buy-in to change by employees. Going back to the alignment model, changing strategy and structure are difficult enough. What is much harder, and takes longer to happen, is changing the organization's culture.

Perhaps the biggest challenge for strategic HR is to create the type of culture that will support the organization's objectives. This is likely to be a culture with a positive work climate, where work practices are adaptable to changing needs and where people are flexible, skilled and committed. Obstacles which prevent the system from operating in this way need to be identified and eliminated. New practices and processes need to be introduced. Managing the change process which this involves can be daunting. Changes come so thick and fast that in many organizations it may be hard to isolate just one change process which needs to be managed. Yet change does need to be managed if the positive benefits of change are to be able to overcome the forces of inertia and resistance which are common to most organizations.

What is meant by 'culture change'?

Culture or the 'way we do things around here' represents the way organizational members behave and the beliefs, values and assumptions which they share. Some of these assumptions may be so taken for granted that they become invisible and only become visible when change threatens them. The assumptions may be apparent in the formal systems, such as the reward scheme, or may be more active in the informal or 'shadow' system in which the grapevine, political behaviour and networks flourish.

Typically, the culture is most visible in manifestations such as the way employees treat one another, how they dress, the size and layout of office space, the appearance of the reception area and how customers are treated. Less visible, but good indicators of culture are the rituals and routines which staff engage in, the amount and nature of political activity and the symbolism of certain aspects of an organization's history.

Types of organizational culture

Certain characteristics of organizational culture may be harder to shift than others. Roger Harrison (1986) has identified four broad categories into which organizational cultures can be classified. Any organization, he argues, has a blend of these types of culture, though some types may be more characteristic of some organizations than others. Each of these types of culture has its strengths and limitations, as well as its 'dark' side where the strength becomes a limitation. He suggests that organizational excellence is achieved through exploiting the dynamic tension between the strengths of these different culture types.

Each culture type has the capacity to empower or disempower people. A *power* culture empowers through identification with a strong leader but can disempower through fear and through an inability to act without permission. A *role* culture, such as in a bureaucracy, empowers through systems which serve the people and the task, reducing confusion and conflict. Such a culture disempowers through restricting autonomy and creativity and erects barriers to cooperation. An *achievement* culture empowers through identification with the values and ideas of a vision; through the liberation of creativity; through freedom to act. It disempowers through burnout and stress; through treating the individual as an instrument of the task; through inhibiting dissent about goals and values. A *support* culture empowers through the power of cooperation and trust; through providing understanding, acceptance and assistance. It disempowers through suppressing conflict; through preoccupation with process; through conformity to group norms.

Organizations as systems

Complexity theories suggest that all organizations, which are essentially complex systems, act as networks of interconnections. These networks, which are basically feedback loops, are not necessarily consciously planned but spring up across the organization in ways which connect different groups of people. While some networks, such as learning groups, may be part of the formal system, the informal system where most networks operate is inherently unpredictable and self-organizing. The way these networks operate is most obvious in the 'corridor conversations' which provide a way of bypassing blockages and act as 'safety valves' for employees. The informal system is a social, political one in which people communicate and learn.

The grapevine is a much faster means of communication than formal systems and, because the grapevine cannot be controlled, it is easy for negative ideas to be embedded there, especially in times of change when anxieties may be running high. The stories circulating via the grapevine often show that high levels of creativity exist within the organization since people will invent what they do not know. Equally, the informal system is subject to the 'ripple effect' of the stone in the pond. When positive messages are implanted there they can also spread like wildfire.

The types of stories which are told can teach employees about how they are expected to behave. In 3M the story about the invention of the Post-it note (which was an accidental discovery in the search for another product) is deliberately told to new employees to encourage them to experiment and learn from their mistakes. In another organization, the story about the appalling way in which a redundancy situation was handled made the organization notorious in the town where it was based and taught employees to expect to be dealt with ruthlessly. Not surprisingly, many 'uncontrolled' departures followed the redundancies.

Formal change programmes tend to set up more resistance than emergent change, especially if they appear to threaten values which employees hold dear. A number of years ago the new chief executive of a small consulting firm, wishing to improve the profitability of the firm, introduced a new reward system based on individual targets and performance-related pay for income generators. This was to replace the flat rate percentage of profits which previously distributed equally to all employees on a collegiate basis. The new reward system threatened to undermine the team-working for which the consulting firm was known. For the first few years there was strenuous staff resistance and for a while there was an uneasy co-existence of the formal and informal system as employees and management tried to reason with each other.

The chief executive persisted with the scheme and gradually resistance gave way to a grudging acceptance of the scheme. Some consultants began to enjoy the individual bonuses. They became reluctant to share leads with colleagues and political games started to be played. Teamworking broke down. Profitability did increase in line with the improved market but only as new staff were brought in to replace those who left because they no longer enjoyed the culture.

How does an organization reach a state where positive change is possible?

Chaos theory suggests that while an organization can exist in a stable or unstable state, the state most productive of change and new possibilities is the 'edge of chaos'. The organization has to have the capacity to be stable, but also to change/evolve. If there is too much stability, however successful the organization, complacency can set in and the organization can become internally focused. Too much change can lead to chaos, lack of coordination and waste. The edge of chaos, where there is experimentation but within a framework, is most conducive to emergent culture change since the people who are likely to be affected by the change are the ones who introduce it. Edge of chaos states are typified by muddling through, searching for error, brainstorming, use of intuition and agenda building.

Factors which affect the direction in which the culture travels (towards stability etc.) are as follows:

- How richly the network is connected – do the feedback loops work across the organization and through the management levels?
- The diversity of 'mindset' of the people within the network
- How quickly, or otherwise, active information flows through the system
- How power differences are used
- How anxiety is contained.

To reach this state, you have to recognize that the formal and informal systems co-exist. Do not over-control or predetermine goals and agendas. The informal networks themselves must generate their own order and change. The role of the senior manager is to articulate ideals, open-ended challenges capable of different interpretations, umbrella concepts and metaphors. Avoid power being either highly controlled or widely distributed and hardly ever use authority. Actively promote a diversity of culture. Create forums where individuals and groups can operate in a spontaneous and self-organizing way. Develop group-learning skills and encourage the development of the informal organization. Provoke challenges which are ambiguous and which may generate conflict; create an environment in which senior managers are open to challenge from subordinates.

Why do people resist change?

Many psychologists have addressed this question and have identified that change can represent a major personal transition, akin to bereavement, during which what is familiar has to be destabilized and 'let go' before people can move on to integrate new learning. For people who like the comfort of the familiar, or who are rather risk averse (which is surprisingly common among senior managers), change can threaten their comfort zones. Of course, change can bring many opportunities for individuals and organizations and there is much research evidence to suggest that people who have a positive approach to change usually manage to make opportunities for themselves during periods of ambiguity.

A qualitative survey carried out by the Spencer Stuart Organization in 1998 highlights the strong cultural resistance to change which was experienced by executives who were hired by utilities companies in the USA to champion moves to a competitive market culture in monopolies. Many of the executives brought in to implement change left within two years. The most common cultural challenges were:

- Resistance to change
- Unfamiliarity with competitive markets
- Aversion to risk
- Lack of responsiveness to risk
- Managers' and employees' sense of entitlement to resources and benefits.

The study also found that 'champions of change' felt that the following were most valuable in overcoming cultural challenges:

- Outstanding communication and persuasion skills
- Taking action to create entirely new programmes and structures
- Managing well in the face of uncertainty
- Flexibility
- Marketing skills and a customer-focused viewpoint
- Knowledge of competitive market finance and accounting.

On the whole, though, organizational change can seem threatening to employees because when the change is imposed top-down, such as in the decision to acquire another company or to sell off part of the organization, employees feel that they have no control over what is likely to happen. This is when the consequences of change can appear profoundly negative to employees. Transformation can threaten people's mental models of how their organization should act, what work should be like and what their own prospects look like. In the early phases of Roffey Park's Career Development in Flatter Structures project, some of the symptoms of employee dissatisfaction came through when people were asked about the effect of delayering on them. Comments included:

- It's unrewarding financially
- Chaos; no-one knows what anyone else is doing
- We've added a tier rather than taking one away
- There's confusion about people's roles
- Ongoing uncertainty with all these changes happening
- People do not know where they are going any more
- Loss of staff loyalty
- Stress levels high
- No accountability
- Turf protection
- Same workload but fewer staff to do it.

Sadly, comments also included criticisms of the role of HR in managing change – 'HR credibility knocked – an example of what not to do'.

Ironically, while so many change projects are introduced in order to bring customer and business benefit, the effect of change on employees can actually lead to a down-turn in profits, at least in the short term. One of the reasons for this is a loss of focus. Organizations can become introspective and cease paying attention to the external business environment. If political behaviour and 'turf wars' break out during the period of uncertainty, the internal focus becomes stronger. Similarly, the rate of change can be so great that employees simply stop working and spend their time in speculation. There may also be a leadership vacuum at the top of the organization because members of the management team are actively involved in managing the business deals rather than the organization.

Approaches to changing cultures

Overcoming resistance to change is a joint effort between HR, line managers and employees and there are no easy answers. Helping employees understand the need for change by sharing information about the business strategy, involving people in data gathering and problem-solving are approaches used in the case studies in this chapter. Helping people to benefit from the change with new development opportunities and aligning reward systems are other ways.

Management writers such as Quinn (1995) argue that most change happens in an evolutionary rather than a revolutionary way. Strategic decision making in 'real-time' business is more akin to logical incrementalism. He suggests that managers have a view of where they want the organization to be in years to come but try to move towards this position in an evolutionary way. They do this by attempting to ensure the success and development of a strong, secure but flexible business, but also by continually experimenting with 'side-bet' ventures. Managers seek to become highly sensitive to environmental signals through constant environmental scanning. They manage uncertainty by testing changes in strategy in small steps. They also encourage experimentation in the organization. Moreover, there is a reluctance to specify precise objectives too early as this might stifle ideas and prevent the sort of experimentation which is desired. This approach takes account of the political nature of organizational life since smaller changes are less likely to face the same extent of resistance as major changes.

Roger Harrison (1986) argues that different approaches to changing an organization's culture may be more or less difficult. In managing change you should intervene no more deeply than is necessary to accomplish your purposes. Strengthening the culture, for instance by doing the same things only better, is perhaps the easiest form of change to implement. This is the best approach when the organization does the 'right things' but not well enough. Balancing the culture to preserve the culture's benefits and to encourage cultural differentiation is more difficult. This is appropriate when the organization's culture is narrow, where the cultural patterns fit the organization's business but the necessary checks and balances are missing. Changing the culture, through, for instance, introducing new values and beliefs or work and leadership styles is the most difficult of all. This is necessary when needed improvements are blocked by the limitations of the current culture.

Other researchers, such as John Kotter (1995), who have made studies of why change efforts often fail, have identified the need for:

- Creating a sense of urgency and 'readiness' for change
- Creating powerful guiding coalitions who are willing to bring about change and letting a clear vision emerge
- Communicating the change continuously and in many different ways
- Coordinating efforts, measuring and communicating progress

- Keeping morale and energy levels around the change project high by celebrating progress so far, and using that energy to tackle the more important issues
- Consolidating improvements while eliminating remaining obstacles to change.

In all of these the role of leaders is vital and HR is a potential partner.

Communication and leadership

In managing change, communication plays a vital part in building an organization which is adaptable and more than the sum of its parts. Communication is about relationship building and has a major role to play in building trust and commitment. It can help create buy-in to new ways of operating. Communication should be considered a key component of change management and is an obvious area for active collaboration between Human Resource professionals and the line.

People need to understand why change is happening

When I first started researching career issues in flatter organization structures in 1994, Europe was deep in the middle of a profound economic recession. I wanted to find out why organizations had restructured by removing management layers – whether it was part of some strategic plan, such as providing better service to customers by removing bureaucracy, or whether delayering was driven by the need to trim costs, regardless of the impact on employees or customers. One of the key findings in the early part of the research was the link between the perceived reason for the delayering and the effect on employees. If people thought that the reason for delayering was simply cost cutting, their morale and motivation tended to be more adversely affected than where there appeared to be a more 'strategic' reason for the change. It seems that failure to communicate a strategic focus for the changing organization, compounded by a failure to communicate progress towards the new business targets, leads people to question the quality of leadership.

Some of the best formal communication schemes we encountered use a wide variety of methods to convey simple messages and include two-way communication processes which are taken seriously. Attitude surveys are widely used but action needs to be seen to be taken on at least some of the findings for such processes to have credibility. Good communication leads to employees feeling 'empowered' to contribute to the development of the organization. Involving employees in decisions affecting business strategy can produce dividends. **Thresher,** for example, has run trial programmes on different working practices for three years. These have led to improvements in morale and performance and the business results of the trial teams speak for themselves. The Thresher case described later in this chapter demonstrates the immense value of collaboration between Human Resources professionals and line managers in developing the organization.

Formal communications typically include some or all of the following:

- Senior management presentations, roadshows, corporate videos
- Team briefings and management cascades
- Help-desks and electronic mail question and answer services
- Staff newsletters.

Communication should be as two-way as possible, with staff being given opportunities to discuss the latest news. Key messages may need to be repeated in many different formats. Staff response to the messages about change should be anticipated and questions-and-answer sessions built into presentations. Marion Devine (1999) suggests that, broadly speaking, formal communications should aim to:

- Inform – about the organizational/personal implications
- Clarify – the reason for the change, the strategy and benefits
- Provide direction – about the emerging vision, values and desired behaviours
- Focus – on immediate work priorities and actions, together with medium-term goals
- Reassure – that the organization will treat them with respect and dignity.

Communications should be honest and should involve all stakeholders. However, formal communication processes alone may not be enough to achieve buy-in. What matters more is how the message is conveyed, especially if the behaviour of senior managers in particular contradicts their verbal messages. In one financial services company, for instance, directors were expected to lead a culture change towards a focus on the customer. They spoke publicly about the virtues of the company values, especially teamwork. Since they were known as being themselves a dysfunctional management team, these separate presentations were received with scepticism by staff. It was only when the CEO threatened the directors with financial penalties for failing to model leadership and teamwork that their behaviour changed and their messages about the need for teamwork became credible.

Trust

During change, the role of leaders is paramount and motivating people to move bravely forward when the destination may be unclear is a challenging task. Leadership credibility can be quickly lost if senior managers are out of touch with what is happening on the ground. As will be seen in the next chapter, senior managers have often been through their own personal change process having had prior knowledge of, and some control over, what is about to happen. They may well be unaware of how staff are feeling and what their needs are. HR professionals can play a key role in keeping the top in touch with the bottom of the hierarchy and acting as listening posts for areas which senior managers should attend to. Top management needs to be seen to care, to act competently and fairly and to keep promises. Leaders should be discouraged from announcing that 'there will be no redundancies': even in good faith this cannot be guaranteed.

Leaders should communicate openly about the situation which, as long as the managers have not built up a legacy of cynicism among employees, should lead to employees trusting top management. Employees are then more likely to suspend judgement and display their trust by going the extra mile. Management teams need to speak with one voice during change since any dissent among the leadership is likely to cause trust to break down and put the change effort back. Similarly, leaders should not be seen to tolerate sabotage of the change effort, especially among their own ranks, but should deal firmly with those who seek to revert to the status quo.

Helps and hindrances in managing change

One UK firm incorporated and became a PLC at the same time in the late 1990s. For partners, and those aspiring to be partners, the implications of the change for their own career aspirations, working practices and the way in which the organization is to be managed are significant. For people who might have expected to have a key role in decision making as well as those who might once have aspired to 'owning' the firm, the changes initially appeared retrograde at a personal level, while being good for the business. A group of senior associates and salaried partners considered what would help them to adjust to the change. While no two change initiatives are alike, their comments hint at some relatively common line management concerns with regard to change. Their suggestions about how the changes which they were experiencing could be better handled were as follows:

What people expected of senior management
- Forward planning
- Professionalism
- Conviction on delivery of the message
- Senior management should 'own' the change
- Managing expectations beforehand
- Immediate feedback
- Openness and honesty
- Having a logical process to manage the change
- Making resources available for the new business strategy
- Reward and benefits should be speedily aligned to the new approach
- Implementing change quickly

Expectations of self and peers
- Flexibility of response
- Develop a support network
- Be focused
- Work with the change
- Build up inner strength
- Create common conviction about light at the end of the tunnel.

The managers also considered what was getting in the way of successfully managing change and the 'hindering' factors were as follows:

- Limited time for reflection
- Emotion
- Detachment of senior management
- No direction
- Aggressive/defensive responses from senior management
- Fudging of issues
- Lack of communication
- Uncertainty
- Dishonesty
- Lengthy deliberation
- 'Surprise' announcements with no explanation
- Inflexibility
- Systems and processes which dull the energy
- Imposed change.

Arguably, their comments point to elements of a strategic HR contribution to managing change. This involves 'reading' the organization and providing senior management with feedback about how employees are receiving the change. Executives often need coaching in the arts of leadership especially during major change. HR needs to be prepared to confront executives if their style is contributing to the problems experienced. Similarly, HR needs to adjust human resource processes and systems to ensure that they are aligned to the change and do not act as 'brakes' on the way forward.

Ensuring that communication processes are working well in different parts of the organization is another key contribution since typically some managers are better than others at keeping employees abreast of the changes and their implications. Helping employees and managers to cope with change and develop flexible approaches is easier said than done, but creating workshops and other forums where people can get together and contribute their ideas to the implementation of change can help. Involving and energizing people is key if people are to stop being doorstep critics and become active proponents of change.

David Waters of **Whitbread** has implemented many change initiatives (see Chapter 15). He uses a hierarchy of proactivity to explain to people what the company needs from people during change. At one extreme are those who wait for guidance before they will do anything. At the other are people who will act without consultation and reflect on their actions afterwards. Given that there are often periods when guidance is not forthcoming, the 'spectators' are unlikely to receive the instructions they need and therefore may hang on to 'old' ways of doing things whether or not these are appropriate. People at every level in an organization can be galvanized into finding new ways forward, as in the case studies which follow, but line managers and HR may have to accept that some people will need a lot more encouragement than others before they will try anything different.

Checklist – Developing a positive climate for change

*   Understand your current culture and what can be strengthened, balanced and changed
*   Link the changes in roles with the business imperative
*   Define future roles
*   Break established patterns
*   Challenge cultural and other sacred cows
*   Set new standards
*   Involve people in designing their future
*   Excite and enthuse people
*   Support people in learning
*   Give people the opportunity to exercise new skills
*   Empower people

Developing a customer-focused culture in Standard Life

Standard Life is a long-established mutual company operating in the UK, Ireland, Canada, Spain and Germany, predominantly in life insurance and pensions. Standard Life UK operating companies include Standard Life Assurance Co., Standard Life Investments, Standard Life Bank Ltd and Prime Health. Despite competition from banks, building societies and many other sources, Standard Life has been through a period of solid growth which has included launching its own investment house and bank in 1998. There are 9700 employees, 7500 of whom are based in Edinburgh. The head office is in Edinburgh where Standard Life is the city's largest private employer.

In recent years, Standard Life has successfully transformed itself from being a relatively staid and paternalistic organization into one which balances dynamic business innovation with effective risk management. On the whole, there is genuine employee ownership of the culture change. The need for change was strong. The drivers for change were typical for the financial services industry:

- Static market growth
- Rising unit costs
- Increased regulation
- Increased competition
- Customer requirements for customer service as well as excellent financial strength.

In the early 1990s, the board of Standard Life agreed that it was essential to increase market share, recover the competitive position as a low-cost provider and maintain financial strength. To achieve this, the board recognized that Standard Life needed to develop a genuinely customer-focused organization and created a forward strategy known as Total Customer Satisfaction (TCS). It was clear that employees were going to be key to delivering the TCS strategy and their behaviour and attitudes had to be transparently customer-focused. The quality programme underpinned by competencies became the mainspring for the new culture.

The management process is derived from the group mission and vision and these are underpinned by a set of values as follows:

From	*To*
Internally driven	Customer-driven
Task	Added value
Parent–child	Adult–adult
Functional	Collaborative
Uniform	Diverse

Operating Principles were also established with three clear areas of focus:

- *Customer* Customers' needs and expectations will drive our actions
- *Process* We will deliver value through processes which we will seek continuously to improve

- *People* We will train and develop all staff to realize their full potential to serve our customers.

Group strategies were developed, together with three-year company plans and corporate scorecards, using the Balanced Scorecard approach which enables progress to be measured. The whole process is cascaded through the organization with divisional scorecards, plans and supporting scorecards. Staff are aware of, and refer to, the operating principles in internal meetings. The competence framework is seen as essential to translating the values into action. Competencies run through all development initiatives, especially leadership development and are also key to contribution (line) management, recruitment, feedback processes, market pricing, provision of learning materials, succession management. The link between these 'soft' people processes and the 'hard' business results is made transparent through the use of the Scorecard.

The role of HR in supporting change

Human Resources has played an important role in bringing about this successful culture change. Initially, responsibility for managing the culture change implicit in TCS lay with the Corporate Development unit. HR took back the initiative for organizational development and training. Stephen McCafferty, Assistant General Manager Resourcing and Development (see Chapter 12) believes that the challenge for HR is to get the match between the environment, the team, the job specification and the job holder right, all within a cultural context. Training has been a key plank of this strategy, with line managers encouraged to take an active performance coaching role.

HR strategic plans were created for each division so that HR can be fully aligned to the business. HR's role is to offer the line best practice, not to interfere. The HR team is organized so that 'Business Consultants' support different parts of the business, helping the management teams link their operational functional plans and their strategic plans with how they will get the best out of their people. With the rapid growth of recent years, a key focus has been recruitment.

With business commitment to improving customer service, an Employee Development Strategy was created which clearly focused on serving customer needs. Elements of the strategy are as follows:

- Build the skills required to become a customer-focused organization
- Enhance the capability of our leaders
- Build 'self-directed/just-in-time' learning
- Build explicit links between employee development and business outcomes
- Create a 'feedback' culture
- Become recognized as an 'Investor in People'.

The Employee Development Strategy has four main components:

- Total customer service training
- Proactive contribution management
- Reverse feedback
- Technical based training.

Some of these are explored in a little more detail as follows:

Total customer service training is largely delivered by the line and has high business credibility. Line managers receive recognition for providing effective coaching for performance improvement to their teams. *Proactive contribution management*, rather than appraisals and backward-looking performance management. This encourages employees to ask themselves:

- What will you contribute to the organization to achieve the goals?
- How will you develop to achieve these and your own goals?
- How will we work in partnership based on competencies to achieve these goals?

The contribution management discussions take place quarterly between employees and their managers. Development priorities are agreed on one or two competencies which are linked to the job. At the end of the year, the discussion involves taking stock and planning for the future.

Workshops offering *reverse* or 180-degree *feedback* are now being run for senior and middle managers. The first workshops were championed by the CEO and top 27 managers. Now into phase 5, with over 300 managers having taken part, the upward-feedback process is producing desired behavioural changes in managers who now take the developmental aspects of managing people very seriously. The process has now become integrated into the cycle of management activity, rather than being seen as a one-off. As with all HR-related activity, upward feedback is timed to suit business needs in the different parts of Standard Life.

Similarly, the feedback process has to be seen to add value. The results of the feedback have to be used. Initially, the feedback forms the basis of an individual action plan which eventually becomes part of an individual's contribution plan. Then the entire team of the person who has received feedback are engaged in a review meeting to discuss the themes of the feedback in more detail, with the support of an individual adviser. There is an agreed action plan for the team which then goes into the manager's contribution plan. At an organizational level, the feedback results are used to direct training and development activity.

Ultimately, the overall feedback results are reported in the Standard Life Organizational scorecard. Measurement is a key feature of the Standard Life approach to organizational change. The Organizational scorecard is used to ensure that cultural shifts, such as changing leadership behaviour, are actually happening. Three-quarters of the executive group have now experienced reverse feedback and their results are fed into the organizational action plan, as well as individual development plans. For internal purposes, the results are also broken down by business unit, with an indication of what is being done to address issues. 'League tables', though, are not made public within the organization since encouraging competition between business units and managers would be seen as counter-cultural. Currently the results are used entirely for developmental rather than assessment purposes, though eventually they could be linked with reward.

A key issue within change is trust between management and employees as a whole. The feedback process suggested that there is a perceived lack of trust between the executives and employees. The managing director has taken this issue seriously. There has therefore been a conscious attempt to build trust by consulting staff openly on issues such as the revised grading system. There is also a deliberate focus on building better relationships between managers and their teams, making better use of manager role models who can coach their peers in new behaviours, and an emphasis on dealing with performance robustly. The scorecard results have started to show the positive effects on business results of good people management practice.

Current and future focus

The HR team has also focused on a range of additional ways of adding value. 'People asset techniques' such as training are receiving serious investment, with 8.5 per cent of payroll including downtime expended on training in 1998. Recognizing that culture change needs to be led from the top, one important area involves training executives. An initial workshop, which involved case studies, psychometrics and discussion groups with observers, provided the impetus for further development. This was followed by action learning sets, teamworking initiatives and a range of specific modules such as for influencing skills, strategic leadership, strategic marketing and finance. This executive programme was run in collaboration with the Management Development Network (MDN), a network established by Standard Life with other major employers in Scotland such as **Scottish Power** and **Motorola**.

Current HR priorities include the use of Open Access Development Centres (described in Chapter 16), leadership development, NVQs and the development of a new induction process. Career development has been a major area of focus and a range of self-assessment and career self-management tools have been developed for use by employees. The HR team are very clear that certain things will become more (or less) important over time as the business changes and they use a framework to keep track of where the priorities are and progress made against them. Clear areas for future focus include the enhancement of the employee brand, consolidation and welfare reform. Priorities within these will include designing the psycho-social elements of the workplace, calling on the skills of the in-house ergonomist, as well as relationship building within the evolving HR function.

Measuring progress – and success

Standard Life believe that investing in people development makes a positive difference to the organization, but, as always, proof is needed. Compared with other large financial institutions

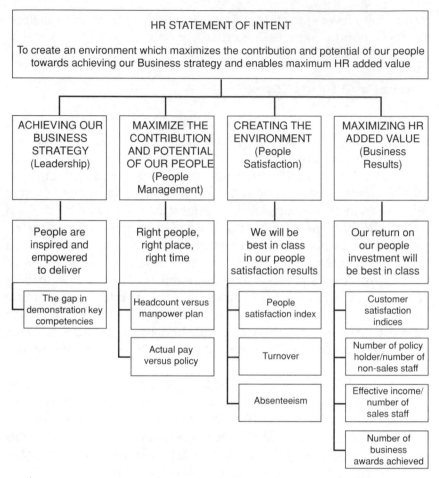

Figure 14.1   *The organizational HR scorecard*

in 1997 (Corporate Leadership Council research) they are ahead of their competitors by spending 8.5 per cent of payroll on employee development. The challenge is to assess whether the spend is justified. The evidence collected suggests that the investment is paying off handsomely.

The team use the organizational HR Scorecard to keep track of progress (Figure 14.1). They believe that they have been able to establish links between improved market share and where HR has made a difference. A number of external benchmarks of success reinforce the team's own assessment. An independent survey of the company's results carried out by the Independent Advisers' Strategy Group has placed Standard Life ahead of its

competitors because of its changed culture. This result represents a startling improvement over the assessment made at the
start of the culture-change period when Standard Life was rated
thirty-seventh out of thirty-nine companies.

On the Customer element of TCS the company won the PIMs
award (the quality award for the financial services industry) in
1996 and has since won it three times more. Employees have
been rewarded with bonuses to celebrate the achievement. On
the Process element, Standard Life has maintained a Triple A
rating for financial strength and unit costs continue to fall. On
the People element, the company has won Investors in People
status for the second time. The HR team are aiming to reach
world class and are using EFQM measures for internal assessment purposes. The team won the 1998 Cranfield Award for
linking HR strategy to business strategy.

In hard business results, Standard Life's share of the total market has shifted from 5.5 per cent in 1995 to 6.9 per cent in 1998,
representing an increase of 25.45 per cent (this excludes Unit
Trust and PEP). This is a remarkable achievement by any standards, but the success of the business strategy has no doubt been
made possible because of a well-aligned and implemented HR
strategy underpinning the culture change. The link between the
'people aspect' and a good return on investment has become clear.

On the 'soft' side of measures, the subtle signs of shifting culture are difficult to pin down but are real for all that. Some of the
more obvious signs of shifting attitudes are evident in 'surprises'.
An IS manager, for instance, who once saw anything concerning
people to be HR's responsibility is now working with HR to plan
for succession, being very aware that without it he cannot succeed
in the future. Measuring values about customer focus could easily concentrate on training, when in fact the processes need to feed
into selection and the way people are managed and rewarded.

Measuring 'people' values highlights the potential for dilemmas
if the needs of staff and customers are different. While aiming for
consistency, the HR team realize that some trade-offs may be necessary between different aspects of the values at different times.
Work patterns, such as a proposed 24-hour banking service, need
to be determined by the needs of customers, though shift patterns
may not suit the needs of existing employees who have been used
to conventional working weeks. This has implications for the
nature of the workforce – permanent, contract, flexible, a mix of
new and existing staff – and for the way people are managed.

Potentially key organizational values around fairness at all times and employee welfare will become the guiding principles for resourcing decisions. Rewarding people by contribution made is now reflected in the breakdown of a common grading system, with a greater emphasis on market pricing of jobs.

The culture change goes on...The company aspires to a culture where people at all levels deal with each other openly and honestly, where promotions are founded on consistent criteria, based largely on contribution and through demonstration of the key competencies and where career development is given prominence. The acid test of whether the values live is when people start to question senior management, as they are now starting to, in an adult–adult way, and receive an appropriate response. There is now ample evidence that the various parties concerned with managing careers, namely individuals, managers and the organization, are beginning to accept their different responsibilities. Individuals in particular are recognizing that they need to take ownership of their own careers and managers at all levels are now beginning to encourage and support that development.

Lessons learned

The HR team believe that certain elements were vital to achieving this successful culture change. These were:

- Top team commitment and focus – and willingness to commit money to achieving culture change
- Listening to the staff – they are HR's customers
- Designing and trialling initiatives to support staff and help them to do their jobs
- Training managers how to coach
- Using competencies to provide clarity about what is needed
- 'Borrowing with pride' – i.e. looking at good practice elsewhere and adapting it to meet the needs of Standard Life.

Change at Thresher – updating the Operations Development Project story

As a case study in change management, the **Thresher** story is worth recapping and updating. The original case study was published in my previous book *Motivating People in Lean Organizations*. This case study demonstrates change management driven from the middle of an organization, rather than initially from the top. It also demonstrates the value of an effective line/HR business partnership.

Since the case was published, circumstances have changed and Thresher has become part of First Quench, a joint venture set up by parent companies Whitbread PLC and Allied Domecq. The success of the Operations Development project (ODP) helped Thresher to be seen as a viable contender in an extremely competitive marketplace. The Operations Director of First Quench, Brian Wisdom, was the Ops Director of Thresher and was one of the prime movers behind the ODP. Brian's challenges will include bringing about a successful new company from the combined forces of Thresher and Victoria Wine.

Thresher (1898–1998) was a successful high street specialist wine and drink retailer with 150 outlets, 10 000 employees and £600 million turnover. Retail brands include:

Thresher Wine Shop
Bottoms Up
Huttons
Wine Rack
Drinks Cabin
Drinks Direct.

A subsidiary of Whitbread PLC, the business had grown via a series of acquisitions, including Peter Dominic (case study featured in Chapter 15).

By the early 1990s, big competitive challenges meant that Thresher was potentially likely to lose market share to the supermarkets and the cross-Channel flood of drinks imports. Consumers were becoming more demanding. Despite the dangers of doing nothing, there was a degree of complacency with regard to change. As a former HR director put it, the approach to running the business was to 'get the money in the pot and sit on it'. Culturally, the organization appeared closed and risk averse. Quality of Worklife surveys suggested that employees perceived there to be a command and control management style and a degree of employee dissatisfaction. Opportunities for personal growth were limited. The ethos was on growth through control, with the effect that there were plenty of 'checkers checking checkers'.

The real challenge was to bring about change in what was perceived to be a successful company. The board's agenda was firmly on aligning Retail strategy and the Operations organization, which comprised the shops. This meant branding differently according to locations and customers. However, operations were not set up in brands and the parallel imperative to reduce overheads seemed in potential conflict with the branding aspirations. After all, a regional structure was more cost effective than a branded one.

The Operations' agenda, in contrast, was also focused on the 'people' aspects of the strategic imperatives. Brian Wisdom and the HR Controller, Chris Johnson, wanted to improve the calibre and skills of people so that growth could be achieved through realizing potential, as much as by cost containment. They wanted to shift from an ethos of control to one which centred on the customer. In particular, they wished to improve systems, processes and working practices to produce better functional integration.

Winning board commitment

At the start of the change project, the board were not really engaged, with the exception of the sales director, Dick Smerdon who acted as a shield to the project. Support for the project gradually grew as data from the field trials helped to convince the board and others of the need for change. Initially, the board did not appreciate the importance of mobilizing the workforce for change. However, the former HR director said 'our people will sink this company because they're unhappy'. As the groundswell of opinion grew, the sales director and HR director prepared to 'take a careful look at the future without taking our eyes off the ball'.

The process of persuasion involved developing a clearly phased change management process which had all the appearance of being well structured, but which allowed a great deal of scope for learning and experimentation. However, it was not simply the board which was subject to this persuasion. All Operations staff were involved in some way with the change process and therefore built a strong sense of personal ownership about the project. The phases were as follows:

• Research and analysis – people's feelings were measured on a range of issues linked with operational effectiveness

- A cycle of blueprinting options
- Trials of new working practices and structures
- The business case – a seventeen-page document outlining the numbers on the proposed changes.

The process of persuasion and building support for the initiative took two years and involved regular presentations to the board not only by the immediate project team but also by junior line managers and others likely to be affected by the proposed changes. Brian Wisdom himself presented the case for eliminating jobs at his own level in the hierarchy – including his own.

Creating the principles for managing change

A key characteristic of this change process was achieving commitment to a set of change principles by the board and the operators. The role of HR was critical in this. The principles were as follows:

- Everyone should be involved
- The change should be owned by Operations
- Cost-savings would be reinvested
- Everything would be measured, both 'hard' and 'soft' targets
- There was to be no 'cherry-picking' of the parts of the change which appeared successful. The project had to be seen as fully integrated, with all the parts – systems, processes, working practices – interlinked.

There needed to be convergence between the board's vision and that of the project team. A set of broader objectives than the original board objectives were agreed which were about helping people to do their jobs more effectively. So they concerned business development, rather than control ('from cop to coach'), the use of information, not just data. This was vital if people were to really support the change and see some benefits from what might otherwise have appeared an imposed set of objectives. The objectives included:

- Getting closer to the customer
- Performance improvement
- Retail strategy

- Flatter, more responsive organization
- Fast, efficient communications
- To develop and energize people.

The trials of new working practices were closely linked with these objectives. They included creating a lap-top environment and an excellent management information system which was genuinely useful to Operators. This meant that the chore of processing volumes of paperwork each week was significantly reduced and the focus was now on providing people with the information they needed to do their jobs. Cross-functioning self-managing teams were established and training provided to get them up and running. Much of the money saved from restructuring was reinvested in training. The ODP was managed as a project with a three-year timescale and the project team ensured that the project kept on track.

The ODP was also a means of creating a more flexible and customer-focused culture than in the past. For many people, especially long-time employees, this might require a change in behaviour. A key facet of the ODP was that a clear set of values underpinned the project. Operators, including managers, were offered 360-degree feedback which helped them to understand how their behaviours matched the values, and recognition was consciously given for changed behaviours in line with the values.

The HR contribution

HR had a key role in making the ODP happen in a number of ways. Chris Johnson, working alongside Brian Wisdom, was able to understand the Operational imperatives and provide business-focused HR support. One contribution was in ensuring that the change was supported by like-minded people with the relevant skills and experience by developing appropriate recruitment and development processes. As detailed in Chapter 7, a strategic approach to recruitment was undertaken which challenged conventional recruitment. This was not a question of filling gaps; rather it was a means of bringing into the organization people who were credible at all levels, especially middle management, who could help mobilize their peers. These 'architects of change' or 'ambassadors' were mainly recruited from outside quite deliberately. Wisdom and Johnson developed a clear picture of what an ambassador needed to be able to do. They looked for people who embodied the new ethos but who had more to offer than a list of conventional competencies. They wanted people who could show what Brian called the 'essence of being'.

Wisdom and Johnson funnelled all the recruitment activity through themselves as well as the support mechanisms for the new recruits, such as the 'bat phone'. This meant that help was on hand for the ambassadors when things became difficult. This practical help and the demonstration of belief in the individuals prevented a high drop-out rate. A completely new induction programme was developed which was not just focused on familiarization but also on personal development. New recruits were introduced to working in self-managing teams and were given access to senior management when Directors hosted induction dinners.

HR also contributed to the many ways in which employees became energized for change. Early in the project, the project team suggested that employees fell into different categories with regard to change. There were the 'spectators' who cautiously preferred to watch from the sidelines, the downright 'cynics', the 'players' who were already involved and the 'question marks' who might never be able to get on board with the change. The task of HR was to create a compelling future so that at least the spectators wanted to become players and ideally a few of the cynics too. This was likely to require some coaching and clarity about what behaviours were required for effective performance.

Getting staff involved in different stages of the project was vital to motivation. Members of the field teams were engaged in the trials and analysis. Getting people involved in experimentation meant that people were more likely to accept and drive forward the change. Experimenting also meant that there were no disasters if the experiment failed, only a better end product. It was important to capture learning from mistakes rather than simply punishing people. This was a 'Trojan horse' approach which helped to create the agenda for change.

The data from the trials suggested that the changes were on the right track and 'made us bolder' according to Brian Wisdom. But this was not involvement in the sense that anything went. The foundations of self-managing teams were laid and each team of six to eight people did a section of the work. Clear handovers or 'baton changes' were arranged between teams working on different phases of project. As people with different skillsets and beliefs started to work together in teams they had to start trusting each other.

Communication, especially of the values, was a major responsibility as people started to live the values and a drip-feed approach was taken to reinforce the messages once people had returned to the field. Wisdom and Johnson preferred to help people to change the culture, and see the benefits, rather than go public on the values without substance. Roadshows, conferences etc. all demonstrated the same philosophy – the project teams themselves mounted the events rather than relying on a conventional top-down presentation. The project teams also presented their findings to the board themselves – after all, what they had discovered, they believed in.

The Operations values were as follows:

- Have the intellectual confidence to keep it simple
- Respect the contribution and potential of our people
- Take pride in the service we offer to customers
- Be honest and open.

The values were underpinned by a set of change principles which emerged in the early phases of the ODP. The principles encouraged people to:

- Develop people to their maximum potential
- Use technology to make things simpler, faster and better
- Value and recognize individual contributions, especially when they benefit the team
- Embrace change and become players not spectators
- Welcome surprises that innovation brings
- Guard against shocks due to negligence.

The principles and values were eventually featured on a motivational video which was used by teams throughout Thresher and which demonstrated the principles in practice.

Capturing the learning

The learning from a change project of this size could easily have been lost had the need to capture the learning not been recognized. Learning was reviewed at the end of each phase of the

ODP, enabling people to gain a sense of progress and to celebrate achievements. A Generic Implementation Guide (GIG)
captured the essence of the change programme and what had
been learned from experience but this was not intended to be a
rigid formula for others to follow. Rather it was a resource to
prevent a lot of wasted effort for future project teams. Learning
was linked with physical actions so that it translated readily into
practice. Some of the learning, such as the need for managers to
be prepared to let go and allow people to grow into new roles,
was painfully acquired. However, the change programme, with
its regular review procedures, had succeeded in creating the right
environment for change.

A success story...

By every measure against success was measured, the ODP more
than fulfilled its promise. The new, vibrant culture of enterprise
and experimentation has enabled many employees to develop
their potential and contribute in new and exciting ways.
Employees report massive boosts to their self-esteem and a 'can
do' attitude is evident. Performance improvement has led to
improved business results (the investment in the ODP had been
paid back within two years). Meanwhile, the ever-burgeoning
cross-Channel trade and increased duties on alcohol continues
to put the business under pressure. One response is to increase
the use of technology to provide alternative means of buying
drinks to having to go to shops. Once again, new working practices are called for which some employees may find threatening.

Yet, the project team admit that the very success of the ODP
highlighted other areas which needed to change. After the project phases ended, the change programme had become the new
way of doing business. Management started to find itself subjected to 'values blackmail' by which individuals would make
demands based on selective use of the Operations values. Some
people picked up on the value linked with the 'potential of our
people' and demanded further development. In some cases it
was felt that managers had transformed themselves so thorough-
ly 'from cop to coach' that controls were not being properly exer-
cised and needed to be reintroduced.

Another area where the success of the project exposed problems was succession planning. In a matter of a few years,

Thresher's reputation as a source of good people had been positively transformed. Now other organizations, especially within the **Whitbread** companies, were recruiting Thresher employees. In the space of a year, Operations lost sixteen excellent players and Brian Wisdom had to carry out some rapid reconstruction. Succession planning was introduced to ensure that at least some provision would be made for turnover of key staff. Internal and external recruits made up the succession pool.

Induction was also improved to prepare new recruits for the relatively sophisticated skills context which they would be entering. After all, few people had prior experience of working in a situation characterized by self-managing teams, technical and coaching skills.

Thresher senior management also had to walk the talk on being open – especially to feedback from members of the self-managing teams. As Brian Wisdom says: 'It can be really tough sometimes working in a flat structure.' The self-managing teams operated at different speeds and some teams became rather dysfunctional. They found it hard to recognize this and needed intensive coaching to address the issues. It was important to create alignment within teams by reinforcing the vision and mission and creating a strong directional focus.

An individual's experience of the change process

In the early stages of the ODP, Alison Ainsworth was an area manager who subsequently moved into Human Resources for a few years. She then became Operations Manager responsible for franchising and has therefore practical insights into the change from both a leadership and 'followership' perspective. Alison describes the range of reactions that people had to the change programme in the early stages:

> People seemed to fall into two groups; they were either enthusiastic or concerned. The ones who were enthusiastic felt highly motivated by what was going on; they felt liberated, challenged and part of something leading edge. The concerned people, by contrast, were uncertain what the future held. They were uncomfortable, felt pressurized and thought that the change was part of a passing fad.

What made the difference was strong role modelling by the Thresher board. The visits to shops by senior managers were inspirational and conveyed their belief in the project. They rewarded people's behaviours by 'thank-you's, bottles of champagne and other small tokens of appreciation. It felt as if the recognition was very personal, which was great. It also felt as if there were no barriers between staff and the board. There was lots of regular communication and the Board asked for feedback. People felt informed and involved. As Alison says:

> It was not just a management theory. The mission, vision and values became wrapped up in what we wanted to do. It felt like a framework within which to work. It was easy to visualize and relate to. People could see where the parts of the jigsaw fell into place. The milestones felt motivational. We felt that Operations had really changed and that, if anything, change in other parts of the business like Marketing or Buying wasn't fast enough.
>
> The self-managing teams went through a lot of storming before they really started to perform. People had to change their mindsets from 'I' to 'we'. The teams sometimes went off at tangents and lost their way. They had to really work hard to get people with different approaches to the values to mesh together. What was particularly interesting was seeing how the culture could change and the benefits of involving people. The personal commitment of managers did motivate the cynics.

Getting the balance right

The ODP demonstrates the value of business and HR strategies complementing each other. Building 'soft' behavioural measures into a medium-term change project was a strategic activity to support broader culture change beyond the ODP. At the same time, those measured activities enabled the business in the short-term to transform its performance and profitability. The Operational imperative for business results, performance measures and action-oriented organizational change were appropriately enhanced by the mode of delivery which was HR reliant. Change was to be delivered by people, whose competencies and skills would grow and result in changed, visible behaviours. These in turn would create an 'organizational conscience' which would guide people's behaviour in the future, without becoming a straightjacket.

1999 and beyond

> Achievement is a Journey without an ending, and the hardest part
> of planning for this Journey is how to arrive at one destination and
> look forward to the next. (Frank Dick, OBE)

The ODP is not the end of the story. As is so often the case,
more change has occurred due to the August 1998 merger
between Thresher and Victoria Wine to produce First Quench.
The merger has effectively doubled the size of both of the previous organizations. First Quench now has 3000 outlets, 20 000
employees and a turnover of £1.3 billion. Retail brands include
Thresher brands and Victoria Wine, Victoria Wine Cellar,
Martha's Vineyard, Firkin Off Licence and Haddows. The
shares are owned 50/50 by Whitbread PLC and Allied Domecq.
The new entity therefore boasts at least two different organizational cultures.

On becoming Operations Director for First Quench, Brian
Wisdom was faced with the challenge of maximizing the potential of the new organization. In order to do that he felt that it is
necessary to take one step back. He recognized that, for the time
being, a more conventional approach to managing the organization was called for and put in place a management layer or two
to consolidate decision making and procedures. Initially, the self-
managing teams were disbanded. For Brian, moving to a hierarchical approach is a challenge and he sees it as a temporary measure to establish one supply chain.

He commissioned an organizational development project
which delivered a new structure for the year 2000 onwards. He
is very clear about what some of the new change programme's
characteristics were to be:

- The change this time will be driven top-down, rather than
  middle-up
- It will be underpinned by a clear Mission, Vision and Values
- It will operate in a Total Quality Management context
- There will be cross-functional involvement.

Organization Project II adopted learning from the ODP and start
at the customer interface. Brian believes that by starting at the
front-line and working back, change will rapidly benefit the customer.

Key learning points

- If you are going to carry out a change project, it must be in a strategic context, so that you can bring the people with you and they understand why they have to change.
- Changing any process in isolation is a fool's errand. There needs to be integration between process and function.
- Structured project management is crucial to the success of a change initiative. There need to be clear milestones and deliverables along the way. People need to know whether the change is working or not, and take corrective action as appropriate. If you are using an external consultant to manage the project, make sure that they 'fit' culturally.
- There has to be a strong business case for the change and measures need to be set and monitored – around both 'hard' and 'soft' targets.
- Communication cannot be overplayed. Too much top-down communication may cause people to stop listening. Find ways to get two-way communication flows and engage people in communicating the change to each other. In the Thresher case, the roadshows and sales conferences were designed, organized and delivered by the teams themselves, with senior managers in 'walk-on' parts. Create motivational messages, videos and other ways of reinforcing the message when the first flush of enthusiasm wears off.
- For change to be really effective, there has to be an active partnership between the business and HR. In the Thresher case, HR helped redesign the structures and create room for the 'architects of change'. HR rebuilt the succession planning processes which had long been moribund.
- Organization design should push decision making as far down the hierarchy as possible and make people accountable. Delayered structures work best in this regard, as long as people have the appropriate skills and behaviours and are provided with the resources, including training, they need to do the job. Each layer should have clear areas of accountability which should be different from other levels.
- Self-managing teams can become high performing and are an excellent way of involving people and tapping into their creativity. They may need support to prevent them losing sight of the bigger picture and starting to compete with one another.
- Remember to celebrate the achievements of all those

involved in the change. In celebrating current success, do not denigrate the past by implication. Motivate people for ongoing change by stabilizing what works.

Checklists on change management

Creating future directions

- What is the vision for the future of the organization?
- What are the values of the organization? To what extent are these values translated into leaders' behaviours and commitment?
- How much do employees believe that the lived values matched the espoused?
- What are the cultural 'gaps'?
- What is the organization's culture, and what are we trying to change?
- What are the aspects of the organization's culture which need to be strengthened, balanced or changed?
- How can we create an adaptable culture in which change is welcome?

Enabling change

- What is our change strategy? Methods? Action plans? Who is involved?
- What are the most effective methods of communication used in the organization? How often do we review these methods to assess if they are still effective?
- What do employees like to know about in practice?
- In what areas are employees asked their views? What follow-up is offered when employees have been consulted?
- How active is informal communication, i.e. gossip, corridor conversations etc. To what extent are these a proxy for formal communications?
- What are the main communication issues stopping our organization from being more effective at the following levels – small group, departmental, business unit, whole organization? What can be done to address these issues?
- What are the main issues which currently or potentially cause difficulties between the organization and its clients, or vice versa?

- What approach to change is taken – evolutionary or revolutionary?
- Are leaders capable of leading the change? If not, how can this be compensated for?
- Is there a guiding coalition who can help drive change forward?
- Are there clear project plans for implementing change?
- Do we have any genuine change agents? How can we engage them in the change process?

Human implications of change

- Have we considered the human implications of change and how we will address these?
- What are the sources and types of resistance to change? How do we overcome resistance to change?
- How can we help people to cope with change?
- What is the impact of our change(s) on customers?

Becoming a change agent

- How can we assess sources of influence?
- Where should change start in our team?
- How well has this team effected change in the past? What has worked? What are the barriers to success?
- How well do we integrate different initiatives into an overall change framework which is coherent?

References

Devine, M. (1999). *A Mergers Checklist*, Roffey Park Management Institute.

Duckler, P. and Shifman C. (1998). *Cultural Crisis Threatens to Derail Deregulation*, Chicago: Spencer Stuart.

Harrison, R. (1986). *Diagnosing Organization Culture*. Harrison Associates.

Kotter, J. P. (1995). Leading change: why transformation efforts fail. *Harvard Business Review*, **73**, No.2, 59–67.

McCurry, P. (1998). Power transformers. *Personnel Today*, 22 October.

Quinn, J. B. (1995). 'Strategic change: logical incrementalism'. In Mintzberg, H., Quinn J. B. and Ghoshal, S. *The Strategy Process*. Englewood Cliffs, NJ: Prentice Hall.

Mergers and strategic alliances

> I know that what looks good on paper can easily turn sour in prac-
> tice, and very many mergers have failed – why? Because a merger
> is ultimately more about people than balance sheets. We need to
> bring together two groups of people and build a new organization
> which is more than the sum of its parts (Sir Michael Bett, former
> First Commissioner of the Civil Service and lately President of
> the Chartered Institute of Personnel & Development).

This chapter is based on the Mergers and Strategic Alliances
research project carried out by Roffey Park Management
Institute since 1997. The first phase of research focused on the
human aspects of mergers and was based on in-depth organizational case studies. Organizations studied from the commercial
sector include examples from the financial services, manufacturing, retail and the oil industry. From the public sector, cases
include a government department, a government agency and two
Further Education colleges. Each case is distinctive and shows
that mergers are rarely identical. A broader group of organizations contributed information to the study anonymously.

The findings suggest that there is a business case for taking
people issues seriously. The starting point for the Roffey Park
research was that while many organizations claim that their
mergers have succeeded, short-term financial measures of success due to rationalization are unreliable indicators of the longer-
term effectiveness of a merger. A study by Hall and Norburn
(1987) of the financial benefits of M&As found that returns to
shareholders are at best 'slight' and at worst 'significantly negative'. Mergers hold out the attractive prospect of increasing earnings per share (EPS) to shareholders. However, the risks

attached to mergers are mainly linked to the Human Resource arena. Interestingly, it is perhaps because of the recognized difficulties of making mergers happen successfully that the UK government pressure on Colleges of Further Education to merge has been replaced by a requirement that colleges work in partnership to achieve many of the same ends.

It is the range of issues relating to people within merging organizations which can determine whether the merger is as successful as it might be, or indeed whether it succeeds at all. While there is increasing awareness that human factors have an influence over the success of the merger, executives are often at a loss to know how to address the different issues. Frequently, they are so absorbed with the nature of the business deal and in securing their own interests that the organizational implications of the deal are only considered once the deal has been struck.

Bungling the handling of a merger can result in losing people – who often constitute the market value which attracts the acquiring organization in the first place. People are a vulnerable asset – and the benefit of this asset can be destroyed if senior managers do not anticipate and prepare for the emotional response of employees at the outset. Meridian Consulting suggest that failure to create additional value through the combination and deployment of the intellectual property gained from the deal represents a new type of risk, known as knowledge risk. They calculate this as follows:

> The knowledge value at risk – that is the amount of shareholder value the firm stands to destroy if they fail to successfully integrate and leverage acquired intellectual property – equals the premium paid multiplied by the acquiring company's price-to-earning ratio, i.e.
> Value at risk = premium $ × P/E ratio

They argue that if the combining organizations are to become capable of achieving shared business goals, three abilities must be grown, i.e.

- The ability to talk with one another
- The ability to work with one another
- The ability to learn from one another.

Roffey research suggests that the way the merger process is handled will have a major impact on how well much people feel able and willing to exercise these abilities. Similarly, the roles, behaviours and attitudes of managers make a big difference to how well employees adjust to a merger. Employees are often hit by multiple waves of anxiety and need to be supported through the transition. Culture clashes between the two organizations are inevitable, especially between companies with apparently similar approaches. These are the most common causes of merger failure. HR has potentially a key role in anticipating and reducing the impact of those culture clashes.

Mergers and acquisitions, when two organizations are brought together, or are required to collaborate as in a strategic alliance, highlight the need for really effective change management. Indeed, mergers should really be thought of as large and complex change projects. If the merger is to succeed, people have to be supported in integrating working practices. Key employees need to be retained and ways of transferring knowledge across the organization found. HR potentially has a critical role to play in bringing about successful new organizations. HR strategy is vitally important during all stages of M&As and needs to be addressed as early as possible. Yet our research suggested that sometimes HR professionals were not involved until late into the merger process when many decisions had been taken (and sometimes damage caused).

The growth of mergers

Mergers are on the increase it seems. There has been a marked increase in merger activity since the mid-1990s, with activity in Europe reaching record levels in 1996. The drivers for such deals are the changing market conditions which require businesses to regroup their activities, deregulation leading to consolidation and availability of capital. Cross-border deals are becoming commonplace and there is a record number of deals between the USA and the UK. In 1997 there were a number of 'mega-deals' such as the $30 billion merger between BP and Amoco. Deal-making goes on with the **BP Amoco** acquisition of **Arco**, further consolidating the marketplace. Arguably the increasing focus on the core business is leading to the current trend of horizontal acquisitions and away from opportunistic acquisitions. These are possibly more problematic than unrelated conglomerate deals.

Every merger is different, yet there are certain common factors. Mergers take place for a wide range of reasons. A deal may be opportunistic such as to refocus on core capabilities and key markets, or defensive, enabling two weaker organizations to compete better together. Typically, mergers occur for a range of the following reasons:

• To increase shareholder value
• Dominate/penetrate new markets
• Develop new products and services
• Defend the organization against a takeover.

In the public housing sector in the UK, for instance, the most common reasons are to extend the geographical spread of Housing Associations' operations, to reduce unit costs and to strengthen the income stream. The rationale for the merger is likely to affect how the merger is managed. Where mergers occur because a company wants to dominate the marketplace with a range of services, such as different fast food outlets, there is much to be said for leaving the operations broadly separate, with integration only at senior management level. Conversely, if a company wishes to swamp the market with a single brand, full integration may be necessary.

Typically, organizations assume that full merger is required and greater upheaval than is necessary may be caused in some cases. Other possible combinations include considering the acquired company as:

• A separate holding
• Requiring strategic control
• A managed subsidiary
• Requiring operational control
• Full integration.

The integration decision should involve assessing the degree of cultural and functional integration required to help the combined company achieve its strategic ambitions. Whatever the rationale for the merger, it seems that the way the process of merging is carried out can have a bearing on whether the organization is able to achieve its business aims. Several cases studied in the Roffey Park research highlight the mistakes made when the acquiring company seeks to impose its procedures onto the acquired company. Ironically, this often results in the acquirer unwittingly snuffing out the vital spark which made the acquired company seem such an interesting proposition.

In other cases, the uncertainty caused when senior managers of the acquired company are to lose their jobs following a merger can result in the employees of that company feeling especially vulnerable. When one pharmaceutical company acquired another, partly in order to absorb the other company's research capability, there was some surprise among managers of the acquiring company when initially exciting research projects failed to materialize. The phenomenon became known in the organization as 'burying the babies', i.e. employees kept their best projects safe in case they needed to jump ship.

The reason for the merger clearly has a bearing on whether the organization's strategy includes a reduction in headcount, relocation or other issues which have a direct impact on employees. The critical thing seems to be not so much whether there are job losses or whether organizations are renamed but *how* these processes are carried out. Open and honest communication and fair principles are very important in maintaining employee commitment.

Similarly, the degree and speed of integration appears to affect employees, with organizations such as **Bristol and West PLC**, which had initiated its own acquisition, being able to phase the impact on employees over time. In theory this should help employees cope better with the 'waves of change' described in this chapter. However, other cases such as the integration of **Peter Dominic** into **Thresher** described later in this chapter suggest that a speedy integration can be highly effective in giving people a clear sense of direction.

What separates merger partners

The relative sizes of partners has a bearing on how employees view the merger. It is often assumed that the larger organization swallows up the smaller one. This is not always the case. One relative newcomer to UK DIY retailing acquired a bigger and longer-established competitor. Typically, employees consider issues such as which head office is closed as indicative of which organization is the dominant partner. Similarly, perceptions about the power dynamics between the companies concerned can cause some employees to consider jumping ship.

Some of the main factors which can undermine successful integration are differences in the two organizations' politics, decision making, cultures, values and leadership styles. Their strategies and structures, including systems and processes, are usually different. Employees are sensitive to those differences which affect them most, especially if they perceive the acquisition to be hostile. Which approaches are adopted and they way in which such decisions are taken can have an effect on employees' morale and willingness to adopt new working practices, especially if the acquired company's employees perceive that these are being imposed on them. One UK building society actively sought a merger partner and was acquired by a large bank. The importance of having a 'fit' at values level between the two organizations was recognized by both sets of senior managers who spent time getting to know one another, and building trust, before the deal was struck. Having taken time to understand each other's skills and attributes, the two organizations found they were complementary businesses and didn't need to fully integrate.

Mergers need managing

Several of the organizations studied by the Roffey Park team draw attention to the need for a skilled team of merger planning experts, and the importance of carrying out an effective human resource due diligence before the merger. Key employees need to be identified and encouraged to stay in the merged organization. The process of recruiting into positions needs to be handled in such a way as to minimize the potential for 'winners and losers'. The role of an influential and skilled Human Resources professional can be critical here.

Each phase of a merger has implications for leadership and for HR. These phases are:

* The 'run-up' or pre-merger
* The immediate transition (the first 100 days or 6 months)
* The integration (the longer-term coming together of the two parties).

Some companies are clearly focused on people issues right from the start of the merger process. They tend to be adept acquirers who have learned from past experience. Some of these companies have succeeded by developing key specialists who handle the merger process. With the full backing of the board, these taskforces are highly adept at getting communications appropriate to the situation and in making sure that the relevant relationships are established early on. The 'run-up' period should be used to carry out an effective HR due diligence and develop an awareness of the likely challenges and pressure points. The 'run-up' team should make a realistic assessment of the probable management workload and find ways of easing the burden somewhat.

The same companies then use a different team to manage the transition, and an effective handover is essential between teams. Typically, as in the **Whitbread** case study which follows, there is a clear 100-day plan which addresses most of the integration issues at the level of human resource matters, systems and processes. Of course, personnel issues, including policies and procedures, are not the only things which need managing. Other critical issues include integrating:

- IT
- Product ranges
- Supply chains
- Head offices.

Senior managers and directors have a key role in leading the change. In many mergers, the roles of one group of directors simply disappear. Where directors survive the merger, the relative positions which directors occupy in the new organization seems to have an impact on whether other employees consider their organization to be a 'winner' or ' loser' in the merger process. Ideally, at least one or two senior managers from the acquired company should be retained to provide other employees with reassurance. Willing collaboration between management teams before and after the merger also seems to make a positive difference to the way the change is handled.

During the transition period, the pace of change is so fierce that keeping an eye on the business is not easy. The research highlights the importance of managing the integration of the organizations as a critical project alongside keeping the business going and customers satisfied. This conscious management of the integration should carry on for as long a period as is necessary. Some companies manage the longer-term integration by training line managers and making them responsible for the real bedding down of the new organization. In the most successful cases, at least one board member takes responsibility for over-seeing the integration for the period of time required for the 'new' organization to have fully emerged.

Even when handled 'professionally', mergers can still backfire. One company closed down its customer support site – when a merger made it obsolete – only to find that a competitor was opening a new facility nearby the very next week. The people whose jobs were made redundant and who had received generous pay-offs went straight into similar jobs with the rival company, taking their expertise and competitor knowledge with them.

Communication

The importance of communication cannot be over-emphasized, particularly in the pre-merger phase. For example, a UK manu-facturing company agreed to be acquired by a Swiss company in early 1998. The management team were pleased and excited as the firm had been 'on the market' for some time. Since then, how-ever, contact between the two companies had dwindled, leaving the UK company's management team unclear about the Swiss company's plans and expectations. Now in a state of limbo, the UK firm is effectively 'off the market'. Some senior managers have already jumped ship because they have no guarantees for the future. There is no new product development, no investment and customer orders are dropping off. Lack of communication has led to suspicion, demoralization, and loss of key personnel and busi-ness, even before the contract has been signed.

Communications are critical throughout, with several man-agement teams learning the hard way that it is better to commu-nicate even when you have nothing to say. HR needs to work alongside or as part of management teams, ensuring that formal communications are effective and that staff are being kept informed. The 1998 Benchmarking survey by Price-WaterhouseCoopers, however, suggests the HR department typ-ically does not focus on communication or motivation issues precisely at the very time when they are most needed – during organizational change such as a merger or demerger. Managers may need to be adept at managing rumours and paying attention to the first impressions which staff in the acquired organization can form, based on their first encounter with employees from the acquiring company. When a merger is under way, communication mechanisms need to be in place which encourage an upwards flow of information in addition to top-down announcements. Open and frank dialogue between parties brings benefits.

The reaction of employees on both sides of the merger will be conditioned by factors such as the clarity and credibility of the messages given publicly and internally – and by their perception of the 'other party': is this a business they want to work for? The starting point for communication is usually the merger announcement, which is nearly always highly sensitive. The Roffey Park research found that employees sometimes found out first when listening to the radio on their way to work. Often, due to a lack of HR involvement in the run-up phase there is no clear communication plan for employees – all the attention has been paid to other stakeholders.

Early contacts set the tone and arrogance is common. 'Them and us' attitudes can easily result from inappropriate first contacts. The reaction of employees on both sides of the merger/acquisition will be conditioned by factors such as the clarity and credibility of the messages given publicly and internally – and by their general perception of the 'other party': is it a business they want to work with/for? In one case, employees in both the acquired and acquiring companies were told on day one why the merger was happening and it was made clear to employees that 'good' people were in no danger of losing their jobs. People were asked to commit to the new company on the basis that 'we'll see you are alright'. None of the senior management from the acquired company survived the merger.

On day two, a presentation by the new chairman and chief executive conveyed an unfortunate impression to employees in the acquired company. The chairman insisted that the previous management had 'got it all wrong' and that his vision would lead to a successful company. While the message was no doubt meant to be motivational, and many 'acquired' employees agreed that they had been constrained by the previous management, the impression of arrogance created by the chairman's speech was confirmed by early attempts to impose one set of working practices on to another. What made matters worse was that there was in fact no plan of attack to support the chairman's claim and personnel matters such as appointments were left in abeyance. Many employees lost patience and left.

Gaining buy-in

Gaining emotional and intellectual buy-in from staff is no easy feat. Employees really need to know why the merger is happening so that they can work out the options for themselves. Issues such as the rationale for the merger, whether it is a proactive or reactive response, how the merger partner was selected, whether this is a merger or a takeover all need addressing. What can help is an early statement about the vision for the merged organization. When the **Halifax** and **Leeds Building Societies** merged they decided that their merger would create 'a Yorkshire-based world-class alternative to the clearing banks'. When the Environment Agency was formed out of up to eighty separate bodies, the aim was to provide ' a better environment in England and Wales for present and future generations'.

Typically, mergers are both mechanical/structural and psychological/cultural. All aspects of the merger need managing. In drawing up a checklist of the mechanical aspects of the merger, which tends to be the focus of director attention, care must also be given to being able to provide answers to employee questions which will set the scene for the psychological/cultural merger.

Merger mechanics	*Psychological impact*
Communication – road shows etc.	What's happening?
	When will I know if I have a job?
	Will there be redundancies and if so, when will they be announced?
Business strategy – loose/ tight coupling	Why is it happening?
	Does it make sense?
	What changes are planned and when will they be announced?
Organizational structure	Where will I be in 6 months?
	Will there be changes in reporting structure? Who will I be reporting to in future?
Appointments and exits	Will I have a job?
Terms and conditions	Will our terms and conditions change? Will I lose out?
Managing performance	What is expected of me?
	Will there be performance Appraisals?
Training and development	Do I have a future?

Fear of the unknown is a major contributor to employee uncertainty. Arguably, finding ways to reduce that uncertainty is a key responsibility of management.

In managing communications around the different phases of a merger, HR should bear in mind the psychological impact on employees of these changes and aim to offer answers to these core questions. While not all of these questions lend themselves to easy answers, people at least need to know when solutions to some of the problems will be worked upon. Some HR processes, such as rationalizing pay and conditions may take time to achieve. While there is no blueprint as to which issues must be tackled in what order, it is important to communicate a broad architecture of the merger process, together with targeted HR and management actions at each stage so that employees and senior managers can be reassured.

Waves of change

Mergers and acquisitions set off 'waves of change' within the organizations concerned. Unless these are managed, business performance can nosedive as a result of employee uncertainty and because senior managers concentrate their time on the merger, to the detriment of the existing business.

In the pre-merger phase, it is essential to explain to employees the strategic business reasons for the merger. Whatever approach is adopted, many organizational cases point to the importance of recognizing and understanding the differences between the organizational cultures as early as possible so that sensitive issues can be carefully handled. Similarly, employee loyalties to their colleagues, ways of working, company brand should not be underestimated. Employees may need to be allowed to 'grieve' the loss brought about by the merger as well as celebrate the new opportunities.

Typically, anxiety is highest at the time of the merger announcement and when the first job losses are announced. The rumour mill is very active at this stage. People wonder how they will be affected, if at all and what their own prospects will look like in the new organization. They are on the alert to signs, such as which company gets the lion's share of the best appointments, which indicate their likely fortune. Employees are hungry for information and this is typically when formal communications are at a standstill (Figure 15.1).

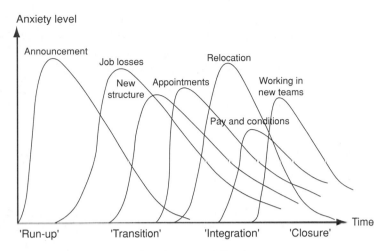

Figure 15.1 *Typical emotional waves following a merger*

Research suggests that over 40 per cent of the changes take place in the first two months. In the immediate transition, major events include the appointment of a new board of directors and key appointments/redundancies. As the new structure emerges, different groups are affected at different times. Often senior managers have been through their own anxiety and emerged the other end. Their focus may be on the next key business issue and it may be hard for them to appreciate the anxieties of people working in a front-line role who are being affected by restructuring in some cases up to two years after the merger. Other key points at which employee anxiety is high are decisions about which head office will be used, especially where relocation is involved, and when terms and conditions are integrated. Head-office staff are often the first to be affected by an early decision to close down an office. Field staff may wait for some time before the merging companies rationalize their outlets.

Communication alone is not enough – as previously stated, mergers need managing, especially the personnel issues. The way difficult personnel issues such as redundancies are handled will have a long-term effect on the morale of survivors and be a telling indication of the values of the new organization. New appointments must be seen to be fair and employees treated with dignity. Personnel processes should be documented and decisions should be open to scutiny. The longer-term integration phase is often the period during which sites are closed or merged and staff are informed about relocations. New terms and conditions may be announced. Often a more fundamental revision of working practices and structures takes place (for more details of such a change, see Chapter 14: the Thresher update).

The case which follows illustrates one approach to managing the pre-merger and transition phases.

The Whitbread case: the integration of Peter Dominic with Thresher

Thresher, part of Whitbread PLC, is a well-known UK major chain of off-licences which since a merger with Victoria Wine in 1998 has become known as 'First Quench'. Back in 1991, the Thresher business was doing reasonably well despite strong competition from other major off-licence chains and the super-markets. Though part of Whitbread, Thresher was effectively run as a stand-alone business, with an experienced board which included Jerry Walton as managing director, Dick Smerdon as sales director, Ralph Hayward as marketing director and David Waters as HR head. The business had been reshaped on the margin side and was run along cost lines.

The need for change

In spring 1991 a market strategy analysis suggested that change was inevitable if the business was to continue to be successful. Increasing competition from the major supermarket chains meant that there was pressure to grow bigger in order to survive and thrive. Similarly, for longer-term success it was clear that there needed to be a stronger emphasis on customer focus and on developing brands. There were other drivers for change too. For David Waters, the existing culture of the organization, with its tendency towards Theory X styles of management, was working against the need to retain and grow good people who would be willing and able to provide excellent customer service.

How much people perceived the need for change at that time is questionable. To some extent in 1991, Thresher risked becoming a victim of the success of the two previous years which had been particularly good in terms of business results. Waters believes that this success was largely due to the efforts of a few key people. Thresher really needed to sell more drink and that, to a large extent, depended on the skills and attitudes of staff at shop level. It became apparent that the business could not continue to operate in this way and would need to be reshaped.

The move towards restructuring along brand lines

The initial move towards reshaping the business came through discussions about how the business could be restructured along brand lines. The business had been developing a segmentation strategy for over a year. A think tank was set up consisting of key members of the HR team and a consulting group. The group brainstormed how the organization could look two or three years down the line. Though by 1998 Thresher has developed a range of brands including Bottoms Up, back in 1991, the existence of brands such as Wine Rack was embryonic.

The group's recommendations were taken to the board for debate in May 1991. The proposals involved splitting out Wine Rack, Thresher (Wine Stores) and the Drink Stores. This focus on brands implicitly carried with it a greater emphasis on the customer. Initially, the board were reluctant to accept proposals which would so radically shift the organization from being centralized to one which was based on a series of brands, each with its own core functions such as Personnel. The board debated long and hard and finally made the decision to restructure operations only along brand lines in June 1991. Once this decision had been taken, a culture shift became inevitable.

The decision to acquire Peter Dominic

As part of Grand Metropolitan, **Peter Dominic** was effectively available for acquisition. For Thresher, Peter Dominic would be a useful complement to the existing business, resulting in substantially more retail outlets and better geographical coverage. The courtship went on throughout the summer, with Thresher becoming more confident of acquiring Peter Dominic by September.

During the courtship phase, financial plans were put together as well as a detailed organization plan. The organization plan needed to be reasonably robust and capable of indicating where profit would come from, if not from sales. While it was clear that the Thresher team were leading the process and that this was an acquisition rather than a true merger, the creation of the organization plan was greatly assisted by the general willingness of the

Dominic managing director and HRD team to collaborate with the planning team.

They shared detailed information about organization charts, roles, key players, systems and practices within Dominic. The disclosure information included job histories, pay rates, training plans, union agreements and methods of communication such as newsletters. The planning team were able to identify possible synergies, assess the numbers of jobs required, design structures and in other ways carry out an effective human resource due diligence. They were able to identify issues which would need resolving such as those relating to the transfer of undertakings, as well as areas which would need to be negotiated with trades unions, since Peter Dominic was unionized, whereas Whitbread was not.

In addition, the planning team were provided with details of the sales histories of each of the stores, together with contracts with outside suppliers. The team were able to identify where the overlaps were and which stores would have to close. A critical decision taken during this time was that some Thresher stores would have to close if they were the less promising option. This subsequently caused some discontent within Thresher employees who found it hard to understand why, if they were on the acquiring or 'winning' side, their sites would have to go.

During this phase, the number of people within Thresher involved in preparing for the merger numbered no more than a dozen. Apart from the board, those actively involved included Chris Johnson the HR controller, the directors of Buying and of Property (estates), people responsible for financial planning, financial services and systems and the security manager. The security manager was considered a vital part of ensuring that business continued as usual during this period of change since it was felt that stock might be lost if management attention was on the merger. In addition, three or four members of Whitbread's corporate team worked closely with the board.

The merger negotiations were well advanced by mid-September. By this time, decisions had been taken about who was going to be on the executive team which made many of the preparations for the transition process much easier. The decision was taken to merge the two organizational cultures as quickly as possible, since the more gradual integration of a previous acquisition had caused significant problems. The board went away for a day to draw up a plan of action and key priorities for the first 100 days following the merger announcement.

The 100-day plan

A number of key action areas were identified and intimate, detailed plans drawn up around these. It was obviously important that the businesses should continue to be run effectively during the period of transition and measures were put in place to ensure this. As one board member put it, 'we want the cash in the bucket and no holes'. The board did not underestimate the symbolic significance of some of their earliest acts, one of which was to spend £50 000 changing the locks on all the store front doors in the first week. However, for the first time managers were handed the keys and the implicit message that they were trusted professional retailers carried weight. The plan also made it possible for promises to be made and kept about investing in security to make employees' jobs safer.

Another important area was retaining key employees, especially the planning team, by creating a sense of security around their own futures. Other areas concerned integrating finances, systems, as well as issues relating to employee pay and communications. Perhaps the main feature of the plan concerned the day of the handover itself, and a great deal of preparation was begun to ensure that employees would hear the news first hand as much as possible and have the chance to raise issues with executives. The aim was to ensure that by the end of the first day, all departments would have been seen. Questions and answers were prepared and executives were given a strict schedule of visits.

The handover

The schedule of visits went ahead on the day of the announcement (31 October). Partnership was very much the order of the day with senior managers from both companies involved in communicating with staff. Jerry Walton, for instance, saw the clerical teams and, though the day was very emotionally charged, a proper handover took place. The senior Thresher managers met the Peter Dominic staff and all the subgroups had the chance to meet the functional teams. Despite the planning team's best efforts, there were some emotional issues and things which could not be disclosed prior to the merger which now needed to be dealt with. This was an important cultural first step – being open and honest with people.

Communications

The symbolism of senior management actions should not be underestimated during a merger. Some significant positive messages were conveyed to the Peter Dominic staff, who saw themselves as having been acquired. Individual members of the Thresher board spent lots of time visiting the Dominic offices and stores. Board meetings which would normally have been held at Thresher head office were now also taking place at the Dominic head office, though this would shortly close. The effect on Peter Dominic was to acclimatize the organization to change. David Waters describes this as dropping 'open secrets' into the 'collective grapevine'.

Not everything went smoothly, however. Following the announcements, question-and-answer sessions and other active communications of the first few days following merger, information continued to flow for five weeks. The planning team had confidently predicted that the merger would be sorted by 1 December and significant progress had been made. However, knowing that Christmas is the busiest trading period in drinks retailing, the planning team let it be known that active communications on progress would be suspended during the Christmas period in order to allow people to concentrate on doing their jobs – selling drinks. What the team had not envisaged was the effect of suddenly turning off the flow of information, even though warning had been given. People assumed that the merger was going wrong and that bad news was to follow.

Winners and losers

There were initially people who perceived themselves to be winners and losers. According to David Waters this is inevitable, no matter what you do. The challenge is to ensure that, as much as possible, 'losers' start to find some advantages in the merger situation for themselves.

In the Thresher case, part of this was accomplished by the actions of senior managers. The company kept the board's promise that people would be told the fate of their job within thirty days. The policy was to forge integration in the shortest time possible. The Peter Dominic board all went and a policy for store closures was drawn up under which stores would be given six months' notice of closure and that closure decisions would be reviewed over two years based on profit. This applied to both Dominic and Thresher stores.

Senior managers took the approach that people whose jobs were going would be actively helped to find others and would demonstrate their interest in people who were leaving asking, for instance, whether they were receiving enough help in finding new jobs. It was decided that the Peter Dominic head office in Harlow would be closed down. Employees were told on 1 December that the office would close seven months later. Until closure, staff working in the redundant office still experienced fresh flowers in reception twice a week and the canteen, though expensive to run, was kept open to the end. There were visits from senior management and other small signs were used to ensure that the board could show they were still valued by the company which they would soon be leaving.

The management team tried to show respect to all staff, whether they were going to be part of the future operation or not. Individuals were offered a variety of forms of career counselling and practical support in finding new jobs. There was a party for employees from both of the original organizations when the Dominic head office finally closed.

Not everybody who might have been considered a 'winner' in the merger was pleased with their lot, however. The Thresher team recognized that some of the Dominic team had the kind of skills they were looking for. What the team soon learned was that just because you offer someone a good job, it does not mean that they will accept the job. Some of the Dominic sales and marketing staff were exactly what Thresher wanted – upbeat and bullish. Many of these people left because they were not willing to accept the package offered by Thresher.

One of the main reasons for people leaving, no matter how well a merger is handled, appears to be that people recognize that a merger throws all the job 'balls' into the air. Wherever the job balls land is likely to stay in place for several years. A number of key people who had considered themselves due a promotion and who did not welcome the advent of more competitors for jobs left the company before the job situation had been finalized.

Some of Thresher middle managers also considered that the allocation of jobs turned them from considering themselves to be 'winners' into 'losers' when they found themselves reporting to a more experienced Peter Dominic manager. They could not understand why, if they were part of the dominant group, they were being asked to change role, and people took the matter to heart. They also blamed senior management, complaining that they had not been communicated with enough and that all the attention was being lavished on Dominic staff.

Similarly, there were a number of 'culturally misaligned' people, who, though skilled at their jobs, were effectively undermining the integration process though their cynical behaviour. It was important to confront such behaviour, allow a little time for people to change their ways or part company. There were also strenuous discussions with unions about pay and conditions (Dominic was unionized whereas Thresher was not). A negotiated settlement produced a compromise deal in which there were some, but different benefits and drawbacks for most employees.

Effective communications are clearly critical during and after a merger. Inevitably there will be some things which cannot be disclosed prior to the merger. For David Waters there are some clear fundamentals of good communication which should not be ignored:

> Keep talking with people every day. Questions and answers in week one need to be the foundation of ongoing good communications. You cannot overcommunicate in the early stages of integration.
>
> No matter what you do, employees will expect a consistency of approach from you which you may not consider appropriate. By and large they will have less information than you about where the organization is going and may be less able to appreciate the subtleties of your approach. Communications should always be looked at from a variety of employee angles. In particular you have to overcommunicate with the 'home team' in the early stages to secure their commitment as you start to know staff from the other organization.

Integration – building on the merger

By Summer 1992 the merger was considered complete. The 100-days plan was completed within 75 days. There were now more brands (four or five were emerging) and the organization structure to support these was in place. Marketing and HR support was aligned to each of the brands. The two cultures were fused together with neither having supremacy over the other. This provided a solid platform for changing things further. This was also helped by the injection of talent from outside into key roles which the new structure made possible. This built up the amount of experience within the company of how to run businesses and change processes. This in turn led to a better calibre of management, with the business as a whole benefiting from this blend of approaches from the main two companies and others. Similarly, the merger provided the catalyst for 'releasing' relatively non-performing people.

A significant benefit was that people, including the board, got used to change. The challenge following a successful merger is to introduce yet more change in order to achieve some of the potential of the combined operation. It was at this point that the Operations Development Project (ODP) came into being. The ODP was a strategic, long-term change project which has brought with it new working practices, energized staff and the release of human potential as well as improved business results. More details of the ODP can be found in Holbeche (1997) and in Chapter 14.

Key learning points

- Be aware that there are some things you can plan for, and you should make every effort to put plans in place for these. However, some things such as predicting the emotional reaction to the news and dealing appropriately with it are easier to plan for than to cope with. Those on the receiving end of other people's reactions may themselves need support, whether this is from other senior managers, members of the planning team, external mentors or others.
- Senior management teams must stay close to the merger during the period of transition and not become shut off – that is when energy gets dispersed.
- While it is important to use appropriate resources and skills during mergers, make sure that, as far as possible, internal staff lead the integration effort, rather than relying on external consultants. According to David Waters, 'the whole thing is about confidence, not over-confidence, that you can carry people with you'.
- When attempting to integrate cultures, start with the people with the right attitude to people – high energy, prepared to confront things.
- Never make promises which you cannot keep.

How HR can help an organization through a merger

From this and other case studies it is clear that the HR function has a potentially key role to play in a merger. Involvement should begin in the run-up phase. Early identification of sensitive issues can reduce their impact over time. Pay and conditions can become a huge issue and in many cases are dealt with early in the transition period. Without a strategic perspective, the HR team is likely to be overtaken by a host of operational and mechanical issues which must be dealt with. Having said that, time must be set aside to work with directors and individuals on the critical HR issues. Help from consultants may well enable HR teams to focus their energies strategically during a critical period. The research suggests that some of the critical contributions which HR can make are as follows:

Being involved in planning, transition and integration teams

- HR professionals need to contribute specific expertise to these teams, enabling the merger to be managed as a project, while keeping the core business going
- Develop effective ways of collaborating with the planning team from the other company in the pre-merger phase, if possible
- Does clear communication exist between members of the negotiating and transition teams? What are the handover issues which will make a difference to the success of the integration?
- If the acquisition is perceived as hostile, identify as early as possible the key information you need to know if a thorough human resource due diligence is not possible. What other ways can the necessary information be obtained?
- What framework is in place for managing the different phases of the merger?
- Find ways in which people from both companies can get to know each other as quickly as possible
- Identify how the emerging organizational vision can best be communicated
- Take a 'best of both' rather than 'equal shares' or 'acquirer dominates' approach to deciding who has which roles, which working practices etc. are adopted
- Decide fair principles on the handling of redundancies.

Identifying the HR issues and carrying out an effective Human Resource Due Diligence by:

- Comparing terms and conditions of employment and salary scales including the structure of share options and to whom they are available, severance terms in contracts, incentive and bonus schemes in terms of immediate and future commitments
- Gathering information about the management team – how critical are they and will they all remain post-acquisition?
- Gaining perspectives of the management team – their view of the company, employees' view of the senior team
- Understanding the existing skills of the present HR team – are they adequate to coordinate proposed changes to the business?
- Understanding the organization structure
- Identifying what is required in terms of manpower plan to achieve the business strategy
- Identifying key personnel and having initial plans for securing ongoing commitment. To what extent is the necessary knowledge and skill critical to running the business vested in a few staff?
- Identifying the likely level of redundancies involved and prospects for early retirements
- Identifying which job descriptions and/or profiles will need to be changed
- Finding out how communication of the sale has been dealt with so far including the processes used for communication
- Comparing ways of working and identifying major differences which will need to be addressed
- Agreeing the management culture of the combined organization and what will need to be done to achieve it
- Considering the size and location of existing offices. Deciding whether office closures will be necessary and whether the provision of new office accommodation will be appropriate or possible
- Finding out details of any industrial disputes etc. and the number of appeals on job evaluations by the Hay Committee within the last 12 months
- Is the organization unionized or does the staff council or similar employee representation group have any negotiation rights and if so, what do these rights include?
- Being realistic about timescales. Does everything have to be

done at once? Many companies attempt to integrate terms and benefits as quickly as possible. If delay is required, there should be a clearly communicated plan so that employees know when key issues will be addressed. Merging cultures may take two years or longer

- Agreeing a clear communication plan for the first 100 days. What clear central message will be sent to all employees?

Carrying out effective HR integration on the following:
- Remuneration
- Benefits
- Terms and conditions
- Culture and management style
- Career and other development issues
- Communication and climate
- Employee relations.

Ensuring that management teams have the skills they need to manage the merger well

Line managers usually play a key role in central project teams. Management teams need to be quickly welded together, with at least a common approach on key Human Resource issues. Some team building may be needed. Management teams need the following:-
- Strategic management skills, especially understanding how to add value to the new business
- Integration skills – being able to make decisions about structure, roles and dealing with sensitive situations
- Change management skills – being able to bring people with them through change
- Cultural skills – being able to understand the dynamics of organizational culture, deal with culture clashes and the emergence of a new culture
- People skills – being able to understand the reactions and concerns of employees and support them through change.

Helping line managers to communicate effectively during the transition phase

Managers also have a key role in sustaining communications about the merger process to all employees even when there is 'no news'. Given the symbolic importance of senior management behaviour, managers may need practical help in understanding how to communicate to employees from both companies in the early days. Managers may need to be made aware of the symbolic power of language to help or hinder the merger process. They may need to recognize that a merger is likely always to be an emotional issue for employees and that employees need to be communicated with, and convinced of the benefits at an emotional not simply rational level.

In the first month of a merger between two professional service firms, line managers were given the chance to reflect on how they were going to help implement the organizational changes. For some the main challenge was 'getting staff into confidence mode – our task is to raise staff morale'. Many managers also felt the need to ask questions of their own directors, rather than assuming that they were being kept in the dark. Some managers recognized the importance of sitting down with their team and personalizing the messages which were largely being conveyed via corporate videos. The managers were mainly concerned about the apathy resulting from apparent lack of change following the merger announcement. They recognized that they would need to prepare their colleagues for the ongoing waves of change which would eventually arise from the merger.

Since managers are in the front line for communication, it is essential that they have the ability to develop two-way communications. HR can provide practical help with team briefings and feedback processes. Managers need to communicate why the merger has taken place, what the organization is trying to achieve and how each person's role contributes to achieving this. They need to have a wide range of management styles appropriate to different circumstances and may need help in developing their coaching ability and flexibility.

Managing individuals with dignity

Chief executives, often very action-oriented, are keen to get through the difficult business of reorganization and job loss as quickly as possible. Speed is helpful as long as it does not compromise dealing with staff fairly and treating them with dignity. The handling of key changes for individuals – such as job changes, appointments and relocations as well as exits – sets the tone for how staff view the new organization. Handling redundancies inappropriately usually results in a morale backlash among 'survivors'.

Developing and implementing actions to retain key employees

Good people have to stay if the two organizations are to learn from each other's strengths. Line managers need to identify and keep close to key staff at all levels and actively involve them in the merger process. If such people are neglected in the early months, they often jump ship. Some organizations develop retention strategies which involve some sort of inducements such as 'golden handcuffs' to encourage people to stay. There appears to be some evidence that, even without financial incentives and firm guarantees, letting people know that they are valued and quickly finding ways of using their talent in the new organization can be sufficient encouragement for some.

Keeping the top in touch with the bottom

HR is uniquely placed to build in upward feedback to keep the boardroom in touch with what is really going on in an organization. In the Roffey Park research senior people described being sucked into the detail of the operational issues and the mechanics of the merger. It was only with the benefit of hindsight that they realized that understanding and managing people's perceptions and expectations were equally vital to promoting a healthy emergent organization. The culture of the new organization begins from day one, not when vision and values statements start to appear.

This is where the special skills of trainers can come into their own. Typically, trainers have good communication skills and are in touch with the 'mood' of employees who are attending courses. Trainers who are able to understand the business dynamics and the sensitivities involved in creating a new culture can provide a useful steer to line managers who are charged with communications in the early days post-merger.

Helping to clarify roles

Once the shape of the new organization becomes clearer, people may need help in clarifying their roles, knowing where they fit in the organization's purpose and how to be successful in the new set-up. This may require them to learn new skills or adjust their working practices. Briefings for line managers and some training for individuals may be necessary. Typically, in the early days of a merger a number of temporary policies and short-term priorities are identified. Line managers often need a basic set of 'tool kit' training sessions which are short and focused. These can help build up managers' confidence where responsibility, reporting lines and roles are still ill-defined.

Alliances

While more and more organizations are developing a range of partnerships with others, the issues involved in managing alliances effectively are relatively little researched. Driving factors for alliances include overcoming the problems of growth industries. There are several telecoms alliances such as **Ericsson** and **Telefonica** (Spain), to overcome the problems of national protectionism. Rapid technological development and innovation is leading to the need for shorter product life cycles. So **Philips** and **Sony** are jointly developing audiovisual CDs.

In more mature industries, the concentration of players is leading to the challenging of monopolies. **Redland Brick** and **Australian CRS** are building material to challenge **BPB**. Governments are also creating pressures for collaboration, for instance on joint research and the transfer of technology in projects such as **Airbus** and **ESPRIT** (European Strategic Programme in Information Technologies which is half funded by the EEC). Other alliances are formed as a defensive measure to prevent other potential alliances.

Different forms of alliance are in evidence which require different forms of strategic human resource activity. These include:

- Licensing arrangements, which are typical of manufacturing industries. Strategic Human Resource Management (SHRM) input would be most likely to involve the training of local managers on-site and the development of technical knowledge
- Franchises which are typical of sectors where there is fast market entry. SHRM input is likely to involve working with franchisees to create a common set of values and behaviours with those of the 'parent' company
- Partnerships, federations and consortia which are typical of situations where organizations wish to share risks and costs.

They are currently growing in sectors such as the UK Further Education sector where there is a need to increase provision and quality of programmes. SHRM contribution is likely to involve facilitating networks, and providing mentoring to create a common vision across the member organizations

- Joint ventures, which allow for specialization or shared added value. The SHRM contribution could include teambuilding, the development of a joint venture culture and the development of flexibility among employees.

Making alliances work

Research by KPMG has shown that 70 per cent of alliances are disbanded prematurely and that in two-thirds of cases, interpersonal factors were blamed as the main cause of failure. Cultural differences, between companies as well as nations, were considered at the core of the difficulties. Other research suggests that common failure factors relate to partners' behaviour before the collaborative agreement is established. These include:

- Lack of clarity in defining the single firm's goals
- Poor choice of partners
- Emphasis on short-term results
- Little involvement by top management in the partnering project
- Incomplete information on potential partners.

Other failure factors related to partners' behaviour during the actual collaboration were:

- Lack of an alliance 'champion'
- Lack of trust among partners
- Lack of communication and information diffusion
- Inadequate human resources allocated to the process
- Lack of management commitment
- Failure of one of the partners to deliver their expected contribution
- Change in the partners' top management
- Conflicting culture and values of partners
- Conflicting objectives of partners
- Lack of collaboration objectives in terms of time, costs, inno-

vative results etc.
- Inflexible people
- Loss of control on certain partners.

The KPMG (1999) research identified four phases through which alliances usually progress. These are similar to the familiar stages of team development, i.e. forming, storming, norming, performing and mourning.

The first stage is the norming or 'politeness' phase when the intentions of partners are explored and attempts are made to converge toward the desired goals. The second 'conflict' or storming phase is where key players conflict with each other at a number of levels. If the conflict, especially with regard to the vision and values underlying the project, remains unresolved, the alliance is unlikely to make progress. In the next 'inquiry' phase, key players start to ask questions which explore each other's vision. If the partners come to understand and respect differences, new insights can be gained. This then leads to the performing or 'energy' phase in which the new mental models and improved trust lead to better understanding between the key players, and better outputs.

The skills required to cope effectively at each stage differ but HR professionals can support alliances through helping make differences explicit. This can be done in a number of ways, through team meetings, team building, a stocktake of working practices etc. HR can also help manage conflict and enable partners to gain positive momentum from the effective resolution of difficulties. Partners need to be helped to retain their objectivity and respect for the views of their counterparts. HR can support partners as they develop ways of understanding each other's perspectives on the underlying vision and values which they are working towards. They can also support partners as they move towards the creation of practical implementation plans to translate the vision into action.

Conclusion

Though mergers and alliances are tricky territory for organizations, what has become clear from the Roffey and other research is that mergers and alliances are most successful when the 'people' issues are well handled. HR practitioners are uniquely placed to help the organization realize its strategic ambitions – by getting their 'people' strategies right. Trust can be built but this requires a special awareness and influence which HR ought to be able to wield. HR needs to be represented on planning and transition teams and use the opportunity to challenge management thinking about what – and who – is required in the new organization.

Real communication, and for an extended period, may be necessary if employees are to feel committed to the new organization. HR may need to act as the line management 'conscience' on communication once there is a semblance of 'business as usual' returning. Individual transitions need to be handled well and employees should be allowed to deal with their bereavement about departing colleagues – and the changing organization. This does not mean holding formal 'wakes' but celebrating the end of one set of working practices formally can help people integrate the new.

If handled well, mergers and alliances can be a lever for introducing major change which brings significant business benefits. They are an opportunity to develop a new management style and culture, as well as to manage and improve costs. They are also an ideal opportunity to put the right people in the right jobs. They provide the rationale for putting performance on the map and for measuring the performance of the business and the success of the integration process following the merger. And of course, in an ideal world, they provide the opportunity to do things differently, while adding value to the business; to deliver excellent service to the client while providing a rewarding experience for all employees. To achieve all this, a strategic HR contribution can be pivotal and the HR practitioner who helps his or her organization achieve these benefits can truly be said to have managed change effectively.

References

Devine, M., Hirsh, W. *et al.* (1998). *Mergers and Acquisitions: Getting the People Bit Right.* Roffey Park Management Institute.

Hall, P. and Norburn, D. (1987). The management factor in acquisition performance. *Leadership and Organization Development Journal,* No.8.

Holbeche, L. (1997). *Motivating People in Lean Organizations.* Oxford: Butterworth-Heinemann, Chapter 6.

KPMG (1999). The art of alliances. *Virtual Library,* April.

If a company has not organized its personnel in a way that allows fast learning and the conditions of 'flocking' (learning in groups), or if it doesn't do, intensively, things like career development, it will be hurt. If it hasn't got the right underlying contract with its people that means, 'I'm interested in your potential, rather than in your immediate output over the next three months', then I think the bell is tolling (DeGeus, 1997).

Senior managers are now faced with a period of ongoing change and uncertainty given the rate of technological change and the scope of market pressures. Irrespective of whether an organization is currently undergoing major change, such as a merger, the impact of the Information Revolution is beginning to be felt and working patterns are likely to be irrevocably changed. In the Information Society, factors of production are no longer land, labour or capital, as in the industrial era, but knowledge. At the heart of the Information Revolution is low-cost computing and communication. This is enabling people to communicate externally and internally on a more extensive basis than ever before. The speeding up of communication is changing the rules of business, bringing new opportunities for creating value and the need for new measures to protect existing value.

New measures of value suggest that the market value of a company is based on financial capital and intellectual capital. Intellectual capital represents the intangible assets of an organization. This breaks down into the 'structural' capital, in which some of the knowledge, processes and procedures can be captured by the organization and held there. The other two forms of capital – 'customer', such as the brand, reputation, relationships and 'human' – represent the real competitive advantage since it is the ongoing development of ideas, products and service which meet customer needs which ensures that the organization is sustainable. According to Gareth Morgan (1993) 'an organization has no presence beyond that of the people who bring it to life'. The challenge of managing intellectual capital is ensuring that it does not walk out of the door.

There is a strategic imperative which suggests that managing knowledge is a key priority since the risks of not doing so are high. They include:

* Duplication of effort
* Wasted time (which managers do not even notice because they are too busy)
* Repeated learning curves
* Slower rate of innovation
* Higher threats to the speed and quality of service.

Conversely, it might be argued that having good structural capital, through which new entrants can experience rapid development could make a company an employer of choice.

Few organizations have a blueprint for the future and are able to accurately predict the precise talents and skills needed for future success. Preparing an organization for change and learning requires not only tight links between the organization's strategies and training but also an underpinning culture in which learning is valued and encouraged. Developing and exploiting some of the knowledge capability within an organization may be one of the few relatively untapped sources of competitive advantage. Some organizations invest heavily in the latest IT systems and are amazed to find that the systems fail to deliver the desired business advantage. What is becoming increasingly evident is that for information systems to work, human beings must be willing to create and generate useful knowledge which is more than just data. Managing knowledge is essentially a people-related activity.

Knowledge management

Knowledge of all forms exists in different parts of an organization, but very few organizations have a 'map' of the knowledge available. The amount and pace of change within businesses today makes it difficult to keep abreast of existing knowledge, let alone identify the knowledge needed for the future. The Chief Executive of **Hewlett-Packard**, for example, has been quoted as saying 'If HP knew what HP knows, we would be three times as profitable'. Thomas Stewart (1997) writing about intellectual capital, suggests how challenging it can be to try and understand what knowledge resources exist within an organization:

> Trying to identify and manage knowledge is like trying to fish barehanded. It can be done...but the object of the effort is damnably elusive.

Managers may therefore be unaware of the vast potential which employees can offer. Traditional accounting systems for valuing organizations typically fail to register the value of that knowledge since it is notoriously difficult to measure and, by its nature is 'implicit', 'tacit' or inside people's heads. The real value of a company is what acquirers are willing to pay to gain access to staff and their skills and knowledge. In sectors such as advertising, fund management and consultancies, many organizations on the acquisition trail have found that they have bought nothing when key staff walk.

So great has been the staff turnover in some sectors that there are often few people left within the business who really know how things can be done. Arnold Kransdorff (1995) studied organizations which formerly had low rates of staff turnover and which now experience a wholesale turnover of staff every four or five years. He coined the term 'corporate amnaesia' to describe the loss of learning to the company when staff left. He found that in some cases, expensive mistakes were repeated while in others, systems which had been developed could no longer be used by staff since they were all new and there was no-one left with the relevant experience who could teach them. Particularly costly was the loss of customer information which was acquired over years by employees who were invited to retire early.

'Explicit' information, as detailed in databases, staff manuals and process maps shows only a small part of the real knowledge assets of a company. The intangibles, such as know-how, information on stakeholder relationships, experiences and ideas, represent the critical knowledge. Such information tends to stay in the informal system of the organization where it is shared by only a few people. Information alone is not the real asset; it is what people do, or are prepared to do with that information which turns it into valuable, shared knowledge. It is how people convert information into knowledge and the way they use that information to shape decisions which represents the real knowledge asset.

Knowledge tends to generate knowledge when ideas are shared and collaboration is in evidence. Flatter structures, with their emphasis on teamwork and smart ways of working should be ideally suited to the generation and sharing of knowledge. The challenge is how to capture knowledge in the context of a flexible, mobile workforce. Knowledge management is about harnessing the knowledge and experience that people have; it's about connecting people and creating a culture where senior people think that knowledge sharing is worth investing in. This reinforces the idea that knowledge management is not the exclusive domain of IT specialists but is of direct relevance to line managers and HR professionals. It is fundamentally about creating the conditions in which human beings create and share information, knowledge and learning.

Barriers to sharing knowledge

However, there are a number of important barriers to organizational learning which prevent organizations from making the most of their intellectual capital. One is the rate of change and the increasingly flexible nature of the workforce. Capitalizing on the skills, knowledge and experience is challenging enough, but capturing the knowledge of a flexible workforce, including consultants, contractors and others whose affiliation to the company many be temporary, is even more difficult.

Another barrier is deeply embedded in the old hierarchical structures and related career progression routes. To some extent conventional career development has been based on individuals becoming knowledgeable – about issues, technical and professional bodies of knowledge and about how the organization works – and being able to use that knowledge to get things done. The axiom 'knowledge is power' is evident when skills and knowledge are in short supply, as are certain types of IT skills currently.

Flatter structures too can reinforce the desire to hoard information. People who were once colleagues are now competitors for scarce promotion opportunities. The internal market value of certain types of knowledge is evident in the political battles being waged in many organizations. While Charles Handy (1997) has identified knowledge as only one of seven forms of power, knowledge can give individuals career trading power which many people would be unlikely to wish to give up, given the ongoing uncertainty of the jobs market.

Similarly, HR and other systems can undercut people's willingness to share information which might be useful to others. One major UK broking firm was concerned about the ways in which they failed to service clients well because the relevant client information was in the head of one individual. If that individual was sick or left the firm, their knowledge was no longer available. A related problem was that clients were becoming increasingly irritated by the numerous contacts they had with the same firm, while employees at the firm were unaware that other employees were in touch with the same client.

The firm installed expensive hardware and software to enable information about clients to be kept up to date. They were puzzled why employees did not update records and use the new resource. This was not a case of 'technophobia' – another common barrier to knowledge management processes. It was only when they recognized that people were individually rewarded for the 'deals' struck that they realized that there was no incentive for people to share information about the client. It was not until rewards were attached to the quality of the client relationship that people's behaviour, and use of the system began to change. Some of the previous main critics of the new system became its champions when they could see advantages to them in ensuring that the information was kept fresh. Any organization seeking to introduce knowledge management systems needs to be clear about potential obstacles to the sharing of knowledge, and address those obstacles so that people can identify the 'what's in it for me?' factor.

Another common barrier to the sharing of organizational learning is that people often focus rather narrowly on their jobs, rather than the purpose of the organization as a whole. There can be a heavy emphasis on the short term which makes the sharing of knowledge for longer-term gains an impediment to getting the job done now. The new CEO of a major electronics company visited all the decentralized business units and was amazed to find that there were many initiatives under way in separate units which would be useful to the work of other units – but no-one apart from the CEO had the full picture. The CEO insisted that interchanges were established so that the organization could benefit more widely from these new approaches.

Making time for reviewing what they have learned can appear an unnecessary luxury. People fail to notice the slight but significant changes in the business environment until it is too late. Teams can engage in 'us and them' mentalities which cause defensive and political behaviour over turf issues. Perhaps the biggest obstacle to shared learning is a blame culture when things go wrong. This is where the tone set by senior management is absolutely critical to the successful implementation of knowledge management strategies.

A key barrier to organizational learning may be embedded in the dominant thought processes in evidence among Western managers. Indeed, some of the leading thinking on knowledge management comes from Japan. Ikujiro Nonaka, co-author with Hirotaka Takeuchi of *The Knowledge-Creating Company* (1995) suggests that Japan is more innovative than the West because the West, with its culture of rationalism, tends to value explicit knowledge. Conversely, the Japanese, with their emphasis on the holistic nature of mind and body, value tacit knowledge, which is both elusive and abstract. Other thinkers agree. Jean Lamimann and Michel Syrett (1999), who carried out Roffey Park research looking at where directors get their ideas from, suggest:

> The foundations on which traditional management is based – rational judgement and decision-making based on sharply expressed definitive ideas – can be counter-intuitive and may shut down all but a fraction of the organization's creative capability.

The interest in recent years in emotional and other forms of intelligence, is starting to percolate through into Western management vocabulary. Roger Leek, former Group Head of Human Resources of **BNFL** believes that training and development can support a culture change from a relatively hierarchical and inflexible system to a more customer-focused culture, by developing the emotional intelligence of senior managers. Roger recognizes the vital role of line managers in championing knowledge management within the organization in their capacity of leaders.

How can barriers to the sharing of knowledge be overcome?

Overcoming all these barriers is a tall order. However, individuals need to be able to identify sharing of knowledge as being in their interest. Sharing knowledge makes existing knowledge more productive and helps to create new knowledge. The more information is used, the more it develops and grows. One of the ways of achieving this is by providing people with the conditions in which information can be shared, and letting them work out the benefits for themselves. In broad terms, knowledge management has to address three key activities:

- Motivating people to share information
- Developing a system for managing and storing information
- Motivating people to use the knowledge available to them.

The first step is to find out what knowledge really is important and who has that knowledge. This may involve brainstorming to find out what knowledge is critical to the organization. The next step is making people accountable for managing that critical knowledge. However, some general conditions need to be in place for knowledge management to be effective. Broadly speaking, these are ensuring that top leaders own the knowledge management agenda, creating a culture of trust and teamwork in which collaboration is the norm and building an appropriate infrastructure to facilitate learning. As Morgan suggests:

> You can't create a learning organization.... But you can enhance people's capacities to learn and align their activities in creative ways.

How HR can create the conditions for knowledge management

1 *Develop a knowledge management framework*
- Decide what kinds of data, information and experience is valuable enough to retain and make available
- Identify what are the strategic management assets and assign someone to manage these
- Produce guidelines about the kind of information which should be stored so as to avoid the danger of overload
- Provide appropriate infrastructure in the form of communications technology, systems design and applications tools
- Decide on a knowledge 'architecture' which gives guidance on what kind of data is valuable enough to retain and make available. This will include not simply product information but also useful knowledge such as lessons learnt from experience with customers, projects etc.

2 *Develop a sharing approach*
- Experiment with building networks
- Share 'best practice' via the intranet, Lotus Notes etc.
- Ensure that usable information is catalogued and stored with the relevant technology
- Allow the majority of employees direct customer contacts
- Give free access to all information to all employees
- Disseminate information in a timely and extensive way.

3 *Spot when knowledge assets are being under-utilized and find ways of getting knowledge onto people's agenda*
- Raise awareness through the use of diagnostics and high-level measurements
- Create a clear understanding of which knowledge is important for delivering strategic objectives
- Map knowledge and its integration with other key processes
- Prioritize important knowledge assets.

4 *Enable people to develop information skills*
- Provide staff with the appropriate technology – Statoil supplies its employees with PCs and advanced communications equipment at home
- The UK government, recognizing that a whole new generation who are conversant with cyberspace communication will enter the job market, has equipped secondary school teachers with laptops
- Universities and business schools are developing various forms of partnerships with business – make appropriate learning links
- Provide training in IT systems to enable people to acquire and share the information they need
- Employees need to be skilled at time management in order to use their time effectively for the creation and sharing of knowledge
- HR can help employees to acquire information skills which will help them to become more employable as well as increasing their value to their employer:
  - Resource investigation skills
  - Networking skills
  - Communication and diagnostic skills
  - A range of learning techniques
  - Team-based problem solving
  - Flexibility
  - Willingness to try new things, take risks and review learning.

5   *Develop a knowledge-friendly culture*
- CEOs need to set the style, ensuring that training and educational activities are both short- and long-term oriented
- Create a clear shared vision and values about the effective creation and dissemination of knowledge
- Trust is a vital component in the human aspects of knowledge management. Leaders need to encourage the sharing of best practice by recognizing and rewarding people when this happens and by being good role models
- Encourage research and development at all levels
- Actively develop and market new ideas to create new products and services
- Ensure that the formal and informal reward systems reinforce the value of creating and sharing knowledge
- Create a physical work environment which facilitates shared learning and knowledge.

6   *Address the 'what's in it for me?' question*
- Find synergies between the individual's need for growth and personal development and the company's needs. Effective career development practices are conducive to the sharing of knowledge since people can see that they do not need to hold on to knowledge in order to progress their career
- For some employees, technophobia prevents them from keeping up in today's workplace. A few years ago, recognizing that some employees needed help, **Marks & Spencer** declared an IT amnesty for staff so that all employees could get up to speed with computers
- Employees need to be able to willing to develop key skills for the workplace of tomorrow, which will enhance their employability. These include confidently seeking knowledge from other people, inside and outside the organization, as well as team skills and the willingness to collaborate with others to create new solutions
- When employees cease to be overloaded with unnecessary data, and start to perceive the benefits of sharing information to their own effectiveness, they are more likely to willingly collaborate in the generation of useful knowledge
- Employees should respect and value their knowledge and experience as an asset that can add value to the business – and not fear sharing that knowledge
- Employees can give and receive honest feedback which can help them and others to develop – and at the same time build trusting relationships.

7   *Develop criteria for successful knowledge management projects*
- Ensure senior management support
- Link the knowledge project to economic performance
- Use appropriate technical and organizational infrastructure
- Develop a standard, flexible knowledge structure
- Use clear purpose and language
- Use multiple channels for knowledge transfer.

8   *Communicate knowledge effectively*
- Communicate at the right level – senior managers often talk at too senior a level to make sense lower down the organization.
- Use the experts to impart information. Involve contractors and flexible workers in communications stategies
- Managers should develop the skills of non-judgemental listening and brainstorming. 'Whacky' ideas should be encouraged
- Make sure that people are rewarded in some way for developing and sharing knowledge.

How organizations are developing intellectual capital

Knowledge management, or the development of intellectual capital, is very much about the creation of an open, collaborative culture in which learning is valued. This is not simply a question of increasing spend on training. Within this culture, the generation of new knowledge through learning needs to be managed, knowledge needs to be captured, shared and communicated, information needs to be organized for easy retrieval and existing knowledge built upon. To some extent, HR is in a position to take a lead role by agreeing with senior managers what the learning culture would look like, and then agreeing actions to move the culture in the desired direction.

A learning culture will be one in which some risk-taking and a few mistakes are tolerated. They are the opposite of what line managers commonly describe as their experience of the 'blame culture' in their organizations. Leaders are influential and have to understand that they are part of a system which they can shape. This is why leaders at all levels need to be behind moves to create a learning culture, or else *ad hoc* initiatives will lead nowhere. HR can help leaders to become open to core skills of feedback and how to leverage knowledge and learning.

For many leaders, accepting emergence, learning and the uncertain future that it implies creates anxiety. Managers need to develop ways of openly examining their individual and collective responses to anxiety as a way of avoiding decisions or actions which may be superficial, ineffective or counterproductive for the purpose of the organization. In the same way, managers should be sensitive to the people processes they use and their own tolerance of risk and ambiguity. Particularly important are managers' attitudes to and ability to handle conflict, debate and tension within the organization.

In the West, a number of companies have acknowledged the importance of the management of knowledge by appointing a 'chief knowledge officer'. Though these are currently few in number in the UK, many have grouped together in networks to share learning on a pan-organization basis. This is not considered to be a breach of confidentiality. What works for one organization does not necessarily work for others, but knowledge officers are honing their own insights as to how to create a culture which is supportive of the management of intellectual capital. HR can also help set up networks that bring communities with a common interest in developing and sharing knowledge together.

Other new roles and responsibilities are being created. In some companies, there is a senior-level 'knowledge sponsor' who can ensure board-level attention for knowledge issues. Then there are knowledge managers/facilitators who offer support to client teams. Knowledge owners provide the expert input, and their responsibility is to keep up to date and keep up with the information flow. On the technical side there are information service providers and webmaster roles.

Some sophisticated companies are developing networks to explore issues of knowledge management and to develop strategies for maximizing the value of the organization through knowledge. One such network is the Knowledge Exchange which aims to put a financial measure on an organization's intellectual capital. Another group of companies including **ICL**, **3M** and **Monsanto** have formed a consortium *Strategic Management of Knowledge and Organizational Learning* which acknowledges the need for organizations to collaborate in order to develop and share know-how on knowledge management. This consortium recognizes that these issues must form part of the top management agenda, if more value and sustainable advantage are to be created through the development of knowledge processes.

Consortium members understand that the strategic management of knowledge and organizational learning are inextricably inter-linked.

The Consortium recognizes that there are key elements and relationships which shape the priorities by which knowledge is selected and focused upon. Without the aligning force of business strategy, knowledge initiatives remain disparate and unco-ordinated. However, with strong business drivers, knowledge can take on a purpose and direction. The Consortium members also recognize that while leveraging of knowledge is driven by the value to be created, and guided by the business strategies/strategic imperatives, people are key to success in all elements and relationships in the model. The management challenge is to implement the processes that will support and liberate their capabilities.

So if knowledge underpins every value-added activity which the organization carries out, this body of knowledge must be managed and developed for its full potential to be realized. This requires identifying the processes of creating and sharing knowledge, and supplying the enabling conditions, i.e. developing the organization's capability through its culture and leadership and providing the supporting technology and infrastructure. Starting with existing projects, and involving people is such a way that they begin to understand the benefits to them, leads to employee ownership of the knowledge process.

There are opportunities for sharing and developing knowledge inside the company and with external stakeholders, such as customers. The company needs to learn about its customers and their needs, as well as learn from them. This learning can become reciprocal if there is trust and a partnership. **NCR** in the UK has developed a Learning Centre which has developed a reputation for thought leadership within the high-technology sector. The facilities are available to clients and leading thinkers address industry gatherings on a range of business and strategic topics. **Du Pont** supplies customers with a Gold Card which gives them access to Du Pont research.

ICL has developed Café VIK (Valuing ICL Knowledge) which is both actual and virtual – 'the global coffee room'. This is both an information service and exchange and a physical location in the UK where employees can meet to share knowledge. Café VIK was developed following extensive staff consultation. Staff were asked 'what kind of information will help you to do your jobs?' so that the knowledge on offer could be made as relevant as possible to the different professional communities within the company. The new service was introduced with roadshows and take-up has been substantial. Information sheets are available on the company intranet. These are both issues sheets and attachments offering solutions based on people's experience. A database on people – their skills/expertise and project experience – facilitates networking. Data warehousing ensures that information is kept up to date.

Moving towards organizational learning

Over and above these knowledge management initiatives, the organization needs to develop its capacity to continuously renew itself in the context of ongoing change. Peter Senge, author of *The Fifth Discipline* (1990), has identified five disciplines which are essential to creating an organization which can learn. These are:

- Systems thinking – which considers the interrelatedness of forces and sees them as part of a common process. 'System dynamics' involves looking for the complex feedback processes which can generate problematic patterns of behaviour within organizations.
- Personal mastery – which acknowledges that we are all a significant part of the systems we work within and 'the most significant leverage may come from changing our own orientation and self-image'. Concepts include personal visioning, treating emotions respectfully and the leader as coach.
- Mental models – which involve the ability to reflect and the theories which make up our current reality. Having the ability to develop and test new mental models will be essential for future-oriented learning and development.
- Shared vision – which involves gaining the commitment and focus which comes when a vision is genuinely shared. The vision should provide clues as to the organization's deep purpose and ways must be found of involving people at every level of the organization to speak and be heard about things which matter to them.
- Team learning – in which collective aspiration gives team members a compelling reason to begin to learn how to learn

together. Learning design can incorporate a team, as well as individual development focus. Following a learning activity, people can be encouraged to consider 'who also would benefit from this?' and transfer relevant and helpful learning to others.

Creating a development culture in a UK local authority

In one local authority, many initiatives to support learning, such as lunchtime seminars, are already under way. These are complemented by a set of supporting activities, such as linking the seminars to the senior management competencies. These form part of a coherent management development strategy. Self-development is a key part of this strategy, supported by targeted use of Learning Resource Centres. Materials linked to the competencies are networked so that people have ready access to learning materials.

Variations on action learning groups have been established at different levels within the organization. These groups are treated as a legitimate business activity rather than a 'nice to have'. Some are cross-level and are proving helpful in breaking down some of the hierarchical barriers which apparently exist. Learning groups are set up around the different competencies and specific projects. This way learning can be shared between people with different forms of experience. Other learning groups are more open-ended, with people carrying out their own development targets with support from other members of their learning group.

The development team are considering whether learning should be accredited to a recognized qualification such as a Diploma in Management Studies and whether to support individuals selectively in their pursuit of qualifications such as MBAs. These can be a tremendous source of learning and stimulus, especially for relatively high flyers who may feel trapped in their current role. Depending on the course chosen, there can be useful organizational benefits to be gained from business-related project work. However, it is very important that people who benefit from such training have the opportunity to use their enhanced knowledge and skills in some way, even if only to run an in-house seminar on their chosen subject.

In this and other ways, the authority hopes to play to people's strengths. The development team are planning to establish a data bank, showing not only what people's development needs are but also their strengths and areas where they are prepared to be a resource to others. Peer mentoring can be a powerful resource and sometimes needs a little formal help in becoming established. While it is not necessary to go the Investor in People route when creating a development culture, this can often provide the organization with additional kudos for what is happening anyway, if these recommendations are adopted.

Networking

In some companies, networking happens accidentally or as part of the informal system. Smokers' rooms are a good example of where new information circuits have been developed in recent years. Some companies deliberately encourage and enable networking as a means of getting people to share ideas. **3M** is well known as a company which encourages innovation. Indeed, every activity revolves around this and individual responsibilities are clear. Networking is the main operating mode and there is a strong culture in which risk-taking is good, innovations can be made by everyone and there is a tolerance of honest mistakes. Informal working, including working at home, and team working are encouraged. In the new corporate headquarters of **British Airways**, the physical environment has been specifically designed to facilitate employee networking. A 'street' complete with coffee bars is intended to create a community environment in which collaboration will naturally take place. This will enable 'structured' networking in which people with specific forms of knowledge can help one another.

Culture change at Sainsbury's Logistics division

The Logistics division of **Sainsbury's** supermarkets is in the vanguard of a cultural shift which aims to align employee and business development. The cultural shift is away from managers making all the decisions to 'empowerment' of employees to make decisions and to take action. The culture should therefore become more flexible and adaptive to changing business conditions and innovative solutions should be readily found. The process works through a combination of team and personal development – from career planning to corporate vision cultural work – performance management tools such as one-to-ones, and the use of a full range of development techniques including training and flexible/home working. Measures are also used to encourage mutual respect and appreciation, and there's a People's Charter and Staff Council.

Open Access Development Centres at Standard Life

Standard Life has created some very successful learning resource centres known as Open Access Development Centres (OADCs). These are based in five sites, having been piloted in Edinburgh where the head office is situated. Standard Life has actively encouraged employees to take responsibility for their development but recognizes that the organization must provide resources to make this possible. The OADCs are one of the ways in which Standard Life is investing in its staff.

Employees are encouraged to create a development plan and negotiate their needs with their managers. Having done this, they can have access to a wide range of resources at the OADC where staff are available to provide help and advice. If employees are unable to visit the centre in person, materials are sent out to them. Teams can also use the centres for development purposes. If development is directly linked to a person's role, it is considered legitimate that they spend work time acquiring the new skill or knowledge. Where possible, materials are provided on similar topics in a variety of formats such as videos, books, CD-ROMs, the Internet, self-assessment tools etc. to suit different learning styles. Copies of management development materials from training programmes are also available.

The OADCs are designed to support five operational objectives:-

- The development of key role and core organizational competencies
- Training by alternative medium
- Corporate initiatives such as the executive learning programme
- Professional studies in line with the company policy
- Vocational qualifications enabled.

They currently cost around £500 000 to run (excluding salaries) and utilization is running at 60 per cent. There have been a number of significant benefits to the business as well as to employees. Staff surveys indicate that there has been a positive impact on retention since employees recognize that Standard Life offers significant opportunities for development. Similarly, there have been cost-benefits in terms of recruitment. In 1998 a modern apprenticeship scheme was launched which has attracted many youngsters who might otherwise have gone to university. A strong selling point to potential recruits was the OADC provision and staff development opportunities. In addition, OADCs provide a tangible demonstration of Standard Life's commitment to developing employees.

Sun Microsystems

All employees are connected through SunWeb, the corporate intranet. Quality staff distribute findings from the Customer Quality Index and the Employee Quality Index, a monthly online survey of 3500 randomly selected employees. This index gauges employee satisfaction and the information it provides is used to target 'performance inhibitors'. Sun University uses the latest technology to train 20 000 employees and the workplace has been designed to facilitate learning and knowledge sharing.

Creating a self-development culture at the National Air Traffic Services (NATS)

The **National Air Traffic Service**, a subsidiary of the Civil Aviation Authority, plans, provides and operates safe and efficient air traffic services. NATS is working towards a public/private partnership and has over 5000 staff. The average length of service is 15 years and there is relatively low turnover. Staff skills have a strong technical bias and, given the safety culture, there is an emphasis on critical, problem-identification and problem-solving approaches.

While employees tend to stay with NATS for a long time, a 1993 staff survey indicated that career satisfaction was low and highlighted a number of employee concerns with regard to career development. These were:

- Lack of information
- Misconceptions about procedures
- Limited movement across functions
- Uncertainty over the future
- Managers' skills and attitudes were not supportive of career development.

Responding to the survey findings, a new framework was put in place for all staff in 1994 based on self-development of the organization's twelve core competencies. A number of initiatives were carried out and measures set to establish whether these initiatives would produce improvements in any of the three areas measured, namely:

- Career satisfaction
- Organizational commitment
- Management support for careers.

Among the initiatives introduced were some practical tools to help people to manage their own development. These were all voluntary and the amount of use made of them is roughly in descending order as follows:

- Personal Development Plans
- Development Options Guide (DOG)
- Career workshops
- Coaching training
- Learning Resource Centre
- Secondment policies and guidance
- Career workbook
- NATS Career planning guide.

Interestingly, all the measures improved though there was relatively little impact on career satisfaction. Employees clearly believed that the company should still manage their career. However, management support for development increased as a result of these initiatives. The lessons learned were that extensive communication about career self-development was needed (due to resource constraint at the time, formal communication had been limited) and that line managers were the lynchpin to making a self-development culture work. It was also essential that these learning and career development initiatives had a non-HR senior sponsor who could help tackle some of the issues raised in the next phase.

In the latest work, the competencies have been revised to include a more commercial focus. In a 1996 programme for managers, using 360-degree feedback, the findings suggested that there were clear differences of perception between what managers thought they did, and what other people perceived. The major differences of perception were around the following competencies:

- Managing people
- Teamworking
- Challenging complacency.

Clearly work needed to be done to help managers to support people development. NATS recognizes that employee satisfaction with regard to career development is important and maintains the strategy of self-development supported by the organization. Therefore to reinforce and support this culture shift, various tools have been introduced to help people carry out a realistic self-assessment, such as using 360-degree feedback. A grid of development methods available has been developed against the competencies. This allows people to identify development options which suit them and other tools, such as a computerized Development Options Guide, provides a steer on training courses and other means of developing the competencies. This also allows the HR team to understand who needs what type of development, so they are better able to focus resources. Career paths, especially for engineer groups, have been developed which should make some development moves possible.

In the move towards a self-development culture, the need for opportunities for people to learn from others, as well as generate new knowledge collaboratively was recognized. A key initiative was the introduction of action learning sets, some of which include managers from other companies. With low turnover, the importance of bringing in new ideas from other organizations has been recognized. Other ways in which development is being moved outside the organization include the use of cross-company mentoring. A new strategy for senior manager development is focusing on leadership, recognizing that if the self-development culture is to become fully embedded, leaders need to role model learning with and from one another.

Conclusion

The turbulent job markets of the 1990s following waves of downsizing and other restructurings have led to an increase in job insecurity among employees and a corresponding loss of trust in employers. The sense of self-preservation is strong and many individuals are likely to hoard information which may be useful to others and use it only for their own benefit. However, in today's complex organizations, competitive advantage for the business is likely to depend on the ways in which employees create and share their knowledge in ways to benefit the bottom-line. The challenge of knowledge management is to ensure that employees also benefit from developing and sharing knowledge.

But this is not simply a question of helping employees to see 'what's in it for me?', even though the ability to share key knowledge effectively is likely to make employees more truly employable. Just relying on people's goodwill and trust in the organization is unlikely to lead to knowledge sharing and the development of exciting new products and services. To do this, employees need to be provided with the appropriate environment and infrastructure. IT and HR systems need to complement each other, and there needs to be a clear strategy with regard to the types of knowledge the organization wishes to develop, store and be able to retrieve. In addition, employees need to be helped to develop the attitude and skills required for the Information Age.

Above all, managers need to take a lead in developing a culture which is conducive to learning and knowledge creation. Their behaviour and responses to critical incidents, such as when an experimental activity backfires, will speak volumes. They need to both encourage others to continuously learn from one another and be prepared to do so themselves. Managers need to make the time to identify, prioritize and develop knowledge assets which need to be integrated into the main business processes. In large companies, tools will need to be developed to enable global sharing. Human Resource development has a critical role to play in identifying skill gaps and planning to overcome them. New roles and responsibilities need to be clarified and ways of connecting people found. Knowledge management is a key area for line/HR partnership in ensuring that the precious human resource can become ever more resourceful.

References

Geus, Arie de, interviewed by Chambers, N. (1997). Does the bell toll for your living company? *HR Focus*, October, **74**, No.10.

Handy, C. (1997). *The Hungry Spirit.* London: Hutchinson.

Kransdorff, A. (1995). Succession planning in a fast changing world. *Training Officer*, **31**, No.2, 52–53.

Lamminam, J. and Syrett, M. (1999). *Innovation at the Top: Where do Directors get their Ideas from?* Roffey Park Management Institute.

Morgan, G. (1993). *Imaginization: The Art of Creative Management.* London: Sage.

Nonaka, I. and Takeuchi, H. (1995). *The Knowledge-Creating Company.* Oxford: Oxford University Press.

Senge, P. (1990). *The Fifth Discipline.* New York: Doubleday Currency.

Senge, P. (1994). *The Fifth Discipline Fieldbook.* London: Nicholas Brealey Publishing.

Stewart, T. A. (1997). *Intellectual Capital: The New Wealth of Organizations.* London: Nicholas Brealey.

Conclusion

So as the new millennium unfolds, will there be a future for HR? The changing patterns of recent years suggest that the jury is still out. My guess is that there will be more not less need for effective HR contributions. In recent years, HR has been at the forefront of thinking about many of the big organizational issues of which line managers are only now becoming aware. The importance of building a learning culture, knowledge management, leadership, skills development and recruitment and retention is now widely recognized in many organizations. HR has been trying to get these issues on the strategic agenda for years, yet somehow the thinking about how these 'HR' issues can contribute to business success has not been aligned in managers' minds. The irony is that they are only being treated as serious business issues now that line managers also see their importance.

That is perhaps one of the key messages of this book. HR can and probably should be the key interpreter, problem solver and resource gatherer with regard to people issues, but responsibility for the design and implementation of people strategies should be shared between the line and HR. Alignment between business and HR strategies begins with a partnership approach. For this to happen, there needs to be give and take on both sides as well as mutual understanding and respect.

For HR the main challenge is to ensure that the HR strategy genuinely supports the business strategy. This requires having a thorough understanding of your business and what it is trying to achieve and being able to communicate in business language rather than professional jargon. This involves understanding the top two or three current executive priorities and developing actions to implement and track solutions to them. This means showing business acumen and thinking in terms of the people outcomes which must be achieved if business success is to follow. These outcomes should be measurable so that the relevent value logic for your organization can be tracked through.

This also means understanding what leads to highly productive work groups in your organization. Typically, the high-performance culture which HR can help to create is one characterized by role clarity, clear and challenging objectives, opportunities for development, effective coaching, recognition of achievement and appropriate rewards. HR can work with line managers to create performance standards which help employees appreciate standards in terms of behaviours and outcomes. Processes can be developed for monitoring and following up results. These ingredients tend to lead not only to high performance but also to high employee commitment which in turn lead to satisfied customers and other stakeholders.

As Dave Ulrich (1997) points out, the proof of effective people management practices is evident when two firms in the same basic industry which have similar results are compared, and where one is considered to have considerably more shareholder value potential than the other. In the future, perceptions of improving shareholder value are likely to be based on the development of intellectual capital, the strength and 'reality' of the brand in practice and the quality of leadership. A Roffey Park focus group (1998) of senior HR managers and directors had straightforward ways of describing what the core role of strategic HR should be:

* Supporting the business objectives of the firm by timely, intelligent and commonsensical HR activities and planning
* Looking at what the organization needs to deliver (medium and long term)
* Ensuring that the organization has the right staff (skills, knowledge, motivation) to deliver
* Creating flexible, broad business people
* Thinking big picture
* Developing integrated policies and processes
* Communicating clearly to people about the things which affect them
* Identifying the support of business decisions across countries and business units

- Creating a cohesive framework/common company language
- Acting as internal change agent – with an eye on strategic business plans and organizational effectiveness
- Making uncertainty manageable.

They also had a strong preference for how HR should operate:

- Simple rather than sophisticated
- Business focused
- Human!
- Making a difference.

HR has a critical role to play in building the leadership of the organization to create shareholder and other stakeholder value. It involves having a global perspective on the business and consciously seeking out global knowledge. This also means not only developing succession for the medium term but also critically evaluating the quality of current leadership. Again, the changing business requirements should drive the assessment agenda. To what extent is the current leadership able to create an adaptable, change-oriented organization in which accountabilities are clear, employees are highly motivated and committed and where the culture is supportive of learning and innovation? Are leaders able to provide a clarity of direction in ambiguous circumstances so that employees are clear what needs to be done and what is no longer relevant? Do leaders develop and manage effective relationships with internal and external stakeholders and are they able to scan the environment for new opportunities for their organization?

To win the mandate for developing the organization, HR has to be good at both the operational personnel processes and practices, however these are delivered, as well as developing a culture change agenda which is strategic and future-focused, rather than reactive and 'picking up the pieces'. Of course, many practitioners will say that their organization is not ready for a strategic HR approach, that what really counts is delivering the 'pieces' well in the here and now. Other practitioners argue that it is precisely because the function contents itself with administration, hiring and firing, that HR is not valued. I would argue that this is a false dilemma. While being an administrative expert is valuable, even day-to-day operations should be carried out within a broad strategic framework if HR is to be able to build employee commitment and capability on to the organizational infrastructure.

In some cases, the apparent dilemma can be reconciled through the way in which HR organizes its delivery. In some organizations, operational HR is delivered through junior staff, through outsourcing, through call centres or service centres. Other organizations consider this to be the core. Typically, strategic areas such as organization design, succession planning, designing strategies to recruit and retain key talent are often the remit of a few senior HR staff. While this may be a sensible way of sharing responsibilities, such divisions may make it difficult for the HR team as a whole to develop a strategic approach and may cause problems when it comes to implementation.

In yet other organizations, strategic delivery is more hybrid. In Sun Microsystems Europe, for instance, HR service delivery is through 'account managers' who provide consultancy support to specific business units. In addition, these HR account managers each take responsibility for developing expertise in one area of the firm's strategic agenda, such as managing mergers, for instance. This more strategic role requires carrying out effective diagnosis of what is needed to deliver the business strategy and an effective corporate translation into practice of HR strategies. Indeed, some pundits suggest that having a separate 'HR' strategy is a mistake; that HR plans should be seen as so integral to the business strategy that they do not need a separate caption. Perhaps this is the surest way of aligning HR and business strategies – making them one!

Whichever approach is taken – segmentation/functionalization – the challenge according to the focus group of senior HR managers and directors is to 'keep the eye on the ball', having worked out what the 'ball' is in the first place. Several comments reveal the commonality of view about what HR needs to focus on:

- 'Anything from not doing "day-to-day" work to looking ahead three years'
- 'Influencing the board and the direction of the company'
- 'Making a difference to the bottom line'
- 'Developing the frameworks, policies and initiatives to move the business forward'
- 'Integrating future business goals/needs with people issues/needs in a plan'
- 'Clear thinking/policies/right direction/motivation of staff'

What is important is to gauge the actual needs and readiness of your organization for what it intends to do strategically. Does it have the core competencies, culture, systems and processes, working practices and human skills to accomplish what it wants to do? If not, what does this imply if the strategic aims are to be accomplished? HR should be able to contribute to the strategic planning processes inventories of not only technical capabilities but also the organization's cultural strengths and weaknesses.

How will HR support the development of a high-performance culture, how will work processes need to be managed to achieve high-quality deliverables, how will the core competencies be activated and what aspects of the organization's culture will need to be strengthened, balanced out or changed? HR teams need to develop their own answers which will fit their current organizational context. This means defining the implications of business strategy for organizational capability, such as the firm's ability to learn, and developing measurable actions to build that capability. If, for example, managing costs is a strategic aim, does the organization have the capability to create high productivity, use resources efficienctly and become a low-cost provider in its marketplace?

By way of example, the HR team of one organization which supplies a UK-wide repair service to individual and corporate customers has analysed the links between business strategy and HR actions as follows:

Business strategy
- Meet customer needs – best service possible – unequalled value for money
- Build on strengths of brand, customer database and IT capability
- Manage for profit and growth

Core values
- Brand
- Courtesy and care
- Stakeholders
- Quality and value for money

Critical success factors
- People
- Financial performance
- Operational performance
- Market share

Translated into Balanced Scorecard
- Vision and strategy

- Customer perspective
- Internal business perspective
- Financial perspective
- People (learning and growth)

Learning and growth measures

- Capability (performance management, succession management)
- Culture and climate (survey measures)
- Skills mix (training and development outputs)
- Capacity for change
- Employee profile (statistics, costs)
- Organization structure.

This organization's HR team has been able to subdivide the staff population, identify the relevant development needs, establish behavioural standards, business skills and the areas of technical and professional mastery required for the current and future business. HR processes and tools such as recruitment and selection, training and development, performance management and reward, employee relations and management standards are fully integrated to support the learning and growth aims. 'Learning and growth' can then fully enable the organization to achieve its strategic aims.

The credibility of HR is based partly on being able to deliver results in a business-like way but also by the ability to build trust and influence at all levels, especially at senior levels. Our focus group data suggests that this ability to influence is critical if HR is to be perceived to add value. In the current state of evolution of HR, there is a perceived need to 'sell' the value of HR. Part of the problem, according to these practitioners lies in the roles of HR. Where HR is organized around specialists, these professionals may not be comfortable about selling the business implications of what they are recommending. Conversely, HR generalists have a good business grounding but may lack the confidence in their ability to add specialist value. Again, a way of reconciling this apparent dilemma is by ensuring that specialists develop business and consultancy skills and relationships, and that generalists develop at least one area of expertise.

Similarly, building an image of professionalism through knowing your business allows HR to usefully introduce best practice thinking – but critically and pragmatically rather than falling into the 'initiative of the month' trap. This requires HR to network with other members of the HR profession and line managers from other organizations, picking up ideas and developing a global idea of what externally judged good practice looks like. This will enable HR to more confidently assert what needs to be done with regard to the people implications of business strategies in their own organization and even recommend potential business opportunities.

There is a great deal that can be done by HR teams themselves to ensure that they have the skills needed to develop and deliver people strategies. The competencies of HR should be a happy blend of what line managers and HR itself believe it should be good at. Influencing through networking should be a key tool of HR. Taking time to learn about employee and senior management issues should be a legitimate priority, yet it is often squeezed out of the daily round due to the pressure of business. Since the HR function is always likely to be thinly resourced, these time pressures may well contain the seeds of functional self-destruction. Team members can be so busy that they do not take time to reflect, to see the wood for the trees and take stock of what needs to be the new focus.

The HR team therefore needs to be able to operate strategically, even if its delivery is currently operational. In some cases, team members will need to develop their own skills to higher levels. Other prerequisites include interpersonal and consultancy skills, planning and implementation skills, and the willingness to learn from other organizations and people. Being able to manage culture involves being willing to challenge the status quo and to have the courage of your convictions. It involves being able to diagnose the kind of culture required to deliver the business strategy and encouraging leaders to walk the talk with regard to the desired culture and values. This in itself may seem a risky thing to do and will require confidence or Ulrich's 'attitude' on the part of HR. According to Jeffrey Pfeffer (1996), this is an area which HR needs to develop: 'the comparatively low power of human resources is often further reduced by the reluctance of its executives to engage in organizational politics.'

Being able to manage change means taking a proactive rather than reactive role in bringing about change. It involves being able to understand how the organization works as a system, identifying where change needs to occur to enable the organization to achieve its goals, and integrating separate initiatives into a change framework. It also requires being willing to assess how well the HR team is equipped to manage change and being prepared to improve the team's capability as appropriate.

Of course, strategic business partnership is not a one-way street. If line managers genuinely believe that HR issues have a critical impact on achieving business success, they should insist on involving HR professionals in the business strategy-making process. That way, expensive mistakes can be avoided and potential opportunities can be identified at the optimum time. This partnership approach needs to extend to implementation. HR must be able to understand the practical implications of delivering people-related business strategies and work with line managers to ensure that HR delivery at all levels is professional and effective. Line managers need to develop the skills and responsibility to deal effectively with devolved HR responsibilities. Arguably, 'HR' strategies are better called 'People' strategies if they are named at all.

Will HR therefore be the best function to deliver 'people' strategies? Various management thinkers (Hastings, 1993) predict that the changing concept of organization is likely to have a radical impact on the future role of HR – in other words, the evolution may become more revolutionary. The predictions include:

- The average company will become smaller and employ fewer people
- Hierarchical organizations will be replaced by organizations of various forms
- Technicians or 'knowledge workers' will become the worker elite
- Vertical divisions of labour will be replaced by horizontal divisions
- The service economy is here to stay
- Work itself will be redefined by constant training

Each of these trends has implications for the skills of employees generally, and for HR in particular. The pundits suggest that the HR function of the future will segment into operational, technical roles carried out by a range of specialists whose affinity is to a network rather than the HR function as a whole, and strategists who will take their seats at board tables. However, the predictions include the strategists being from a range of backgrounds, of which the HR route may be only one. In preparing for the future, HR professionals may therefore need to broaden and deepen their skills. This may indeed result in the clearest alignment between HR and business strategies, when the managers involved have similar experiences and understanding of what needs to be done and where professional expertise is a value add.

So if HR does matter, it is important to be able to answer the question 'What is the purpose of HR?'. Wayne Brockbank (1997) suggests that 'if HR as a whole is unclear about its purpose, what can be expected from the rest of the company about the purpose of HR?'. He offers a range of criteria for developing a departmental point of view which include:

- Is it formally stated or is it *ad hoc* and assumed?
- Does it comprehensively cover the whole organization thereby encouraging the corporate whole to be greater than the sum of the parts?
- Is it linked to issues which are critical to long-term corporate success?
- Does it create explicit and measurable results?

Becoming clear about how HR can add value in your organization is part of the process of making a difference.

No HR practitioner would claim that delivering a strategic and value-added contribution is easy. However, I suggest that many of the practitioners featured in this book demonstrate that success is possible. Each of them is responding in their own way to the challenges of understanding their own organization's changing needs and developing and implementing aligned and integrated HR agendas which equip their organizations for the future. If Lester Thurow (1992) is right when he asserts that 'In the 21st century, the education and skills of the workforce will end up being the dominant competitive weapon', then the Human Resources function should be the key enabler of organizational success in years to come.

References

Brockbank, W. (1997). HR's future on the way to a presence. *Human Resource Management*, Spring **36**, No.1, 65–69.

Hastings, C. (1993). *The New Organisation: Growing the Culture of Organisational networking.* New York: McGraw-Hill.

Pfeffer, J. (1996). When it comes to 'Best Practices' why do smart organizations occasionally do dumb things? *Organizational Dynamics*, Summer.

Stroh, L. K. and Caligiuri, P. M. (1998). Increasing global competitiveness through effective people management. *Journal of World Business*, **33**, No.1.

Thurow, L. C. (1992). *Head to Head: The coming of economic battle among Japan, Europe and America.* London: Nicholas Brealey.

Ulrich, D. (1997). *Human Resource Champions: The Next Agenda for Adding Value and Delivering Results.* Cambridge, MA: Harvard Business School Press.

Ulrich, D., Brockbank, W., Yeung, A. K. and Lake, D. G. (1995). Human Resource competencies: an empirical assessment. *Human Resource Management*, Winter.

Ulrich, D. and Lake, D. (1990). *Organizational Capability: Competing from the inside/out.* New York: Wiley.

Index

Other Roffey Park books and research reports

Devine, M. (2001), *Mergers and Acquisitions Checklist*. £11.00
Devine, M. and Hirsh, W. (1998), *Mergers and Acquisitions: Getting the people bit right*. £50.00
Evans, C. (1997), *Managing the Flexible Workforce. A source book for change* £42.00
Evans, C. (1998), *Managing the Flexible Workforce. Enhancing performance by aligning organisational and individual needs*. £40.00
Evans, C. (2000), *Developing a Knowledge Creating Culture*. £30.00
Garrow, V. (1997), *360 Degree Feedback. Do we really want to know?* £15.00
Garrow, V. (1998), *Self Managed Learning: Development for the 21st century*. £20.00
Garrow, V. (1999), *A Guide to the Implementation of 360 Degree Feedback*. £6.95 plus p&p
Garrow, V., Devine, M., Hirsch, W. and Holbeche, L. (2000), *Strategic Alliances: Getting the People Bit Right*. £60.00
Garrow, V., Glynn, C., Tarpy, S. and Whatmore, J. (2000), *Contemporary Approaches to Team Working*. £20.00
Garrow, V. and Holbeche, L. (2001), *Mergers and Acquisitions*. £50.00
Glynn, C. (1999), *Enabling Balance: The importance of organisational culture*. £30.00
Glynn, C. (2000), *Work-Life Balance, Careers and the Psychological Contract*. £20.00
Glynn, C. (2000), *Young People's Attitudes to Work, Careers and Learning*. Free
Glynn, C. and Holbeche, L. (1999), *The Management Agenda* £25.00
Glynn, C. and Holbeche, L. (1999), *Towards Global Leadership. Recruiting and developing international managers*. £40.00
Glynn, C. and Holbeche, L. (2000), *The Management Agenda 2000*. £30.00
Glynn, C. and Holbeche, C. (2001), *The Management Agenda 2001*. £30.00
Hamilton, F. (2000), *Interpersonal Conflict at Work*. £30.00
Holbeche, L. (1997), *Career Development in Flatter Structures. The impact of flatter structures on careers*. £80.00 plus p&p
Holbeche, L. (1997), *Motivating People in Lean Organisations*. £21.00
Holbeche, L. (1998), *High Flyers and Succession Planning in Changing Organisations*. £50.00
Holbeche, L. (2000), *The Future of Careers*. £50.00
Lammiman, J. and Syrett, M. (1998), *Innovation at the Top. Where do directors get their ideas from?* £50.00
Lammiman, J. and Syrett, M. (2000), *Entering Tiger Country: How Ideas are Shaped in Organisations*. £60.00

To purchase any of the publications listed above please contact The Research Department on 01293 851644 or email pauline.hinds@roffeypark.com

Roffey Park has over 50 years experience of developing innovative approaches to management development and understanding the human dimension of organisational issues. Areas of expertise include organisational and management development at all levels, managing change, training developers and interpersonal skills development. Roffey Park offers a wide range of services including short residential open programmes, in-company development and consultancy, weekend workshops, an MBA, Post Graduate Diploma in Management and MSc in People and Organisational Development.

Roffey Park Institute, Forest Road, Horsham, West Sussex, RH12 4TD, United Kingdom
Tel: +44 (0) 1293 851644   Fax: +44 (0) 1293 851565
www.roffeypark.com   email:info@roffeypark.com

Roffey Park Institute Limited is a Charity, Registered No: 254591 VAT No: 201-9601-03